ASIAN AMERICAN CULTURE

ASIAN AMERICAN CULTURE

FROM ANIME TO TIGER MOMS

VOLUME 2: J–Z

Lan Dong, Editor

Cultures of the American Mosaic

GREENWOOD™

An Imprint of ABC-CLIO, LLC
Santa Barbara, California • Denver, Colorado

Library of Congress Cataloging-in-Publication Data

Names: Dong, Lan, 1974– editor.
Title: Asian American culture : from anime to tiger moms / Lan Dong, editor.
Description: First edition. | Santa Barbara, California : Greenwood, An
    Imprint of ABC-CLIO, 2016. | Series: Cultures of the American mosaic
Identifiers: LCCN 2015025999 | ISBN 9781440829208 (set) | ISBN 9781440845451
    (vol. 1) | ISBN 9781440845468 (vol. 2) | ISBN 9781440829215 (set : ebook)
Subjects: LCSH: Asian Americans—Encyclopedias. | United
    States—Civilization—Asian influences—Encyclopedias. | BISAC: SOCIAL
    SCIENCE / Ethnic Studies / Asian American Studies. | HISTORY / Asia /
    China.
Classification: LCC E184.A75 A8265 2016 | DDC 973/.0495—dc23
LC record available at http://lccn.loc.gov/2015025999

ISBN: 978-1-4408-2920-8 (set)
ISBN: 978-1-4408-4545-1 (vol. 1)
ISBN: 978-1-4408-4546-8 (vol. 2)
EISBN: 978-1-4408-2921-5 (set)

20 19 18 17 16   1 2 3 4 5

This book is also available on the World Wide Web as an eBook.
Visit www.abc-clio.com for details.

Greenwood
An Imprint of ABC-CLIO, LLC

ABC-CLIO, LLC
130 Cremona Drive, P.O. Box 1911
Santa Barbara, California 93116-1911

This book is printed on acid-free paper ∞

Manufactured in the United States of America

CONTENTS

Alphabetical List of Entries

Some entries include one or two supplementary sidebars, which are shown here, under the entry each accompanies.

GUIDE TO RELATED TOPICS

Following are the entries in this encyclopedia, arranged under broad topics for enhanced searching. Readers should also consult the index at the end of the encyclopedia for more specific subjects.

Art, Music, and Theater

Arts and Artists (Visual), Asian American
Asian Indian American Dance
Asian Indian American Performing Arts and Artists
Asian Indian American Visual Arts and Artists
Cambodian American Performing Arts and Artists
Chinese American Visual Arts and Artists
Chinese Calligraphy
Dance, Asian American
Filipino Folk Music
Japanese American Arts and Artists
Korean American Arts and Artists
Musical Theater, Asian American
Music and Musicians, Asian American
Theater, Asian American
Vietnamese American Arts and Artists
Youth and Arts, Asian American

Education and Politics
Activism, Asian American
Chinese Americans and Education
Chinese Heritage Language Schools
Japanese Americans and Education
Model Minority
Politics, Asian Americans in
Proposition 209 (1996)
Scientists, Asian American
Tiger Mom

Family and Community
Adoption of Asian Children
Asian Indian American Children and Family
Asian Indian American Community Organizations
Cambodian American Children and Family
Cambodian American Community Organizations
Chinatown (New York City)
Chinatown (San Francisco)
Chinese American Children and Family
Filipino American Children and Family
Filipino American Community Organizations
Hawai'i, Asian Americans in
Interracial Marriage
Japanese American Children and Family
Japanese Community Organizations
Korean American Children and Family
Korean American Community Organizations
Koreatowns
Little Manilas
Little Saigons
Little Tokyo (Los Angeles)
Vietnamese American Community Organizations

Food
Asian Indian American Food
Chinese American Food
Chop Suey
Filipino American Food
Fortune Cookie

Fusion Cuisine
Japanese American Food
Japanese Tea Ceremony
Kimchi
Korean American Food
Pho
Sushi
Thai American Food
Vietnamese American Food

Gender and Sexuality
Cambodian American Women
Chinese American Women
Comfort Women
Dragon Lady and Lotus Blossom
Filipino American Women
Japanese American Women
Korean American Women
LGBTQ Asian Americans
Picture Bride
Vietnamese American Women
War Brides Act (1945)
Women, Asian American

History and Immigration
Asian American Studies
Asian American Transnationalism
Asian Indian American Immigration
Chinese American Immigration
Chinese Exclusion Act (1882)
Demographics, Asian American
Discrimination against Asian Americans
Filipino American Immigration
Hmong American Immigration
Japanese American Immigration
Japanese American Internment
Korean American Immigration
Transcontinental Railroad
Vietnamese American Immigration

Holidays, Festivals, and Folk Traditions
Acupuncture
Asian Indian American Festivals
Asian Indian American Folklore
Cambodian American Folklore
Chinese American Folklore
Festivals and Holidays, Asian American
Filipino American Folklore
Ghost and Spirit
Guan Yu
Japanese American Folklore
Korean American Folklore
Lunar New Year
Monkey King
Traditional Healing and Medicine, Asian American
Vietnamese American Folklore

Literature and Culture
Asian Indian American Fiction
Asian Indian American Literature
Asian Indian American Poetry
Autobiographies, Asian American
Bangladeshi American Culture
Bhutanese and Nepalese American Culture
Burmese (Myanmar) American Culture
Cambodian American Literature
Children's and Young Adult Literature, Asian American
Chinese American Autobiographies
Chinese American Fiction
Chinese American Literature
Chinese American Poetry
Comics and Graphic Narratives, Asian American
Fiction, Asian American
Filipino American Literature
Hmong American Culture
Indonesian American Culture
Japanese American Autobiographies
Japanese American Fiction
Japanese American Literature
Japanese American Poetry

Korean American Literature
Laotian American Culture
Literature, Asian American
Malaysian American Culture
Mongolian American Culture
Pakistani American Culture
Singaporean American Culture
Sri Lankan American Culture
Thai American Culture
Tibetan American Culture
Vietnamese American Literature

Media, Sports, and Entertainment

Anime
Asian Indian American Films and Filmmakers
Boxing and Wrestling, Asian Americans and
Cambodian American Films and Filmmakers
Chinese American Films and Filmmakers
Comedy and Humor, Asian American
Fashion, Asian Americans and
The Internet and Asian Americans
Japanese American Films and Filmmakers
Judo
Karate
Korean American Films and Filmmakers
Linsanity
Popular Culture, Asian Americans and
Sports, Asian Americans in
Tae Kwon Do
Tai Chi
Television, Asian Americans on
Video and Online Games, Asian Americans and
Vietnamese American Films and Filmmakers
Yoga

Religion, Spirituality, and Belief

Asian Indian American Religions and Beliefs
Buddhism
Cambodian American Religions and Beliefs
Confucianism

Daoism
Filipino Catholicism
Hinduism
Hmong American Religions and Beliefs
Islam
Pakistani American Religions and Beliefs
Religions and Beliefs, Asian American
Shamanism
Theravada Buddhism
Traditional Polytheistic Religions
Vietnamese American Religions and Beliefs

PREFACE

ASIAN AMERICAN CULTURE IS IN A CONSTANT STATE of change. The great variety of oral, textual, visual, and other modes of productions are historically informed and transnationally influenced. The first and foremost aim of *Asian American Culture: From Anime to Tiger Moms* is to guide the ways in which teachers, students, and general readers understand the diverse and complex Asian American cultural forms. The essays included in these two volumes also hope to inspire further inquiries and explorations in Asian American culture. To this end, each essay includes cross-references and resources for further reading; Volume 2 includes a carefully selected bibliography of recommended resources.

Asian American Culture is unique in its scope. Even though there are reference books, encyclopedias, and sourcebooks devoted to a particular field of Asian American studies—such as Asian American literature, history, and religion, among others—this book is the first seeking to offer a comprehensive view of numerous Asian American cultural forms. These two volumes provide reliable, up-to-date, and thorough information about a broad range of topics in Asian American culture. They not only address the general commonalities in Asian American culture but also include rich details about the historical origins, regional practices, and diverse variations within specific cultural expressions. The entries provide comprehensive coverage of a variety of Asian American cultural forms: folk tradition, popular culture, literary and artistic productions, and other forms of shared expression.

Current state social studies standards recommend that courses present culturally diverse historical viewpoints that include the Asian American experience.

Colleges and universities across the nation have implemented general education curricula, requiring students to broaden their knowledge about the distinctive, complex, and diverse peoples of the United States. Materials presented in this book are particularly valuable for understanding the history, complexity, and contemporary practices in Asian American culture. The entry essays included in these two volumes are written for undergraduate students at colleges and universities (especially those taking classes on race, ethnicity, multiculturalism, and Asian American studies), high school students, book club members (who are reading books by or about Asian Americans), and general readers. This book will be a useful reference for school and public libraries in addition to academic libraries at colleges and universities and research libraries.

This book covers the broad roots of Asian American culture, including living traditions, rites of passage, art, literature, folk culture, popular culture, subcultures, and other forms of expression. By discussing history and origins, expressive forms in contemporary culture, and regional practices, traditions, and artifacts, the entry essays collectively provide in-depth coverage of Asian American cultural forms and present culturally diverse historical viewpoints regarding the Asian American experience in the United States. In addition, the sidebars, short text boxes accompanying some entries, highlight significant facts, give biographies of key figures, and describe influential artifacts as well as important events and rituals. Readers of *Asian American Culture* will notice the following features of the 170 essays and 118 sidebars:

- They provide readers with an understanding of the variety and commonalities in Asian American culture, enabling a fuller comprehension of Asian American history, experiences, and cultural expressions.

- They introduce not only major figures with national and international recognition but also lesser-known and emerging practitioners.

- They use interdisciplinary approaches and offer broad and in-depth coverage in accessible writing, making the book suitable for general readers as well as specialists in the field.

- They offer overviews of ideas, organizations, movements, and practices as well as highlight particular differences and achievements through biographies of key figures, historical events, legal cases, and significant artifacts.

- They suggest a number of additional resources to facilitate further reading and research.

This work collects research by professionals hailing from North America, Europe, and Asia, including both well-established specialists and emerging scholars. Their expertise in many academic disciplines and interdisciplinary fields ensures the coverage and depth of the entry essays that address a wide range of topics in Asian American culture, such as Cambodian American literature, the Chinese Exclusion Act of 1882, fashion and Asian Americans, Filipino folk music, fusion cuisine, Hmong American immigration, the Internet and Asian Americans, interracial marriage, LGBTQ Asian Americans, model minority, picture brides, shamanism, and Asian American theater, among others. The 69 contributors' diverse backgrounds and authority in their respective fields are also crucial for a balanced representation of significant events, landmark works, key individuals, and underrepresented forms and groups in Asian American culture.

The entries in these two volumes are organized alphabetically in standard A–Z encyclopedia format. At the front along with an alphabetical list of the essays and sidebars is the Guide to Related Topics, listing all related entries under broad topics such as art, music, and theater; education and politics; family and community; food; gender and sexuality; history and migration; holidays, festivals, and folk tradition; literature and culture; media, sports, and entertainment; and religion, spirituality, and belief. Finally, *Asian American Culture: From Anime to Tiger Moms* features a comprehensive index at the end of Volume 2, providing further access for readers.

While the entry essays represent a wide range of perspectives and approaches, when appropriate most follow a standard arrangement, beginning with an introduction to history and origins, then providing an overview of regional practices, traditions, and artifacts and discussing particular expressive forms in contemporary culture. Each essay has a "See also" section at the end that helps the reader identify related topics included in these volumes. For example, the cross-references provided in the entry "Sushi" directs the reader to other entries discussing Asian and Asian American food, their origins, regional variations, and cultural influences (for instance, "Chop Suey," "Filipino American Food," "Kimchi," "*Pho*," and "Thai American Food"). This "See also" section also points to other entries related to Japanese American experiences and cultural forms (such as "Japanese American Immigration" and "Japanese Tea Ceremony").

Sources are listed under "Further Reading" sections, which include additional sources for further reading and research. These materials range from scholarly books, journal articles, and book chapters to statistics, websites, and media sources, providing broad and up-to-date coverage of resources. At the end of Volume 2, along with the comprehensive index, the Recommended Resources lists carefully selected print, media, and online resources that are helpful for students, educators, scholars, and general readers to further explore particular topics related to Asian American culture. Volume 2 closes with the index.

Lan Dong

ACKNOWLEDGMENTS

THIS PROJECT WOULD NOT HAVE BEEN POSSIBLE without the support of Kim Kennedy-White, Anne Thompson, Barbara Patterson, and the staff at ABC-CLIO. The editorial and marketing teams worked tirelessly to keep the project on schedule. Their dedication made everything proceed smoothly. My gratitude goes to Monica Chiu, Rocío Davis, and Julia Mickenberg for being role models and for their advice and mentorship over the years. Thank you Cathy Schlund-Vials, Jonathan H. X. Lee, Ymitri Mathison, Grace Yoo, Judy Wu, Kathleen Nadeau, and Marie-Therese Sulit for being generous in contributing your expertise, mentoring student contributors, and supporting me and cheering me on during the past three years. You and many other scholars in Asian American studies have inspired me and continue to do so. Numerous colleagues at the University of Illinois, Springfield, have provided intellectual camaraderie and friendship at various points along the way: Meagan Cass, Donna Bussell, Tena Helton, Kristi Barnwell, Holly Kent, David Bertaina, and Peter Shapinsky. My gratitude goes out to all the contributors in the United Kingdom, the Netherlands, Italy, Darussalam, China, Hong Kong, India, Canada, and the United States who hail from different academic communities: anthropology, art, education, English, ethnic studies, gender and sexuality studies, history, media studies, music, religion, sociology, and many other fields. Their expertise in various disciplines and interdisciplinary fields ensure the coverage and depth of the great variety of Asian American cultural forms included in these two volumes. It has been a humbling learning experience through the process of working with all the contributors. I extend special thanks to my editorial assistant Nicole Overcash, who generously and patiently offered assistance during the lengthy process of completing this ambitious project. All errors and faults are my sole responsibility. Last but not least I thank my family, who understand and tolerate my workaholic tendency and continue to love and support me.

INTRODUCTION

ASIAN AMERICAN EXPERIENCES AND CULTURAL FORMS

ACCORDING TO U.S. CENSUS DATA, THE ASIAN AND PACIFIC Islander population in the United States has increased dramatically over the past few decades, from 1.5 million in 1970 to 3.7 million in 1980, 7.3 million in 1990, 11.9 million in 2000, and 17.3 million (including Asian alone and multiple-race Asian) in 2010 ("We the Americans: Asians" 1993, 1; Hoeffel, Rastogi, Kim, and Shahid 2012, 3). Recent data also reveals a fast-growing rate of the Asian multiple-race population. From 2000 to 2010, this group grew by about 1 million people; the 2010 census counts about 15 percent of the Asian population in this country as Asian in combination with one or more additional races (Hoeffel, Rastogi, Kim, and Shahid 2012, 4). These statistics suggest not only the changing demographics of Asian Americans as a general minority group but also the complexities and diversities within Asian American communities.

The term "Asian American" came out of the civil rights era in the 1960s. An umbrella term, it reflects a collective awareness of immigrants from a wide range of Asian countries and regions and Americans of Asian heritage. Historically, many have tended to believe a cohesive and shared culture among Asian Americans. While the broad Asian American culture shares some commonalities, rich variations are important to understand specific cultural expressions. This two-volume *Asian American Culture: From Anime to Tiger Moms* addresses Asian American culture broadly defined to encompass the historical as well as contemporary cultural practices and productions related to Asian Americans. As indicated by the Guide to Related Topics, the entry essays introduce to the reader regional, national, and transnational cultural forms in many fields of study: art, music, and theater; education and politics; family and community; food; gender and sexuality; history and migration; holidays, festivals, and folk tradition; literature and culture; media, sports, and entertainment; and religion, spirituality, and belief. The accompanying sidebars highlight significant events, legal cases and documents, individuals, geographic locations, texts, and other objects in Asian American history and experiences.

When studying Asian American culture, it is crucial to recognize its integral connection to history, legislation, and politics. As living forms of expression, cultural practices and productions derive from and in turn reflect particular sociohistorical contexts.

If Asian American communities were already diverse when early immigrants arrived in North America, they have become more varied and complex in recent years. As Huping Ling (1956–) has pointed out, such increasing diversity "poses new challenges not only to communities affected but also to the academic field of Asian American studies," and the consequent new shifting directions in the study of Asian Americans will have "an impact on federal and local policies," which in turn affects Asian Americans in this country (2008, 4). While the past few decades have seen a growing number of studies on Asian Americans, most of the works focus on the history and experiences of the groups with large numbers of population such as Chinese, Japanese, Korean, Filipino, and Asian Indian Americans. In comparison, studies on underrepresented groups—for example, Burmese, Indonesians, Singaporeans, Laotians, Thai, Cambodians, and Tibetans—are recent and relatively few in number. Multiple essays in this encyclopedia are devoted to introducing historically underrepresented Asian Americans and their cultural practices and forms to the reader. Pairing the entries "Hmong American Immigration" with "Hmong American Culture" and "Hmong American Religions and Beliefs," for example, provides a broad historical survey of the Hmongs' long history of immigration to other countries, including the United States, and its connection to regional and international conflicts; it also offers in-depth discussion of traditional Hmong clans, community celebrations, and faith practices. Cross-referencing the entries "Cambodian American Performing Arts and Artists," "Cambodian American Folklore," "Cambodian American Literature," and "Cambodian American Films and Filmmakers" outlines a comprehensive overview of the rich traditions and cultural forms of Cambodian Americans.

Reflecting the diversity, disparity, and complexity within Asian American communities, this encyclopedia includes both overviews and in-depth studies of specific topics. On the one hand, the overview essays provide readers with a general introduction to well-known as well as emerging practices and works and help them form a historical snapshot of particular areas in the broad spectrum of Asian American culture. For example, the entry "Demographics, Asian American" outlines how government legislation and classification in population surveys help shape Asian American demographic patterns historically and nowadays. It also discusses the implications of census data and examines in detail particular groups based on countries of origin. On the other hand, essays addressing monumental events, landmark works, controversial cases, and other specific topics offer in-depth studies of cases that have significant impact on the formation of Asian American identities and communities and the development of Asian American culture. For instance, the entry "Guan Yu" presents a thorough study of a prominent figure in Chinese American folklore and literature through introducing his origin in Chinese history, literature, folklore, and theater performances; discussing this character's long-lasting presence in Chinese American communities in the forms of worshipping, festivals, and celebrations; and addressing the strong influence of his legacy on contemporary Asian and Asian American writers, artists, and filmmakers. Essays such as these highlight the importance of a comprehensive understanding of Asian American culture and its historical, regional, and ethnic diversity.

The entries included in these volumes address the reigning ideas and frameworks in studies of American culture and at the same time challenge the established paradigms. While recognizing the established frameworks and landmark works, this encyclopedia also outlines new directions, recent trends, and controversial practices and productions. It enables readers to incorporate Asian American cultural productions into their studies of arts, music, theater, literature, folklore, history, politics, religion, and popular culture. Entries such as "Discrimination against Asian Americans," "Chinese Exclusion Act (1882)," and "War Bride Act (1945)" offer glimpses into the exclusionary laws and diplomatic agreements that have had significant impact on Asian immigration and the formation and development of Asian American communities in the United States. By passing the Chinese Exclusion Act in 1882, Congress fundamentally changed American immigration policy. As historian L. Ling-chi Wang has stated, "Up until 1882 America was open to everybody who wanted to come. We welcomed everybody. The only people that we excluded by law, at that time, were prostitutes, lepers and morons, and in 1882 we added the Chinese to that list" (qtd. in *Becoming American* 2003). The act had a significant impact on the Chinese American population. The Chinese population declined at the end of the 19th century and continued to decrease for the next few decades. By 1940, the number of American-born Chinese had outgrown those born in China (Wong 2013, 284). The act was finally repealed by the Magnuson Act in 1943, allowing Chinese nationals residing in the country to become naturalized citizens.

Exclusion and discrimination have stemmed from not only economic concerns but also cultural and racial differences; they are not just a legal matter but are prevalent in other areas. Since the 19th century, media representations of Asians and Asian Americans in the United States have been problematic in many cases. As the entries "Popular Culture, Asian Americans," "Comics and Graphic Narratives, Asian American," and "Television, Asian Americans on" indicate, racial stereotypes and misrepresentations continue to permeate American popular culture and have significant impact on Asian Americans. Studies such as these contextualize common stereotypes, show how they recur and transform, and demonstrate the nuances and complexities within them. Contributors to these volumes also critically examine high-profile and controversial cases in such entries as "Model Minority," "Linsanity," and "Tiger Mom" and introduce Asian American productions that provide counternarratives and nuanced representations of Asian American people and culture. In addition, researchers included in these two volumes direct the reader's attention to previously less known areas in entries such as "Fashion, Asian Americans and," "Video and Online Games, Asian Americans and," "The Internet and Asian Americans," and "Fusion Cuisine," thus charting new territories in the understanding of Asian American cultural forms.

For Asian immigrants and their American-born offspring, preserving cultural elements from their ancestors' countries of origin is of great importance. As living and evolving forms, cultural practices change and transform as they are implemented in the United States. Since the early immigration years, Asian immigrants have formed support groups and community organizations. As the number of Asians and Asian Americans grew in the United States in recent decades, more and more community organizations came into being. Preservation and celebration of Asian American culture have expanded well beyond Asian American communities nationwide. Representatives Frank Horton (1919–2004) of New York and Norman Mineta (1931–) of California and Senators Daniel Inouye (1924–2012) and Spark Matsunaga (1916–1990) introduced resolutions asking the president to declare the first 10 days of May as Asian/Pacific Heritage Week in 1977. President Jimmy Carter signed a joint resolution designating the annual celebration. President George H. W. Bush proclaimed the month of May to be Asian/Pacific American Heritage Month in 1990 ("Asian-Pacific American History Month," 2015). The publication of *Asian American Culture,* as part of the new Cultures of the American Mosaic series, reflects the increasing awareness of and interests in Asian American culture among general readers. These two volumes are designed as a guide to the great variety of Asian American cultural expressions.

Lan Dong

Further Reading

"Asian-Pacific American History Month." Library of Congress, http://asianpacificheritage.gov/index.html.

Barnes, Jessica S., and Claudette E. Bennett. "The Asian Population: 2000." U.S. Census Bureau, February 2002, https://www.census.gov/prod/2002pubs/c2kbr01-16.pdf.

Becoming American: The Chinese Experience. A Bill Moyers Special for Public Affairs Television. DVD, 2003.

Chan, Sucheng. *Asian Americans: An Interpretive History.* New York: Twayne, 1991.

Hoeffel, Elizabeth M., Sonya Rastogi, Myoung Ouk Kim, and Hasan Shahid. "The Asian Population: 2010." U.S. Census Bureau, March 2012, http://www.census.gov/prod/cen2010/briefs/c2010br-11.pdf.

Ling, Huping. "Introduction: Emerging Voices of Underrepresented Asian Americas." In *Emerging Voices: Experiences of Underrepresented Asian Americans,* edited by Huping Ling, 1–13. New Brunswick, NJ: Rutgers University Press, 2008.

Smith, Marcus T. "Fact Sheet: The State of Asian American Women in the United States." Center for American Progress, November 2013, https://www.americanprogress.org/issues/race/report/2013/11/07/79182/fact-sheet-the-state-of-asian-american-women-in-the-united-states/.

Takaki, Ronald T. *Strangers from a Different Shore: A History of Asian Americans.* Boston: Little, Brown, 1989.

U.S. Department of Commerce, Economics and Statistic Administration, Bureau of the Census. *We the Americans: Asians.* Washington, DC: U.S. Government Printing Office, 1993, https://www.census.gov/prod/cen1990/wepeople/we-3.pdf.

U.S. Department of Commerce, Economics and Statistic Administration, Bureau of Census. *We the Americans: Pacific Islanders.* Washington, DC: U.S. Government Printing Office, 1993, http://www.census.gov/prod/cen1990/wepeople/we-4.pdf.

Wong, K. Scott. "Chinese and Chinese Americans, 1870–1940." In *Immigrants in American History: Arrival, Adaptation, and Integration,* edited by Elliott Robert Barkan, 279–289. Santa Barbara, CA: ABC-CLIO, 2013.

J

JAPANESE AMERICAN ARTS AND ARTISTS

History and Origins

There is very limited documentation of Japanese American arts and artists in the early immigration years. Chiura Obata (1885–1975) is a recipient of the Order of the Sacred Treasure, 5th Class, for promoting goodwill and cultural understanding between the United States and Japan. Born in Japan, Toshi Shimizu (1887–1945) arrived in Seattle in 1907 and later moved to New York. He exhibited in New York, Chicago, and Paris. Born in Okayama, Japan, Yasuo Kuniyoshi (1893–1953) came to the United States when he was a teenager. He first lived on the West Coast and then moved to New York City. His early artwork combines elements of American folk tradition, Japanese prints, and European modernism. In 1948 the Whitney Museum of American Art in New York held a retrospective of his work, the first solo show for a living American artist and the first for an Asian American artist at Whitney.

Japanese American Visual Arts and Artists

Numerous Japanese American artists have made important contribution to the development of modern arts, including among others painter and collagist Paul Horiuchi (1906–1999); painter Jimmy Mirikitani (1920–2012); sculptor Ruth Asawa (1926–2013); screen-printer Arthur Okamura (1932–2009); painter, illustrator, and architect Shusaku Arakawa (1936–2010); renowned landscape architect Robert Murase (1938–2005); and comics artist and animator Jeff Matsuda (1970–).

Isamu Noguchi (1904–1988) is a prominent Japanese American artist and landscape architect. His notable works include among others the Japanese Garden at United Nations Educational, Scientific and Cultural Organization (UNESCO) headquarters in Paris; the Gardens for IBM headquarters in Armonk, New York; the Billy Rose Sculpture Garden at the Israel Museum in Jerusalem, Israel; the bust of Martha Graham at the Honolulu Museum of Art in Hawai'i; sculpture for First National City Bank building in Fort Worth, Texas; and Moerenuma Park in Sapporo, Japan. He was awarded the Edward

Known for his sculptures and public works, Isamu Noguchi's representative work is *Red Cube* **at the HSBC Building in the Financial District of New York City, April 11, 2010. (Sean Pavone/Dreamstime.com)**

MacDowell Medal for Outstanding Lifetime Contribution to the Arts in 1982, the National Medal of Arts in 1987, the Order of the Sacred Treasure from the Japanese government in 1988, and many other honors and awards. His works are collected in numerous museums around the world and at the Noguchi Museum in New York City. His obituary in the *New York Times* considered him "a versatile and prolific sculptor whose earthy stones and meditative gardens bridging East and West have become landmarks of 20th-century art" (Brenson 1988).

Sueo Serosawa (1910–2004) is best known for his modernist artwork. Serosawa was born in Yokohama, Japan, and his family moved to the United States in 1918. They lived in Seattle and Los Angeles. During World War II, they moved to Chicago and then New York and then returned to Los Angeles after the war in 1947. He painted a portrait of American actress Judy Garland (1922–1969) around 1940. His works have been included in the collections of the Metropolitan Museum of Art in New York and the Smithsonian Institution in Washington, D.C.

Miné Okubo (1912–2001) is known for her paintings, portraits, murals, and *Citizen 13660* (1946), a book of drawings and text narratives documenting her experience in Japanese American internment camps during World War II. Born and raised in California, she moved to New York City after World War II. She is the recipient of the Bertha Taussig Memorial Traveling Fellowship, the American Book Award, the Lifetime Achievement Award from the Women's Caucus for Art, and many other honors and awards.

Many organizations have played a vital role in the development of Japanese American arts during the past few decades. For example, the Japanese Art Society of America (JASA) traces its origin to a group of collectors around the New York City area in 1973. During the past few decades, JASA has been offering and developing its programs for members as well as the general public. Besides hosting exhibitions, gallery shows, and lectures, JASA organizes a variety of programs and events and publishes *Impressions Journal* and newsletters. Located in Los Angeles, California, the Japanese American National Museum hosts exhibitions, develops projects, offers research resources, and provides art education programs for adults and children.

Japanese American Performing Arts and Artists

Japanese American performing arts have roots in traditional Japanese performing arts. Performing arts in varied forms have a long history in Japan. The widely known forms include *noh* theater, *kabuki* dance drama, and *bunraku*. *Noh* is one of the oldest theater performances in the world. A highly stylized form of drama, it combines various performing elements, including dance, chanting, and music. The main character in *noh* is usually masked. A *noh* program commonly includes *noh* plays with comic *kyōgen* plays in between.

Kabuki is known for its stylized drama and the elaborate makeup of the performers. The three main categories of *kabuki* plays are *jidai-mono* (historical stories), *sewa-mono* (domestic stories), and *shosagoto* (dance pieces). It was particularly popular during the Edo period (1603–1868) in Japan and began to decline by the beginning of the Meiji era (1868–1912). *Kabuki* was inscribed on the United Nations Educational, Scientific and Cultural Organization Representative List of the Intangible Cultural Heritage of Humanity in 2008.

Bunraku is a form of puppet theater in Japan and can be traced to the 17th century. It commonly features three kinds of performers: the puppeteers, the chanters, and the musicians. In modern times, there have been many efforts to preserve and continue traditional performing arts in Japan, including the

National Theater in Tokyo completed in 1966, the National Noh Theater established in 1983, and the National Bunraku Theater in 1984, among others.

In the United States, many organizations have played an important role in the development of Japanese American performing arts. Various institutes and groups host, sponsor, and organize a variety of performances, promote and support Japanese and Japanese American performing artists and professionals, and facilitate other programs. For example, the Japan Foundation New York (JFNY) offers a number of grants and programs to support the introduction of Japanese performance arts to local communities in the United States and Canada. The JFNY has funded over 200 projects. The Japan Foundation Los Angeles (JFLA) manages arts and culture grants for the 13 states west of the Rocky Mountains: Alaska, Arizona, California, Colorado, Hawai'i, Idaho, Montana, Nevada, New Mexico, Oregon, Utah, Washington, and Wyoming. The JFLA offers programs supporting museums and art institutions in its efforts to introduce and develop Japanese arts and culture outside of Japan. Its Performing Arts Japan program provides financial assistance for performances and coproductions in North America. The Japanese American Citizens League, the oldest and largest Asian American civil rights organization in the United States, has been supporting students through its National Scholarship and Awards program since 1946, including creative and performing arts. Funded by the Japan-US Friendship Commission, the Noh Training Project provides intensive, extensive, and performance-based training in *noh*.

Lan Dong

See also: Japanese American Folklore; Japanese American Immigration; Japanese American Literature

Further Reading

Brenson, Michael. "Isamu Noguchi, the Sculptor, Dies at 84." *New York Times*, December 31, 1988, http://www.nytimes.com/1988/12/31/obituaries/isamu-noguchi -the-sculptor-dies-at-84.html.

Chang, Gordon H., Mark Dean Johnson, Paul J. Karlstrom, and Sharon Spain, eds. *Asian American Art: A History, 1850–1970.* Stanford, CA: Stanford University Press, 2008.

Doss, Erika. *Twentieth-Century American Art.* Oxford and New York: Oxford University Press, 2002.

Hoeffel, Elizabeth M., Sonya Rastogi, Myoung Ouk Kim, and Hasan Shahid. "The Asian Population: 2010." U.S. Census Bureau, March 2012, http://www.census .gov/prod/cen2010/briefs/c2010br-11.pdf.

The Japanese American National Museum, http://www.janm.org/.

Japanese Art Society of America, http://www.japaneseartsoc.org/.

The Japan Foundation Los Angeles, http://jflalc.org/.

The Japan Foundation New York, http://www.jfny.org/.

"Kabuki Theatre." UNESCO, 2008, http://www.unesco.org/culture/ich/index.php?lg=en&pg=00011&RL=00163.

Khalid, Farisa. "For Heritage Month, Remembering 'One of a Kind' Painter Yasuo Kuniyoshi." Asia Society, May 10, 2013, http://asiasociety.org/blog/asia/heritage-month-remembering-one-kind-painter-yasuo-kuniyoshi.

Noh Training Project, http://www.nohtrainingproject.org/.

Yang, Alice. *Why Asia? Contemporary Asian and Asian American Art.* New York: New York University Press, 1998.

JAPANESE AMERICAN AUTOBIOGRAPHIES

Japanese American autobiographies began to appear half a century after the first group of Japanese landed on Hawai'i in 1868. Early Japanese American autobiographies include *Daughter of Samurai* (1925) by Etsu Inagaki Sugimoto, *Holy Prayers in a Horse's Ear* (1932) by Kathleen Tamagawa, and *Restless Wave: My Life in Two Worlds* (1940) by Ayako Ishigaki. Born into a prestigious family in 1874, Sugimoto immigrated to the United States as the wife of a Japanese merchant. In *Daughter of Samurai,* Sugimoto introduces Japanese culture that was not fully understood in the United States at the time. Born to an Irish mother and a Japanese father, Tamagawa narrates her identity and the ways in which other people perceive her and her mixed race in *Holy Prayers in a Horse's Ear.* Her book also reflects her experiences living in several countries including Japan because of her father's and husband's businesses. Ishigaki, daughter of a professor and wife of a painter, narrates her political perspectives in *Restless Wave* using a mixed genre of autobiography, fiction, and reportage. While these early autobiographies are unique texts in their own way, their perspectives are limited to the realm of the upper middle class. The authors' socioeconomic status led to the book being removed from the majority of Japanese Americans who were plantation laborers, farmers, and small business owners at that time.

During World War II, over 11,000 Japanese Americans on the West Coast were forcibly interned in various camps as enemy aliens. The trauma experienced during this period has profoundly affected Japanese American autobiographies. In the postwar era, Nisei (second-generation Japanese Americans) who were born in the United States and were fluent in English began to write autobiographies reflecting their experiences and expressing their feelings toward the incarceration.

Nisei Daughter (1953)

Nisei Daughter is widely recognized as one of the first autobiographies written by a Nisei writer. In this autobiography, Monica Sone (1919–2011) recollects her childhood and helping her parents run a hotel in Seattle, Washington. During her childhood and adolescent years, Sone constantly had to negotiate her Japanese American identity. In the first chapter, she expresses a shocking discovery at the age of six that she is indeed Japanese. She must adjust herself to two different worlds: an active American in a regular school on weekdays and a passive Japanese in an ethnic school on the weekends. Consequently, she struggles for a sense of belonging and fails to completely assimilate into Japanese and American culture. On the one hand, a trip to Japan exposes cultural differences between her and her relatives and convinces her that her home is the United States. On the other hand, she experiences racial discrimination in the United States when her family is not allowed to move to the suburbs. *Nisei Daughter* also documents her family's incarnation at the Minedoka Camp in Idaho during World War II. Through reflecting on her experiences in the camp and attending college after her release, the narrator eventually comes to terms with her Japanese American identity.

During the late 1960s, the civil rights movement inspired some Nisei to write their autobiographies, although it consisted of a small number of publications. As a war hero of the 442nd Regimental Combat Team and a politician, the late senator Daniel Inouye (1924–2012) wrote his success story, *Journey to Washington* (1967), in collaboration with Lawrence Elliott. In *American in Disguise* (1970), Daniel Okimoto (1942–), who was born during the Japanese American internment, tells the story of how he pursued education as a means of overcoming racial discrimination. In *The Two Worlds of Jim Yoshida* (1972), Jim Katsumi Yoshida (1921–), in collaboration with Bill Hosokawa (1915–2007), documents his life as a Kibei (Japanese Americans who were born in the United States, received education in Japan, and then returned to the United States) who was detained during his visit to Japan and drafted by the army and his legal struggles in 1953 to regain his U.S. citizenship. Bill Hosokawa (1915–2007) published two autobiographies. *Thirty-Five Years in the Frying Pan* (1978) is about his internment experience at the Heart Mountain Camp in Wyoming, and *Out of the Frying Pan* (1989) is about his observations of Japanese American communities as a journalist. Yoshiko Uchida (1921–1992), who is the author of several children's books, published an autobiography, *Desert Exile: The Uprooting of a Japanese American Family* (1982). It documents

Farewell to Manzanar (1973)

Farewell to Manzanar is Jeanne Wakatsuki Houston's (1934–) collaborative autobiography with his husband, writer James Houston (1957–). Jeanne Houston was born in 1934 in Long Beach, California. Her narrative reveals how Pearl Harbor and World War II changed her and her family's lives. Without a full understanding of her surroundings, she observed her father's psychological damage caused by the war. The FBI regarded him as a suspected collaborator with Japan; he became a violent alcoholic after being released from the detention camp. Sometimes Houston narrates traumatic incidents with a child's naïveté. For example, she recalls her relocation to Manzanar Camp with excitement as a child as if she is going on a vacation. In the camp, she continually searches for a space to fit into through extracurricular activities. After the war, an 11-year-old Houston fights against racism by empowering stereotypes and winning a beauty contest. A prominent theme during her adolescence is the sense of acceptance. Decades later, Houston is unable to detach herself from the trauma of the war and decides to revisit the site of Manzanar Camp with her husband and children in 1972. Once there she finally releases her repressed memory and pain and manages to leave these issues behind at the camp.

her life at the Topaz Camp in Utah and reflects her struggle with Japanese American identity.

Inspired by the civil rights movement, Japanese Americans lobbied for an investigation of the unconstitutional treatment of Japanese Americans during World War II. In 1980, the Japanese American Redress Movement promoted awareness in the U.S. government that eventually established the Commission on Wartime Relocation and the Internment of Civilians. This series of redress movements helped Japanese Americans negotiate with their traumatic experiences. Former internees tend to regard their internment as shameful and often refuse to talk about it. The redress movement also helped Sansei (third-generation Japanese Americans), many of whom were born after the war, learn about their cultural heritage and the internment. Thus, the redress movement became the inspiration for Sansei writers as well as the turning point of Japanese American history.

In the 1990s, Japanese American autobiographies demonstrated the diversity of its authors and narratives. In *Turning Japanese: Memoirs of a Sansei* (1991), David Mura (1952–) narrates how his understanding of his Japanese American identity transformed during his stay in Japan. He further examines how his sexuality is intertwined with being an ethnic minority in *Where the Body Meets Memory: A Odyssey of Race, Sexuality, and Identity* (1996). In *Taking High Monks in the*

Snow: An Asian American Odyssey (1992), Lydia Minatoya (1950–) writes about how she changed the view of her ethnicity through her experiences abroad in Japan, China, and Nepal. Garrett Hongo (1951–), a Yonsei (fourth-generation Japanese American), combines his family's history with the natural history of his Hawai'ian hometown in *Volcano: A Memoir of Hawai'i* (1995). Farmer David Mas Masumoto (1954–) narrates a one-year story of farming along with his family's history and the coexistence with nature in *Epitaph for a Peach: Four Seasons on My Family Farm* (1995). Actor George Takei's (1937–) autobiography *To the Stars: The Autobiography of George Takei, Star Trek's Mr. Sulu* (1994) recollects memories of his childhood at the Rohwer Camp in Arkansas.

Japanese American autobiographies published in the 2000s inherit many of the themes from the previous decade as well as address new topics emerging in the new millennium. Well-known activist Yuri Kochiyama (1921–2014) recollects her internment experience at the Jerome Camp in Arkansas along with her lifelong activism for civil rights in *Passing It On* (2004). In *The Heartland: My Japanese Girlhood in Whitebread America* (2006), Linda Furiya writes about her childhood isolation as an ethnic minority in a white-dominated area, her father's story as a Kibei, and an ethnic identity gained through a Japanese culinary heritage. Kyoko Mori, a former international student and now a Shin-Issei (new first-generation Japanese American), narrates her traumatic past in Japan as well as her new life in the United States as a student, wife, and teacher in *Yarn: Remembering the Way Home* (2010). Born in Hawai'i and of mixed heritage, Rahna Reiko Rizzuto recollects her research and interviews with atomic bomb survivors in *Hiroshima in the Morning* (2010).

Yuki Obayashi

See also: Autobiographies, Asian American; Chinese American Autobiographies; Japanese American Internment; Japanese American Literature; Japanese American Women

Further Reading

Austin, Allan W. *From Concentration Camp to Campus: Japanese American Students and World War II.* Urbana: University of Illinois Press, 2004.

Bloom, Harold, ed. *Asian-American Writers.* New York: Chelsea House, 1999.

Daniels, Roger. *Concentration Camps, North America: Japanese in the United States and Canada during World War II.* Revised ed. Malabar, FL: R. E. Krieger, 1981.

Sherman, Mark, George Katagiri, and Lawson Fusao Inada, eds. *Touching the Stones: Tracing One Hundred Years of Japanese American History.* Portland: Oregon Nikkei Endowment, 1994.

Wong, Sau-ling Cynthia. *Reading Asian American Literature: From Necessity to Extravagance.* Princeton, NJ: Princeton University Press, 1993.

JAPANESE AMERICAN CHILDREN AND FAMILY

For the first wave of immigrants from Japan to the United States at the end of the 19th century, typically family was most prominent in their lives and central to their everyday experiences and decision making. The vast majority of this first generation of Japanese Americans (known as Issei) immigrated to the United States in search of employment and planned to return to Japan when economic circumstances warranted. In part because they perceived their time in the United States as temporary, culturally the Issei remained fully Japanese, and few learned English. Their Japanese culture and its strong Confucian influences, then, were the foundation for their belief that family was the most important social unit. Indeed, family was thought to be protection from and even a weapon against a hostile world, and family ties and continuity were considered critical components of a quality life. As a result, for the Issei the well-being of their children was paramount and considered key to both maintaining strong family ties and perpetuating their family and the family's name through time. For these reasons many sacrifices were made for children, and children were expected to be well educated and self-disciplined, as these characteristics were thought to be fundamental to success in an ever-changing world.

In stark contrast, Japanese Americans coming of age today, several generations after the Issei arrived from Japan, have assimilated to such a degree that most have virtually no contact with people in Japan; do not speak, read, or understand Japanese languages; and are not familiar with historical or contemporary Japanese culture. Moreover, for the most part their family-related values, structures, and behaviors mirror those of the larger population in the United States. In fact, even for the children of the Issei, the second generation of Japanese Americans (known as Nisei), assimilation was extensive. For example, most Nisei spoke English unless interacting with their parents. This alarmed many Issei, as speaking Japanese was considered crucial to a Japanese identity and to navigating and maintaining the close-knit communities of Japanese Americans that existed prior to World War II. Because Issei were intent on their children identifying as Japanese and having Japanese values and sensibilities, many Nisei were sent to Japanese-language schools.

The Nisei, though, had begun to adopt attitudes about family prevalent in the United States at the time. Although family ties remained important to the Nisei, this generation did not view those ties as essential for their survival. However, Nisei rarely married outside of their ethnic and cultural group. If needed to ensure this, it was acceptable for sons to secure picture brides from Japan, often with the encouragement and financial support of their parents. Picture brides were women from Japan who were brought to the United States to marry first- and second-generation Japanese American men who had remained unmarried for some time. The term "picture bride" refers to the fact that families only had a picture of the son's wife-to-be in advance of relocating her to the United States. By the time the third generation of Japanese Americans (known as Sansei) came of age, the rate of intergroup marriage had risen sharply, with approximately one in every four marriages among Japanese Americans including a spouse with little or no Japanese heritage. This rate doubled for the next generation, with nearly 50 percent marrying someone with no Japanese ancestry. The internment of Japanese Americans during World War II was thought to be a key factor in this rapid rise in interethnic and cultural marriages, as anyone with one drop of Japanese blood could be interned. Hence, Japanese Americans found themselves living in restricted communities with people outside of their previously homogenous enclaves, and many interethnic marriages followed.

The internment of Japanese Americans had other profound effects on Japanese American family life. For example, with their jobs, careers, and material possessions gone or out of reach during internment, many Japanese American men seemed to experience an identity crisis of sorts, as their roles as head of household and provider were gone. In addition, the internment led to a substantial reduction in the number and size of Japanese American enclaves. When released, Japanese Americans had to make their homes wherever they could, as many had lost their businesses and possessions upon being interned. The upheaval associated with internment, then, in terms of employment, material wealth, gender roles, and place of residence is thought to have led to a more rapid and comprehensive assimilation into American culture for Japanese Americans than would have otherwise occurred.

Indeed, contemporary parenting philosophies and practices among Japanese Americans are mostly indistinguishable from other American parents today. Just a few prominent and traditional features of parenting in Japan can still be discerned. In terms of child development, while European Americans tend to emphasize independence, self-reliance, and self-actualization in their children, Japanese American parents are more likely to value adaptability to group norms and work, impulse control, harmony, and obedience in their children. Well-known Japanese expressions reflective of these child-rearing differences remain commonplace, even among fourth-generation Japanese American parents. These include *gaman,* which means that one should set aside one's own goals and endure the circumstances, and *enryo,* which means keeping one's desires to oneself. In addition, Japanese American children are more likely to downplay their accomplishments and present modesty when compared to European American children. Such modesty is intended to enhance their ability to get along in groups.

Indeed, another traditional Japanese expression popular among contemporary Japanese American parents is that "the nail that sticks out gets hammered down."

The prominence of the parent-child relationship over the marital relationship also is more common in Japanese American families than European American families. On average, in Japanese American families the connection between mother and child is often more intertwined, and the mother generally contributes more to the socialization of children than Japanese American fathers do and more than the larger population of American mothers do on average. At the other end of the life cycle, older Japanese American widows are much more likely to live with their adult children when compared to non-Hispanic white widows in the United States. However, when compared to contemporary widows in Japan, Japanese American widows are much less likely to live with their adult children. In essence, then, contemporary Japanese American families are nearly indistinguishable from the larger population of American families with respect to everyday family life, family values, and family structure, yet some remnants of traditional Japanese family practices and philosophies remain.

Melanie Moore

See also: Japanese American Immigration; Picture Bride

Further Reading

Kitano, Harry H. L. *Japanese Americans: The Evolution of a Subculture.* Englewood Cliffs, NJ: Prentice Hall, 1976.

Lee, Lauren. *Japanese Americans.* Tarrytown, NY: Benchmark Books, 1996.

Modell, John. "The Japanese American Family: A Perspective for Future Investigations." *Pacific Historical Review* 37(1) (1968): 67–81.

O'Brien, David J., and Stephen S. Fugita. *The Japanese American Experience.* Bloomington: Indiana University Press, 1991.

Yanagisako, Sylvia. *Transforming the Past: Tradition and Kinship among Japanese Americans.* Stanford, CA: Stanford University Press, 1985.

Yoo, David K. *Growing Up Nisei: Race, Generation, and Culture among Japanese Americans of California, 1924–49.* Urbana: University of Illinois Press, 1999.

JAPANESE AMERICAN FICTION

Japanese American fiction is often associated with internment literature. Numerous writers have captured poignant moments and memories of how their lives were forever changed as a result of the Japanese American internment during World War II. The literature may not be categorized as "resistance," but

John Okada (1923–1971)

John Okada was a Japanese American writer known primarily for his novel *No-No Boy* (1957). Set in Seattle and the Pacific Northwest, the novel examines the harrowing sociological and psychological impact of the Japanese American internment during and after World War II. Okada contextualizes his novel from the point of view of a 25-year-old Nisei (second-generation) Ichiro forced to withstand prejudice and racism based on his ethnicity. The character is imprisoned for two years, having answered "no" to questions 27 and 28 of the loyalty questionnaire of 1943: "Are you willing to serve in the armed forces of the United States on combat duty, wherever ordered?" and "Will you swear unqualified allegiance to the United States of America and faithfully defend the United States from any or all attack by foreign and domestic forces, and forswear any form of allegiance or obedience to the Japanese Emperor, or any other foreign government, power, or organization?" Throughout the novel, Okada subtly directs attention to the creation of a phantasm, an evil imaginary figure routinely constructed through government propaganda. This remains the underlying theme of Okada's work—the discrimination and racism that existed not only toward Japanese Americans but within the Japanese American community itself. Though Okada's novel was not widely received upon publication, his work is widely used and referenced not only for Asian American studies classes but also for courses that study social injustice nowadays.

authors such as John Okada (1923–1971), Yoshiko Uchida (1921–1992), Jeanne Wakatsuki Houston (1934–), and many others have crafted narratives that help the reader comprehend the injustice that Japanese Americans endured not only in the 1940s but also in postwar eras. These narratives of social injustice conveyed the pain of articulate silences, a theme that runs through the work of Wakako Yamauchi's (1924–) *Songs My Mother Taught Me* (1994), Hisaye Yamamoto's (1921–2011) *Seventeen Syllables* (1988), and Joy Kogawa's (1935–) *Obasan* (1981). As scholar King-Kok Cheung (1954–) notes, these writers convey how emotions are expressed not simply through Western verbal structures but also through gestures, expressions, and subtle nuances that provide readers with a glimpse of comprehending Japanese American culture. The work of Yamauchi and Yamamoto offers lyricism and denies normative, linear movement, as their stories highlight the angst and grace of characters who were interned, often with no definitive conclusion at the end of their stories.

In "The Legend of Miss Sasagawara," a story in *Seventeen Syllables*, Yamamoto creates an allegory whereby the protagonist is treated as a spectacle by

Yoshiko Uchida (1921–1992)

Yoshiko Uchida was a prolific Japanese American writer. Her first two publications, *The Dancing Tea Kettle and Other Japanese Folk Tales* (1949) and *New Friends for Susan* (1951), are based on Japanese folklore. Having spent at least two years in Japan, she immersed herself in the study of Japanese arts. Such experience serves as the foundation for primary themes in her work. Having written over 30 books, she is perhaps best-known for adolescent and children's literature. Arguably, her most critical text was her autobiography *Desert Exile: The Uprooting of a Japanese American Family* (1982) in which Uchida explores how the internment has lasting effects on the structure of family. Her work voices the silences that continue to hold intergenerational trauma for the Issei, Nisei, and Sansei (first-, second-, and third-generation) communities. These silences provide context for how individuals and families endured the unjust treatment of internment and how they attempted to assimilate into mainstream American culture. Uchida's primary audiences were children and young adults, as her desire was to transmit themes of an enduring attitude. Her works honor several generations through positive values. Some of the major themes she has written about include humor in the face of adversity, one's ability to endure treacherous circumstances, and resilience.

other internees who ridicule her for eccentricities and "odd" verbal communication. The parallel to the U.S. government and its treatment of Japanese Americans before, during, and after World War II provides questions regarding social justice that were earmarked but remain unanswered. Yamauchi's, Yamamoto's, and Kogawa's works raise the question of what exactly constitutes an American and how one can achieve this status or privilege if one is consistently treated as an enemy alien. Similarly, Lawson Fusao Inada's (1938–) family was interned in Colorado, Arkansas, and Fresno, California, during World War II. His poetry illuminates not only the emotional turmoil of internment but also the physical hardships of living in harsh environments.

Milton Murayama's (1923–) *All I Asking for Is My Body* (1975) chronicles how assimilation was different in Hawai'i from those who lived on the continent. This novella focuses on a protagonist who leaves Hawai'i and enters the military in order to prove his allegiance to the U.S. government. At the same time, the book offers images and dialogues that contextualize plantation life in Hawai'i. It is arguably one of the first books to challenge the idyllic lifestyle of the islands and underscores social injustice within a stratified, hegemonic system. Perhaps a distinction between Japanese American fiction told from a mainland or continental perspective and Japanese American fiction of Hawai'i is the usage of language. The seminal work of Eileen Tamura and Charlene Sato in the 1980s and 1990s dispelled disturbing stereotypes that those who spoke Hawai'ian Creole English suffered from learning disabilities or speech impediments. Their efforts enabled local artists of Hawai'i to write about their experiences in a language that is natural to them.

Lee Tonouchi (1972–), Lois-Ann Yamanaka (1961–), and others provide a distinct sound to the dialogue in their works. Tonouchi challenges arguments regarding standard English in his fiction and scholarly endeavors. He wrote his master's thesis in Hawai'ian Creole English (also known as pidgin) and continues to experiment with the rhythm and sound of the language in his stories. His work broaches the fact that languages are complex in origin and history, and usage and dialect vary from one location to the other and one generation to the next. Speaking Hawai'ian Creole English has become part of the discursive strategy through which Japanese American writers from Hawai'i reconstruct their identities in relation to their culture and home language.

Yamanaka is a prolific Japanese American writer who has published *Saturday Night at the Pahala Theatre* (1993), *Wild Meat and the Bully Burgers* (1996), *Blu's Hanging* (1997), *Heads by Harry* (1998), *Name Me Nobody* (1999), *Father of the Four Passages* (2001), and others. Since the 1990s, her work has gained critical acclaim. The controversy surrounding *Saturday Night at the Pahala Theatre* and *Blu's Hanging* appear regularly in discussions of Japanese American fiction among scholars and general readers. Some readers accuse these novels of contributing to harmful stereotypes of Filipino Americans.

Candace Fujikane's work "Sweeping Racism under the Rug of Censorship" (2002) propelled scholars, creative writers, graduate students, and teachers to examine their own place in a reified hierarchical system in which the Japanese and Chinese communities established a foothold of hegemonic privilege in Hawai'i. Since then Japanese Americans and scholars in Asian American studies continue to pose questions regarding social justice and Japanese American internment in the 1940s.

Amy Nishimura

See also: Japanese American Autobiographies; Japanese American Folklore; Japanese American Immigration; Japanese American Internment; Japanese American Poetry

Further Reading

Cheung, King-Kok. *Articulate Silences: Hisaye Yamamoto, Maxine Hong Kingston, Joy Kogawa*. Ithaca, NY: Cornell University Press, 1993.

Murayama, Milton. *All I Asking for Is My Body*. Honolulu: University of Hawai'i Press, 1988.

Okihiro, Gary. *Whispered Silences: Japanese Americans and World War II.* Seattle: University of Washington Press, 1996.

Sumida, Stephen H. *And the View from the Shore: Literary Traditions of Hawaii.* Seattle: University of Washington Press, 1991.

Sumida, Stephen H. "Postcolonialism, Nationalism, and the Emergence of Asian/Pacific American Literatures." In *An Interethnic Companion to Asian American Literature,* edited by Kink-Kok Cheung, 274–288. New York and Cambridge: Cambridge University Press, 1997.

Takezawa, Yasuko. *Breaking the Silence: Redress and Japanese American Ethnicity.* Ithaca, NY: Cornell University Press, 1995.

Yamamoto, Hisaye. *Seventeen Syllables and Other Stories.* New Brunswick, NJ: Rutgers University Press, 2001.

Yamanaka, Lois-Ann. *Blu's Hanging.* New York: Avon Books, 1997.

JAPANESE AMERICAN FILMS AND FILMMAKERS

Japanese American actors and actresses have been active in the film industry since the early years. Some of the pioneers include Sessue Hayakawa (1889–1973), Tsuru Aoki (1892–1961), Jun Fujita (1888–1963), Reiko Sato (1931–1981), James Shigeta (1929–2014), Mako Iwamatsu (1933–2006), and Nobu McCarthy (1934–2002). Besides acting, Japanese Americans have also made significant contributions to directing, cinematography, screenwriting, and other aspects of filmmaking.

Tak Fujimoto (1939–) is a cinematographer of many Hollywood films including *The Silence of the Lambs* (1991), *The Sixth Sense* (1999), and *The Manchurian Candidate* (2004). Born in Hawai'i, Kayo Hatta (1958–2005) was a filmmaker, writer, and activist. She is best known for directing and cowriting the film *Picture Bride* (1995), winner of the Sundance Film Festival Audience Award for best dramatic film. Rokuro Bob Kuwahara (1901–1964) was an animator for Walt Disney and Terrytoons from the 1930s to the 1960s and creator for the *Hashimoto-san* series. Robert A. Nakamura (1937–) is a filmmaker, teacher, and cofounder of Visual Communications, the first community-based Asian Pacific American media arts organization in the United States.

To some degree, Japanese American film productions are influenced by the history of Japanese American immigration and Japanese Americans' experiences in the United States. For instance, documentary filmmakers have produced numerous films about Japanese Americans' experiences during World War II, focusing mainly on two aspects: Japanese American soldiers in combat and Japanese American internment. Loni Ding's (1931–2010) *The Color of*

Sessue Hayakawa (1889–1973)

Born in Chiba, Japan, Sessue Hayakawa was the first Asian actor who found stardom in the United States and Europe. His acting career lasted more than half a century, from the 1910s to the 1960s. He starred in more than 80 films and was the first Asian actor who played leading roles in the early American film industry. He was among the highest-paid actors at the time. During his long career in the film industry, he faced racial barriers. The Production Code came into effect in 1930 and forbade portrayals of miscegenation in films. Hayakawa was repeatedly typecast as a villain or an exotic and forbidden lover. His first film, *The Typhoon* (1914), was an instant success. His role in *The Cheat* (1915), directed by Cecil B. DeMille (1881–1959), made Hayakawa a romantic idol to women across America and a top leading man in romantic dramas in the 1910s and 1920s. His role in *The Bridge on the River Kwai* (1957) earned him an Academy Award nomination for best actor in a supporting role. His first sound film is *Daughter of the Dragon* (1931), in which he starred opposite Asian American actress Anna May Wong (1905–1961). He retired from the film business in 1966. Besides acting, he was also a director, screenwriter, theater actor, and zen master. He formed his own production company, Haworth Pictures Corporation, in 1918 and produced over 20 films. After he passed away in 1973, he was buried in the Chokeiji Temple Cemetery in Toyama, Japan.

Honor: The Japanese American Soldier in WWII (1987) and *442: For the Future* (1997), Junichi Suzuki's (1952–) *442: Live with Honor, Die with Dignity* (2010), and Vince Matsudaira's *America at Its Best: Legacy of Two Nisei Patriots* (2003) for the Nisei Veterans Committee of Seattle are a few examples of the documentary films portraying Japanese Americans in armed services during the war. A number of filmmakers also have produced documentaries about the internment experiences, such as Steve Rosen's *Beyond Barbed Wire* (1997), Stephen Holsapple's *Children of the Camps* (1999), Janice D. Tanaka's *When You're Smiling: The Deadly Legacy of Internment* (1999), Jeffrey S. Betts's *Democracy under Pressure: Japanese Americans and World War II* (2000), Konrad Aderer's *Enemy Alien* (2011), Lina Hoshino's *Caught in Between: What to Call Home in Times of War* (2004), and Andrea Palpant Dilley and Dave Tanner's *Take Me Home: A Child's Experience of Internment* (2005).

In addition, a number of feature films also reflect Japanese Americans' experiences in combat and in internment camps during World War II. *If Tomorrow Comes* (1971), directed by George McCowan (1927–1995), is a made-for-television film following the interracial relationship between a Nisei (second-generation Japanese American) man and a Caucasian women at the

Sessue Hayakawa in *The Bridge on the River Kwai* (1957). His role in the film earned him an Academy Award nomination for Best Actor in a Supporting Role. He is the first Asian actor to become a film star in the United States and Europe. (Columbia Pictures/Photofest)

beginning of World War II. *Farewell to Manzanar* (1976), a film made for television and directed by John Korty (1936–), is an adaptation of Jeanne Wakatsuki Houston's (1934–) memoirs of her experience before the war, in the Manzanar camp, and after the war. *Come See the Paradise* (1990), directed by Alan Parker (1944–), features an interracial family separated by the internment. *Day of Independence* (2003), directed by Chris Tashima (1960–), follows a Nisei teenager whose parents decided to return to Japan instead of staying in the internment camp. *American Pastime* (2007), directed by Desmond Nakano (1953–), portrays how the internees use baseball as a source of entertainment in the camp.

Younger generations of Japanese Americans continue to contribute to filmmaking and other media productions. Chris Tashima (1960–) is an awardwinning director, actor, and stage set designer. He is best known for directing, cowriting, and starring in the film *Visas and Virtue* (1997), which won an Academy Award for live-action short films. He cofounded Cedar Grove Productions in 1996. Iris Yamashita (1966–) is the screenwriter for Clint Eastwood's (1930–)

film *Letters from Iwo Jima* (2006). She was nominated for the Academy Award for original screenplay and the Chicago Film Critics Association Awards for best original screenplay. Ryan Higa (1990–) is a YouTube celebrity. His comedy videos have over 2 billion views, and his YouTube channel has millions of subscribers. He started posting YouTube videos when he was in high school. In 2012, he established his own production company, Ryan Higa Production Company.

Lan Dong

See also: Anime; Japanese American Immigration; Japanese American Internment; Japanese American Literature; Picture Bride; Popular Culture, Asian Americans and; Television, Asian Americans on

Further Reading

Chan, Sucheng. *Asian Americans: An Interpretive History.* New York: Twayne, 1991.

Chin, Frank, ed. *Born in the USA: A Story of Japanese America, 1889–1947.* Lanham, MD: Rowman and Littlefield, 2002.

Feng, Peter X. *Identities in Motion: Asian American Film and Video.* Durham, NC: Duke University Press, 2002.

Feng, Peter X., ed. *Screening Asian Americans.* New Brunswick, NJ: Rutgers University Press, 2002.

Hoeffel, Elizabeth M., Sonya Rastogi, Myoung Ouk Kim, and Hasan Shahid. "The Asian Population: 2010." U.S. Census Bureau, March 2012, http://www.census .gov/prod/cen2010/briefs/c2010br-11.pdf.

Miyao, Daisuke. *Sessue Hayakawa: Silent Cinema and Transnational Stardom.* Durham, NC: Duke University Press, 2007.

Ono, Kent A. "Re/Membering Spectators: Meditations on Japanese American Cinema." In *Countervisions: Asian American Film Criticism,* edited by Darrell Y. Hamamoto and Sandra Liu, 129–149. Philadelphia: Temple University Press, 2000.

U.S. Department of Commerce. "Asian/Pacific American Heritage Month: May 2013." U.S. Census Bureau, March 27, 2013, http://www.census.gov/newsroom /releases/pdf/cb13ff-09_asian.pdf.

Wee, Valerie. *Japanese Horror Films and Their American Remakes: Translating Fear, Adapting Culture.* New York and London: Routledge, 2014.

JAPANESE AMERICAN FOLKLORE

History and Origins

Japanese American folklore comes mostly from Japan, and though the exact origins of any given folk practice or story is still debated, most can be traced to indigenous, East Asian, or South Asian sources. Indigenous beliefs and legends

Inugami

One Japanese folkloric belief of particular significance to Japanese Americans is the concept of *inugami*. The belief is that a shaman kills a dog, turning it into an *inugami* (dog spirit); the shaman becomes an *inugami-mochi* (dog spirit holder) by taking control over the spirit. The shaman is then able to sic the *inugami* on people he or she is angry with, possessing them and causing them to act as if they were dogs. As noted by Yukiko Kimura in *Issei: Japanese Immigrants in Hawaii* (1988), this folk belief persisted among immigrants from Hiroshima, Yamaguchi, and Okayama on the far west side of Japan's main island from their arrival until long after World War II (259). Because of the spirits' volatile nature and the cruelty involved in their creation, people suspected of having an *inugami-mochi* in their family were generally shunned by society and were considered unmarriageable.

According to Stephen Sumida's *And the View from the Shore: Literary Traditions of Hawai'i* (1991), in the wake of Pearl Harbor there was an outbreak of *inugami* possessions on Kaua'i. He argues that Japanese immigrants, who had toiled endlessly to give their children a future in the United States only to find that all they had worked for was suddenly in jeopardy, were exhibiting signs of collective anxiety. Kaua'i would have felt this anxiety more acutely, he says, as it had a higher proportion of Japanese priests and cultural leaders, many of whom would soon be rounded up as potential spies. He argued that being "possessed" gave victims a way to express their pain and offered them attention and comfort from the priests who might soon not be available to them (227).

from throughout the Japanese and Ryukyuan Islands provided the basis for much contemporary lore, and while these cultures were highly diverse, they were almost universally animistic, which is reflected in the folk stories (as is the cultural importance of repaying debts and obligations). Additionally, South Asian and East Asian folklore as well as Buddhist mythology and parables were imported via China and Korea, and they both modified and were modified by indigenous belief.

For instance, one of the best-known creatures from folklore among Japanese Americans is the *oni*, an ogre-like creature most often depicted as a muscled red-, green-, or blue-skinned hairy humanoid with at least one horn. While their origin is almost certainly indigenous, their appearance is likely derived from Indian demons, introduced to Japan through Buddhist artworks. And the name of the legendary Tengu, a creature with a human body and a bird's face, is taken from *tiangou*, a demon dog from Chinese legends. However, its bird-like appearance and behaviors were invented in Japan.

The stories, creatures, and beliefs that comprise Nikkei (Japanese diaspora) folklore were almost universally brought over from Japan by Issei (first-generation immigrants). Subsequent generations continue to teach folk stories to their children as a way to connect them to their cultural heritage, often through English-language children's books or through Nikkei community institutions (i.e., cultural programs hosted by community centers and Japanese Buddhist and Christian churches).

Hero myth stories are among the best-known and most popular folktales in Japan, as they are in most places throughout the world. For example, the story of Momotaro tells the tale of an old couple who cannot have children but are gifted a child by the gods when they find a giant peach floating in a river and, upon trying to eat it, are startled to find a child inside. They name the child Momotaro (peach boy), and he grows up to be strong and virtuous. Eventually he saves his village from *oni* (ogres) by traveling to their island and defeating them. The story of Issunboshi also begins with an old childless couple being gifted a baby by the gods (one of the most frequent motifs in Japanese folktales). In this case, the boy is birthed by the old woman (in some tellings through a welt on her thumb), and he turns out to be very small, about an inch tall. He eventually, though, saves a princess from an *oni* and receives a magic hammer that make him normal-sized, at which point he marries the princess and they live happily ever after. While the hero stories are fairly universal, there are themes in equally popular tales that are more distinctly Japanese.

Ongaeshi (debt-repayment) stories, in which humans receive rewards for kindness to animals or other spirits (and punishment for crossing them), may be the most common kind of folktale in Japan. These stories follow a pattern: a human rescues, rears, feeds, or otherwise helps an animal (a dog, sparrow, mouse, cat, raccoon, dog, or even *oni* in some stories). The animal then rewards the person, often by taking him or her to a secret location where the person receives gold or some other precious object or by receiving a magical object that helps the person generate wealth. In these stories, the human often shares the story with a greedy person, who attempts to gain the same reward by repeating the first person's actions. However, instead of receiving a reward, the greedy person is punished for being dishonest, greedy, or calculating.

In some of the most famous stories, the person who assists the animal and the one who betrays the animal's trust is one and the same. For instance, one of the best-known Japanese folk stories is Urashimataro. It tells of a boy who rescues a turtle and is then, as a reward, taken by the turtle to the sea king's underwater castle, where he is feasted and betrothed to the king's daughter. After three days the boy yearns to return to land to visit his family, and he is permitted to do so. However, before he leaves, the princess gives him a box and tells him never to look inside it. When the boy arrives at his home, he finds that 300 years have passed and everyone he ever knew has passed away. Breaking his promise, he opens the box, which, it turns out, contained his youth, and he instantly ages 300 years.

Another popular story tells of a man who rescues a crane. The crane later returns to him in human form, though she keeps her identity a secret. They wed, and she makes him wealthy by weaving beautiful garments. However, she forbids him from viewing her while she is weaving. The man eventually breaks his promise and discovers that she is in fact a crane. She then disappears, and he never sees her again. (Tragic marriages/amorous unions between humans and animals or other spirits is another common motif.) There is a variant of the story where it is an old couple who finds the crane, and the crane returns in the form of a human child and becomes their adoptive daughter rather than the man's wife.

Themes and Creatures

There is significant overlap between these various themes of Japanese folktales, with many themes appearing in combination in different stories. For instance, the very popular Kaguya-hime (Princess Kaguya) story involves an old couple who cannot have children and find a baby in a glowing bamboo shoot (the childless old couple motif). The girl, named Kaguya (meaning "glowing night"), grows up to be beautiful and has many suitors, including the emperor himself. However, she rejects even him, explaining that she comes from another world. Eventually she reveals that she comes from the moon and returns there (the doomed relationship between a human and a supernatural being motif).

In addition to these folktales, there are many folkloric creatures who are widely known among Nikkei. Possibly the best known is the *kappa*, a kind of water sprite. Their enduring popularity might be attributed to their memorable and unique appearance. They look like a humanoid turtle, and they have a dish of water on the top of their heads that, if emptied, causes them to dehydrate and die. They are also said to be extremely fond of cucumbers, and the association between the mythical beasts and the vegetable is so strong that cucumber sushi rolls are called *kappa maki*. Another potential explanation for their persisting popularity among Nikkei is that when parents introduce their children to sushi, they have occasion to relate the story.

Other well-known creatures are the *tanuki* and *kitsune*, which are both actual animals (Japanese raccoon dog and fox, respectively). However, folkloric belief imbued them with so many supernatural powers, most notably shape-shifting powers, that they are considered mythic creatures in their own right.

Additionally, there are still a few beliefs not associated with any particular story or creature that are still widely known in the Nikkei diaspora. For instance, the *obon* festival is still widely practiced by Japanese Americans. It is a Buddhist custom adopted and localized in Japan to honor ancestor spirits. The festival is held most often at Buddhist temples in the mid to late summer, when it is believed that the spirits of ancestors come to visit. In the United States, they are the Japanese Buddhist temples' most public event. Like in Japan, the temple events often include a bazaar with food and games in addition to the Japanese folk dance and music that are at the heart of the celebration, though some of the songs and dances have been modified since coming across the Pacific.

Collecting and Recording Japanese American Folklore

Doubtless, Nikkei created their own folklore in all the places they immigrated to. However, the only extensive record of folk beliefs of Japanese American origin is the work of Glen Grant. According to Grant's research, immigrants to Hawai'i from Japan, Okinawa, China, and Korea shared animistic beliefs and nature and ancestor veneration with the native peoples of Hawai'i, so the newly arrived laborers readily accepted Hawai'ian beliefs and vice versa. The various groups' beliefs intertwined to the point where Hawai'i residents of all ethnicities began to use the Japanese word *obake*, which means "supernatural creatures."

Despite the pervasiveness of islands spirituality, only a handful of people other than Grant—such as anthropologist H. Arlo Nimmo, folklorist Dr. Katharine Luomala, and archaeologist William Kenji "Pila" Kikuchi—have made an effort to research it. Grant collected firsthand tales of supernatural encounters, publishing them in collections of ghost stories sometimes in fictionalized form though mostly as straightforward accounts of the supernatural told by local people. The works include reports of sightings of *kappa* and Japanese faceless ghosts, records of Shinto exorcisms, and encounters with various kinds of otherworldly creatures, some of which have no precedent in Japanese folklore at all.

Ben Hamamoto

See also: Japanese American Immigration; Japanese American Literature

Further Reading

Grant, Glen. *Obake Files: Ghostly Encounters in Supernatural Hawaii.* Honolulu: Mutual Publishing, 2000.

Green, Thomas A. *Asian American Folktales.* Westport, CT: Greenwood, 2009.

Kimura, Yukiko. *Issei: Japanese Immigrants in Hawaii.* Honolulu: University of Hawai'i Press, 1988.

Lee, Jonathan H. X., and Kathleen M. Nadeau, eds. *Encyclopedia of Asian American Folklore and Folklife.* Santa Barbara, CA: ABC-CLIO, 2011.

Luomala, Katharine. *Oceanic, American Indian, and African Myths of Snaring the Sun.* Honolulu: The Museum, 1940.

Sumida, Stephen H. *And the View from the Shore: Literary Traditions of Hawai'i.* Seattle: University of Washington Press, 1991.

JAPANESE AMERICAN FOOD

Traditions and Practices

Far more than any other culture, Japan prizes raw fish and has developed its preparation into an internationally renowned art form. The preparation of raw fish for sashimi and sushi requires skilled knife work. Dipping sauces for the sashimi and sushi typically consist of soy sauce and may include additional flavorings. Sashimi, made of raw fish without rice, typically includes elaborate garnishes that add color, texture, flavor, and aroma to the finished dish. When raw fish is paired with rice, it becomes sushi. One of the most popular Japanese dishes in the United States, sushi was developed as a way of preserving fish, which was salted and packed in cooked rice. Eventually it came to be associated with fresh fish served on top of rice held together with rice vinegar or wrapped with vinegar-splashed rice and seaweed. One of the most popular forms of sushi is made with tuna. Typical sushi accompaniments include soy sauce, wasabi, and vinegar-pickled ginger. In addition to tuna, prized seafood for sashimi and sushi includes conger eel, abalone, shrimp, yellowtail, squid, sea bream, octopus, sea urchin roe, and salmon roe. In addition to being served raw, fish may be grilled, pan-fried, steamed, simmered, or deep-fried; made into salads, soups, or stews; or dried for use as a protein-rich condiment.

As in many other Asian cultures, rice appears at every Japanese meal unless it consists of a one-pot noodle dish. In addition to being steamed and served as a base for everyday meals, rice is transformed to make three of the basic flavoring agents in Japanese cooking: mirin (a sweet rice wine), vinegar, and miso (fermented bean paste). It is also made into the popular beverages sake (dry wine) and *shochu* (alcohol). Cakes made from glutinous rice (known as *mochi*) play an essential role at every ceremonial meal. Noodles, whether made from a mixture of buckwheat and wheat (*soba*) or wheat (*udon* and *ramen*), are the Japanese equivalent of fast food; they are easy and inexpensive to make into a hearty one-pot dish. Noodles can be served in a simple broth on their own or with a wide range of additions and toppings. A few of the most popular toppings include tempura (lightly battered and fried food), eggs, poultry, seafood fritters, fried tofu, raw or cooked vegetables, seaweed, and breaded fried pork (*tonkatsu*). Noodles can also be stir-fried or boiled and served cold with a dipping sauce. In addition to wheat and buckwheat, Japanese noodles are also made from rice, mung beans, and yams.

Dashi, a delicate broth made from kelp and dried bonito (a type of tuna) flakes, serves as the foundation for nonvegetarian soups, simmered dishes, and sauces. A basic vegetarian broth is made from shiitake mushrooms, boiled with or without kelp. Soups are classified as clear broth or miso broth; the latter is thickened with miso. Clear broths are made into soups with the addition of a piece of protein such as tofu, fish, or chicken; a sliver of seasonal vegetable; and a seasoning or garnish such as soy sauce or an herb. Miso soups are heartier and may contain seasonal vegetables and tofu. *Nabe*, a hearty one-pot dish, might be made with monkfish and mizuna or with chicken, watercress, and shiitake. Similar to the Mongolian hotpot, *shabu-shabu* is a dish of sliced meat and vegetables that is cooked by diners in a communal pot that simmers on the table.

Favored vegetables for pickling include daikon radishes, Chinese cabbage, carrots, burdock, zucchini, cucumbers, eggplants, and turnips. One of the most important pickles in Japanese cuisine, *umeboshi* is made from *ume* fruit, an apricot that is generally referred to as "Japanese plum" in English. *Ume* plum vinegar is one of the most popular souring agents in Japanese cuisine. In addition to being pickled and fashioned into vinegar, *ume* is often added with sugar to a mild-flavored alcohol to make the popular cordial *umeshu*. Another fruit, *yuzu* (a variety of citrus), is a key ingredient in *ponzu*, a staple dipping sauce made often of equal parts of *yuzu* juice and soy sauce.

Favorite meat dishes in Japanese cuisine include simmered pork belly; pork and flowering mustard stir-fry; miso-marinated pork that is rolled, coated in panko crumbs, and deep-fried; sweet and sour braised pork with pickled plums (*umeboshi*); steamed pork with *ponzu* sauce; and pan-seared dumplings stuffed with pork and cabbage. Beef *sashimi* is the Japanese version of carpaccio, finely ground or diced raw beef. Thinly sliced beef is pan-simmered with vegetables, mirin, and soy sauce to make the hearty stew sukiyaki. Like beef and pork, chicken is cooked in a wide variety of ways. It may also be diced finely and served raw.

Contemporary Forms

Although it had been decimated by the War Relocation Act, the Little Tokyo area of Los Angeles had recovered by the 1950s to become the main hub of Japanese American life in California. Residents from cities such as Los

Angeles, San Francisco, and Monterey began frequenting Japanese restaurants in significant numbers during the 1950s. The majority of the first non-Asians to dine at Japanese restaurants were American soldiers who had been stationed in Japan during the Allied occupation from 1945 to 1952. Having developed a taste for Japanese food, many returning soldiers, accompanied by friends and family, sought out Japanese restaurants. Not surprisingly, the majority of the first restaurants to draw non-Asians specialized in dishes that catered to the American palate such as sukiyaki (a stew often served as a one-pot meal), teriyaki (marinated meat or fish that has been grilled or broiled), tempura, and shabu-shabu (thin slices of meat cooked in simmering broth at the table). Riding on this wave, Tokyo Sukiyaki restaurant opened at San Francisco's Fisherman's Wharf in 1954. It would draw almost 500 diners a day.

Los Angeles businessmen were first introduced to sushi at the Kawafuku Restaurant in Little Tokyo, which opened in 1966. Japanese businessmen so enjoyed the sushi that they soon brought their American clients. During the 1970s, a decade when Japanese businesses began expanding into the United States, sushi bars that catered to Japanese businessmen and their American clientele began to open throughout the country. With the invention of the California roll by the mid-1970s, Japanese sushi was officially Americanized. One origin myth for the California roll claims that a chef at Los Angeles's Tokyo Kaikan invented the combination because *toro*, the fresh fatty tuna belly much prized by Japanese, was hard to come by in the United States. So, the chef took advantage of the abundance of fatty avocados and rich crab to create a roll that he could serve when *toro* was unavailable.

As far back as the 1930s, intrepid New Yorkers had ventured on occasion to Japanese restaurants that served Western palate–friendly menus. Manhattan saw its first sushi bar in 1957, when Moto Saito (d. 1989) opened Saito restaurant. During the 1960s, Americans outside of California would slowly become acclimatized to Japanese food through a series of Japanese American ventures. Prime among these would be Benihana of Tokyo. The brainchild of Hiroaki "Rocky" Aoki (1938–2008), a former alternate for Japan's Olympic wrestling team, Benihana opened in New York in 1964. The original eatery, which was housed in a former Chinese restaurant, served *tappanyaki* (a term designating a dish that has been cooked on a steel griddle) to patrons at a total of four large tables. Cloaked in an aura of authenticity, Benihana served decidedly Americanized dishes that featured large amounts of beef, lobster, and chicken. Diners who were seated around metal grills watched as the chef theatrically prepared the dishes they ordered, using lightning-speed knife skills and flamboyantly tossing ingredients into the air. As much about entertainment as about food, Benihana quickly earned a favorable review from dining critic Clementine

Paddleford (1898–1967), and New Yorkers took heed. Today, Benihana boasts over 70 restaurants in the United States.

Gently introduced to "Japanese-style" dining by Benihana, Americans soon developed a taste for more "authentic" Japanese food, and enterprising chef-entrepreneurs ventured to the United States in order to meet the growing demand. One of the famous celebrity chefs and restauranteurs, Matsuhisa Nobuyuki (1949–), would arrive from Japan via Peru. He would eventually open 14 high-end Japanese restaurants in the United States, including one co-owned by Robert De Niro (1943–)—Nobu in New York. Today, Americans have become so enamored with traditional Japanese cookery that they clamor to dine on specialized *kaiseke* meals (multicourse seasonally driven menus) and order snack foods while sipping on sake and *shochu* at *izakaya* (drinking houses that offer foods meant to be consumed with alcoholic beverages).

Alice L. McLean

See also: Asian Indian American Food; Chinese American Food; Filipino American Food; Korean American Food; Sushi; Thai American Food; Vietnamese American Food

Further Reading

Corson, Trevor. *The Zen of Fish: The Story of Sushi, from Samurai to Supermarket.* New York: HarperCollins, 2007.

Cwiertka, Katarzyna J. *Modern Japanese Cuisine: Food, Power and National Identity.* London: Reaktion, 2006.

Hachisu, Nancy Singleton. *Japanese Farm Food.* Kansas City: Andrews McMeel, 2012.

Kondo, Sonoko, and Louis Clyde Stoumen. *The Poetical Pursuit of Food: Japanese Recipes for American Cooks.* New York: C. N. Potter, 1986.

JAPANESE AMERICAN IMMIGRATION

History and Origin

Japanese American immigration dates back to the 19th century. After the 1868 Meiji Reform, Japan underwent substantial political, cultural, and social changes. Early Japanese immigrants coming to the United States around the turn of the century were predominantly male; they provided a replacement for Chinese laborers who were barred by the 1882 Chinese Exclusion Act. During World War II, an estimated 120,000 Japanese Americans, immigrant and American-born, were interned in relocation camps in Arizona, Colorado, Wyoming, Arkansas, California, Idaho, and Utah. Japanese American communities suffered physical and mental stress as well as financial losses. As a result of the

"The Gentlemen's Agreement"

Regulations in San Francisco that required Japanese students to attend separate schools created international tension between the United States and Japan. The Japanese government regarded it as a challenge against the entire empire of Japan and demanded racial equality for Japanese Americans. Moreover, Japan gained political and military power in the world by winning two major wars: the First Sino-Japanese War (1894–1895) and the Russo-Japanese War (1904–1905). Therefore, the U.S. government could not ignore school segregation in San Francisco as merely a provincial incident. President Theodore Roosevelt pressured the school board to overturn the decision but failed to change their minds. The Japanese government wanted to avoid a worst-case scenario such as the Chinese Exclusion Act to which the Chinese government had succumbed in 1882. Yet President Roosevelt negotiated with the school board to overturn the decision by compromising Japanese immigration. In 1907, the Japanese government agreed not to grant passports to Japanese who wished to immigrate to the U.S. mainland for the purpose of employment. In return, families of already immigrated Japanese including their parents, wives, and children could be granted passports to enter the U.S. mainland. This diplomatic negotiation is called "The Gentlemen's Agreement." It was a mutual agreement between the United States and Japan initiated by President Roosevelt.

McCarran-Walter Act of 1952, Japanese and immigrants from other Asian countries were eligible to become naturalized U.S. citizens. After the 1965 Immigration Act, Japanese professionals and family members arrived in America, contributing to an increase of the Japanese American population. According to the 2010 U.S. census, the Japanese American population is over 1.3 million. Large numbers of them live in California (southern California in particular), Hawai'i, New York, Washington, Illinois, and Ohio.

The Japanese Meiji period (1868–1912) promoted modernization and contributed to the overseas mobility of Japanese after the Edo period (1603–1868) ended its long-lasting feudalism and *sakoku* policy (1639–1854), which prohibited Japanese to travel abroad and limited their diplomatic relationships and trading with other countries.

Thus, Japanese began to immigrate to Hawai'i as plantation laborers. In 1868 Eugene Miller Van Reed, the consul-general of Hawai'i in Japan, operated the first migration of 153 people, who were titled *gannen mono* (first-year persons). Yet the new Meiji government did not admit this migration officially. In 1885, Japan and the Kingdom of Hawai'i signed a treaty of immigration that officially allowed Japanese to work in Hawai'i. For the next 10 years, the

The 442nd Regimental Combat Team

In 1943, Japanese American internees were challenged to answer a questionnaire about their loyalty to the United States and their willingness to serve in the U.S. Army. In spite of being deprived of their rights as U.S. citizens at internment camps, some Nisei voluntarily enlisted in the U.S. Army. Soon after, the 442nd Regimental Combat Team consisting of Japanese Americans was activated and started its training at Camp Shelby, Mississippi. Meanwhile, the 100th Infantry Battalion, which consisted primarily of Japanese Americans from Hawai'i who were already in the military before the war, were fighting battles to liberate Italy from Nazi Germany and were nicknamed the "Purple Heart Battalion" because of their accomplishments. The 100th Infantry Battalion was incorporated into the 442nd Regimental Combat Team, which later landed in Italy. After fighting several battles, the 442nd Regimental Combat Team was ordered to rescue the 1st Battalion (originally the Texas National Guard), which had surrendered to the Germans in the Vosges Mountains. During the rescue mission, the 442nd Regimental Combat Team suffered heavy casualties. Along with other accomplishments in battle, the 442nd Regimental Combat Team is the most decorated team in the U.S. Army. The members of 442nd Regimental Combat Team—with a motto of "Go for Broke"—showed their loyalty and patriotism to the United States by risking their lives and proved the injustice of the internment camps.

---

population of *kanyaku imin* (government-contracted immigrants) protected under the treaty expanded toward 30,000. However, in 1894 the *kanyaku imin* system ceased, and Japanese who wished to work in Hawai'i contracted with private companies as *shiyaku imin* (self-contracted immigrants). In both cases, the Japanese government issued passports to them under the conditions that the contract terms were clear and that their safe return to Japan was guaranteed. The Japanese who wished to return to their homeland with their fortunes were called *dekaseginin* (migrant workers).

Hawai'i was annexed to the United States in 1898 and became a territory of the United States in 1900. This changed the lives of Japanese in Hawai'i, as laws in the United States applied to the Hawai'ian territory. First, contract laborers were prohibited, and then following 1900 Japanese were allowed to immigrate to the United States more freely. Second, although Chinese began to immigrate to Hawai'i and the U.S. mainland before Japanese did, the Chinese Exclusion Act of 1882 was applied to Hawai'i and excluded the entry of Chinese laborers. This racial discrimination against Chinese resulted in a demand for Japanese laborers as their substitutes. The annexation of Hawai'i allowed the Japanese in Hawai'i to move to the U.S. mainland for further opportunities.

Consequently, the Japanese population in the United States reached the West Coast and the states of Washington, Oregon, and California. This increasing emergence of the Japanese population in the United States became a target of racial discrimination. In 1893 the San Francisco Board of Education passed a resolution, with the purpose of segregation, to order all Japanese children to attend Chinese school (no schools for Japanese existed at the time). Sutemi Chinda, the consul-general of Japan, opposed the decision by the Board of Education for being a direct humiliation toward Japanese and pressured for an eventual reverse decision. However, educational segregation was nationally supported by the U.S. public. Thus, the idea of racial segregation in school for Japanese children appeared again after the 1906 San Francisco earthquake. Historian Roger Daniels claims that the earthquake created an accelerating atmosphere of hysteria and racism. Nonetheless, in 1906 San Francisco's school board again ordered all Japanese children to attend Chinese school.

U.S. immigration officials examine Japanese immigrants at the Angel Island Immigration Station, located in San Francisco Bay, California, 1931. Immigration officials detained, inspected, and examined an estimated one million immigrants at Angel Island between 1910 and 1940. (Corbis)

In the beginning of the 20th century, Japanese started to settle on U.S. soil and began to start families. In 1900 the Japanese population was approximately 24,300, and the majority were Issei (first generation). Twenty years later, the population reached 111,000. The ratio of Nisei (second generation) to Issei became 1 to 2.8. The contributing factor of the increasing population was picture brides who immigrated to start new families with their husbands. The Japanese American community had a gender imbalance with an excess of male populace resulting from the fact that the majority came to the United States as male laborers. These Japanese men sent their photos to matchmakers in Japan, and marriages were arranged for couples who had never met before. By 1920, 70 percent of Japanese Americans lived in California and contributed to the economy, especially in farming.

During the 1910s and the 1920s, Japanese Americans faced laws based on racial discrimination that continued to deprive them of their rights. In 1913 California passed the Alien Land Law, which prohibited Issei, who were "aliens ineligible to citizenship," from owning land. Influenced by California, the states of Arizona, Washington, Oregon, Idaho, Montana, and Kansas followed by passing similar laws. The Naturalization Act of 1870 already defined Asians, including Japanese, as "aliens ineligible to citizenship." The Issei tried to overcome this racial discrimination and used a loophole: Issei parents used their American-born citizen children as landowners. In 1920, California revised the original Alien Land Law and restricted the loophole and prevailing custom. Although the California Supreme Court invalidated the revision in 1922, it was clear that an anti-Japanese movement was stirring due to the economic competition with Japanese farmers, which was initiated by the restriction of their land ownership.

The Immigration Act of 1923 prohibited "aliens ineligible to citizenship" from immigrating to the United States, which particularly targeted the Japanese. Although "aliens ineligible to citizenship" indicated those from Asian countries, the majority of Asians were already excluded by the previous laws of the Chinese Exclusion Act of 1882 and the Asiatic Barred Zone Act of 1917. (Filipinos were exempt from the exclusion because they were U.S. nationals.) In 1921, the Japanese government voluntarily stopped issuing passports to picture brides in order to mitigate the anti-Japanese movement and its growing tension during the 1920s. However, the Immigration Act of 1923 officially reinforced a racially homogenous stance that did not welcome Japanese as well as other Asians to the United States.

Over the next two decades, Japanese Americans shifted from chiefly Issei to mostly Nisei. In 1930 the total population of Japanese Americans, approximately 138,000, was almost equally divided into Issei and Nisei. In 1940 the number of Nisei exceeded that of Issei: approximately 80,000 to 47,000. The prohibition of immigration from Japan in 1923 had affected the demographic transition of generations and the decline of the entire population in 1940. During this period, over 10,000 Nisei children were sent to Japan to receive education. The Kibei (those returning to America) came back to the United States with Japanese linguistic excellence; however, they faced a difficulty in adjusting to U.S. culture again and an identity crisis from being marginalized in both countries.

The Japanese military attack on Pearl Harbor on December 7, 1941, immediately and drastically changed the lives of Japanese Americans. President Franklin Roosevelt (1882–1945) and Federal Bureau of Investigation director J. Edgar Hoover (1895–1972) did not find any proof that Japanese Americans assisted the attack on Pearl Harbor or were a threat to the United States. Yet Major Karl Bendetsen and Lieutenant General John L. DeWitt publically questioned Japanese American loyalty to the United States and consequently received strong support from the media and Americans who were infused with war hysteria and racial prejudice. On February 19, 1942, President Roosevelt signed Executive Order 9066, which gave authority to the secretary of war to intern all Japanese Americans (regardless of their U.S. citizenship status) in the West Coast to camps. Each person was only allowed to bring two suitcases to a camp. Thus, after a short notice of relocation, Japanese Americans unavoidably sold their possessions for much cheaper than their value or were forced to leave them behind. Over 110,000 Japanese Americans were ordered to relocate to 10 different internment camps located in deserted areas (Gila River and Poston in Arizona, Jerome and Rohwer in Arkansas, Manzanar and Tule Lake in California, Granada in Colorado, Minedoka in Idaho, Topaz in Utah, and Heart Mountain in Wyoming).

With the end of World War II, Japanese Americans changed their settlement patterns geographically and demographically. After being released from the internment camps, some returned to their homes or areas where they used to live, while others chose to migrate to the Northwest, the Midwest, and the South, where few Japanese Americans previously resided. Likewise, the War Brides Act of 1945 allowed Japanese women to immigrate to the United States as spouses of U.S. military personnel. As a result, these Japanese spouses went on to live scattered throughout the nation.

Contemporary Forms

In the 1950s and 1960s, Japanese Americans started to gain legal rights. In 1952, the McCarran-Walter Act dramatically changed the lives of Japanese

Americans and immigration, along with the lives of other Asian Americans. Japanese were then allowed to immigrate to the United States through the quota system; however, their quota number was much smaller than the number for Europeans. Moreover, Issei became eligible for U.S. citizenship under the act, as the Alien Land Law of California of 1923 was reversed for being unconstitutional; other states that enacted similar laws soon followed. Finally, in 1965 the Immigration Act allocated an equal quota number for Japanese and Europeans.

Inspired by the civil rights movement, the story of Japanese American internment camps was given historical attention. Thus, a younger generation of Japanese Americans, Sansei (third generation), began to learn about what happened to their parents and grandparents during World War II. Prior to this, the former internees silenced the past and did not tell their stories due to shame, trauma, and a desire to forget and move on with their new lives. On the other hand, while some Japanese American activists lobbied for compensation due to the internment, these survivors began to speak out about their buried pasts. In 1981, over 750 people (former internees, former government officials, and scholars) were witnesses during hearings by the Commission on the Wartime Relocation. In 1983, the Commission on the Wartime Relocation concluded that the internment was caused by "race prejudice, war hysteria, and a failure of political leadership" ("Education Code Section 13000"). Further, during the presidency of Ronald Reagan, the Civil Liberties Act of 1988 granted repatriation to the former internees. The surviving internees were paid $20,000 for each following year (yet the amount of compensation was smaller than the materialistic and psychological loss that the internees endured).

Today, the backgrounds of Japanese Americans are more intricate than ever. Since the 1960s, the number of Japanese American marriages with non-Japanese and non-Asians has been increasing. This marriage percentage is the highest among all other Asian Americans. Furthermore, the Japanese American community that was established toward the end of the 19th century went on to welcome a future generation of new Japanese immigrants who came as students and businesspeople and eventually settled in the United States. They are called Shin-Issei (new first generation) in order to distinguish their backgrounds and history from those of the original Issei.

Yuki Obayashi

See also: Japanese American Children and Family; Japanese American Women

Further Reading

Daniels, Roger. *Asian America: Chinese and Japanese in the United States since 1850.* Seattle: University of Washington Press, 1988.

"Education Code Section 13000." Official California Legislative Information, http://www.leginfo.ca.gov/cgi-bin/displaycode?section=edc&group=12001-13000&file=13000.

Hoeffel, Elizabeth M., Sonya Rastogi, Myoung Ouk Kim, and Hasan Shahid. "The Asian Population: 2010." U.S. Census Bureau, March 2012, http://www.census.gov/prod/cen2010/briefs/c2010br-11.pdf.

Hosokawa, Bill. *Nisei: The Quiet Americans.* Revised ed. Boulder: University Press of Colorado, 2002.

Ichioka, Yuji. *Issei: The World of the First Generation Japanese Immigrants, 1885–1924.* New York: Free Press, 1988.

Murray, Alice Yang. *Historical Memories of Japanese American Internment and the Struggle for Redress.* Stanford, CA: Stanford University Press, 2008.

Spickard, Paul. *Japanese Americans: The Formation and Transformations of an Ethnic Group.* Revised ed. New Brunswick, NJ: Rutgers University Press, 2009.

JAPANESE AMERICAN INTERNMENT

After the bombing of Pearl Harbor on December 7, 1941, and U.S. entrance into World War II, the U.S. government decided that the incarceration of its Japanese American population was justified by wartime needs. During World War II, over 110,000 Japanese American citizens and residents on the West Coast as well as a smaller number of Japanese Latin Americans, German and Italian immigrants, and Native Americans were forcibly relocated into military-run internment camps or deported. This series of events would later be identified as a clear injustice in American history and used as a warning about how pervasive racism in public and media discourse works in connection with wartime hysteria. Mutual support between Japanese American and Arab American groups has arisen due to historically familiar threats of profiling, detention, and deportation in response to fears of terrorism and espionage.

The list of justifications for the necessity of removing all free persons of Japanese ancestry from the West Coast region, from Washington State in the Northwest extending inland to Arizona, was long. Loyalty to the United States was automatically called into doubt, as Japanese American noncitizens (first-generation Issei) were named as enemy aliens and American-born citizens (second-generation Nisei) were named as enemy nonaliens. Fear that locations on the West Coast would be targeted was compounded by a belief that Japan would be secretly aided by Japanese Americans. This verdict was supported by reports that a Japanese pilot who crash-landed in Hawai'i during the Pearl Harbor attack was assisted by three Japanese Americans. Seemingly to placate

Executive Order 9066

The program of removal of Japanese Americans began on February 19, 1942, when President Franklin D. Roosevelt signed Executive Order 9066 authorizing the secretary of war and designated military commanders the power to define large geographic areas as zones of exclusion where categories of people could be forcibly removed. Essentially, this granted the military broad authority over civilians in specific places. The stated purpose of the order was to support national defense by preventing espionage and sabotage. Despite its contradiction of the Fourth, Fifth, and Fourteenth Amendments that protect property from unwarranted seizure and guarantee the right to due process, only limited official opposition came from the Department of Justice and the Federal Bureau of Investigation. Congress passed the order into law on March 21, 1942, and added fines and prison terms for resistance to military demands. In the following months, over 110,000 Japanese Americans were forcibly removed from their homes and properties on the West Coast and incarcerated in relocation camps. The order was rescinded in 1945. The 1944 U.S. Supreme Court case *Korematsu v. United States* challenged the constitutionality of the order, but the Court ruled 6 to 3 in favor of the government. In his dissent, Justice Frank Murphy called this ruling a "legalization of racism."

criticism about the legality of mass incarceration, claims were made that this removal was necessary to protect the Japanese American population from mob violence.

Several groups campaigned for this removal, including military officials who sought to contain potential threats, opportunistic regional farmers and business owners who thought that the removal of Japanese competitors would be beneficial, and a general populace fueled by alarmist and racist messages in the media. Although Hawai'i would seem like a logical choice to protect from further attack, the removal of Japanese Americans there was deemed impossible, since they composed nearly a third of the state's population. Furthermore, Hawai'ian politicians and businesses interpreted removal as being harmful to their economy.

On February 19, 1942, President Franklin D. Roosevelt signed Executive Order 9066 authorizing the secretary of war and giving military commanders the power to define large geographic areas as zones of exclusion where categories of people could be forcibly removed. No specific groups of people or states or regions were named in the order, but who it targeted was evident. General John DeWitt, the military commander in charge of the Western Defense Command,

Hirabayashi v. the United States

In May 1942 Gordon Kiyoshi Hirabayashi, a 23-year-old University of Washington student, protested the violation of his civil rights by disobeying the military curfew and exclusion orders. All Japanese Americans on the West Coast were subject to curfew restrictions whereby they had to remain in their homes from 8:00 p.m. to 6:00 a.m. Exclusion orders entailed compliance with relocation proceedings, since they could not be freely present in these geographic areas. Hirabayashi turned himself in to the authorities, stating that his defiance was based on his belief in his constitutional rights as an American citizen. Hirabayashi was imprisoned and tried in a state court five months later, where he was found guilty and given two concurrent 90-day sentences. The decision was appealed and sent to the U.S. Supreme Court, where in 1943 the case was decided against Hirabayashi primarily based on the curfew violation. The judges agreed unanimously that curfew restrictions were justified by wartime needs. However, in a concurring opinion Justice Frank Murphy warned that "no less than 70,000 American citizens have been placed under a special ban and deprived of their liberty because of their particular racial inheritance. In this sense it bears a melancholy resemblance to the treatment accorded to members of the Jewish race in Germany and in other parts of Europe" (*Kiyoshi Hirabayashi v. United States,* 1943). This case was cited in support of the *Korematsu v. United States* decision. The convictions were overturned in 1987, with findings that the federal government withheld evidence from the Court.

---

described "all individuals of Japanese descent as 'subversive,' as belonging to 'an enemy race' whose 'racial strains are undiluted'" ("Was Internment Constitutional?," 1944). The order granted the military the authority to carry out its plans without hindrance from other agencies and with the support needed to rapidly relocate and house large numbers of people, with the process policed by armed military personnel. DeWitt went on to issue over 100 military orders that applied to a population deemed genetically guilty that was largely composed of American-born citizens and young children. After Congress enacted the order into law on March 21, 1942, these additional orders made disobeying removal procedures punishable by jail time.

Two agencies—the Wartime Civil Control Administration and the War Relocation Authority (WRA)—ordered all Japanese Americans on the West Coast to report to locations where they would first be transported to temporary assembly centers before being transferred to 10 long-term WRA internment camps, referred to as relocation centers. Under short notice, in some cases as little as a few days, individuals and families could only bring whatever

The Mochida family, wearing identification tags and waiting for an evacuation bus to take them to a remote internment camp on May 8, 1942. President Franklin Roosevelt signed Executive Order 9066 in 1942, which authorized the evacuation of over 110,000 Japanese Americans during World War II. (Everett Collection Inc/ Alamy Stock Photo)

possessions they could carry by hand. Attempts to sell businesses, possessions, and homes at fair values were rarely successful. Overall property loss has been estimated at about $1.3 billion.

The assembly centers were constructed hastily on public spaces such as racetracks, sporting arenas, and fairgrounds. The conditions in some locations, such as the Tanforan and Santa Anita centers in California, were particularly bad, where people were housed in horse stalls. The duration of this temporary detention was a long as several months. Although families were permitted to stay together in most cases, individuals were transferred to specific WRA internment camps based on random factors, including geography and perceived loyalty to the United States. The internment camps and detention facilities were built on federally owned land, some on Native American reservations, recalling a precedent of forced removal of communities. The harsh conditions due to climate, inadequate construction, and lack of privacy in the makeshift barracks hindered any illusion of normal community life, with internees assigned labor tasks such as farming and construction.

In 1943, all internees were required to complete a questionnaire whose intent was to separate out the disloyal from the loyal via problematic means of self-reporting. Questions number 27 and 28 were especially controversial: number 27 asked if the individual would be willing to serve in the U.S. military. At the end of 1943, the U.S. Army reversed its earlier decision to bar Japanese Americans from service when it created a racially segregated military battalion (later becoming the highly decorated 442nd Regimental Combat Team that fought in Europe). This loyalty registration process was used to locate volunteers from the camps. Some respondents who answered "no" to this question feared that they would be separated from parents who needed care, while others refused to serve given that their families were unjustly imprisoned.

Question 28 seemed to entail undesirable consequences, asking "Will you swear unqualified allegiance to the United States . . . and forswear any form of allegiance or obedience to the Japanese emperor, to any other foreign government, power or organization?" Adequate clarification was not provided when inquiries were made, and any qualifications that they wrote alongside their answers were ignored. Respondents who answered "no" to this question also did so for a variety of reasons. Some thought that this was a trick question posed with the intent of providing evidence that they had previously acted as agents for the Japanese government. Others thought that this would render them effectively without a state, since those born in Japan were barred from U.S. citizenship. John Okada's 1957 novel *No-No Boy* centers on a young Nisei man who is imprisoned for answering "no" to both questions and describes his conflicts with those in the community who answered "yes" and volunteered to serve in the U.S. military. Those who answered "no" were named disloyal troublemakers; consequently they and their families were transferred to the Tule Lake Segregation Center, the largest and most heavily guarded internment camp.

Resistance

Given the context, it was unsurprising that army recruitment was low in the camps. At the start of 1944, the military decided to make all Nisei men in the camps subject to the draft. Resistance was not supported widely in the camps, but at the Heart Mountain and Poston camps there were public discussions and statements issued about the legality of this obligation. Three hundred fifteen men from 8 of the 10 camps did not comply with induction orders and faced federal charges. Most were convicted and served from six months to over three years in prison. In 1947, President Harry S. Truman (1884–1972) pardoned all draft resisters.

The Renunciation Act of 1944 was passed to enable the deportation of disloyal Nisei along with Issei who agreed to be repatriated. In Tule Lake, some internees were misled into renunciation under the belief that this was required in order to remain in the camp until the end of the war. In 1945 Wayne Collins, a San Francisco ACLU attorney, delayed a mass deportation of voluntary and involuntary "native American aliens," arguing that these renunciations were made under duress. Cases for the restoration of citizenship to nearly 5,000 Japanese Americans went through the courts in the years following, as late as 1968.

Legal Challenges

Four cases led by Nisei plaintiffs challenging the constitutionality of military actions were brought before the U.S. Supreme Court in 1943 and 1944. The 1943 cases *Yasui v. United States* and *Hirabayashi v. United States* challenged the military curfew and relocation orders. The Court chose to focus on the military decision to institute curfews during wartime and upheld the legality of these orders. The 1944 Supreme Court case *Korematsu v. United States* challenged the constitutionality of Executive Order 9066, but the Court ruled 6 to 3 in favor of the government. In his dissent, Justice Frank Murphy called this ruling a "legalization of racism." The 1944 case *Ex parte Mitsuye Endo*, testing the constitutionality of incarcerating loyal citizens, was the only decision ruled in favor of the plaintiff. In a unanimous decision, the Court decided that loyal citizens could not be imprisoned without cause. Soon after in January 1945, the internment program officially ended, and the camps began to close.

Communities were not easily reestablished on the West Coast, and many people were resettled in various locations in the Midwest and on the East Coast, including Denver, Chicago, and New York. However, by the 1950s the Japanese American population on the West Coast approached prewar levels. The nature of the communities changed significantly, with occupations shifting away from farming to jobs such as domestic service and gardening.

Repercussions

In the 1960s activists started campaigning for redress, which would involve formal apologies from the state and reparations to individuals who went through this experience. In 1980, Congress created the Commission on Wartime Relocation and Internment of Civilians (CWRIC) to investigate the civil rights violations experienced by Japanese Americans and the Native American Aleut people who were also forcibly removed during World War II. The CWRIC report, titled *Personal Justice Denied* (1992), determined that the government's decision to support the internment program was not based on any legitimate national threat but rather "race prejudice, war hysteria and a failure of political leadership." The CWRIC's findings supported the passage of the 1988 Civil Liberties Act, which awarded financial reparations and apologies to surviving internees. Legal decisions were also reevaluated, and in the 1980s the convictions against Fred Korematsu and Gordon Hirabayashi were overturned by U.S. district courts in California and Washington.

While there were many Japanese Americans whose politics mirrored the conservative, assimilationist Japanese American Citizens League—condemning draft resisters and advocating cooperation with the government—others were motivated to become civil rights activists working toward a realization of social justice for all. Yuri Kochiyama in New York became an ally of Malcolm X, and Roy Aoki became one of the founding members of the Black Panthers in California.

Discussions about Japanese American internment are of particular importance in both legal classes and Asian American studies. Literary texts such as Okada's *No-No Boy* and Jeanne Wakatsuki Houston's 1972 memoir *Farewell to Manzanar* are frequently chosen for study. Julie Otsuka's 2002 novel *When the Emperor Was Divine* also details one family's experience of internment. George Takei, now a social media celebrity best known for playing a prominent Asian American role on the TV show *Star Trek,* is producing a Broadway musical titled *Allegiance,* also about a family's experience during internment.

In 1998, an Ellis Island museum exhibit on Japanese American internment was titled *America's Concentration Camps: Remembering the Japanese-American Experience,* referring to the camps in a way that has fallen into disuse due to its near-exclusive association with the Holocaust and genocide. Although the camps were called concentration camps by both American military personnel and internees up until contemporary times, there was concern that the dramatic revival might cause confusion or unintentional offense to Jewish communities. Negotiations that followed allowed for the exhibit to use this title accompanied by clear statements about its use. What this highlighted was how government use of euphemisms to refer to controversial acts—"relocation" and "internment"—has operated both in the past and the present.

Despite many years of denial, in 2007 the U.S. Census Bureau confirmed suspicions that there was a breach of confidentiality terms in 1943. Researchers had uncovered papers proving that names and addresses were provided in response to a request from the Treasury Department. This discovery demonstrates how government surveillance needs to be looked at critically when threats to national security are overused as justification.

Ann Matsuuchi

See also: Japanese American Immigration

Further Reading

Densho Encyclopedia, http://encyclopedia.densho.org/.

Hayashi, Brian Masaru. *Democratizing the Enemy: The Japanese American Internment.* Princeton, NJ: Princeton University Press, 2008.

Howard, John. *Concentration Camps on the Home Front: Japanese Americans in the House of Jim Crow.* Chicago: University of Chicago Press, 2008.

Irons, Peter H. *Justice at War: The Story of the Japanese American Internment Cases.* Berkeley: University of California Press, 1993.

Jones, Jennifer Locke, ed. "A More Perfect Union: Japanese Americans & the U.S. Constitution." Smithsonian National Museum of American History, 2001, http://amhistory.si.edu/perfectunion/experience/index.html.

Kiyoshi Hirabayashi v. United States. United States Supreme Court, No. 870, June 21, 1943, FindLaw, http://caselaw.findlaw.com/us-supreme-court/320/81.html.

Nakamura, David. "Japanese Americans: House Hearings on Radical Islam 'Sinister.'" *Washington Post,* March 8, 2011, http://www.washingtonpost.com/wp-dyn/content/article/2011/03/08/AR2011030802876.html.

Ng, Wendy L. *Japanese American Internment during World War II: A History and Reference Guide.* Westport, CT: Greenwood, 2002.

United States. *Personal Justice Denied: Report of the Commission on Wartime Relocation and Internment of Civilians: Report for the Committee on Interior and Insular Affairs.* Washington: U.S. Government Printing Office, 1992, http://www.archives.gov/research/japanese-americans/justice-denied/.

"Was Internment Constitutional?" Digital History, 1944, http://www.digitalhistory.uh.edu/disp_textbook.cfm?smtid=3&psid=49.

JAPANESE AMERICAN LITERATURE

Immigration and internment define much of Japanese American literature. The most recent example is Julie Otsuka's (1962–) *The Buddha in the Attic* (2011). Fellow writer Dolen Perkins-Valdez praises *The Buddha in the Attic* for its portrayal of picture brides: "Otsuka's passionate exploration of history inspires me to reach for higher emotional truths in my own work" (qtd. in Elle 2014). Karen Tei Yamashita's (1951–) *Through the Arc of the Rain Forest* (1990), *Brazil-Maru* (1992), *Tropic of Orange* (1997), and *Circle K Cycles* (2001) also decentralize the North American Nikkei (diasporic Japanese) experience. *Through the Arc of the Rain*

Hisaye Yamamoto (1921–2011)

Hisaye Yamamoto stands out in the history of Japanese American literature for her portrayal of farm and family life, internment, racism, and female characters who refuse to act passively. After internment Yamamoto worked for the *Los Angeles Tribune,* where she was confronted by African Americans' experiences with racism. As noted in Yamamoto's obituary, in order to widen her perspective, she quit the newspaper to travel across the country (Woo 2011). In one of Yamamoto's stories, "Seventeen Syllables," the character Mrs. Hayashi writes haiku for a Japanese-language newspaper. For this, Mrs. Hayashi's husband chastises her. As Sau-ling Cynthia Wong interprets in *Reading Asian American Literature: From Necessity to Extravagance,* "Patriarchy is obviously responsible for Mrs. Hayashi's banishment from her family and from Japan, as well as Mr. Hayashi's stringent concept of wifely propriety" (1993, 168). For Mrs. Hayashi, art allows her to be something more than a silently enduring wife. Yamamoto's other work highlights internal conflicts on the basis of racism. For example, "Wilshire Bus" explores the responsibility that Asian Americans have toward others through the character Esther, a silent bystander who witnesses a white passenger harassing a Chinese American couple. Yamamoto is also known for "Yaneko's Earthquake," which appears in the collection *Seventeen Syllables and Other Stories* (2001).

Forest addresses the effects of globalization on Brazilians. *Circle K Cycles* depicts the overseas workers of Japanese heritage who travel from Brazil to Japan, where they experience lower social status than the Naichi (mainland Japanese). Japanese Canadian writer Ruth Ozeki's (1956–) *All Over Creation* (2003) uses settings in Idaho to highlight the social issues of genetically modified organisms.

Early Japanese American literature focuses on the immigration experience. Etsu Inagaki Sugimoto's (1874–1950) *A Daughter of the Samurai: How a Daughter of Feudal Japan, Living Hundreds of Years in One Generation, Became a Modern American* (1926) details the social life and customs of early 20th-century Japan and those of a well-to-do immigrant who becomes the object of curiosity among white female passengers. The protagonist, who is of samurai social class standing in Japan, is sent to live in the United States with her husband. In the United States, she becomes modernized and Americanized. The bride can be interpreted as a metaphor of Japan's transition from a feudal society to modernity. *A Daughter of the Samurai* has been translated into several languages, a testament to its popularity across the racial and cultural divide.

Lydia Minatoya's (1950–) *Talking to High Monks in the Snow* (1991) is the winner of the Pacific Northwest Bookseller Award and the PEN American

Center's Jerad Fund Award. Minatoya is also the author of *The Strangeness of Beauty* (2001), which is about Etsuko Sone and her niece Hanae's travel to Japan. The character Sone was born in 1897 into a family with over 20 generations of samurai; tragically, her mother Chie rejects Sone and sends her to be raised by another family. Later in her life, Sone relocates to Seattle's Japantown. Minatoya, born in Albany, New York, is a community college counselor based in Seattle. She earned her doctorate from the University of Maryland and spent two years teaching in Japan and China. She dreamed of being a writer since she was seven years old; among her favorite books is Toni Morrison's (1931–) *The Bluest Eye* (1970).

Displacement and alienation are two of the important themes of Japanese American literature. Sau-Ling Cynthia Wong (1993) identifies two major events that led to an overall feeling of alienation among Japanese Americans: the Immigration and Nationality Act of 1924 and Japanese American internment during World War II (110). John Okada's (1923–1971) *No-No Boy* (1957) revisits war resisters who answered "no" to two of the questions on the loyalty questionnaire that the U.S. government distributed to internees during World War II: would you serve in the U.S. armed forces, and would you swear allegiance to the American presidency? *No-No Boy* tells the story of Ichiro Yamada, who returns to postwar Seattle after being released from prison. The book not only offers a commentary on what it means to be nonwhite in postwar American society but also tells the story of alienation from within the Japanese American community.

A number of Japanese American literary texts portray the forced relocation of 110,000 Japanese Americans, such as Monica Sone's (1919–2011) *Nisei Daughter* (1953), Jim Yoshida's (1921–) *The Two Worlds of Jim Yoshida* (1972), Yoshiko Uchida's (1921–1992) *Desert Exile* (1982) and *The Invisible Thread* (1987), Ken Mochizuki's (1954–) *Baseball Saved Us* (1993), George Takei's (1937–) *To the Stars* (1994), Lawson Fusao Inada's (1938–) anthology *Only What We Could Carry* (2000), and Julie Otsuka's (1962–) *When the Emperor Was Divine* (2002). Joy Ogawa's (1935–) novel *Obasan* (1981) provides a story of internment from a Japanese Canadian's perspective. Similar to *Baseball Saved Us* and Ogawa's *Naomi's Road* (1986), Cynthia Kadohata's (1956–) *Weedflower* (2006) is written for young readers.

Monica Sone's *Nisei Daughter* is a coming-of-age autobiography set in prewar Seattle, Washington. In addition to detailing the humiliation that internment conferred upon Kazuko Sone (born Kazuko Monica Itoi) and her family, *Nisei Daughter* documents the author's experiences with racism in everyday life. The narrator, Kazuko, would take steps to decrease tension and conflict by any means necessary. She avoided socializing with her peers in public so as to avoid attracting any attention from white Americans. In addition to books such as *Nisei Daughter*, for more than 40 years Bill Hosokawa (1915–2007) contributed to a weekly column known as "From the Frying Pan" for the *Pacific Citizen* newspaper. His writing helped the Japanese American community process the internment camp experience. Hosokawa also published a number of books, including *Nisei: The Quiet Americans* (1969) and *Thirty-Five Years in the Frying Pan* (1978).

Japanese American literature is noted for its variety of works, including short fiction. Collectively these stories help the reader question the racialized and gendered status quo. Lonny Kaneko's (1939–) story "The Shoyu Kid," published in 1976 in *Amerasia* journal, deals with the castration of Japanese American men. The characters discover that their friend who supplies them chocolate earns this small prize in return for sexual favors performed on a red-headed internment camp guard. Toshio Mori's (1910–1980) story "The Chessmen" was adapted into a film of the same title in 2005. In this story, the naive George Murai and the aging Nakagawa-san vie for the same position of gardener-grower in a California-based carnation business. Both characters are cut off from their loved ones while working on the secluded farm, a situation amplifying their alienation. This story, published in Mori's collection *Yokohama, California* in 1949, paints a picture of the San Leandro and Oakland Japanese American communities in the 1930s and 1940s. Another story from Mori's collection, "The Woman Who Makes Swell Doughnuts," honors first-generation Japanese Americans through veneration of the quotidian, in this case the tasty doughnuts that "Mama" makes for the community. Mori's other works include *Woman from Hiroshima* (1978), a tribute to his mother; *The Chauvinist and Other Stories* (1979); and *Unfinished Message* (2000), published posthumously. Mori himself was born in Oakland, California, but relocated with his family to the Topaz, Utah, internment camp during World War II.

Poetry

Japanese American poetry is as varied as fiction. Yone Noguchi (1875–1947) is an early poet who lived near Stanford University. It was in Palo Alto, California, where he began writing poetry. In 1906 Noguchi published *The Summer Cloud* and three years later published *The Pilgrimage*. Violet Kazue Matsuda de Cristoforo's (1917–2007) *Poetic Reflections of the Tule Lake Internment Camp, 1944* (1987) brings to life her experiences during the internment. After the war, de Cristoforo participated in the redress movement as a result of the maltreatment her interned husband and brother encountered. She credits poetry for helping keep herself together during the trying times, including her visits to her severely burned mother in Hiroshima, Japan. Another poet, Janice Mirikitani (1941–), is also an activist. Her poems highlight sexual abuse as well as the trauma of internment as major themes. *Awake in the River* (1978) and *Shedding Silence* (1987) earned Mirikitani the distinction of being San Francisco's second poet laureate. James Masao Mitsui's (1940–) *From a Three-Cornered World* (1997) contains 60 poems that centralize family history, migration, and assimilation. Mitsui's *Journal of the Sun* (1974) received the Pacific Northwest Booksellers Award in 1974. Sharon Hashimoto (1953–), also from the Pacific Northwest, is the author of *The Crane Wife* (2003), which earned the Nicholas Roerich Poetry Prize. Hashimoto obtained her master's degree from the University of Washington and currently teaches at Highland Community College.

Japanese American Writers and Hawai'i

A number of Japanese American writers are from or write about Hawai'i. Juliet Sanae Kono's (1943–) *Hilo Rains* (1988) is largely autobiographical. It addresses her family's history on a sugarcane plantation. Milton Murayama's (1923–) *All I Asking for Is My Body* (1975) demonstrates what it was like to grow up as a Japanese American at the height of Hawai'i's plantation society. Sylvia Watanabe's *Talking to the Dead* (1992) was a finalist for the PEN Faulkner Award. It is set in the islands of Hawai'i and features a colorful cast of characters, including a grandmother who makes quilts from stolen laundry. Born in Ho'olehua in Moloka'i (meaning "the friendly island"), Lois-Ann Yamanaka (1961–) is a productive writer. Her book of poetry *Saturday Night at the Pahala Theater* (1993) addresses child abuse, an unfortunate part of life that unsettles the postcard image of Hawai'i. Much of Yamanaka's work is comedic and direct, utilizes Hawai'ian Creole English, and addresses racism and poverty. She has also written *Wild Meat and the Bully Burgers* (1996), which was adapted into the film *Fishbowl* (2005), directed by Kayo Hatta; *Blu's Hanging* (1997); *Heads by Harry* (1998); *Name Me Nobody* (1999); *Father of the Four Passages* (2001); *The Heart's Language* (2005); and *Behold the Many* (2006). *Wild Meat and the Bully Burgers* showcases racism and classism, while *Blu's Hanging* problematically portrays a Filipino sexual predator. *The Heart's Language* is a children's book that helps young readers understand autism.

Drama

Drama constitutes another part of Japanese American literature. An early play-wright by the name of Carl Sadakichi Hartmann (1867–1944) studied with Walt Whitman (1819–1892). Hartmann wrote his first play, *Christ*, in 1893. Wakako Yamauchi (1924–) is a playwright from California; her parents were immigrants living in southern California. The Yamauchis were interned in Poston, Arizona, during World War II. After the war, Yamauchi found a job in a candy factory based in Chicago, where she viewed plays. Yamauchi's plays *And the Soul Shall Dance* (1974) and *The Music Lessons* (1980) take place in desolate places, similar to the environment of the internment camps. *12-1-A* (1982)—Yamauchi's par-ents' address in the Poston camp (Block 12, Barrack 1, Unit A)—tells the story of the author's farming days as well as her family's attempts to address their mar-ginal social status. Momoko Iko (1940–) is also an early playwright; she honed her writing skills at the University of Illinois at Urbana–Champaign and the University of Iowa. Iko's first play, *Gold Watch* (1970), was shown on television in 1975 and brings to life Japanese Americans' resistance to forced relocation. Iko also wrote *Flowers and Household Gods* (1975), which deals with the haunting memories of internment, and *Boutique Living and Disposable Icons* (1987). Philip Kan Gotanda's (1951–) *The Wash* (1985) explores patriarchal power and chang-ing notions of family through a couple who eventually divorce in postwar Amer-ica. Gotanda, a third-generation Japanese American, was born in Stockton, California. He also wrote *The Avocado Kid or Zen in the Art of Guacamole*, which the Los Angeles–based East-West Players staged in 1978. His other theatrical works include *A Song for a Nisei Fisherman* (1981), *The Dream of Kitamura* (1982), *Yankee Dawg You Die* (1988), and *Fish Head Soup* (1991). Velina Hasu Houston (1957–) represents the second generation of Japanese American playwrights. She is well known for *Tea* (1987), about Japanese war brides who make sense of their lives in a Kansas town. Her contemporary Amy Hill (1953–), who had a role in *All-American Girl* (1994), wrote *Tokyo Bound* (1990), an autobiographical per-formance about the culture shock Hill experiences in Japan.

Joy Takako Taylor

See also: Japanese American Autobiographies; Japanese American Immigration; Japanese American Internment; Japanese American Women; Literature, Asian American

Further Reading

"14 Great Female Authors Recommend Their 41 Favorite Female Authors." Elle.com, April 1, 2014, http://www.elle.com/pop-culture/reviews/chick-lit-versus-lit-chicks -great-novel.

Lilienfeld, Jane. "Where in the World Is Transnational Feminism?" *Tulsa Studies in Women's Literature* 23(1) (2004): 91–105.

Wong, Sau-ling Cynthia. *Reading Asian American Literature: From Necessity to Extravagance.* Princeton, NJ: Princeton University Press, 1993.

Woo, Elaine. "Hisaye Yamamoto Dies at 89; Writer of Japanese American Stories." *Los Angeles Times,* February 13, 2011, http://articles.latimes.com/2011/feb/13/local/la-me-hisaye-yamamoto-20110213.

Yogi, Stan. "Rebels and Heroines: Subversive Narratives in the Stories of Wakako Yamauchi and Hisaye Yamamoto." In *Reading the Literatures of Asian America,* edited by Shirley Geok-lin Lim and Amy Ling, 131–150. Philadelphia: Temple University Press, 1992.

JAPANESE AMERICAN POETRY

Japanese American poetry consists of numerous and heterogeneous elegiac customs and immensely dissimilar, characteristic poetic modes. These qualities in part reflect chronological circumstances, geographic dissimilarities, and demographic transforms that have formed the materialization and growth of poetry by Japanese Americans. While the phrase "Japanese American literature" was first used during the early 1970s, current research has traced the genesis of it to the 1850s, when Japanese immigrant neighborhoods were established in the

Lawson Fusao Inada (1938–)

Born in 1938 in Fresno, California, Lawson Fusao Inada, together with his family, was interned in California, Arkansas, and Colorado during World War II because of his Japanese heritage. He studied at Fresno State University; the University of California, Berkeley; the University of Oregon; and the University of Iowa. He was also a jazz musician. Jazz and his experience in the internment camps provide inspirations for his poetry. Inada's collection *Legends from Camp* (1994) won the American Book Award, and *Drawing the Line* (1997) won the Oregon Book Award. He also published *Before the War: Poems as They Happened* (1971) and *Just Into/Nations* (1996), among other works. Inada received poetry fellowships from the National Endowment for the Arts, a Guggenheim Fellowship, and a Creative Arts Grant from the Civil Liberties Public Education Fund; won the Stafford/Hall Award for Poetry in 1997; and was named Oregon's fifth poet laureate in 2006.

Lan Dong

David Mura (1952–)

David Mura is a Japanese American poet, memoirist, writer, and artist. His poetry collections include *After We Lost Our Way* (1989), winner of the National Poetry Series contest in 1989; *The Colors of Desire* (1995); and *Angels for the Burning* (2004). He also published memoirs *Turning Japanese: Memoirs of a Sansei* (1991) and *Where the Body Meets Memory: An Odyssey of Race, Sexuality, and Identity* (1996) as well as novels and other works. Common themes of his writing are race, sexuality, and Japanese American identity. He is a recipient of several prestigious fellowships and awards, including National Endowment for the Arts literature fellowships, a U.S.-Japan Creative Artist fellowship, Bush Foundation fellowships, and a Discovery/The Nation Award, among others. He lives in St. Paul, Minnesota.

Lan Dong

United States and started to circulate bilingual and Japanese-language newspapers that regularly ran fiction, spoofs, verse, and fashionable rhymes and songs. The history of the Japanese people in the United States exceeds one century, with its beginnings in settlement mostly in the state of California, especially in San Francisco, and the establishment of a literary community that practiced two traditional poetic forms: haiku and tanka.

Twentieth-century Japanese American poetry makes use of a set of repeated themes: customary Japanese mores, the thought of the United States as the "Gold Mountain," education, the spinster culture of Japantown, the feminization of Japanese society, and ethnic inequity. In addition to their thematic and prescribed heterogeneity, the physical sites of these poets—San Francisco, New York City, Chicago, Los Angeles, Santa Fe, Portland, Seattle, and Honolulu as well as many others—and their famous careers point out that Japanese American poems are no longer limited to Japantown or dispersed to Japanese American ghettos exclusively. Japanese American poets no longer exist in the physically surrounded limits of ordinary American civilization and society. On the other hand, the multicultural features of Japanese American poems are not merely straight indications of the bards' ethnicity or communal place. To a certain extent, the prescribed and stylistic conventions of Japanese American poetry, such as its thematic apprehensions, are the consequence of the writer's dialogues with numerous poetic traditions in battles of absorption by Eurocentric mores and in exploration of novel manners of implementing language and shape to connect with social matters and to re-create poetry.

Poet Kimiko Hahn reading at the 12th Annual Poetry Walk in New York City, June 11, 2007. She is the winner of many prestigious awards including the American Book Award. (Roger Kisby/Getty Images)

Victoria Chang has noted that one sign of the growing assortment of Japanese American poets is that it has become harder to identify artists by their surname only. A few examples that Chang draws on are Brenda Shaughnessy, who is "half-Japanese and half–Irish American," as well as Brian Komei Dempster and Lee Ann Roripaugh, who both have "half-Japanese, half–European American" parentage (2004, xxvi). Chang goes on to list a variety of Thai, Filipino, Norwegian, and Chinese poets whose ancestry is a combination of Asian and other cultures.

Edith Marcombe Shiffert and Yuki Sawa's *Anthology of Modern American Japanese Poetry* (1972) is one of the first collections that details the development of Japanese American poetry. In this canonical text that demonstrates the tense assortment and growth of Chinese American verse, the editors incorporate a variety of poetic forms including free verse, tanka, and haiku as well as an introduction that situates the texts in their appropriate chronological circumstance, permitting the audience to take pleasure in the book both for its literature and as a guide to the educational history of Japan. Selections cover writers such as Kōtarō Takamura (1883–1956), Sakutarō Hagiwara (1886–1942), Murō Saisei (1889–1962), Tatsuji Miyoshi (1900–1964), Tsunao Aida, Takako Hashimoto, Shigenobu Takayanagi, and about a dozen other Japanese American poets. Also, the text's back matter includes detailed biographical notes, a selected bibliography, and an index of poets.

Japanese American poet Kimiko Hahn's (1955–) haiku "Utica Station" from *An Old World Made New: The Narrow Road to the Interior* (2006) makes use of the very short structure of haiku. As John Givens notes, Hahn uses a variety of transformations and expansions of travel to discover a personal retort to the past. The corporeal expedition is portrayed as an artistic pilgrimage to exact spaces (2010). Hahn's poem, like the traditional haiku form, allows no room for unnecessary words or philosophy.

Japanese American poetry is an important aspect of the U.S. multiethnic mix. It symbolizes freedom, equality, and the attainability of the America Dream for everybody. Its style demystifies and creates a unison within the United States while at the same time establishing a picturesque portrait of Japanese culture and lifestyle. The contribution that Japanese American poetry has made to the American canon demonstrates the striving for inclusiveness that has become synonymous with American culture as a whole.

Gerardo Del Guercio

See also: Japanese American Literature; Literature, Asian American

Further Reading

Bloom, Harold, Henry W. Berg, and Albert A. Berg, eds. *Asian American Writers*. New York: Chelsea House, 1998.

Chang, Victoria M. "Introduction." In *Asian American Poetry: The Next Generation*, xv–xxx. Urbana: University of Illinois Press, 2004.

Givens, John. "An Old Road Made New: The Narrow Road to the Interior by Kimiko Hahn." *Cerise Press: A Journal of Literature Arts and Culture* 1(3) (2010), http://www .cerisepress.com/01/03/an-old-world-made-new-the-narrow-road-to-the-interior-by -kimiko-hahn.

Hahn, Kimiko. *An Old Road Made New: The Narrow Road to the Interior*. New York: Norton, 2006.

Keene, Donald, ed. *Modern Japanese Literature: From 1868 to the Present Day*. New York: Grove, 1956.

Shiffert, Edith Marcombe, and Yuki Sawa, eds. *Anthology of Japanese Poetry.* Rutland, VT: Charles E. Tuttle, 1972.

Tanaka, Ronald. *The Shino Suite.* New York: Authors Choice Press, 1981.

Wright, Richard. *Haiku: the Last Poems of an American Icon.* New York: Arcade Publishing, 1998.

JAPANESE AMERICAN WOMEN

History

In 1882 President Chester A. Arthur (1829–1886) signed the Chinese Exclusion Act, the first race-based federal immigration law in American history. It substantially curtailed the number of Chinese laborers entering the country, thus creating the need for a new labor force. Japan underwent dramatic political, cultural, and social changes as a result of the 1868 Meiji Reform. Early Japanese immigrants coming to the United States around the turn of the century were predominantly male; they provided a replacement of Chinese laborers who were barred by the 1882 Exclusion Act. Although Japanese women

Patsy Takemoto Mink (1927–2002)

A third-generation Japanese American born and raised in Hawai'i, Patsy Takemoto Mink was the first woman of color elected to the U.S. House of Representatives. She was also the first woman elected to Congress from Hawai'i. She served in the U.S. Congress for a total of 12 terms, from 1965 to 1977 and from 1990 to 2002, representing Hawai'i's 2nd Congressional District. She was one of the principal authors and sponsors for the Title IX Amendment of Higher Education Act, which prohibits gender discrimination by federally funded institutions. She also introduced the first comprehensive Early Childhood Education Act and the Women's Educational Equity Act and sponsored many influential coalitions in Congress. President George W. Bush renamed the Title IX Amendment of Higher Education Act the Patsy T. Mink Equal Opportunity in Education Act in 2002. In recognition of her work on civil rights, women's rights, justice, peace, and integrity, the Patsy Takemoto Mink Education Foundation was established in 2003, aiming to carry on her commitments to educational access, opportunity, and equity for low-income women and educational enrichment for children.

began arriving in the United States in the late 19th century, their numbers remained small. After Japan and the United States signed the Gentlemen's Agreement in 1907, allowing wives to join their husbands in the United States, a number of Japanese women entered the country as so-called picture brides. The majority of Japanese women immigrants went to Hawai'i in the late 19th and early 20th centuries. They faced long working hours, limited English-language skills, isolation, and other hardship in America. Their arrival and settlement in America changed the Japanese American community. A number of Japanese American literary works address the life experiences of these pioneer women, including among others Cathy Song's debut poetry collection *Picture Bride* (1983) and the novels *Picture Bride* (1987) by Yoshiko Uchida, *Honolulu* (2009) by Alan Brennert, and *The Buddha in the Attic* (2011) by Julie Otsuka.

During World War II Japanese American women, together with men and children, were interned shortly after the attack on Pearl Harbor. As a result of Executive Order 9066, an estimated 120,000 Japanese Americans, immigrant and American-born, were interned in relocation camps in Arizona, Colorado, Wyoming, Arkansas, California, Idaho, and Utah. Japanese American communities suffered physical and mental stress as well as financial losses.

With the McCarran-Walter Act of 1952, Japanese and immigrants from other Asian countries were eligible to become naturalized U.S. citizens. After the 1965 Immigration Act, Japanese professionals and family members arrived in America, contributing to the increase of Japanese American population. According to the 2010 U.S. census, the Japanese American population is over 1.3 million. Large numbers of them live in California (southern California, in particular), Hawai'i, New York, Washington, Illinois, and Ohio.

Like China, Japan has traditionally been influenced by Confucianism. Traditional Japanese families follow patriarchal orders: men are breadwinners working outside the home and heads of the families, while women take care of domestic duties such as child rearing and household chores. Parents look after their children when they are young; children take care of their parents when they become elderly. When Japanese immigrants came to the United States, they preserved some of the traditional practices and at the same time changed others to adapt to American culture. During the early years of Japanese immigration, a number of women worked in sugarcane plantation fields and farms alongside men besides taking care of child rearing and household chores. Some women helped with family business; others took up jobs to supplement family income, thus gaining more financial independence. In recent years, women professionals have become an important part of Japanese American communities across the country. Generally speaking, first-generation

Japanese immigrants held on to many of the traditions, while the younger American-born generations show less influence by Japanese culture and more acculturation to American life.

Japanese American men and women practice a wide range of religions. The two main religions among Japanese Americans are Buddhism and Protestantism. Other religious beliefs include Catholicism and Shintoism. Due to the long history of Buddhism and Shintoism in Japan, some of the cultural traditions associated with them are still influential in Japanese American communities. The annual summertime Obon Festival provides an opportunity for celebration, community building, and reconnection with Japanese Americans' cultural roots. The Japanese Evangelical Missionary Society was founded in 1950 and includes four ministries: the International Mission Ministries in Japan and South America; the Campus Ministry: Asian American Christian Fellowship; Specialized Ministries: Mount Hermon Summer Conference; and the Support Coordination Ministry.

Representative Patsy Takemoto Mink, a Democrat from Hawai'i, puting a nameplate on the door of her new office in Washington, D.C., December 2, 1965. The first woman of color elected to the U.S. House of Representatives, Mink served 12 terms. (Bettmann/Corbis)

Japanese American women have made significant contributions to many areas in contemporary America, including music, arts, literature, entertainment, and others. Midori Gotō (1971–) is a famous violinist. Born in Osaka, Japan, she moved to New York City in 1982. A talented musician, she made her debut at the age of 11. She founded Midori and Friends in 1992, an organization that aims to bring music education to inner-city children in New York City. She later started other community-based projects: Partners in Performance, the University Residencies Program, and the Orchestra Residencies Program. She was the recipient of the Suntory Music Award in 1993. In 2001, she received the prestigious Avery Fisher Prize.

Japanese American women artists and curators have contributed to the development of contemporary art. Born in Japan in 1933, Yoko Ono is known for her avant-garde art, music, and filmmaking. She moved to New York in 1953 and soon became involved with the city's artist groups. Much of her art work is experimental. She married John Lennon, and the couple collaborated on some albums. She released her first solo album, *Yoko Ono/Plastic Ono Band,* in 1970 as a companion to Lennon's *John Lennon/Plastic Ono Band.* She was also an experimental filmmaker, active in the 1960s and 1970s. Ono has been criticized for her influences on Lennon, his music, and the breakup of the Beatles. She received the Golden Lion Award for lifetime achievement from the Venice Biennale in 2009 and the Oskar Kokoschka Prize for applied contemporary art in 2012. Ono has been active in preserving Lennon's legacy and contributing to philanthropy, including the Strawberry Fields memorial in New York City, the Imagine Peace Tower in Iceland, and the John Lennon Museum in Saitama, Japan, among other efforts. From May to September 2015 Ono had her first exhibition, a one-woman show, at the Museum of Modern Art in New York.

Mine Okubo (1912–2001) is best known for *Citizen 13660,* a memoir made of black-and-white drawings and text narratives documenting Japanese American internment during World War II. When the war broke out, Okubo was studying in Europe on an art fellowship. She later made her way back to the United States. After the attack on Pearl Harbor, she and her brother were sent to Tanforan Assembly Center and then the Topaz War Relocation camp. After the war she went to New York, where she continued to work as an artist. First published in 1946, *Citizen 13660* was one of the first book-length works reflecting Japanese Americans' experiences in the internment camps. Okubo won many awards for her contribution to art and Japanese American culture.

Japanese American women writers and their works have become frequent subjects in academic studies as well as among general readers. Jeanne Wakatsuki Houston (1934–) is best known for her memoir *Farewell to Manzanar*

(1973), coauthored with her husband James D. Houston (1933–). Houston was born in California. After the attack on Pearl Harbor, her family was relocated to Manzanar as a result of Executive Order 9066. Her book documents her family's experiences before World War II and in the internment camp. The book was adapted into a film in 1976; Nobu McCarthy (1934–2002) played both Houston as an adult and her mother.

Yoshiko Uchida (1921–1992) was a second-generation Japanese American writer. Her novel *Journey to Topaz* (1971) draws inspiration from her personal experiences in the internment camp during World War II. Her autobiography *Desert Exile* (1982) not only documents Japanese American internment experience but also reflects how such experience affects her own identity formation. Many of her other works also address such topics as race, ethnicity, and identity. She was a prolific writer and published more than 30 books, including fiction, nonfiction, and children's and young adult literature. She won many awards and honors, including the American Library Association Notable Book citation, the Children's Spring Book Festival honor award, the Commonwealth Club of California medal, and the Friends of Children and Literature award.

Karen Tei Yamashita, born in Oakland, California, in 1957, is a professor of literature and creative writing at the University of California, Santa Cruz, where she teaches Asian American literature and creative fiction writing. She is the author of *Through the Arc of the Rain Forest* (1990), *Brazil-Maru* (1992), *Tropic of Orange* (1997), *Circle K Cycles* (2001), *I Hotel* (2010), and *Anime Wong: Fictions of Performance* (2014), all of which were published by Coffee House Press. In *I Hotel,* the story begins in 1968 against the backdrop of the Martin Luther King Jr. and Bobby Kennedy assassinations, student demonstrations, and the Vietnam War. It won the California Book Award, the American Book Award, the Asian/Pacific American Librarians Association Award, and the Association for Asian American Studies Award and was a finalist for the National Book Award.

Japanese American women athletes have achieved remarkable accomplishments in American history. Born and raised in California, Kristi Yamaguchi (1971–) won the World Figure Skating Championships in 1991 and 1992, the U.S. Figure Skating Championships in 1992, and the Olympic Gold Medal for ladies' singles in 1992. She was an accomplished figure skater in both singles and pairs, winning world and national titles in both categories. She founded the Always Dream Foundation to provide funding for after-school programs, summer camps, literacy programs, back-to-school clothes, and other things for underprivileged children and children with disabilities. In 2005, she was inducted into the U.S. Olympic Hall of Fame. She worked as a local commentator on figure skating for San Jose TV station KNTV during the 2006 Winter

Olympics and served as a special correspondent for NBC's *Today Show* during the 2010 Winter Olympics. In 2008, she was the champion in the sixth season of the television show *Dancing with the Stars.* She also published children's books and created a woman's active-wear line.

Japanese American women have also been active in the entertainment business. Born in Ottawa, Nobu McCarthy was a Japanese Canadian actress. She moved to the United States in 1955. She made her debut in *The Geisha Boy* (1958) and appeared in many films and television shows. She played the leading role in *Farewell to Manzanar* in 1976, a film based on Jeanne Wakatsuki Houston and James D. Houston's memoir under the same title and documenting Japanese American internment during World War II.

Lan Dong

See also: Japanese American Folklore; Japanese American Immigration; Picture Bride; Women, Asian American

Further Reading

Asian Women United of California, ed. *Making Waves: An Anthology of Writing by and about Asian Women.* Acton, MA: Beacon, 1989.

Chan, Sucheng. *Asian Americans: An Interpretive History.* New York: Twayne, 1991.

Hoeffel, Elizabeth M., Sonya Rastogi, Myoung Ouk Kim, and Hasan Shahid. "The Asian Population: 2010." U.S. Census Bureau, March 2012, http://www.census .gov/prod/cen2010/briefs/c2010br-11.pdf.

Hune, Shirley, and Gail Nomura, eds. *Asian Pacific Islander American Women: A Historical Anthology.* New York: New York University Press, 2003.

Kawaguchi, Yoko. *Butterfly's Sisters: The Geisha in Western Culture.* New Haven, CT: Yale University Press, 2010.

Matsumoto, Valerie J. "Apple Pie and Makizushi: Japanese American Women Sustaining Family and Community." In *Eating Asian America: A Food Studies Reader,* edited by Robert Ji-Song Ku, Martin F. Manalansan IV, and Anita Mannur, 255–273. New York: New York University Press, 2013.

Yamamoto, Traise. *Masking Selves, Making Subjects: Japanese American Women, Identity, and the Body.* Berkeley: University of California Press, 1999.

Yoshimizu, Ayaka. "'Hello, War Brides': Heteroglossia, Counter-Memory, and the Auto/Biographical Work of Japanese War Brides." *Meridians: Feminism, Race, Transnationalism* 10(1) (2010): 111–136.

JAPANESE AMERICANS AND EDUCATION

Education is traditionally significant in the Japanese American community. The first Japanese immigrants to arrive in numbers to the United States arrived during the Meiji era (1868–1912), which marked Japan's movement from isolation to trade and interaction with the rest of the world. Universal education was a critical aspect of Meiji reformation, and many Issei (first-generation immigrants) had educational experiences that were influenced by exposure to teachers and curricula influenced by the West. As a result, Japanese immigrants were often more educated than immigrants from other nations who came to the United States between the 1880s and early 1900s. However, because of language barriers and prejudice, they were frequently relegated to domestic, menial, and physical labor. In the early years of post-Meiji emigration, it is estimated that students were 5–20 percent of emigrants leaving Japan. Historical accounts report that the first bachelor's degree awarded to a Japanese America dates to 1914, and the early years of the 1930s saw a Japanese American alumni association established at a California university.

Education was seen as the road away from labor and toward employment opportunities beyond the plantations of Hawai'i and the fields of California and was seen as the means of leaving the laundries and food service work of their parents. At the height of the second wave of Japanese immigration, most Issei parents encouraged their children toward American assimilation and standards of excellence and success. To that end, Nisei (second-generation) children were told about the importance of school and education—how knowledge could never be taken away and that learning could be the ladder toward success, security, and equality. By 1940, the median education level of Nisei was 12 or more years as compared to 10 years for American-born white children.

In the years prior to World War II, many Nisei attended the American school by day and the Japanese school in the evening to keep up their Japanese-language skills as well as their English-language skills. Some were given the opportunity to go to Japan to study to escape the possibilities of discrimination in admission and ill treatment. Before World War II, Nisei men who held college degrees in engineering, pharmacy, or accounting were seldom hired in their fields. Instead they found jobs as assistants in family businesses or as clerks in local markets. Some may have found employment in the Japan-based businesses in communities where such businesses thrived, but even in these positions their acceptance was inconsistent.

Passed in February 1942 and in effect until January 1945, Executive Order 9066 prescribed military areas to be overseen by the secretary of war where Japanese and Japanese Americans would be held. Executive Order 9066 ultimately led to the relocation of Japanese citizens particularly on the West Coast and had a drastic impact on Japanese American education, as the traditional mainstream educational experience was disrupted by relocation to internment camps. People created a life within the camps, and life began to follow a routine that included schools and the related extracurricular sports and other activities. For many Nisei, education was the way out of the internment camps before the war was over. Many of them were granted permission to attend colleges throughout the United States, but the volume of applications to be processed created a long wait for final approval. Sometimes the decision took years. The Pacific War ended in August 1945, but the last mass detention camp did not close until October 1946, and the last special internment camp did not close until 1952. The interruption in education, along with the large-scale loss of home and financial security, resulted in a situation whereby most Nisei could no longer afford to go to college because of the need to support and rebuild the family and community. In the years following internment, education was seen as the way to reestablish individual self-respect as well as community and professional stability.

In the 1950s and 1960s, the majors chosen by Japanese Americans in college reflected an interest in knowledge that would translate into business ownership or a midlevel profession, including business management and accounting. Although their pay was not commensurate with white Americans who held the same jobs and education, by 1960 Nisei had exceeded the educational levels of all other ethnic groups in the United States. During the mid-1960s, Japanese Americans were emerging as what some called the model minority largely because of educational achievements. By 1970, they had one of the highest educational levels of any ethnic group in the country, with a median of 12.4 years of schooling (Takahashi 1997, 158).

Standardized test scores earned by Japanese American students, particularly in math and reading, often exceed the national averages. Japanese Americans have the largest showing of any ethnic group in nationwide advanced placement testing each year. This early educational success continues to college-level study and postbaccalaureate study. A large majority of Japanese Americans obtained postsecondary degrees.

There is an equal distribution of Japanese Americans in the sciences, mathematics, arts, and humanities. Although their numbers have declined slightly in recent years, Japanese Americans are still a prominent presence in the top colleges and universities in the United States, including Ivy League schools and the top University of California campuses, including UC Berkeley and UCLA. In 2010 the U.S. Census Bureau reported that more than 40 percent of Japanese Americans held a college degree.

The focus on education in the Japanese American community follows the chronology that details their experience in the United States. Specifically, the Issei are noted for primary and secondary education. The Nisei were encouraged to excel in high school and to seek college degrees. The Sansei (third generation) earned college degrees and sought postbaccalaureate study, and the Yonsei (fourth generation) continued the tradition of study after college and success in graduate study at some of the most well-known colleges and universities in the country.

Joni L. Johnson Williams

See also: Japanese American Immigration; Japanese American Internment; Model Minority; Proposition 209 (1996); Tiger Mom

Further Reading

Chan, Sucheng. *Asian Americans: An Interpretive History.* New York: Twayne, 1991.

Fugita, Stephen S., and David J. O'Brien. *Japanese American Ethnicity: The Persistence of Community.* Seattle: University of Washington Press, 1994.

Inada, Lawson Fusao, ed. *Only What We Could Carry: The Japanese American Internment Experience.* Berkeley, CA: Heyday Books, 2000.

Ogunwole, Stella U., Malcolm P. Drewery Jr., and Merarys Rios-Vargas. "The Population with a Bachelor's Degree or Higher by Race and Hispanic Origin 2006–2010: American Community Survey Briefs." U.S. Census Bureau, May 2012, www.census .gov/prod/2012pubs/acsbr10-19.pdf.

Okihiro, Gary. *Margins and Mainstreams.* Seattle: University of Washington Press, 1994.

Spickard, Paul R. *Japanese Americans: The Formation and Transformations of an Ethnic Group.* New Brunswick, NJ: Rutgers University Press, 2009.

Takahashi, Jere. *Nisei/Sansei: Shifting Japanese American Identities and Politics.* Philadelphia: Temple University Press, 1997.

Tamaki, Ronald. *Strangers from a Different Shore: A History of Asian Americans.* Boston: Back Bay Books, 1998.

Uchida, Yoshiko. *Desert Exile: The Uprooting of a Japanese American Family.* Seattle: University of Washington Press, 1982.

Weinberg, Meyer. *Asian American Education: Historical Background and Current Realities.* New York and London: Routledge, 1997.

Yamanaka, K. Morgan. "Japanese American Life in the Twentieth Century: A Personal Journey." In *The Asian Pacific American Heritage: A Companion to Literature and Arts,* edited by George J. Leonard, 85–112. New York: Garland Publishing, 1999.

JAPANESE COMMUNITY ORGANIZATIONS

History and Origins

Japanese community organizations started to appear more frequently after World War II. Organizations did exist prior to this period but were more localized groups who disbanded or became less active during the war. Shortly after the war ended, a resurgence of organizations occurred because many Japanese living in the United States were put into camps during the war, and there was a need for assistance. When the war was over, many Japanese were relocated and felt a sense of noncommunity and isolation. Older organizations were revived, and new community groups were founded to fill the void for the Japanese Americans and to promote their well-being. These community organizations are still active today and take on the new concerns and promote the intellectual and social growth of Japanese Americans.

The oldest Japanese community organization is the Japanese American Citizens League (JACL), which was founded in 1929 in California. The JACL is also regarded as one of the largest Asian American civil rights organizations in the United States and has grown to include many non-Asian groups who have had their civil rights threatened. The JACL vision statement explains that the

Officials of the Japanese American Citizens League posting signs notifying the public that all residents of Japanese heritage must register themselves and their families, Seattle, Washington, March 11, 1942. Founded in 1929, JACL is the oldest and largest Asian American civil rights organization in the U.S. (AP Photo)

organization "strive[s] to promote a world that honors diversity by respecting values of fairness, equality, and social justice." The JACL's overall mission is to stop prejudice and bigotry. This organization has had many significant milestones throughout its history. During World War II, the JACL tried to ensure the protection of Japanese who were living in government camps. The JACL also fought for the rights of Japanese Americans who wanted to serve in the U.S. military. This led to the formation of the 442nd Regimental Combat Team, which merged with the 100th Battalion in Hawai'i and became one of the most decorated units in U.S. military history. After World War II, the JACL helped many of the dislocated Japanese relocate to new areas and become citizens. In 1947 the JACL fought to amend the Soldier Bride's Act, which did not allow Japanese wives of U.S. servicemen to enter the United States. Even though the JACL was primarily located on the West Coast, in 1946 it formed a special antidiscrimination committee office in Washington, D.C. The committee's goal was to promote the civil rights of all Japanese Americans. The JACL began to grow, and two years later in 1948 it achieved its greatest feat. The organization helped to form the Leadership Conference on Civil Rights, which brought together all of the major U.S. civil rights organizations.

Today the JACL is still an active community organization. It has played a vital role in promoting scholarship and leadership in the Japanese community. The JACL now has approximately 108 chapters in most of the major metropolitan U.S. cities. The JACL has expanded its mission to not only protect the rights of Japanese and Asian Americans but also to protect the rights of all individuals.

Another organization, the Japanese American Association of New York (JAA), originally called the Japanese Mutual Aid Society in 1907, was reestablished after World War II. At first this organization was spearheading efforts to send aid such as food and clothing to Japan, but once living conditions in Japan improved, the organization focused its efforts on helping Japanese Americans in the United States, primarily in the New York City area. Today the JAA is still focusing on the well-being of Japanese Americans. It now offers free legal and medical consultations, delivers meals to the elderly, and sponsors community activities for all ages. The JAA works with other New York organizations and formed the Committee on Aging Issues. This committee addresses the increasing needs of elderly Japanese Americans.

Japanese American organizations continue to grow. The Japanese American Cultural and Community Center (JACCC) was founded in 1971 to enhance Japanese community, cultural, and art programs. The JACCC's mission is to bring the Japanese cultural arts to a more diverse audience while instilling pride in Japanese Americans. Today this organization provides a place for cultural enrichment as well as establishing an outlet to showcase Japanese American achievements in the arts.

In addition to these organizations, there are also organizations that promote the international relations between Japanese Americans and Japan. One such group, the Nippon Club, was established in 1905 by Dr. Jokichi Takamini. The club, which is the only Japanese social club, promotes a sense of community by providing a place for Japanese Americans to socialize and form a bond with their culture. The club holds numerous athletic and cultural events as well.

One of the most recently formed organizations is the Japanese American Network (JA*NET), which was founded in the summer of 1995. Even though the Internet contains a plethora of information, there seemed to be a lack of information about Japanese Americans. JA*NET wanted to fill this gap and provide a site that individuals could visit to learn more about Japanese American history and accomplishments.

In 1971, a resurrection of the Japan Society (originally founded in 1907) occurred. The organization's mission is to enhance people's understanding of Japanese American culture. Its headquarters is located in the first building in New York designed by a Japanese architect, Junzo Yoshimura. Today this organization is a flourishing center for global leaders, scholars, and educators.

In 1990 the National Association of Japan America Societies (NAJAS), a nonprofit organization that provides educational, cultural, and business professional programs to the community, was formed. The NAJAS's goal is to promote a good communication network for all Japan America Societies throughout the United States. The Japan America Societies started to form in 1917 in many metropolitan cities to promote stronger bonds between America and Japan and currently have chapters throughout the United States. Japanese American organizations have been with us for over 100 years. Their continued growth and the emergence of new organizations will strengthen the Japanese American community.

Candy A. Henry

See also: Japanese American Immigration

Further Reading

Flewelling, Stan. *Shirakawa: Stories from a Pacific Northwest Japanese American Community.* Auburn, WA: White River Valley Museum 2002.

Fugita, Stephen S., and David J. O'Brien. *Japanese American Ethnicity: The Persistence of Community.* Seattle: University of Washington Press, 1991.

Japanese American Association of New York, Inc. www.jaany.org.

Japanese American Citizens League, www.jacl.org.

The Japanese American Cultural and Community Center, www.jaccc.org.

Japanese American Network, www.janet.org.

Levine, Gene N., and Colbert Rhodes. *The Japanese American Community: A Three-Generation Study.* New York: Praeger, 1981.

Matsumoto, Valerie J. *Farming the Home Place: A Japanese American Community in California, 1919–1982.* Ithaca, NY: Cornell University Press, 1993.

National Association of Japan America Societies, www.us-japan.org

JAPANESE TEA CEREMONY

History and Origins

The Japanese tea ceremony, *chado,* as we know it today has its roots in the 16th century. It was initially influenced by Chinese practices of drinking powdered green tea (*matcha*) and by Zen Buddhism. It was enjoyed primarily by privileged members in society, such as respected warriors and wealthy merchants. In the mid-16th century, a tea culture unique to Japan began to take shape and infiltrate all aspects of life. This expansion into wider social circles was partially due to the emergence of tea masters such as Sen no Rikyū (1522–1591), who was deified as the god of tea in the Edo period (1600–1867) and is still a revered figure in Japanese tea culture. Among other things, he advocated the use of more rustic ceramic vessels from Korea and Japan instead of refined ones from China and further developed the *wabi* aesthetic, which emphasizes simplicity and beauty and is still central to the Japanese tea ceremony today.

Although tea plays a key role in *chado,* the Japanese tea ceremony is not just about consumption. Instead, the ceremony also speaks to a distilled attitude toward life and is seen as an aesthetic, philosophical, and spiritual experience. The *wabi* ceremony, for example, embodies the essence of the following four principles put forward by Sen no Rikyū: harmony (*wa*), respect (*kei*), purity (*sei*), and tranquility (*jaku*). It often takes place in a simple but elegant room decorated with hanging scrolls (*kakemono*). In the ceremony, tea drinking is said to become a transformative and transcendental experience in which the tea drinkers may reach a meditative state that forgoes awareness of the self.

In a Japanese tea ceremony, one can assume the role of either host or guest. Often, the host receives the guests in a special tea room, the door of which is

The tea ceremony has a long history in Japan, dating back to the 16th century. At first available predominantly to men, it is now largely practiced by women. (Akiyoko74/Dreamstime.com)

designed so that the guests have to bow when making an entrance, thus showing humility. The tea ceremony begins with the host elegantly cleaning the tea-serving utensils. After the process is complete, the host adds scoops of green tea powder to the tea bowl and pours in hot water. When the tea has properly steeped, it is presented to the guests, who receive the cups with care and respect. Due to its intricacy and complexity, the art of the Japanese tea ceremony may take years of practice to master. Many people in Japan opt to take formal classes to learn how to be a graceful host and an appropriate guest. Students can even earn certificates for mastering the different procedures of a traditional tea ceremony, and the true student may spend a whole life perfecting the artistry of *chado.*

Tradition and Practices

In the early periods of its development women were largely excluded from *chado,* as it was an activity restricted to the predominantly male spheres of

Buddhist monasteries and later the court and the military. Women only played a peripheral or at best supportive role in the tea ceremony during this time, such as preparing the tea utensils.

Two events in Japanese history were instrumental in changing the role of women within *chado*. The first was the Meiji Restoration (1864) and increased contact with the Western world associated with this period in Japanese history. As a result of the transformations that occurred in Japanese society at this time, the study of *chado* was opened up to social classes that were previously excluded from the activity as well as to women, who were tasked with teaching children the art of the traditional tea ceremony. Job opportunities also became available to women at this time, especially those from the upper class, who were hired to teach *chado* to women from all social strata in order to prepare and train them to be suitable wives.

World War II also had a large effect on women's roles in the Japanese tea ceremony. In the aftermath of Japan's humiliating defeat in the war, *chado* was considered a cultural practice that had important connections to Japanese values and its history. Women were thus encouraged to participate in reestablishing the significance of the art of the tea ceremony in society.

Today, classes on *chado* are arranged in a myriad of places, such as classrooms, tea houses, and museums. The teachers tend to be women, who may also teach other traditional Japanese arts and practices such as gardening and flower arrangement. Thus, an activity that was at first only available to men is now largely practiced by and associated with women. The changing social significance and symbolism of the Japanese tea ceremony is a remarkable example of how a traditional practice can evolve to accommodate historical and social changes.

Tammy L. M. Ho

See also: Chop Suey; Filipino American Food; Fortune Cookie; Fusion Cuisine; Kimchi; *Pho;* Sushi; Thai American Food; Vietnamese American Food

Further Reading

Kondo, Dorinne. "The Way of Tea: A Symbolic Analysis." *Man* 20(2) (1985): 287–306.

Mori, Barbara. "The Tea Ceremony: A Transformed Japanese Ritual." *Gender and Society* 5(1) (1991): 86–97.

Pitelka, Morgan, ed. *Japanese Tea Culture: Art, History, and Practice.* London and New York: Routledge, 2003.

Varley, Paul, and Kumakura Isao, eds. *Tea in Japan: Essays on the History of Chanoyu.* Honolulu: University of Hawai'i Press, 1989.

Willmann, Anna. "The Japanese Tea Ceremony." Heilbrunn Timeline of Art History, Metropolitan Museum of Art, 2000, http://www.metmuseum.org/toah/hd/jtea/hd_jtea.htm.

JUDO

History and Origins

Judo developed from jujutsu. The three basic categories are *kokoro* (mind), *waza* (technique), and *kata* (form). In modern times, judo is best known for *nage-waza* (throwing technique) and *katame-waza* (grappling technique). Judo emphasizes free practice in its pedagogy. Contest is also an important aspect of judo. Tournaments started as early as the 1880s, and various championship events and competitions continue to develop nowadays.

Jigoro Kano (1860–1938), the father of judo, conducted a comprehensive study of the ancient self-defense forms and integrated some of them into Kodokan judo in the 1880s. Kodokan judo highlights maximum efficiency and minimum effort and has three general aims: physical education, contest proficiency, and mental training. Kano was the first member of the International Olympic Committee from Asia at the beginning of the 20th century. He worked to promote judo to the world and received a doctorate degree in judo. In 1935 he was awarded the Asahi Prize in recognition of his outstanding contribution. Judo became an official event in the Olympic Games of Tokyo in 1964.

Traditions and Practices

In judo, the objective is to take down and immobilize the opponent. Strikes, thrusts, and grappling are used. A judo practitioner is known as a judoka. Traditionally, a judoka wears a white uniform called a judogi. Sometimes a colored judoji is also used. It is usually made with heavy cotton and fastened by a belt. Similar to karate and tae kwon do, the color of the belt corresponds to the ranking in judo. The ranking in judo follows the kyu-dan system, starting with the white belt and moving up the levels to the black belt. There are variations among different organizations and countries. Jigoro Kano developed this system based on the ranking system of the game *go*. The judo ranking system has direct influence on the ranking in karate. Judo has had a noticeable impact on mixed martial arts (MMA). Well-known judo-trained MMA fighters include Hidehiko Yoshida (1969–), Naoya Ogawa (1968–), Makoto Takimoto (1974–), Satoshi Ishii (1986–), and Ronda Rousey (1987–), among others. Other

Judo became an official Olympic event in 1964. (Stef22/Dreamstime.com)

martial art forms related to or derived from Kodokan judo directly or indirectly include Brazilian jiu-jitsu, Kosen judo, Russian judo, and Sambo, among others.

Based in Tokyo, Japan, the Kodokan Judo Institute follows Jigoro Kano's teaching closely. Kodokan stands for an "institution to teach people the way of life" and helps them use both spiritual and physical power.

The International Judo Federation (IJF) is the worldwide governing body for judo and has representatives in many countries and regions across the globe. Members of the IJF include the African Judo Union, the Pan-American Judo Confederation, the Judo Union of Asia, the European Judo Union, and the Oceania Judo Union. The IJF organizes international competitions and hosts the World Judo Championships.

Based in Ontario, Oregon, the United States Judo Federation (USJF) provides national standards and guidelines for the teaching and development of judo. Its members and affiliated clubs have a presence in many states across the country. The USJF sanctions many events each year and offers various scholarships regularly to facilitate the learning and development of judo.

The United States Judo Association (USJA), based in Tarpon Springs, Florida, provides information, products, and services to club leaders, athletes, and students of judo. It includes over 300 chartered clubs across the country. The USJF and the USJA collaborate on the Grassroots Judo initiative, aiming to grow judo, encourage people to contribute to society, and facilitate a way for instructors, competitors, coaches, and referees to give back to judo through both organizations.

Lan Dong

See also: Karate; Tae Kwon Do; Tai Chi

Further Reading

Dando, Justin. *Judo.* London: Ward Lock, 1990.

Harrington, Patricia. *Judo Basics: Principles, Rules, and Rankings.* New York: Kodansha, 2002.

Hoare, Syd. *A History of Judo.* London: Yamagi Books, 2009.

International Judo Federation, http://www.ijf.org/.

Kano, Jigoro. *Mind over Muscle: Writings from the Founder of Judo.* Tokyo: Kodansha International, 2005.

Kodokan Judo Institute, http://kodokan.org/e_basic/faq.html.

Norwood, W. D., Jr. "Judo as Poetic Way." *Southern Quarterly: A Journal of the Arts in the South* 9 (1971): 191–212.

United States Judo Association, http://www.usja-judo.org.

United States Judo Federation, http://www.usjf.com.

Wood, Alix. *Judo.* New York: PowerKids, 2013.

K

KARATE

History and Origins

Karate, also known as karate-do, is a martial art that originated in the Ryukyu Islands in present-day Okinawa, Japan. A karate practitioner is known as a karate-ka. Karate was first developed in the Ryukyu Kingdom (1429–1879) with influences from Chinese martial arts and Ryukyan indigenous martial arts. Even during its early stage of development, there was more than one style. Karate was brought to the Japanese mainland at the beginning of the 20th century. In 1924, the first university karate club was established at Keio University. Karate became popular among American troops stationed in Okinawa after World War II. Karate schools began to appear in the United States in the 1940s and 1950s. Bruce Lee and martial arts films in the 1960s and 1970s helped popularize martial arts originating from Asian countries in the United States, including karate. Nowadays karate schools and organizations offer classes and sanction competitions for youths and adults across the country. Karate is not yet an official sport for the Olympic Games.

According to the International Ryukyu Karate-jutsu Research Society, Kanga Sakugawa (ca. 1733–ca. 1815) is a martial arts master and major contributor to the development of *te*, the precursor to modern karate. One of his students, Sōkon Matsumura (ca. 1809–ca. 1899), developed *te* further, incorporating the Shaolin style from China. Matsumura's style is known as Shorin-ryu. A student of Matsumura, Ankō Itosu (1831–1915) is considered the grandfather of modern karate. He developed the style further and simplified it for beginners. At the beginning of the 20th century, Itosu helped introduce karate to public schools in Okinawa. Important masters in the history of karate also include Higaonna Kanryō (1853–1915), Kanbun Uechi (1877–1948), Gichin Funakoshi (1868–1957), and Arakaki Seishō (1840–1918), among others.

Traditions and Practices

Karate focuses on striking using punches, kicks, knee and elbow strikes, and hand techniques. It emphasizes lifelong training, self-development, and discipline. Generally speaking, karate training includes fundamental skills, forms, and sparring. The karate training uniform is called karate-gi, which is often white and sometimes black or in other colors. These uniforms are usually light and loose fitting for the purpose of easy movement in training. Ranking of karate practitioners correlates with the belts they wear. In the United States most karate schools follow the kyu-dan system, starting with white belts and moving up the levels to black belts.

The World Karate Federation (WKF) is the largest sport karate organization. It is recognized by the International Olympic Committee, and includes many affiliated national WKF organizations. Formed in 1996, The USA National Karate-do Federation (USA-NKF) is the national governing body for karate. It is recognized by the U.S. Olympic Committee as well as the World Karate Federation and the Pan American Karate Federation. The largest karate organization in the United States, USA-NKF selects junior and adult karate athletes who represent the United States at international events and competitions such as the World Championships, the Pan American Games, the World Cup, the Junior World Championships, and the Junior Olympics, among others.

Karate has historically been associated with Asians and Asian Americans, particularly in U.S. popular culture. Jim Shooter created fictional character Karate Kid Val Armorr, son of a Japanese father and an American mother, for DC Comics' *Adventure Comics* in the 1960s. In the 1970s, Karate Kid was featured in a bimonthly series, published by DC Comics. John G. Avildsen's (1935–) film *The Karate Kid* (1984) portrays the mentorship and friendship between Daniel (Ralph Macchio, 1961–) and Mr. Miyagi (Pat Morita, 1932–2005). Avildsen later made two sequels: *The Karate Kid, Part II* (1986) and *The Karate Kid, Part III* (1989). Herald Zwart (1965–) directed a contemporary version of *The Karate Kid* (2010), starring Jackie Chan (1954–) and Jaden Smith (1998–).

Lan Dong

See also: Judo; Tae Kwon Do; Tai Chi

Further Reading

Buckley, Thomas. *Karate.* Chanhassen, MN: Child's World, 2004.

Chapman, Kris. "Ossu! Sporting Masculinities in a Japanese Karate Dōjō." *Japan Forum* 16(2) (2004): 315–335.

Craats, Rennay. *Karate.* Mankato, MN: Weigl Publishers, 2002.

Healy, Kevin. *Karate.* London: Connections, 2011.

International Ryukyu Karate-Jutsu Research Society, http://www.koryu-uchinadi.com/.

USA National Karate-do Federation, http://www.teamusa.org/USA-Karate.

The World Karate Federation, http://www.wkf.net/.

KIMCHI

History and Origins

Kimchi is a Korean dish in which vegetables are fermented in a mixture of vinegar and spices that often include garlic, salt, and chili pepper. Kimchi can be eaten as an isolated dish but is often used as a garnish for rice or noodles. The provenance of the dish extends back into the ancient history of the Korean Peninsula and the origins of pickling as a form of preservation in agriculture. As crops would not grow during the winter, farmers were forced to innovate methods of curing vegetables so they would have enough food to last until the following spring. Kimchi thus joins *surströmming* (soured herring) in Northern Europe and other such dishes as a foodstuff innovated by peoples facing difficult winters and possible starvation in a cold climate, foodstuffs that would eventually become ingrained in cuisine as staples or even delicacies.

The Korean Diaspora

The 20th century witnessed much turmoil on the Korean Peninsula, starting with the Japanese invasion and rule in 1910 and conscripted labor during the Japanese occupation of Manchuria and World War II and culminating in the Korean War and the subsequent division into communist and nationalist countries. As a result of these upheavals, numerous Koreans left the peninsula in search of better political conditions and economic opportunities. Many traveled to nearby China and Japan, while still others journeyed to Australia, Canada, and, following the removal of race- and ethnic-based quotas for immigration in 1965, the United States. Although these countries represent the destination for the bulk of the diaspora, Koreans reached all corners of the globe, setting up thriving expatriate communities in cities such as Paris, London, Buenos Aires, and São Paulo. These communities are referred to as *jaeoe gungmin* (citizens abroad) or *dongpo* (brethren) by Koreans, indicating a continued bond that transcends national boundaries. Such immigrants have brought aspects of their culture to their adoptive countries. For instance, recent aspects of Korean culture that have served to impact American pop culture include food (kimchi), gaming (StarCraft), and music (Psy's song "Gangam Style" and other K-pop hits).

With kimchi, farmers with excess vegetables innovated curing methods involving preservation in salt, brine, or even alcohol. With the opening up of spice routes between east and west and eventually global trade following the European discovery of the Americas, vinegar and pepper began to be used as agents, acting not only as preservatives but giving kimchi a spicier and more distinctive flavor. Kimchi as it appears today, however, did not come along until the end of the 18th century, when cabbage began to predominate as the vegetable base and red pepper the central ingredient in giving the dish its hot, spicy flavor. Although it is not known for sure, the name "kimchi" probably derived initially from the Korean word *shimchae* (salting of vegetables).

Traditions and Practices

The history of kimchi on the Korean Peninsula as well as its appearance in other countries following the Korean diaspora is highly correlative to time and location. During the Koryeo dynasty, several different types of radish-based kimchi were predominant, including *sunmu sogeumjeori* (radish preserved in salt) and *jangajji* (radish preserved in soy sauce). Slowly but surely, vegetables and other foodstuffs began to be pulled into the kimchi orbit, including cucumbers, bamboo shoots, mushrooms, mustard leaves, and Chinese cabbage. Garlic joined salt and soy sauce as a common agent of taste and preservation. The complexity and type of kimchi continued to diversify during the Joseon dynasty, in large part due to the increased trade that brought new vegetables from the brassica family to Korea, including broccoli, cauliflower, and cabbage. It would be the latter that would eventually grow to serve as the vegetable base for the vast majority of different forms of this dish. The Joseon dynasty also saw a diversification of ingredients added to kimchi, including not only different spices but also the genesis of dishes that employed fish, seaweed, and other imports from the coastal regions. Trade with the Portuguese from the 16th century on brought corn, potatoes, sweet potatoes, and red pepper to the Korean table. Although all were incorporated into kimchi on some level, the introduction of red pepper was transformative in the evolution of the dish, as it quickly became one of the go-to preservatives used in numerous forms.

With such a long history, it is no surprise that there should be some cultural traditions surrounding the preparation and eating of kimchi. One such tradition is an event in Korea called the Gimjang, during which lots of kimchi is prepared in the fall to be consumed in the winter months. Even though kimchi has not been the starvation food of its origins for quite some time, this tradition has endured into contemporary times but is in decline in Korea, as cabbage and other vegetables can now be obtained year-round. Although generally not practiced in expatriate communities around the world, Gimjana is somewhat reflected in that making kimchi for special occasions is often a cross-generational affair among, for instance, Korean American families.

Contemporary Forms

From the earliest recorded Korean writings regarding pickling vegetables over 2,000 years ago, the history of kimchi has been synonymous with the history of Korea's placement in local, regional, and global trade, with different vegetable bases, garnishes, and preservative spices reflecting specific aspects of time and place. By the mid-19th century, there were over 100 separate and distinct forms of kimchi. Today there are in excess of 200, each with multiple variations. Due to its popular association with Korean cuisine and unique properties of preservation, kimchi has become the de facto national food of Korean expatriates worldwide. Since the mid-19th century, the Korean diaspora has brought waves of Korean immigrants to China, Japan, the United States, Canada, and other countries. These immigrants have brought with them aspects of their cuisine, most notably kimchi, a food largely without analogue in any of these adoptive cultures. In the United States it has remained very popular with Korean Americans, some of whom are known to say "kimchi" instead of "cheese" when a group photograph is taken. With the United States transitioning to a culture where numerous meals are consumed outside of the home and a general interest in cultural diversity prevails, the dish has begun to filter into the American mainstream consciousness and can be found in a growing number of fusion- and international-themed restaurants and is even used as toppings on such foods as burgers, hot dogs, and pizza.

Perhaps one reason for its growth in popularity in the United States involves the identification that kimchi is one of the healthiest foods one can eat. The high spice and vinegar content helps to raise metabolism, and the varieties that feature cabbage are high in fiber while being low in fat. Most notably, kimchi is high in vitamins and lactobacilli, the latter of which is one of the good bacteria associated with long life in locations with high yogurt consumption. These bacteria, which aid in digestion and boost immunoresponse, are also known to inhibit obesity, diabetes, and various forms of gastrointestinal cancer.

Andrew Howe

See also: Chop Suey; Fusion Cuisine; Korean American Food; Korean American Immigration; *Pho;* Sushi; Thai American Food

Further Reading

"History of Kimchi." Recipes of Asia, September 2012, 2014. www.asian-recipe.com /korea/history-of-kimchee.html.

"History of Kimchi." Visit Korea Website, 2014, http://english.visitkorea.or.kr/enu/FO/FO_EN_6_1_2_1.jsp.

McPherson, Joe. "Kimchi: A Short History." Zenkimchi Website, 2014, http://zenkimchi.com/FoodJournal/top-posts/kimchi-1-short-history/.

KOREAN AMERICAN ARTS AND ARTISTS

History and Origins

Korean American immigration dates back to the 19th century. A small number of Korean diplomats, merchants, and students came to the United States after the United States–Korea Treaty of Peace, Amity, Commerce, and Navigation (1882). Yet it was not until the beginning of the 20th century that Korean immigrants began to arrive in America in notable numbers. Early immigrants were mostly men who went to Hawai'i to work on sugarcane plantations. As a result of the McCarran-Walter Act of 1952, Koreans and immigrants from other Asian countries are eligible to become naturalized U.S. citizens. After the 1965 Immigration Act, Korean professionals and family members arrived in America in increasing numbers, contributing to the continuing growth of the Korean American population since the 1970s. According to the 2010 U.S. census, the Korean American population is over 1.5 million. Korean American art nonetheless has a comparatively short history.

There is very limited documentation of Korean American arts and artists in the early immigration years. Whanki Kim (1913–1970) was one of the first Korean artists who lived and worked in the United States. He lived in New York City from 1963 to 1970. His paintings show a strong influence from French abstract expressionist works as well as the traditional Korean color palette used for temples. Nam June Paik (1932–2006) was one of the early conceptual and performance artists of Korean descent. He worked in Europe, Japan, and the United States. Korean American artistic productions did not gain much recognition until the early 1980s. Since then Korean Americans have continued to contribute to the development of arts.

Korean American Visual Arts and Artists

In the 1980s, several Korean American artists came of age. For the most part, they grew up or were educated in the United States. Some of their works address ethnicity, politics, and gender as major themes. Born near Seoul, Korea, in 1953, Yong Soon Min moved to the United States in 1960. Her works take interdisciplinary approaches to examine representation, cultural identity, and the intersection between history and memory. She has produced numerous artworks and also has curated many projects. She has received numerous honors, awards, and grants, including the Fulbright Senior Research Grant, the Anonymous Was a Woman Award, and the National Endowment for the Arts Visual Artist Award in New Genre.

Theresa Hak Kyung Cha (1951–1982) was born in Busan, Korea, and grew up in California. She studied literature and arts in the United States and France and is well known for her mixed-genre artistic and literary works. She has published *Dictee* (1982), *The Dream of the Audience* (2001), and *Exilée and Temps Morts: Selected Works* (2009) and has produced numerous films, videos, performances, and mixed media pieces. She was murdered in New York City in 1982.

In the 1990s, younger generations of Korean American artists began to gain recognition. Byron Kim (1961–) has produced minimalist paintings that examine racial identities. His contribution to the Whitney Biennial Exhibition in 1993, titled *Synecdoche,* is composed of 400 small monochromatic paintings. These paintings depict the skin color of different individuals. Generally speaking, Kim's artwork reflects the influence of minimalists; it has a strong racial and political dimension. *Black & White* (1993), a collaborative project by Kim and Glenn Ligon (1960–), criticizes the prejudices of art material.

Michael Joo (1966–) investigates identity and knowledge in his artworks. He has done solo exhibitions at the Aldrich Contemporary Art Museum in Connecticut, Blain/Southern in London, the Anton Kern Gallery in New York, the Palm Beach Institute for Contemporary Art in Florida, and many other prestigious art venues.

Born in South Korea, Yu Yeon Kim is an independent art curator based in New York City and Seoul, Korea. She is known internationally for curating and commissioning distinguished contemporary art exhibitions, such as *Corporeal/ Technoreal,* a media art project for the Poland Mediations Biennale; *Los Puntos del Compas,* an exhibition of Korean contemporary art in Cuba; *Counterpoint,* an international exhibition of art at Bund 18 in Shanghai, China; and *In the Eye of the Tiger* at Exit Art/The Third World, New York. From 2001 to 2003, she curated the controversial exhibition *Translated Acts—Performance and Body Art from East Asia* at the Haus der Kulturen der Welt in Berlin, the Queens Museum of Art in New York, and the Museo de Carrillo Gil in Mexico City.

Many organizations have played a vital role in the development of Korean American arts during the past few decades. Founded in 1989, the Korean American Artists Association of Washington State (KAAW) strives to encourage and support Korean American artists in their pursuit of artistic endeavors, enrich community life, and promote and celebrate diversity in the arts. The KAAW provides resources to artists, offers art scholarships to Korean Americans in Washington State, organizes community activities, and hosts annual exhibitions for KAAW members and other exhibitions. Since 1994, the KAAW has organized the Pacific Northwest Student Art Competition for K–12 students each year.

Sponsored by the National Endowment for the Humanities, the E. Rhodes and Leona B. Carpenter Foundation, the Korea Foundation, and individual contributors and donors in the region, the Museum of Fine Arts in Houston, Texas, hosted the exhibition *Treasures from Korea* to celebrate the artistic achievements of the Joseon dynasty of Korea (1392–1910) from October 2014 to January 2015.

Korean American Performing Arts and Artists

Korean American performing arts have roots in traditional Korean performing arts. Folk dances, ritual court dances, masked dances, and puppet plays have a long history in Korea. *Gu gug* (old plays) became popular in Korea in the 19th century and combines dramatic songs with dance moves and gestures. In the early 20th century, *shimpa* (new school) plays were performed. After World War II, a new National Theatre was established in Seoul. In South Korea, subsidies and other forms of support encourage the development of musical dramas, folk dance, and traditional music. Western-style opera, ballet, and modern dance are also staged regularly. In North Korea, performing arts are generally required to represent socialist and nationalistic ideals.

In the United States, many organizations have played an important role in the development of Korean American performing arts. Various institutes and groups such as the Korea Society in New York, the Korean Cultural Center in Los Angeles, the Korean Cultural Service New York, and the Korean Cultural Center in Washington, D.C., host, sponsor, and organize a variety of performances on a regular basis, promote and support Korean and Korean American performing artists and professionals, and facilitate other programs.

Founded in 1986, the Korean Traditional Arts Community changed its name to the Korean Traditional Performing Arts Association in 1993 and then to the New York Korean Performing Arts Center (KPAC) in 2010, when it built the studio near Koreatown in Manhattan, New York. KPAC offers space for artists, outreach programs for local communities, and music and dance classes for students of all ages.

Sarah Chang (1980–) is recognized as "one of the world's great violinists" (Chang 2008). Her parents are musicians who moved from Korea to the United States. Chang studied music at the Juilliard School and has played with the New York Philharmonic, the Los Angeles Philharmonic, the Philadelphia Orchestra, the Chicago Symphony, the Boston Symphony, the Cleveland Orchestra, the

Montréal Symphony Orchestra, the Berlin Philharmonic, the Vienna Philharmonic, and many others. She recorded her first album, *Debut*, when she was only 10 years old. She has had performances and recitals at Carnegie Hall, the Kennedy Center, the Hollywood Bowl, and the Walt Disney Concert Hall. She has performed around the world in France, the United Kingdom, Germany, the Netherlands, China, South Korea, and Japan. She has received many honors and awards in recognition of her musical talent and contributions, including Gramophone Magazine Young Artist of the Year, the Avery Fisher Prize, and the Hollywood Bowl's Hall of Fame.

Nam June Paik (1932–2006) was a Korean American artist who is considered the founder of video art. Born in Seoul, Paik fled Korea with his family during the Korean War, first to Hong Kong and then Japan. He studied music in Germany and moved to New York in 1964. His debut exhibition *Exposition of Music—Electronic Television* was held at Galerie Parnass in Wuppertal, Germany, in 1963. Many of his early works are collected in *Nam June Paik: Videa 'n' Videology 1959–1973* (1974). He has received many honors and awards

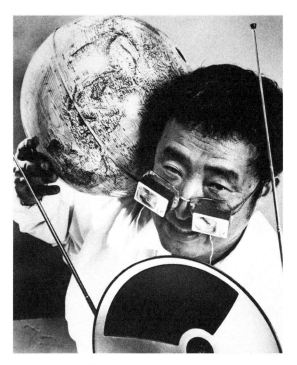

Korean-born artist Nam June Paik, featured here in October 1986, is the founding father of video art. He brought East and West together in a mix of taped and live events from Seoul, Tokyo, and New York, simultaneously in a 90-minute show. (AP Photo)

in recognition of his contributions to art and his influence on the younger generations of artists, including the Order of Cultural Merit, the McDowell Colony Medalist in Visual Art, the Lifetime Achievement in Contemporary Sculpture Award, the Kyoto Prize in Arts and Philosophy, and the Picasso Medal, among others.

Lan Dong

See also: Korean American Folklore; Korean American Immigration; Korean American Literature

Further Reading

Doss, Erika. *Twentieth-Century American Art.* New York and Oxford: Oxford University Press, 2002.

Farver, Jane, et al. *Across the Pacific: Contemporary Korean and Korean American Art.* Queens, NY: Queens Museum of Art in cooperation with SEORO Korean Cultural Network, 1993.

Hoeffel, Elizabeth M., Sonya Rastogi, Myoung Ouk Kim, and Hasan Shahid. "The Asian Population: 2010." U.S. Census Bureau, March 2012, http://www.census .gov/prod/cen2010/briefs/c2010br-11.pdf.

Kelly, Michael. "The Political Autonomy of Contemporary Art: The Case of the 1993 Whitney Biennial." In *Politics and Aesthetics in the Arts,* edited by Salim Kemal and Ivan Gaskell, 221–263. New York and Cambridge: Cambridge University Press, 2000.

Kim, Yu Yeon. *Korea Transfer: 13 Contemporary Korean Artists in New York.* New York: Korean Cultural Service, 2006.

"Korean American Art." Korean American Museum, 2014, http://www.kamuseum .org/culture/base.htm.

Korean Cultural Center DC, http://www.koreaculturedc.org/En/Index.asp.

Korean Cultural Center in Los Angeles, https://www.kccla.org/english/home.asp.

Korean Cultural Service New York, http://www.koreanculture.org.

Korea Society in New York, http://www.koreasociety.org/.

Sarah Chang website, http://sarahchang.com/.

Yang, Alice. *Why Asia? Contemporary Asian and Asian American Art.* New York: New York University Press, 1998.

Yong Soon Min website, http://www.yongsoonmin.com/.

KOREAN AMERICAN CHILDREN AND FAMILY

Korean Americans, a rapidly growing ethnic minority, have carved out a special place in America. Family, along with its different components, plays a crucial role in making Korean immigrants and Korean Americans an integral part of the ever-changing American society.

Family plays a crucial role in the life of Korean Americans. Although the nuclear family living arrangement has become the standard practice in recent years, the existence of extended families living together is still not uncommon. When immigration from Korea accelerated after the Immigration Act of 1965 took effect, extended families were the norm. Apart from husband, wife, and children, grandparents, brothers and sisters of the husband, and sometimes dependent relatives would stay in the same family unit. Obedience to superiors is emphasized in family life—wife to husband, children to parents, and the young to elders—and so is sacrificing oneself for the family. The father is the head of the family per traditional Confucian tradition, and it is his duty to provide for the family. His decision regarding any family matter is final. The traditional role of the mother is to take care of the children and the household chores. Confucianism emphasizes duty, loyalty, honor, filial piety, and mutual dependence among the kin. Family members share the ups and downs of life.

The rite of passage of Korean American children starts 100 days after birth. Parents give cakes made of rice to family members and relatives symbolizing long life for the baby. In the *dol* ceremony for his or her first birthday, the child is dressed in traditional Korean attire and picks up one of the three objects: a thread, a book, and money. They symbolize long life, scholarship, and wealth, respectively. A child pays tribute to his or her father and mother on the parent's 60th birthday (*hwan gap*), which is celebrated with a big feast. The name of a child is generally made up of three characters: family name followed by given name. Some Korean Americans put their given names first, according to American tradition.

Korean American children are encouraged to be acquainted with folktales, myths, legends, and fables as well as Korean culture. Some of the popular Korean stories include *Dan-Gun, Go Zu-Mong, The Magic Mallet,* and *The Heavenly Lady and the Woodcutter,* among others. Korean American literature related to children includes Frances Carpenter's *Tales of a Korean Grandmother* (1947), Lucy Herndon Crockett's *Pong Choolie, You Rascal!* (1951), Faith Norris and Peter Lum's *Kim of Korea* (1955), Helen Doss's *A Brother the Size of Me* (1957), Linda Sue Park's *A Single Shard* (2002), and An Na's *A Step from Heaven* (2002). Some of the folktales and novels are published in a bilingual format. Many Korean American children are acquainted with Korean tales from an early age. These stories inculcate ethical values for a meaningful life.

The dietary habits of Korean American families include traditional dishes such as steamed rice, hot soup, fish or meat, and kimchi (the spicy cabbage and vegetable dish). They are also acquainted with Western-style food. Korean

A one-year-old, dressed in traditional clothes, celebrating his first birthday with his family. Korean birthday celebrations (known as *dol*) are an important part of Korean culture. People usually celebrate a child's first birthday with prayer, special food, and *dol-bok* objects. (Richard Levine/Alamy Stock Photo)

American families keep up their bonds of kinship by interacting with one another at different cultural events, family functions, and festivals. These community gatherings give Korean American families an opportunity to reinforce their cultural identity as well as help each other when needed.

Confronted with American family values that emphasize individual interests and independence, some Korean immigrants have had a difficult time reconciling individualism with Confucian collectivism and trying to keep a balance between the two. The degree of acculturation varies from generation to generation, which sometimes leads to conflicts between generations. A large percentage of Korean Americans, however, are Protestant Christians (61 percent), with some Catholics (10 percent), according to "Asian Americans: A Mosaic of Faiths," a Pew Research Center report in 2012. This is no doubt due to active missionary work by Christians in China and Korea beginning in the 19th century.

Generally speaking, Korean American children learn or adapt to the American way of life easily because they spend a lot of time at school and with friends. Some parents disapprove of their children's behaviors that are against their Korean heritage. The traditional role of women is changing in Korean American families. Apart from supplementing the family income, a wife is looking beyond Confucian ideals. The divorce rate among Korean Americans is increasing due to the burden on working women who have to deal with work-related pressure as well as meet the demands of family members at home.

Many Korean American children are encouraged to learn both Korean and English. Korean-language schools are in abundance in the United States. In southern California there are about 300 Korean-language schools; the Bay Area alone has around 80. Apart from language learning, children also are encouraged to learn about Korean heritage and culture. Some of the children are sent to South Korea during the summer to hone their Korean-language skills and experience life in Korea firsthand. Many Korean American parents leave no stones unturned for a meaningful education of their children, hoping that it will take them to high ranks at work and raise their social status.

The adoption of Korean children by American families has resulted in inculcation of American values by the children as they grow up, although there are now more Korean American young adults, adopted by non–Korean American families, who are seeking their original Korean families and taking on more Korean culture. Overall, Korean American families have adapted to the life and culture of America while keeping their ethnic identity and traditional values alive.

Patit Paban Mishra

See also: Adoption of Asian Children; Korean American Community Organizations; Korean American Immigration; Korean American Women

Further Reading

"Asian Americans: A Mosaic of Faiths." Pew Research Center, July 19, 2012, http://www.pewforum.org/2012/07/19/asian-americans-a-mosaic-of-faiths-overview/.

Hurh, Won Moo. *The Korean Americans.* Westport, CT: Greenwood, 1998.

Jones, Maggie. "Why a Generation of Adoptees Is Returning to South Korea." *New York Times Magazine,* January 14, 2015, http://www.nytimes.com/2015/01/18/magazine/why-a-generation-of-adoptees-is-returning-to-south-korea.html?_r=0.

Lee, Lauren. *Korean Americans.* New York: Marshall Cavendish, 1995.

Lehrer, Brian. *The Korean American.* New York: Chelsea House, 1996.

Min, Pyong Gap. *Changes and Conflicts: Korean Immigrant Families in New York.* Boston: Allyn and Bacon, 1998.

Oak, Susan, and Virginia Martin V. *American/Korean Contrast: Patterns and Expectations in the U.S. and Korea.* Elizabeth, NJ: Hollym, 2000.

Park, Kyeyoung. *The Korean American Dream: Immigrants and Small Business in New York City.* Ithaca, NY: Cornell University Press, 1997.

KOREAN AMERICAN COMMUNITY ORGANIZATIONS

Although the United States and Korea signed a Treaty of Amity and Commerce, which allowed Koreans to immigrate to America in 1882, the first immigrants did not arrive until 1903. Then in 1924, the Nationality Origins Act banned Korean and Japanese immigration to the States. This act stayed in effect until after the passing of the Immigration and Nationality Act of 1965. Now there are over 1 million people of Korean ancestry in the United States.

One of the oldest Korean American nonprofit organizations is the Korean American Association of Greater New York (KAAGNY), which was established in 1960. Even though this organization was founded to work for the betterment of Korean Americans living in New York, it advocates for the rights and interests of all Korean Americans. KAAGNY holds workshops and seminars on job training and other employment topics to help Korean Americans prosper economically. In addition, today KAAGNY organizes community events, sponsors cultural activities, and distributes information on social service programs and has joined together with other ethnic organizations to participate in additional cultural activities to promote a deeper sense of Korean American pride.

On the West Coast, the Korean American Coalition was established in 1983 and now has chapters throughout the United States. This organization promotes its chapters to participate in legislative, civic, and community affairs to give a voice to the Korean American population.

Also on the West Coast in the state of Washington, the Korean American Historical Society (KAHS) was established in 1985. Washington has a high population of Korean Americans, but there was not a lot of information gathered in one location about their cultural heritage. The KAHS wanted to preserve the Korean American heritage for future generations. Their mission statement (2014) is "to collect, maintain, and transmit the Korean American heritage and achievements of Koreans in the United States and Abroad." Initially, the KAHS was founded to record the current and past achievements of Korean Americans in Washington, but over time it has expanded to include the history of Korean Americans in the United States. One of the organization's projects is the journal *Occasional Papers*, which includes oral histories, book reviews, and critical essays dealing with Korean Americans. In addition, the KAHS has created a library that includes books, photographs, and other artifacts representing the Korean American experience in the United States.

In the early 1990s, Proposition 187 was passed in the state of California and created many hardships for all immigrants. Throughout the state there were small Korean American groups, but because of their size, they were powerless; however, in 1994 many of the local community groups united and formed the National Korean American Service & Education Consortium (NAKASEC). This organization's main goal was to give Korean Americans a voice in promoting a national movement for civil rights and social change. Today NAKASEC is active on both coasts; it has headquarters in both California and Virginia, and its chapters span the states.

In addition to Proposition 187, the civil riots in California made many Korean Americans realize that there was no national voice for them; therefore, the National Association of Korean Americans (NAKA) was formed in 1994 to help secure civil rights, promote cooperation with other racial and ethnic groups, and fight against racism and discrimination. Today NAKA still upholds these goals, but it also addresses issues within Korean American families such as generational differences brought about by cultural differences. Through activities and workshops, NAKA has tried to bridge the gap between the generations.

The Korean American organizations do not limit themselves to helping only those in the United States. The Korean American community also tries to help Koreans in other parts of the world. The Korean American Sharing Movement (KASM), established in 1997, first began as a direct response to the famine crisis in North Korea but since then has broadened its outreach to other troubled areas around the world. Starting in 2003, the KASM has also dedicated itself to helping young Koreans by hosting a yearly leadership conference for Korean and Chinese students in Washington, D.C. This conference provides opportunities for learning more about colleges and other contemporary issues. According to the KASM website, the "goal of this program is helping the participants to grow as future leaders by raising awareness of their role in society."

Helping Korean Americans prosper in society is also the main goal for the Korean American Community Foundation (KACF), which is headquartered in New York City. The KACF was formed in 2002 to promote volunteerism, philanthropy, and community connections. According to the KACF website, its mission is to "raise awareness of the needs and issues, foster a culture of giving, and promote self-sufficiency." The basis for this mission is the idea that the more Korean Americans prosper, the more they can assist other Korean Americans in their community. Through fund-raisers and private donations, the KACF has provided individual grants to other organizations and groups that address the needs of the Korean American community. The main projects that the KACF funds are economic security, safety, senior citizen well-being, health, employment opportunities, and intercultural development. As stated on its website, as of 2014 the KACF had awarded nearly $3 million in grants to other nonprofit organizations that are assisting Korean Americans to become healthier, safer, and economically more self-sufficient.

Today in many of the larger metropolitan areas, Korean American organizations have developed to create more opportunities for professional networking. Some examples of these are the Korean American Professional Society in the San Francisco area and the Young Korean American Network in New York City. These organizations support educational programs, community service, and professional networking.

Candy A. Henry

See also: Korean American Immigration; Koreatowns

Further Reading

Hoeffel, Elizabeth M., Sonya Rastogi, Myoung Ouk Kim, and Hasan Shahid. "The Asian Population: 2010." U.S. Census Bureau, March 2012, http://www.census .gov/prod/cen2010/briefs/c2010br-11.pdf.

Korean American Coalition, www.kacatl.org.

Korean American Community Foundation, www.kacfny.org.

The Korean American Historical Society, www.kahs.org.

The Korean American Professional Society, www.kaps.org.

The Korean American Sharing Movement, www.kasm.org.

National Association of Korean Americans, www.naka.org.

National Korean American Service and Education Consortium, www.nakasec.org.

Totten, George O., and H. Eric Schockman, eds. *Community in Crisis: The Korean American Community after the Los Angeles Civil Unrest of April 1992.* Los Angeles: Center for Multiethnic and Transnational Studies, University of Southern California, 1994.

The Young Korean American Network, www.ykan.org.

KOREAN AMERICAN FILMS AND FILMMAKERS

Korean Americans have been active in the film industry since the early years. The best-known pioneer is Philip Ahn (1905–1978), who was the first Asian American actor to receive a star on the Hollywood Walk of Fame.

Many Korean American actors and actresses have made their mark in the film and television industries. Margaret Cho (1968–) and Ken Jeong (1969–) are among those who have established their fame in comedy. Korean American directors and filmmakers include Joy Dietrich, Alexandra Bokyun Chun

Philip Ahn (1905–1978)

Philip Ahn was born in California three years after his parents came to the United States from Korea. While attending the University of Southern California (USC), he served as the president of the USC Cosmopolitan Club, chairman of the All University Committee on International Relations, and assistant to the dean of male students. After two years, Ahn dropped out of college to pursue acting. His first film was *A Scream in the Night* (1935). He also appeared in *Anything Goes* (1936), *The General Died at Dawn* (1936), *Stowaway* (1936), *Love Is a Many-Splendored Thing* (1955), *Around the World in Eighty Days* (1956), *Paradise, Hawaiian Style* (1966), and *Thoroughly Modern Millie* (1967). Ahn starred opposite Anna May Wong (1905–1961) in *Daughter of Shanghai* (1937) and *King of Chinatown* (1939). He played Korean characters in films about the Korean War such as *Battle Circus* (1953) and *Battle Hymn* (1956). From the 1950s to the 1970s, Ahn was active in many television shows, including *Crossroads, Jefferson Drum, Richard Diamond, Private Detective, The Eve Arden Show, Adventures in Paradise, Hawaiian Eye, Follow the Sun, Stoney Burke, Perry Mason, I Spy,* and *M*A*S*H*. Among his television appearances, he was probably best known as Master Kan in the series *Kung Fu*. Ahn was the first Asian American actor to receive a star on the Hollywood Walk of Fame. Besides his long career in acting and contributions to the motion picture industry and television, he was involved in Korean American communities in the Los Angeles area. During World War II, he enlisted and served in the Special Services.

(1967–), Alexander Sebastien Lee, and Chris Chan Lee, among others. Some of the most widely known Korean American actors and actresses are Sung Kang (1972–), who played roles in *The Motel* (2005), *Better Luck Tomorrow* (2002), and *The Fast and the Furious: Tokyo Drift* (2006); Patricia Ja Lee (1975–), who appeared in the *Power Rangers* series (1997–1999); and Ki Hong Lee (1986–), who is best known for his character Minho in *The Maze Runner* (2014). Sandra Oh (1971–), a Korean Canadian actress, has been in a number of U.S. films, including *Sideways* (2004), *Rabbit Hole* (2010), and *Tammy* (2014), although she may be best known for her television role as an American surgeon in *Grey's Anatomy* (2005–2014).

Contemporary Forms and Practices

Christine Choy (1954–) is a renowned Asian American filmmaker. She joined Newsreel, a film workshop in New York City, in 1972. She was the founder of

Third World Newsreel, a distributor of foreign films, civil rights films, feminist films, and community activist documentaries. She was appointed chair of New York University's prestigious Graduate Film School in 1994, the first Asian American to hold this position. Her film *Who Killed Vincent Chin?* (1987) was nominated for an Academy Award for best documentary. Her other films include *Homes Apart: The Two Koreas* (1991), *Out in Silence* (1994), *In the Name of the Emperor* (1994), *The Shot Heard 'Round the World* (1997), and *Long Story Short* (2008).

John Yohan Cho (1972–) is perhaps the best-known Korean American actor nowadays. He was born in Seoul, South Korea, and moved to the United States when he was six years old. His acting career began with his work with the Asian American theater company East West Players. He starred in the critically

In *Daughter of Shanghai* (1937), Philip Ahn (featured here with his co-star Anna May Wong) played Kim Lee. Ahn is the first Asian American actor to receive a star on the Hollywood Walk of Fame. (Paramount Pictures/Photofest)

acclaimed *Harold & Kumar Go to White Castle* (2004), *Harold & Kumar Escape from Guantanamo Bay* (2008), and *A Very Harold & Kumar 3D Christmas* (2011) as one of the title characters, Harold Lee. Cho played the character Hikaru Sulu in *Star Trek* (2009) and *Star Trek: Into Darkness* (2013). He has played roles in *American Pie* (1999), *American Pie 2* (2001), *American Reunion* (2012), *Better Luck Tomorrow* (2002), *Yellow* (1998), and *Total Recall* (2012). He has also made appearances in television shows, including ABC's *FlashForward,* the WB network's *Off Centre,* Fox's *Sleepy Hollow,* and ABC's *Selfie.*

As an actress, Lela Lee (1974–) has appeared in films and television shows, including *Yellow, Better Luck Tomorrow,* NBC's *Scrubs,* the Sci Fi Channel series *Tremors,* and HBO's *Curb Your Enthusiasm.* She is also the creator of the comic strip *Angry Little Girls* and the animated cartoon the *Angry Little Asian Girl.*

Jamie Jilynn Chung (1983–) was born and raised in San Francisco, California. She gained recognition as a cast member on the MTV reality series *The Real World: San Diego* in 2004. She has appeared in a number of films and television shows, including *Grown Ups* (2010), *Premium Rush* (2012), *Sorority Row* (2009), *The Hangover Part II* (2011), *The Hangover Part III* (2013), *Sucker Punch* (2011), *Sin City: A Dame to Kill For* (2014), *Princess Protection Program* (2009), ABC's *Samurai Girl* (2008), and ABC's *Once upon a Time* (2012–). She played the lead role in the independent film *Eden* (2012) about domestic human trafficking.

In the field of animated films, Korean American directors and producers have made remarkable contributions. Peter Sohn (1977–) was born and raised in New York. He worked for Walt Disney Company and Warner Bros. before becoming an animator, story artist, and production artist at Pixar Animation Studios. He has worked on well-known films such as *Finding Nemo* (2003), *The Incredibles* (2004), *Ratatouille* (2007), and *WALL-E* (2008). He directed the short film *Partly Cloudy* (2009) and codirected the English-language version of *Ponyo on the Cliff by the Sea* (2009). He is also a voice actor.

Born in Seoul, South Korea, Tommy Yune became the creative director at Harmony Gold USA in 2001 and directed the animated film *Robotech: The Shadow Chronicles* (2006). His film credits include the opening title animation of *Gen* (2000) and the opening and episode titles of *Robotech: Remastered Extended Edition* (2003). He is also a comics artist and writer and video game producer.

Lan Dong

See also: Comedy and Humor, Asian American; Korean American Immigration; Korean American Literature; Popular Culture, Asian Americans and; Television, Asian Americans on

Further Reading

Chung, Hye Seung. *Hollywood Asian: Philip Ahn and the Politics of Cross-Ethnic Performance*. Philadelphia: Temple University Press, 2006.

Coleman, Craig S. *American Images of Korea: Korea and Koreans as Portrayed in Books, Magazines, Television, News Media, and Film*. Elizabeth, NJ: Hollym International, 1997.

Feng, Peter X. *Identities in Motion: Asian American Film and Video*. Durham NC: Duke University Press, 2002.

Feng, Peter X., ed. *Screening Asian Americans*. New Brunswick, NJ: Rutgers University Press, 2002.

Hamamoto, Darrell Y., and Sandra Liu, eds. *Countervisions: Asian American Film Criticism*. Philadelphia: Temple University Press, 2000.

Hoeffel, Elizabeth M., Sonya Rastogi, Myoung Ouk Kim, and Hasan Shahid. "The Asian Population: 2010." U.S. Census Bureau, March 2012, http://www.census.gov/prod/cen2010/briefs/c2010br-11.pdf.

National Association of Korean Americans. "A Brief History of Korean Americans." Naka.org, 2003, http://www.naka.org/resources/history.asp.

KOREAN AMERICAN FOLKLORE

History and Origins

Folklore refers to a collection of readily available, broadly identifiable forms of expressive culture, including oral and written narratives, artwork and crafts, dances, songs, poems, chants, jokes and wordplay, motifs and symbols, superstitions and other ritual practices, and everyday beliefs that define the guiding ethos of a specific group of people. Korean Americans have access to a national tradition in the form of peninsular Korean culture as well as the broader multicultural matrix of the United States. This scenario allows for a variety of living situations and hence variable access to folkways: ethnic enclaves where a lot of cultural exchange with non-Koreans is unnecessary, mixed ethnic communities where intercultural negotiations are frequent, and integration into a larger Euro-dominant society that may not acknowledge the existence or importance of Korean American identity, let alone its folklore.

For many, especially earlier generations, ties to the Korean mainland have been maintained through immigration experiences, language, strong family ties, increasingly convenient avenues of travel, and accessible forms of communication such as radio, television, films, telephone, print journalism, and the Internet. Folklore tends to be transmitted mostly by word of mouth, as suggested by scenes in literary texts where myths such as the fox spirit emerge

Fox Girl

The fox girl, or *gumiho,* is a legendary figure in Korean culture that is both ancient and contemporary. Lurid tales of these disguised women who infiltrate families and disrupt the traditional patriarchal order demonstrate the character's ongoing cultural relevance. Fox girls, often with nine tails, emerge in popular expressions that are usually pejorative. Calling a female a *yuwoo* suggests that she is clever, sneaky, promiscuous, or unstable, as transformative powers are characteristic of fox spirits. In film, television, literature, and comics, she embodies excitement and vitality but also palpable danger, especially to men. In traditional Korean usage she tends to be a demoness, but in recent literary forms authors have endowed her with a broad range of humanizing characteristics.

Traditionally, fox girls emerged as temptresses, seeking shelter from lonely men and especially scholars. The roots of the figure, folklorists suggest, are in the Chinese fox myth of the *huli jing,* visible in many works by Asian North American writers (for instance, Lensey Namioka's short story "Fox Hunt," Larissa Lai's novel *When Fox Is a Thousand* [1995], and Marilyn Chin's collection of prose *The Revenge of the Mooncake Vixen* [2009]). A transnational phenomenon, the seductive figure coincides as well with Japanese mythology. The fox legend is often alluded to in works by contemporary Korean American writers including Nora Okja Keller, whose second novel is titled *Fox Girl* (2002).

through oral storytelling. While anthropologists and other academics have worked to compile and organize folklore, the source of its constant revitalization lies in the folk—the people themselves.

When early immigrants left to start new lives in the United States largely as laborers and later brides of these laborers, they experienced a constant awareness of political strife back in Korea. At the forefront was a rigorous campaign of cultural erasure by Japanese colonizers. Also concerning was economic instability in the new land. Dislocation and homesickness led to an atmosphere of immense psychological pressure. Folklore would be one way of relieving the tensions of inhabiting a foreign land. Although they did not bring much by way of material goods to such places as Hawai'i and California, the new immigrants certainly brought their language and their awareness of what Korea was to them, not the ideas transmitted through Japanese propaganda about the inferiority of their native land and peoples. As such, folklore was a form of retaliation, a way of using indigenous customs, assumptions, and attitudes to bridge the chasm of space and comfort between former and current countries of residence.

Regional Practices and Traditions

The cultural endangerment and annihilation of Japanese annexation cannot be overstressed. Although aware of neighboring countries' geopolitical interests, "The Land of the Morning Calm" was by no means a new country. Indeed, it was a nation steeped in ancient spiritual practices, including shamanism, Buddhism, and Confucianism. Many of the teachings and values implicit in these belief systems appear in folklore, such as stories detailing the teachings of Buddha and his disciples. While shamanism offered an understanding of natural forces that were interwoven into the human world, Buddhism set forth a model for understanding how spirituality also infused that world in a cycle of accountability and unseen power. Confucianism enunciated collective values such as filial duty, obedience, accountability to family (and in turn to the country), women's subservience to men (namely fathers, husbands, and eldest sons), and the importance of education and hierarchical order. It was a philosophy that was a guiding force in the social arena and also served as fodder for didactic stories, especially for children. Most recognizable include folktales such as "Sim Chung, the Dutiful Daughter" who selflessly strives to obtain sight for her blind, elderly, and poverty-stricken father. After having procured the bags of rice needed as an offering to Buddha, Sim Chung goes to the sea with sailors who need a maiden as a sacrifice. After her willing death, she is rewarded with the favor of the Sea King, and later the king of the land makes her his queen. Upon their tearful reunion at court, the father's sight is miraculously restored.

One of the staples of Korean folklore that has continued relevance in Korean American culture is the presence of ghosts and spirits. The ghosts can take many guises (especially as mistreated or violated females), but they can also be spirits of disrespected relatives or ambulant souls who seek human contact for company or as victims (for instance, the *gumiho,* or fox spirit). The fox figure (usually female but not exclusively) refers to a nine-tailed animal that displays most—if not all—of the following characteristics: supernatural powers such as the capacity to shape-shift and assume human form; the desire to be human and the drive to achieve this feat through extreme measures, usually acts of cannibalism such as consuming human hearts and livers; the ability to interact with humans easily, usually in the guise of an attractive female who seduces, weds, and even bears children with her human partner; and a transcendental quality, such as long life (usually 100 or 1,000 years) that crescendos into the achievement of full humanity.

Some of the other spirits are tricksters and malevolent (for instance, goblins and ogres). The ghost story of Arang is a notable folktale that continues to surface in contemporary films (e.g., the horror thriller *Arang* by Korean director Ahn Sang-hoon in 2002) and also a television miniseries, *Arang and the Magistrate*, in 2012. Arang was a magistrate's daughter during the Choson dynasty (1392–1897) who, through trickery and malice by those close to her, was raped and murdered. Her tragedy led to the downfall of the entire family. Her ghost has troubled every incoming replacement to her father's position until one joins forces with her to root out the culprit and bring peace to her spirit. The tale not only features revenge, a powerful motif in many morality tales, but also stresses the importance of personal and family honor, two Confucian values that many traditional Korean American parents instill in their offspring.

This spirit world is also integral to understanding the work of the *mudang,* or shaman. In Korea, encroachment by foreign missionaries and a widening influence of Christianity (with its injunctions against divination) negatively affected attitudes toward the shamans and their long-standing indigenous presence as spirit mediators. The prevailing attitudes toward psychics and clairvoyants in the West are far from universally respectful, but *mudangs* (or *manshins* as some prefer to be called) are inextricable from an understanding of folk spirituality in Korea. A documentary, *Mudang: Reconciliation between the Living and the Dead* (2003) directed by Park Ki-Bok, explores elaborate rituals, song, chants, dance, and initiation ceremonies. To foreign and domestic clients alike, these individuals (who are usually female) may play the role of fortune tellers, astrologers, necromancers, and spiritual counselors, serving the public through ceremonies called *kut* and one-on-one consultations. They may be contacted privately and advertised through word of mouth or personal websites, although most *mudangs* are not wealthy and tend to come from the working and lower classes. Some American customers will pay to consult by telephone in matters such as romantic compatibility and auspicious days for activities such as weddings or operations. Shamans often figure in literary depictions of Korean immigrant experience. In Nora Okja Keller's novel *Comfort Woman* (1997), the protagonist's mother, Akiko (a survivor of sexual slavery by the Japanese during World War II) is a *mudang* in Hawai'i, allowing her access to an entire cosmology of spirit helpers as she seeks healing from her (de)formative traumas. Her mythological analogue is Princess Pari, read by some to be the ultimate shaman figure because she helps ferry spirits between the realms of the living and the dead.

Whether at home, at church, among community groups, or at Korean-language school (*hangul hakyoh*), many Korean Americans might encounter didactic stories that encourage moral behavior, hard work, respect for elders, and generally honorable lifestyle choices. Among the more prevalent forms of folklore is the etiological fable, or story of how things came to be. The most famous creation story is that of the founding of Korea: the Heavenly King sends his son down to Earth to found the nation. Two animals—the bear and the tiger—wish to become human, so they are charged with abstaining from light and following a severely restricted food regimen. While the tiger cannot cope and flees into the forest, the bear perseveres and morphs into a radiant maiden, later taken as the wife of the Heavenly Prince. Their son eventually becomes the leader of the country, with his father turning into a mountain god upon retirement. While there are various versions of this founding legend, most of the features are similar and stress a harmony between heaven and Earth, commitment and reward. This Ur motif of balance can be seen on the very flag of the nation, and the perseverance demonstrated by the bear might be compared to the rigors of Korean immigrants enduring transformation in a new land such as America.

Many folktale collections exist in translated, illustrated form for Korean American and other readers. One that is readily available is Horace Newton Allen's collection *Korean Tales* (1889). A missionary, physician, and foreign secretary in Korea during the 19th century, Allen brings together many of the most recognizable tales: the trickster antics of the rabbit, the story of Sim Chung, the tale of "dancing girl" Chung Yang, and the familiar good brother/ bad brother pairing of Hyung Bo and Nahl Bo, duly rewarded or punished for their respective benevolence and greed.

Contemporary Forms

Many Korean American writers feature folklore in their texts. Keller's aforementioned *Comfort Woman* includes the story of Princess Pari, a daughter who goes down to the land of the dead in spite of the fearsome death messenger Saja to retrieve her parents. This is despite the fact that the royal couple—disappointed at having no sons—sacrificed her to an ancestral spirit. Although there are many versions of the tale, Keller has this seventh daughter bring them to heaven to reside with her in Lotus Land, thereby underscoring her conformity to filial duty, a virtue cardinal among Confucian values.

There is also the "Heavenly Toad" tale, which involves the familiar motif in many folktales (for instance, the Japanese folktales the "Grateful Stork" and "Momotaro: The Peach Boy") where nonhuman offspring are brought up by a (usually elderly) couple as their own. In Keller's retelling, the Heavenly Toad feels slighted for being rejected as a suitor by a wealthy family in the neighborhood. He devises a clever sleight of hand whereby it appears by heavenly edict that a daughter from that family be given to him as a bride. When the youngest one acquiesces, he asks her to stab him in the back. As a reward for her obedience, a handsome young man emerges from the amphibian's leathery garment, whisking his new wife and his adoptive parents up to his heavenly kingdom.

Keller also retells the story of Little Frog that also pivots upon the relationship between children and parents. A mother frog finds that her son is inclined to do the opposite of what she says. In order to ensure proper funeral arrangements, she advises him emphatically to bury her in the river, not in the mountains. That way, she hopes that her body will be safely interred. Unfortunately, upon her death her son decides to finally comply with her request and buries her in the flowing river, leading him to groan and lament whenever it rains because her body and soul are restless and wandering. The etiological fable explains a natural phenomenon—frog song—as the frog son's concern for the welfare of his mother even after death.

The fox spirit is a case study that illustrates the transnational power of folklore to connect Korea with members of the U.S. diaspora. American folklorist Heinz Insu Fenkl's autobiographical novel *Memories of My Ghost Brother* (1996) evokes the fox spirit when Heinz's uncle Hyongbu offers stories of the cannibalistic demon as part of an overall misogynistic attitude about women. The fox in the oral tale disrupts the family life and fortune through cannibalistic mayhem until her once uxorious husband discovers her infamy and sets the house afire with her inside. This blaze leads to the genesis of the first mosquito, an etiological angle that underscores the pesky, vampiric nature of its female originator.

Keller's second novel, *Fox Girl* (2002), highlights this theme of transformation by examining the precarious lives of young female prostitutes servicing American GIs in the aftermath of the Korean War (1950–1953). The main character, Hyun Jin, encounters folklore through the tales of her father. Her friend and half sister Sookie, whom Hyun Jin identifies as a fox girl, imparts a story about a fox who wants to be human but cannot transform because of her animal nature and the savagery it unleashes. Many of the comparisons hinge on the dichotomy of beauty in ugliness and vice versa. Their mother, Duk Hee, also questions the prevailing interpretations that view the fox as evil and duplicitous rather than empowered and resourceful.

Alexander Chee's award-winning debut novel *Edinburgh* (2002) identifies itself as a fox story in its prologue and casts the fox demon as a leitmotif throughout the text. With Lady Tammamo, Chee combines the folk figure of the vulpine seductress who has nine tails and the capacity to transform herself into a human across two countries. In interviews, the author has referred to a combination of Korean and Japanese myths; his protagonist Fee, however, is half Korean and half Scottish. The American boy learns about the folklore from his father. Chee's innovation on the fox myth is to suggest that the fox need not be a female; indeed, Fee notices red hairs growing in his black beard and wonders about his own moral nature and metamorphic potential. Secrecy too surrounds not only the fox character's life among the humans but also Fee's experience with molestation and later his grappling with life as an Asian American gay man.

Apart from literary renditions, popular media from South Korea complements the awareness of folklore traditions. In 2010, the Korean Broadcasting Corporation aired a popular television miniseries focused on young love called *My Girlfriend Is a Nine-Tailed Fox*. Another dramatic miniseries called *Grudge: The Revolt of the Gumiho* (2010) focused on a feudal-era fox woman's quest to become human amid the complications of a broken conjugal promise, the desire for revenge, and ensuring the welfare of her half-fox and half-human child. The Munhwa Broadcasting Corporation released a miniseries in 2012 called *The Thousandth Man* that follows a young fox woman in search of her 1,000th liver; the catch, of course, is that she only kills the men she actually loves, complicating her desire to be human with the desire to be in a rewarding relationship.

In terms of films, a horror thriller titled *Gumiho* (1994) was the special effects–driven debut of director Park Heon-Su, while the animated feature *Yobi, the Five-Tailed Fox* (2007) focused on themes such as sacrifice and friendship in a form palatable for younger audiences. Korean Americans are able to access these productions easily with access to current online streaming services and the inclination to explore such familiar characters and themes from this folklore-rich ancestral land.

Nancy Kang

See also: Korean American Immigration; Korean American Literature

Further Reading

Allen, Horace Newton. *Korean Tales*. New York: Putnam, 1889.

Fenkl, Heinz Insu. "Fox Wives and Other Dangerous Women." Journal of Mythic Arts Archived Articles, December 2012, http://www.endicott-studio.com/rdrm/fordangr .html.

Grayson, James Huntley. *Myths and Legends from Korea: An Annotated Compendium of Ancient and Modern Materials*. Richmond, Surrey, UK: Curzon, 2001.

Kendall, Laurel. *Shamans, Housewives, and Other Restless Spirits: Women in Korean Ritual Life*. Honolulu: University of Hawai'i Press, 1987.

Lee, Jonathan H. X., and Kathleen M. Nadeau, eds. *Encyclopedia of Asian American Folklore and Folklife*. 3 vols. Santa Barbara, CA: ABC-CLIO, 2011.

KOREAN AMERICAN FOOD

Tradition and Practices

Korean cooking shares two main characteristics that differentiate it from Chinese cooking and align it with that of the Japanese—namely a fondness for raw seafood and a penchant for raw vegetables. A wide variety of fish as well as squid and abalone are consumed raw. Unlike in Chinese cookery, deep-frying is not a common method of cookery. Egg-battered vegetables are typically pan-fried as opposed to deep-fried. A few of the most popular vegetables among Koreans include radishes, spinach, mustard leaves, scallions, and seaweed, which may be dressed with red pepper powder, sesame oil, and rice vinegar or with fish sauce, sugar, and garlic. In addition to being served raw, parboiled, or lightly sautéed, Korean vegetables are often pickled. The Korean penchant for pickling extends to seafood, which may be salted and served as a side dish or as a condiment. Every traditional meal will include at least one pickle dish if not more. In addition to its pervasive use of pickles, Korean cuisine is characterized by the prevalence of grilled meats and flavorful barbecue sauces. In fact, many Korean barbecue restaurants have grills built into each table so that diners can prepare their own meat and vegetables. Serious home cooks would also have a smokeless grill that can be used at the dining table.

As in Japanese cookery, soups are placed into two categories: thin, or *guk*, and thick, or *tang*. Korean stews (*jigae*) are typically spicy concoctions that have been seasoned with either soybean paste or chili paste and may contain vegetables, seafood, or meat. *Tang* and *jigae* can be served as a side dish, a main dish, or even a one-dish meal. One of the most popular seafood dishes comes in the form of a spicy stew laden with crab, clam, shrimp, fish, radish, chili pepper paste, and green onion and garlic. Many beef broth soups use bone broth, which is made by boiling the bones to extract vital nutrients. During the hot summer months, cold soups are common. Summer standards include cucumber, seaweed, and roasted chicken and sesame. Most noodle dishes, whether hot or cold, are served in broth.

Korean noodles are made from rice, wheat, buckwheat, and sweet potato, the latter of which features in *japchae*. For this simple dish, sweet potato or cellophane noodles are tossed with stir-fried vegetables. For a refreshing snack or lunch, buckwheat noodles are drenched in cold beef broth and topped with beef, cucumber, pear, and egg. Steamed rice appears at every meal unless it consists of a one-pot noodle dish. Ground rice is used to thicken sauces and to make a batter for such iconic dishes as the seafood and scallion pancake *haemul pajeon*. Pan-fried pancakes are made with a variety of meats and vegetables.

Kwang Lee (left) and John Kim dining in a Korean restaurant in Palisades Park, New Jersey, May 21, 2008. Koreans are known for their fondness of seafood, grilled meat with barbeque sauce, and *kimchi* (pickled vegetables). (AP Photo/Mike Derer)

Marinated or lightly salted meat and seafood are often grilled over a high flame or broiled. Perhaps the most popular fruit in Korean cooking would be the Asian pear, which is an essential ingredient in the marinade typically used for meat and poultry. The pear's juice acts as a tenderizing agent. In addition to being grilled, meat and fish are also simmered in soy sauce–flavored liquids, a method that not only tenderizes but also seasons the main ingredients. As is witnessed in Korean American restaurants, Koreans have a fondness for beef that far surpasses the rest of Asia. Beef is finely minced; mixed with soy sauce, honey, garlic, and sesame oil; and served raw with egg yolk, pine nuts, and Asian pear. Pork also plays a key role in contemporary Korean cuisine. A popular way of preserving beef, pork, and crab is to marinate it in a soy sauce, sugar, and rice wine mixture.

Three of the most popular Korean meat dishes in the United States include *bulgogi* (thinly sliced and grilled beef or pork that has been marinated in soy sauce, pear juice, garlic, and green onion), *galbi* (grilled beef or pork ribs with a sugar, soy sauce, and garlic marinade), and fried chicken. Rather than achieving a crisp finish like southern fried chicken, the Korean version is fried twice and then slathered in a sticky sweet and hot sauce. Other popular chicken dishes include grilled ginger chicken, baked chicken wings, and braised chicken with shiitake mushrooms. Similar to Vietnamese, Koreans often wrap thin slices of grilled meat in lettuce or *perilla* leaves. Rice and boiled pork are also eaten in tidy leaf-wrapped packages, known as *ssam,* and served with a variety of dipping sauces.

Contemporary Forms

According to 2010 U.S. census data, the recent spike in the number of Korean and Korean fusion restaurants as well as the Korean taco truck craze correspond to an increase in the population of Korean Americans, which has grown twentyfold since 1970 to reach 1.4 million in 2010. Before 1970 few Americans had eaten at a Korean restaurant, in part because so few existed in the United States. Despite the large Korean population in the Los Angeles area, Korean restaurateurs largely ran Chinese-style restaurants until the 1970s. Opened in 1965, Korea House became the first Korean restaurant in Los Angeles to achieve mainstream success. With such illustrious patrons as the mayor of Los Angeles and Republic of Korea president Park Chung-hee (1917–1979), Korea House provided a glamorous introduction to Korean cuisine. What some scholars believe may have been the first Korean restaurant in Manhattan, Mi Cin, opened in 1960. By the end of the decade, three more had opened their doors. This number more than quadrupled during the 1970s.

Like Chinese restaurant owners, the first Korean restaurants offered two types of dishes—those for American customers and those for Korean immigrants. Koreatown restaurants catered primarily to the Korean palate, while those outside of Koreatown created dishes more attuned to the American taste, such as using less fermented fish. Korean restaurants that began to proliferate in the 1980s often specialized in meat dishes, several of which soon held a strong crossover appeal to the American palate. However, it is not until the early 21st century that Korean food gained acceptance within mainstream Americans, albeit a hip, urban, well-heeled swath of the mainstream.

Although the first Korean restaurants needed to Americanize their menus to reach non-Asian diners, the past decade has seen a remarkable change. For example, the suburbs surrounding Washington, D.C., have seen a sharp rise in Korean restaurants of late. Many of these newcomers specialize in a particular dish, such as stews, soups, rice bowls, or ribs. Given that large Koreatowns inevitably boast a vibrant nightlife, some restaurants specialize in communal dishes, which are traditionally shared at Korean drinking parties. Many of the Koreatown restaurant owners are foreign-born Korean Americans. Hee-sook Lee, owner of the chain BCD Tofu House, arrived in the United States in 1989 and opened the first Tofu House in 1996, where she served one simple dish in several different ways. Her original versions of soft tofu soup (*soon dubu*) were so popular that her first restaurant not only draws Asian and non-Asian customers but also serves as a tourist destination for South Koreans. Since 1996, Lee has expanded the menu and also expanded her venture into an international chain, with restaurants in New Jersey, New York, Tokyo, and cities throughout South Korea.

Alice L. McLean

See also: Asian Indian American Food; Chinese American Food; Filipino American Food; Japanese American Food; Kimchi; Thai American Food; Vietnamese American Food

Further Reading

Hepinstall, Hi Soo Shin. *Growing Up in a Korean Kitchen: A Cookbook.* Berkeley, CA: Ten Speed, 2001.

Hoeffel, Elizabeth M., Sonya Rastogi, Myoung Ouk Kim, and Hasan Shahid. "The Asian Population: 2010." U.S. Census Bureau, March 2012, http://www.census.gov/prod/cen2010/briefs/c2010br-11.pdf.

Kim, Kwang Ok, ed. *Re-Orienting Cuisine: East Asian Foodways in the Twenty-First Century.* New York: Berghahn Books, 2015.

Oum, Young Rae. "Authenticity and Representation: Cuisines and Identities in Korean-American Diaspora." *Postcolonial Studies* 8(1) (2005): 109–125.

Pettid, Michal J. *Korean Cuisine: An Illustrated History.* London: Reaktion, 2008.

KOREAN AMERICAN IMMIGRATION

Korean American immigration to the United States can be divided into roughly three waves. The first wave began with the official immigration from Korea to Hawai'i from 1903. These immigrants were mostly men who came to work on the sugar plantations. Approximately 2,500 men came in this wave. The second wave of Korean American immigration began in 1945 and lasted until 1965. This wave consisted mostly of refugees, orphans, and war brides and was precipitated by the Korean War. Finally, the third wave started in 1965. This wave was much more diverse than the previous ones and has slowed down in recent years.

In 1884, Korea and the United States signed the Treaty of Amity and Commerce. This 14-article treaty established mutual friendship and assistance in case of attack, granted most favored nation trade status, and addressed the extraterritorial rights for American citizens in Korea. Broadly speaking, this treaty established diplomatic ties between Korea and the United States and set the base for Korean immigration to America.

The first wave was composed of Koreans, mostly men, who came to Hawai'i. From 1903 to 1905, the Korean government as well as the Sugar Planters Association encouraged Korean men to move to Hawai'i to work on the plantations. They promised the men good wages and a better life. The Sugar Planters Association needed new workforces because Japanese and Chinese laborers who had previously worked on the plantations were now banned by the Chinese Exclusion Act and the Gentleman's Agreement from immigrating to the United States. Korean immigrants were motivated to move to Hawai'i for several reasons: political turmoil in Korea, including two revolts; a poor economy, made worse by a drought in 1901; and the encouragement of American missionaries. Dr. Horace H. Allen (1858–1932) was the most prominent missionary who later rose to the position of diplomat and was instrumental in initiating Korean immigration to Hawai'i.

Once in Hawai'i, these men found that conditions on the plantations were harsh and that their wages were not as high as promised. They were eventually able to move from the plantations to the cities, where they established businesses ranging from grocery and furniture stores to tailoring and cleaning shops. These early Korean immigrants were mostly men, but from 1911 to 1917 they were joined by approximately 1,000 women through the picture

The Korean War

The Korean War lasted for three years, from June 25, 1950, to July 27, 1953. Immediately after World War II, the Korean Peninsula was bifurcated at the 38th Parallel. In the north, the Soviet Union backed a Stalinist regime led by Kim Il-sung (1912–1994). In the south, the United States supported an administration headed by the U.S.-educated Syngman Rhee (1875–1965). Several bloody skirmishes occurred along the 38th Parallel for several years until June 25, 1950, when the Korean People's Army invaded the Republic of Korea and sparked the beginning of the war. Although fighting ended on July 27, 1953, the Korean War is not officially over. An armistice agreement has been signed that, among other things, established a demilitarized zone, now the de facto border between North and South Korea.

There are no exact numbers for the casualties caused by the Korean War. An estimated 10 percent of the Korean population died during the course of the three years, and many war crimes were committed on both sides. In addition, the South Korean economy and infrastructure were left in ruins. The Korean War led to the second wave of Korean American immigrants, which was composed mostly of refugees, orphans, and war brides.

bride system. A man would send his picture to friends and relatives in Korea, who would then show the pictures to young unmarried women they knew. Women would pick their future husbands based on these pictures and come to Hawai'i, where they would be officially married. Oftentimes the women would be surprised and disappointed by their husbands when they met, because the pictures they sent were very different from how they actually looked. Some of the picture brides decided to return to Korea, but many stayed and started families with their husbands.

Many immigrants struggled to adjust to life in America. Approximately 1,000 eventually moved back to Korea, while another 1,000 migrated to California. However, many other immigrants decided to stay. They moved from the plantations to the cities, where they quickly moved up the socioeconomic ladder. These immigrants had one of the highest rates of educational attainment and professionalization among other minority groups, despite racial barriers and other difficulties. They established not only businesses but also Christian organizations and Korean-language schools. Associations for the independence of Korea were also prominent in Hawai'i. In 1905 Japan made Korea a protectorate and then in 1910 officially annexed Korea, turning it into a colony. The independence groups in Hawai'i were not able to provide direct assistance, but they were still able to raise money and send it to the independence movement in Korea.

These organizations played an important part in the life of the early Korean community. They provided financial assistance and also preserved to the best of their ability Korean language and culture. This was especially important for the younger generations who were born in Hawai'i and knew nothing about Korea. In 1905, official immigration to Hawai'i ended because of the Korean government's concerns about bad conditions on the plantations and Japan's annexation of Korea.

The second wave of Korean American immigration began after 1945, when World War II and, consequently, Japanese colonization of Korea ended. The composition of this second wave was very different from the first wave. While the first wave was composed of laborers, mostly men, this wave was composed of wives of U.S. military servicemen, refugees, and orphans. In 1950 Korea was plunged into the Korean War, which lasted for three years and caused untold damage to the country. The war created refugees who lost their homes as well as orphans who lost their families. Many of these orphans were adopted by American families, creating a phenomenon of transnational (and transracial) adoption. In addition, large numbers of Korean women married U.S. soldiers during and after the Korean War and moved to America, where they subsequently sponsored their relatives' immigration. An estimated 100,000 women came to the United States as war brides. They are responsible for paving the way for Korean American immigration after the Korean War.

The third and final wave of Korean American immigration began after 1965. The Immigration and Nationality Act of 1965 repealed the National Origin Quota System Act. This limited the number of immigrants who could come to the United States annually based on their country of origin. Once this quota system was repealed, immigrants were admitted to the United States based on several different categories, including relative preference, people with special skills or training, and family reunification. Although immigration has slowed in recent years, these post-1965 immigrants continue to arrive. New immigrants are mostly middle-class professionals. Overall, they are better educated and better off financially than their predecessors. In spite of the fact that South Korea is now the 11th-largest economy in the world, these immigrants come to the United States because they are motivated by the image of the American Dream.

According to the 2010 census, there are approximately 1.7 million people of Korean descent living in the United States today. The United States contains the second-largest Korean population outside of Korea, after the People's Republic of China. The highest numbers of Korean Americans live in California, followed by New York, New Jersey, and Virginia. In California, the largest concentration of Korean Americans resides in the Greater Los Angeles Area.

Korean Americans have one of the highest rates of educational attainment in the United States. The 2010 census reported that 51.6 percent of Korean Americans ages 25 and older have at least a bachelor's degree, a rate exceeded only by Chinese Americans and South Asian Americans. In addition to this high educational attainment, Korean Americans also exhibit high rates of self-employment, particularly in small business ownership. However, this concentration in self-employment is dominant mostly among first-generation immigrants. Second-generation Korean Americans predominately occupy the mainstream job market. Korean Americans began small business ownership as labor-intensive family-run operations, but these businesses have since expanded in numbers as well as in revenue and scale. The number of Korean-owned firms grew 113-fold from 1972 to 1997, and by 2005 the *Joong An Ilbo L.A.* (Korea Daily) listed 25,000 businesses in its business directory. Another mark of the growing Korean American economy is the number of Korean American banks that have sprung up over the years. As of 2005, 11 Korean American full-service banks operated in Los Angeles, 4 of which are listed in the Nasdaq Stock Exchange.

In spite of these glowing statistics, the Korean American community still faces difficulties. It is a largely insulated community that derives support

The 1992 Los Angeles Riots

The 1992 Los Angeles Riots were a series of civil disturbances that occurred from April 29 to May 4, 1992. They were precipitated by the ruling in the Rodney King trial. King, a black motorist, had been repeatedly kicked and beaten by LAPD officers. Although a video of the attack was aired repeatedly on television news stations, the jurors in the case acquitted all of the officers, and rioting broke out.

More than half of the Korean American businesses in Los Angeles suffered damages during the riots. Many people interpreted this as a sign of tension between African American and Korean American communities, particularly in light of the verdict in the Soon Ja Du case. Du, who ran a liquor store, had shot Latasha Harlins, a black teenager, in the back of the head. Du only received probation, sparking outrage in the African American community. The media showed images of Korean Americans defending their stores with guns during the unrest and described them either as model minorities defending themselves or as lawless vigilantes. Otherwise, Korean Americans were left out of mainstream media's discussion of the events, leading to the rise of Korean American participation in politics in the aftermath.

from within. For example, *kye*, a rotating credit system, is a common way for Korean Americans to raise money. While this insulation strengthens ethnic solidarity, it also keeps Korean Americans isolated from mainstream society. One side effect of this isolation is the low rate of English proficiency in the Korean American community. In addition, not all Korean Americans have achieved socioeconomic mobility in America. There is a relatively high income disparity in the Korean American community. Various events have also impacted the Korean American community negatively. Among them is the 1992 Los Angeles Riots, which destroyed numerous Korean-owned businesses.

Today, formal emigration from Korea has declined. However, the Korean American community is still growing and changing. It has become a community composed not only of immigrants and their U.S.-born children but also those who come to the United States only temporarily and even those who move back and forth between South Korea and the United States. These changes have worked to create a transnational Korean American community.

Ashley Elisa Truong

See also: Korean American Children and Family; Korean American Literature; Korean American Women; Koreatowns; Picture Bride; War Brides Act (1945)

Further Reading

Abelmann, Nancy, and John Lie. *Blue Dreams: Korean Americans and the Los Angeles Riots.* Cambridge, MA: Harvard University Press, 1995.

"A Brief History of the Koreans in Hawaii." Yuji Ichioka Papers, 1880–2002. Special Collections Department, UCLA Charles E. Young Research Library, Los Angeles.

Cho, Grace M. *Haunting the Korean Diaspora: Shame, Secrecy, and the Forgotten War.* Minneapolis: University of Minnesota Press, 2008.

Choy, Bong-Youn. "The History of Koreans in America, Part I: Leaving the Land of the Morning Calm." *Korean Culture* 3(2) (1982): 34–45.

Cumings, Bruce. *Korea's Place in the Sun.* New York: Norton, 2005.

Hoeffel, Elizabeth M., Sonya Rastogi, Myoung Ouk Kim, and Hasan Shahid. "The Asian Population: 2010." U.S. Census Bureau, March 2012, http://www.census.gov/prod/cen2010/briefs/c2010br-11.pdf.

"Korean War." History.com, July 2013, http://www.history.com/topics/korean-war.

Patterson, Wayne. *The Koreans in America.* Minneapolis: Lerner Publications, 1986.

Patterson, Wayne. "Upward Social Mobility of the Koreans in Hawaii." *Korean Studies* 3 (1979): 81–92.

Yu, Eui-Young. "Korean Community in the United States: Socioeconomic Characteristics and Evolving Immigration Patterns." In *Korean Economy and Community in the 21st Century,* edited by Eui-Young Yu, Hyojoung Kim, Kyeyoung Park, and Moonsong Oh, 31–66. Los Angeles: Korean American Economic Development Center, 2009.

KOREAN AMERICAN LITERATURE

History and Origins

Compared to early Chinese immigrants whose first wave arrived after the mid-19th century with the discovery of gold in northern California, the Korean presence in the United States is more recent. The arrival of the first group of workers to Hawai'i in 1903 marks the beginning of migration, integration, assimilation, community building, and relocation for a little over a century. The population was concentrated on the West Coast and later the East Coast as well. The cultivation and spread of Korean culture—including its folklore and the production of Korean American literature—in the United States have been complicated by major historical events, premier among them the colonial imposition by the Japanese starting in 1910.

After victories in the Sino-Japanese War (1894–1895) and the Russo-Japanese War (1904–1905), Japan was able to put its longtime interests in the

Chang-Rae Lee (1965–)

After moving to the United States with his family at age three, Chang-Rae Lee attended Phillips Exeter Academy, Yale University, and the University of Oregon. He is best known as a novelist who published several novels and won numerous honors, including the PEN/Hemingway Award, the American Book Award, the Barnes & Noble Discover Award, the ALA Notable Book of the Year Award, the Anisfield-Wolf Literary Award, the Gustavus Myers Outstanding Book Award, and a finalist for a 2011 Pulitzer Prize.

Native Speaker (1995) focuses on Henry Park, a Korean American in a troubled relationship with his Caucasian wife, Lelia, and father to a deceased seven-year-old for whom he cannot grieve openly. Park realizes that his endemic sense of alienation stems from his uncomfortable position between the world of his hardworking immigrant parents' generation and his outsider status in America.

A Gesture Life (1999) extends the discourse of immigrant life by tracing the experiences of Franklin "Doc" Hata, a Japanese man of Korean ancestry who served as a medic in the Japanese Imperial Army during World War II. Now living in the United States, the retired shopkeeper struggles through an erratic relationship with his adopted mixed-race daughter and agonizing memories of a Korean comfort woman in Burma whom he loved but failed to save.

Aloft (2004) features Italian American Jerry Battle, an early retiree, widower, and suburbanite who enjoys the solitary hobby of flying. The novel satirically explores his checkered family dynamics and meditates upon what it means to be apart from others and yet still a part of them.

The Surrendered (2010) brings disparate characters together through historical catastrophe. The narrative follows June Han, an orphan survivor of the Korean War now dying of stomach cancer. Seeking out her estranged son in Europe, she enlists the help of emotionally eroded former American GI Hector Brennan, the child's father. The links between June and Hector are both tenuous and deep, all tying back to the atrocities of war and the fragility of life.

peninsula into an explicit form. With the goal of crushing Korean sovereignty, language, culture, and history, all the while benefitting from the land and work of its people, the annexation amplified the sense of nationalism not only in the occupied territory but also among those who managed to come abroad at that time. The growing instabilities on the domestic front were a major concern for those who came to the United States to work on the sugarcane plantations. Once arrived, many Korean immigrants were beset by troubles, including nativism and racism from white Americans, limited professional and educational

Nora Okja Keller (1965–)

Of German and Korean ancestry, Nora Okja Keller resides in Hawai'i. Raised primarily by her mother, Keller came to the United States at age three with her family. She went to the University of Hawai'i and the University of California, Santa Cruz. A self-identified Korean American writer, she focuses on responses to historical traumas in Korea, particularly experiences of women under oppressive regimes where they have been sexually exploited or otherwise dehumanized.

Numerous interviews have cited Keller's inspiration for her first novel as a speech she heard by Keum Ja Hwang, a comfort woman during World War II and survivor of the underacknowledged wartime atrocity. Keller's novels— *Comfort Woman* (1997) and *Fox Girl* (2002)—have received numerous honors, including the American Book Award, the Elliot Cades Award, and the Hawai'i Award for Literature. She has also edited *Yobo: Korean American Writing on Hawai'i* (2003) and coedited *Intersecting Circles: The Voices of Hapa Women in Poetry and Prose* (1999) with fellow writer Marie Hara.

Comfort Woman follows the story of Akiko, a Korean woman who survived sexual slavery in Japanese military brothels. Her daughter Beccah, whose father is an American missionary, reflects on her mother's sometimes opaque experiences, including Akiko's frequent plunges into shamanic trances. Set in Hawai'i, the novel shuttles back and forth between two countries, two voices, and various drastic, devastating memories that include rape, murder, abortion, hauntings, and spiritual rebirth.

Fox Girl is set in an "America Town" or marginalized area in Korea frequented by American GIs and Korean prostitutes during the 1960s. The main characters are of mixed race, a source of ostracism on top of their being the children of sex workers. Hyun Jin, initially a model student, finds herself disowned and thrown out of her home. She scrapes together a life with her best friend Sookie and their friend-turned-pimp Lobetto. Hyun Jin finds her birth mother and later becomes a mother to Sookie's child, eventually relocating to Hawai'i and an unknown future. Mother-daughter relationships are a powerful thematic continuity in Keller's novels.

---

opportunities due to linguistic difficulties and citizenship requirements, exclusionary laws preventing naturalization and intermarriage, and the difficulty of finding widespread supportive communities. Apart from those who settled in Hawai'i, a number moved to the mainland, congregating in cities such as San Francisco and later Los Angeles, where aid societies sprang up through church and political interests. These provided some solace for the loneliness of living in a new land. The bulk of new immigrants were men, but the importation of brides, especially to Hawai'i, helped to even out the ratio of Korean men and women and allow for the limited growth of families. This was set back by the 1924 Immigration Act, which aimed to restrict Asian immigration and maintain the integrity of the U.S. populace.

After the defeat of Japan in World War II, the Korean War (1950–1953) led to major changes in U.S.-Korean relations, with immigration taking the form of war brides married to American GIs (after passage of the War Brides Act of 1945) and orphans as well as adoptees (including biracial children of GIs, often ostracized in their native land). The partition at the 38th Parallel that created North and South Korea through the geopolitical machinations of the United States and Russia led to a renewed need for soul-searching and national defini-tion both in and outside of the "hermit kingdom." A diverse group of immigrants arrived after the Immigration and Nationality Act of 1965. The United States, known as *mi-gook* (the beautiful land), became a desired destination for many and remains so, with financially able Korean parents sending their children as *yu-hakseng* (study abroad students) to test the waters and others seeking oppor-tunities as immigrant investors. While many professionals arise especially from the second and later generations, others function as part of the working class, owning small businesses (such as groceries, liquor stores, convenience stores, and dry cleaning shops) that suffered massive destruction during the 1992 Los Angeles Riots. While the population of Korean Americans remains relatively small (less than 1 percent of the U.S. population and around 1.7 million accord-ing to the 2010 census), the group's literary production cannot be ignored.

Many Korean immigrants (*yi-min*) did not have the time or ability to engage in literary art upon arrival. Some may have been writers in their native tongue and continued to craft reflections in Korean, but the rigor of work and the lack of easy access to publishing venues made widespread literary production a virtual impossibility. Much of what is considered Korean American literature today comes from descendants of immigrants; by and large, the designation applies to texts available in English. The field can be divided into two groups: work by immigrant writers and work by native-born Americans of Korean descent. A number of theoretical questions inform the definition of Korean American literature, among them how to differentiate it from Korean literature. Some scholars argue that there is a postnational seamless connection between the writers of Korean descent in the United States and those living in Korea; others argue that Korean Americans have unique preoccupations that cannot be compared to (or subsumed by) the concerns of peninsular Koreans.

This differentiation points to the heart of what it means to be Korean Amer-ican as opposed to a transplanted Korean in America. For instance, the racial tensions between African Americans and Asian Americans explored in Leonard Chang's novel *The Fruit 'N Food* (1996) are not experiences that would exist in contemporary Korea, which is itself partitioned into two distinct national societies, North Korea and South Korea. As such, many readers and critics would agree that Korean American literature cannot be described merely as Korean literature written in or translated into English. Some Korean American writers are not fluent in Korean and do not even identify strongly with the culture or country. Specific concerns relating to life in the United States include reactions to direct or indirect immigrant experience, surviving racism in a majority white society, the effects of stereotyping from without and generational pressures from within, and the balance of self-determination with collectivism in "the land of the free."

Regional Practices and Traditions

Literary critics such as Elaine H. Kim, author of the foundational *Asian American Literature: An Introduction to the Writings and Their Social Context* (1982), have strived to delineate Korean American literature from both Korean and coethnic Asian American literatures. Korean American writing began largely with the meditations of educated exiles fleeing from occupied Korea. The earliest novelist was Younghill Kang (1903–1972), author of *The Grass Roof* (1931), a lyrical bildungsroman about young Chungpa Han's rustic early life and later resistance to Japanese colonial rule. Kang followed up with the creative memoir *East Goes West: The Making of an Oriental Yankee* (1932), which follows Han's hard-knock life in New York City during the 1920s through a series of uninspiring jobs and disheartening (yet illuminating) interpersonal relationships. Among other achievements, Kang taught in the Comparative Literature Department at New York University and won a Guggenheim fellowship.

Fellow Harvard alumnus Richard Eun-Kook Kim (1932–2009) came to the United States as a student, earning a series of degrees and later publishing *The Martyred* (1964), an existential novel set during the Korean War that attempts to solve the mystery of why a group of Christian ministers were murdered. His second novel *The Innocent* (1968), which failed to receive comparable acclaim, continued the military theme, asking questions about how best to negotiate the moral extremities of war. Kim's *Lost Names: Scenes from a Korean Boyhood* (1970) is a series of vignettes based on the author's recollections of Japanese occupation.

While Kang and Kim are often associated with robust masculine perspectives, Korean American women writers have also earned acclaim, among them

Nora Okja Keller with her award-winning *Comfort Woman* (1997), an intergenerational novel of a former sex slave for Japanese troops during World War II. This novel is set in Hawai'i, just like Margaret Pai's *The Dreams of Two Yi-Min* (1989), which details her father's entrepreneurial exploits, her mother's nationalist activism, the social context behind such milestones as the March 1st independence movement in Korea in 1919, and the sometime rivalry between leaders Syngman Rhee and Yong-man Park.

Quiet Odyssey (1990) by Mary Paik Lee (1900–1995) details the rugged life of a pioneer whose exiled family came to Hawai'i before settling in various locales throughout the fertile agricultural regions of southern California. Recent memoirs by Korean Americans include Helie Lee's *Still Life with Rice* (1996) and *In the Absence of Sun* (1998), about how the 38th Parallel separating North and South Korea continues to affect her family, and K. Connie Kang's expansive family chronicle *Home Was the Land of Morning Calm* (1995). Jane Jeong Trenka, a Korean-born adoptee and adoption activist from Minnesota, has written about the search for self in *The Language of Blood* (2005) and *Fugitive Visions: An Adoptee's Return to Korea* (2009). Marie Myung-Ok Lee has also considered the Korean adoption legacy through her novel *Somebody's Daughter* (2005).

Born in Los Angeles in 1926, Kim Ronyoung (Gloria Hahn) wrote the Pulitzer Prize–nominated novel *Clay Walls* (1987) before succumbing to cancer the year of its publication. The triple-voiced text follows a family of immigrants to Los Angeles through the early 20th century up until World War II: Haesu, a woman of the aristocratic *yangban* class who is involved in the Korean independence movement but struggling with unfulfilling jobs and an incompatible marriage; her hot-tempered working-class husband Chun; and their American-born eldest daughter Faye. Their struggles are emblematic of many early immigrant experiences on the West Coast: the quest for meaningful employment, combating racism, seeking financial stability for one's children, and dealing with loss across generations and national lines.

Sook Nyul Choi captures the immigrant experience and other coming-of-age rites in her books for children and young adults, including *The Year of Impossible Goodbyes* (1991). Children's book author Linda Sue Park won the 2002 Newbery Medal for *A Single Shard* (2001), a narrative about an inquisitive Korean boy, his interest in pottery, and the art of persistence.

Contemporary Forms

Among the most famous contemporary writers is Theresa Hak Kyung Cha (1951–1982), who was also a performance artist, filmmaker, and photographer. Best known for her array of talents in visual art and theoretically dense multimedia experimentation, Cha was born in Pusan, South Korea. She immigrated to the United States at age 12 and attended the University of California, Berkeley, where she earned undergraduate and graduate degrees. Her period as a student coincided with the political activism of the late 1960s, including the student strikes and antiwar protests in the Bay Area. The counterculture atmosphere and Cha's desire to explore widely may have catalyzed her insurgent intellectual and artistic spirit.

Cha moved to Paris, France, where she immersed herself in studies of European film theory, psychoanalysis, and the work of poststructuralist intellectuals such as Roland Barthes and Jacques Derrida. When she returned to the United States, she integrated performance art with print genres such as poetry, prose, sculpture, film, and video. Her work combined cultural traditions from Korea (e.g., an awareness of tumultuous colonial history and indigenous rituals such as shamanic trance) with those of Europe (ancient mythology and contemporary cultural theory). Linguistic fluidity and generic hybridization are among the techniques that defined her diverse output.

Cha published *Dictée* in 1982, an autobiographical novel in collage form whose nine sections represent the Greek muses or goddesses of artistic inspiration: Clio, Calliope, Euterpe, Thalia, Melpomene, Erato, Urania, Terpsichore, and Polymnia. Some of the prevailing themes are historical loss, familial honor, intersecting mythologies, women's experiences, and the powers of myth, time, and exile. Cha highlights the intersection of women's suffering with martyrdom, freedom fighting, and rebellion; her mother's story is entwined with that of the Greek goddess Demeter and her imprisoned daughter Persephone, French saint Joan of Arc, and young anti-imperialist demonstrator Yu Gwan Soon. Shortly after the publication of *Dictee,* Cha was raped and murdered in New York City. The University of California–Berkeley Art Museum and Pacific Film Archive serves as the repository for her materials. Her posthumous publications include *The Dream of the Audience* (2001) and *Exilée and Temps Morts: Selected Works* (2009).

Also woman-centered are the quirky comedic novels by Hawai'i-born Willyce Kim, *Dancer Dawkins and the California Kid* (1985) and *Dead Heat* (1988). The majority of the characters are white lesbians, but Ta Jan the Korean, a diner owner from Oahu with an incredibly gifted dog, plays a key role as they experience adventures with madmen and Mafiosi in the Bay Area.

Depictions of Hawai'ian life are central to the oeuvre of half Korean poet Cathy Song (1955–) in *Picture Bride* (1983) and *Frameless Windows, Squares of Light* (1988). The state also appears prominently in the stories and novels of Gary Pak, including *The Watcher of Waipuna* (1992), *A Ricepaper Airplane* (1998), and *Children of a Fireland* (2004). Another longtime academic (but now full-time writer) is Ty Pak, who immigrated to the United States in 1965 with a law degree and experience as a journalist. Pak published the short story collections *Guilt Payment* (1983) and *Moonbay* (1999) as well as the novel *Cry Korea Cry* (1999), all the while serving as a literary spokesperson for Korean Americans and the integrity of their experiences amid uprooting and resettlement.

Another notable academic and creative writer is Heinz Insu Fenkl, a biracial novelist, folklorist, translator, and editor. He published the autobiographical novel *Memories of My Ghost Brother* (1996) and coedited *Kori: The Beacon Anthology of Korean American Literature* (2002) with Walter K. Lew, a scholar, poet, and intermedia artist is known for *Treadwinds* (2002) and other cross-genre and performance-based pieces. Lew's movietelling hearkens back to the Korean practice of having a running commentator guide audiences during silent films. *Century of the Tiger: One Hundred Years of Korean Culture in America* (2002), coedited by Fenkl, Jenny Ryun Foster, and Frank Stewart, features such writers as Suji Kwock Kim, whose much anthologized poems straddle the written word, song, drama, and multimedia performance. Her first book of poetry was *Notes from the Divided Country* (2003).

Chang-Rae Lee is among the most decorated of contemporary Asian American novelists, with four novels thus far: *Native Speaker* (1995), *A Gesture Life* (1999), *Aloft* (2004) and *The Surrendered* (2010). Other contemporary writers include Patti Kim, whose novel *A Cab Called Reliable* (1997) broaches such topics as favoritism of boys within Korean and Korean immigrant families, domestic abuse and parental abandonment, alcoholism, and the redemptive powers of the creative imagination. Many writers such as Kim and Susan Choi, Pulitzer Prize–nominated author of *The Foreign Student* (1998), *American Woman* (2003), and *A Person of Interest* (2008), evoke transnational and intergenerational themes such as unresolved tensions between parents, children, and comrades; failed idealism; the horrors of wartime memory; emotional turmoil in the face of accusation; and the bitter resolve that characterizes the Korean concept of *han*.

Others such as Leonard Chang, author of *The Fruit 'N Food* (1996), write about interracial tensions but also blend in humor and generic experimentation. For instance, his mystery/noir trilogy (*Over the Shoulder, Underkill*, and *Fade to Clear*) features a Korean American detective named Allen Choice, with "Choice" symbolically replacing the typical Korean surname "Choi." Don Lee, former editor of the literary magazine *Ploughshares*, has published short story collections such as *Yellow* (2001) that feature an array of provocative Asian American relationships in the fictional Californian community of Rosarita Bay and novels such as *Country of Origin* (2005), *Wrack and Ruin* (2008), and *The Collective* (2012).

Writer Chang-Rae Lee at a book signing at the National Book Festival on the National Mall in Washington, D.C., September 25, 2010. He has received many honors, including the American Book Award, PEN/Hemingway Award, and ALA Notable Book of the Year Award. (Jeff Malet Photography/Newscom)

The breadth and diversity of Korean American literature has been growing, especially since the last decades of the 20th century as descendants of first-generation immigrants are increasingly making their voices heard. Particular themes—immigration, family dynamics, racism and racial difference, reconciling Asianness with Americanness, and discourses about authenticity in a changing global society—remain prevalent. A larger chorus of voices has been emerging, even allowing for graphic novelists and cartoonists (including Jim Lee, Derek Kirk Kim, and Frank Cho) to join the field as well as more LGBT writers such as Alexander Chee, author of *Edinburgh* (2001). The trajectory of Korean American literary production is one that will likely remain historically conscious but vibrant, intrepid, and future oriented.

Nancy Kang

See also: Korean American Folklore; Korean American Immigration

Further Reading

Foster, Jenny Ryun, Frank Stewart, and Heinz Insu Fenkl, eds. *Century of the Tiger: One Hundred Years of Korean Culture in America, 1903–2003*. Honolulu: University of Hawai'i Press, 2003.

Hur, Won Moo. *The Korean Americans*. Westport, CT: Greenwood, 1998.

Kim, Elaine H., and Chungmoo Choi, eds. *Dangerous Women: Gender and Korean Nationalism*. New York and London: Routledge, 1997.

Kim, Elaine H., and Eui-Young Yu, eds. *East to America: Korean American Life Stories*. New York: New Press, 1996.

Kim-Renaud, Young-Key, R. Richard Grinker, and Kirk W. Larsen, eds. "Korean American Literature," George Washington University Sigur Center Asia Papers, 2003, http://www2.gwu.edu/~sigur/assets/docs/scap/SCAP20-KoreanWriters.pdf.

KOREAN AMERICAN WOMEN

Historically, Korea did not have much interaction with the West until the 19th century. After the United States–Korea Treaty of Peace, Amity, Commerce, and Navigation in 1882, a small number of Korean diplomats, merchants, and students came to the United States. It was not until the beginning of the 20th century that Korean immigrants began to arrive in more notable numbers. Early immigrants, mostly men, went to Hawai'i and worked on sugarcane

Mary Paik Lee (1900–1995)

Born in Pyongyang (nowadays the capital city of North Korea), Lee was named Paik Kuang Sun. She arrived in Hawai'i in 1905; her father, although an educated man in Korea, was a sugarcane plantation worker in Hawai'i. A year later, her family moved to California; she spent the rest of her life there. Over the years she and her family faced many challenges, including poverty and discrimination. She is best known for her memoir *Quiet Odyssey: A Pioneer Korean Woman in America* (1990), one of the early autobiographical writings by Asian American women. The book covers a long time span, from her childhood to the end of the 20th century. It provides valuable and rare documentation of Korean immigrants' experiences in the early years. On the one hand, it tells stories about her and her family's struggles and survival in the United States; on the other hand, the book suggests the narrator's strength and humor.

plantations. Most of them did not bring their families with them. Korea became a protectorate of Japan after the Russo-Japanese War of 1904–1905 and was annexed by Japan in 1910. When Japan and the United States signed the Gentlemen's Agreement in 1907, allowing wives to join their husbands in the United States, some Korean women entered the country as picture brides. Most of them went to Hawai'i. They faced long working hours, limited English-language skills, isolation, and other hardships in America. A number of Korean American literary works address the lived experiences of these pioneer women.

In the mid-20th century, particularly after the War Brides Act of 1945, many Korean women and children entered the country. According to the National Association of Korean Americans, it is estimated that around 100,000 military brides came over between 1950 and 1989. About 300,000 children have been adopted since 1953. Since the 1980s the number of Korean adoptees has been declining. As a result of the McCarran-Walter Act of 1952, Koreans and immigrants from other Asian countries are eligible to become naturalized U.S. citizens.

After the 1965 Immigration Act, Korean professionals and family members arrived in America as well, contributing to the dramatic increase in the Korean American population since the 1970s. According to the 2010 U.S. census, the Korean American population is over 1.5 million. Large numbers of them live in California, New York, New Jersey, Illinois, Washington, Texas, Virginia, Maryland, Pennsylvania, Georgia, and Hawai'i.

Like China and Japan, Korea has traditionally been influenced by Confucianism. Traditional Korean families follow patriarchal orders: men are breadwinners working outside the home and heads of the families, while women take care of domestic duties such as child rearing and household chores. When immigrants came to the United States, they preserved some of the traditional practices and at the same time changed others to adapt to American culture. Women took up jobs to supplement family income, thus gaining more financial independence. Korean American women were politically active in supporting and organizing protests against Japanese occupation during World War II. In recent years, women professionals have become an important part of Korean American communities across the country. Generally speaking, first-generation Korean immigrants held on to many of the traditional practices, while the younger American-born generations show less influence by Korean culture and more acculturation to American life.

The two main religions among Korean American men and women are Christianity and Buddhism. There are many Korean churches (mostly Catholic or Protestant) across the United States that not only serve religious and spiritual purposes but also act as service centers for Korean American communities. In comparison, Korean Buddhist temples are fewer in number, commonly around metropolitan centers. They serve a small portion of the Korean American population.

On June 27, 2002, the U.S. Senate passed resolution S.R. 185 recognizing the 100th Anniversary of Korean immigration to the United States. President Bush issued a proclamation on January 13, 2003, commending Korean Americans for their "important role in building, defending, and sustaining the United States of America." Korean American women played a significant role during that process. They have been active in contemporary American arts, literature, entertainment, and many other areas.

Korean American women artists and curators have contributed to the development of contemporary art. Yu Yeon Kim, born in South Korea, is an independent art curator based in New York City and Seoul, South Korea. She has curated and commissioned many renowned contemporary art exhibitions in Europe, America, Africa, and Asia, including among others *Translated Acts: Performance and Body Art from East Asia* in Berlin, New York, and Mexico City in 2001–2003; *Counterpoint,* an international exhibition of art in Shanghai, China, as well as Seoul, Korea, and Poznan, Poland, in 2007; the media art project *Corporeal/ Technoral* for the Poland Mediations Biennale in 2008; and the exhibition of Korean contemporary art *Lose Puntos del Compas* (The Points of the Compass) at the Fundacion Ludwig de Cuba and other locations in Havana, Cuba, in 2008.

Korean American women writers and their works have become frequent subjects in academic studies as well as among general readers. Theresa Hak Kyung Cha (1951–1982) was born in South Korea during the Korean War. Her family moved to California in 1962. Cha lived and studied in California and Paris, France, and became a renowned novelist, poet, and artist. Her works include poetry, fiction, media production, performances, and mixed genre. She is best known for her novel *Dictee* (1982). Shortly after *Dictee* was published, she was raped and murdered in New York City.

Korean American women have also been active in the entertainment business. Margaret M. Cho (1968–) is best known for her stand-up comedy. Her shows often make social and political commentaries and address such issues as racial stereotypes, LGBTQ rights, and others. She received the American Comedy Award for Best Female Comedian in 1994. She has also appeared in television shows and films.

Lan Dong

See also: Comfort Women; Korean American Folklore; Korean American Immigration; War Brides Act (1945)

Further Reading

Asian Women United of California, ed. *Making Waves: An Anthology of Writing by and about Asian Women.* Acton, MA: Beacon, 1989.

"A Brief History of Korean Americans." National Association of Korean Americans, 2003, http://www.naka.org/resources/history.asp.

Chan, Sucheng. *Asian Americans: An Interpretive History.* New York: Twayne, 1991.

Hoeffel, Elizabeth M., Sonya Rastogi, Myoung Ouk Kim, and Hasan Shahid. "The Asian Population: 2010." U.S. Census Bureau, March 2012, http://www.census.gov/prod/cen2010/briefs/c2010br-11.pdf.

Hong, Christine. "Korean Folklore in the Lives of Korean American Christian Women." In *Asian American Identities and Practices: Folkloric Expressions in Everyday Life,* edited by Jonathan H. X. Lee and Kathleen Nadeau, 221–234. Lanham, MD: Lexington Books, 2014.

Hune, Shirley, and Gail Nomura, eds. *Asian Pacific Islander American Women: A Historical Anthology.* New York: New York University Press, 2003.

Kim, Ai Ra. *Women Struggling for a New Life.* Albany: State University of New York Press, 1996.

Kim, Jung Ha. *Bridge-Makers and Cross-Bearers: Korean American Women and the Church.* Atlanta: Scholars Press, 1997.

Kwon, Ho-Youn, Kwang Chung Kim, and R. Stephen Warner, eds. *Korean Americans and Their Religions.* University Park: Pennsylvania State University Press, 2001.

Pak, Jenny Hyun Chung. *Korean American Women: Stories of Acculturation and Changing Selves.* New York and London: Routledge, 2006.

Song, Young I. *Battered Women in Korean Immigrant Families: The Silent Scream.* New York: Garland, 1996.

Song, Young I., and Ailee Moon. *Korean American Women: From Tradition to Modern Feminism.* Westport, CT: Greenwood/Praeger, 1998.

KOREATOWNS

A Koreatown is a Korean ethnic enclave, usually in a city or metropolitan area, outside of the Korean Peninsula. There are usually Korean restaurants, stores, and other businesses in a Koreatown. Koreatowns came into being in the 19th century after Koreans started to immigrate to other countries. Store signs in Korean language are commonly seen in a Koreatown. These ethnic enclaves appear in many countries around the globe where Korean immigrants and their decedents as well as short-term residents live, such as China, Indonesia, Japan, the United Kingdom, Australia, Argentina, Mexico, Canada, and the United States.

In the United States, the largest number of Korean Americans live around the Los Angeles area in California. Its Koreatown commonly refers to the neighborhoods of Wilshire Center, Harvard Heights, and Pico Heights. Its center is located in central Los Angeles, near 8th Street and Western Avenue. After the 1965 Immigration Act, the Korean American population has increased dramatically. A number of them moved to this area and established various businesses. There are annual festivals such as the Korean Festival and Parade on Olympic Boulevard as well as community service organizations and centers, such as the Koreatown Immigrant Workers Alliance. According to the *Los Angeles Times* Mapping L.A. Project, more than half of the population in Koreatown is Latino, and 68 percent of the total residents were foreign born. During the 1992 Los Angeles Riots, sparked when police officers were acquitted of serious charges in severely beating unarmed Rodney King, many Korean and other Asian American stores around Koreatown were targeted, looted, and burned. Korean American store owners organized armed security groups to protect their properties. The violence and severe damage led to the Korean American community's increased political awareness and activism.

Koreatown, located around 32nd Street and Broadway in New York City. There are Koreatowns in Los Angeles, Chicago, Dallas, and other cities in the United States. (Daria Wilczynska/Dreamstime.com)

According to the 2010 U.S. census, the Korean American population in Manhattan nearly doubled since 2000, reaching 20,000. Koreatown in Manhattan is around 31st and 33rd Streets and Fifth and Sixth Avenues. Many Korean restaurants, bakeries, grocery stores, hair and nail salons, and other shops are concentrated here. The center, known as "Korea Way," is located on 32nd Street between Fifth Avenue and Broadway. More than half of Korean Americans in New York City live in Queens. The Long Island Koreatown is one the largest and fastest-growing enclaves since the 1980s.

The Albany Park neighborhood in Chicago, Illinois, has been known as a Koreatown since the 1980s. A Korean television station (WOCH-CD Channel 41), a Korean radio station (1330 AM), and two Korean-language newspapers are located in the neighborhood. Most Korean stores are on Lawrence Avenue between Kedzie and Pulaski. In December 1992, the Chicago City Council unanimously approved an ordinance designating the stretch of Lawrence Avenue from Western to Pulaski as "Seoul Drive" in order to honor the Korean business owners who have helped revitalize the local business strip. The street's official name remains unchanged. The council also named a portion of the surrounding neighborhood Koreatown but later rescinded that decision.

The concentrated area of Korean businesses and community centers in the San Francisco Bay Area is along Oakland's Telegraph Avenue between 20th and 35th Streets. Known as Koreatown-Northgate, the neighborhood has a large African American population. Dallas has the largest Korean American population in Texas. Besides the majority of Korean American business presence, there are also some Chinese and Vietnamese stores in this area. Koreatowns also exist in Philadelphia, Denver, and Washington, D.C., as well as other areas.

Lan Dong

See also: Chinatown (New York City); Chinatown (San Francisco); Korean American Immigration; Little Saigons; Little Tokyo (Los Angeles)

Further Reading

Hoeffel, Elizabeth M., Sonya Rastogi, Myoung Ouk Kim, and Hasan Shahid. "The Asian Population: 2010." U.S. Census Bureau, March 2012, http://www.census .gov/prod/cen2010/briefs/c2010br-11.pdf.

Joravsky, Ben. "Sign of the Times: In Albany Park, A Dispute over 'Seoul Drive' and 'Korea Town.'" Chicago's Official Reader, April 29, 1993, http://www.chicagoreader .com/chicago/signs-of-the-times-in-albany-park-a-dispute-over-seoul-drive-and -korea-town/Content?oid=881859.

Kwak, Tae-Hwan, and Seong Hyong Lee, eds. *The Korean-American Community: Present and Future.* Seoul, Korea: Kyungnam University Press, 1991.

"Mapping L.A." *Los Angeles Times,* 2000, http://maps.latimes.com/neighborhoods/.

Totten, George O., and H. Eric Schockman, eds. *Community in Crisis: The Korean American Community after the Los Angeles Civil Unrest of April 1992.* Los Angeles: Center for Multiethnic and Transnational Studies, University of Southern California, 1994.

L

LAOTIAN AMERICAN CULTURE

Even though some immigrants had moved from Laos to the United States before the 1970s, most Laotian immigrants began to arrive in America shortly after the Vietnam War. The majority of Laotian Americans residing in the United States were refugees who escaped Laos during the war and its chaotic aftermath in the 1970s and 1980s. The passage of the Indochina Migration and Refugee Assistance Act in 1975 led to the growing number of immigrants from Laos. Their number increased dramatically in the 1980s and continued to grow in the 1990s, although at a slower rate. By 2000, the Laotian American population reached 167,792 (Bankston and Hidalgo 2007, 625). According to the 2010 U.S. census, Laotian Americans make up 0.08 percent of the total U.S. population (Hoeffel, Rastogi, Kim, and Shahid 2012). These census data include Hmong immigrants from Laos. Because Hmongs have distinct cultural traditions, languages, and identity, they are generally identified as Hmong Americans instead of Laotian Americans. The largest Laotian American populations reside in California, Texas, Minnesota, Washington, Tennessee, Illinois, North Carolina, Georgia, Florida, and Oregon.

Tradition and Practices

Many Laotian Americans retain their traditional values in the United States. The family is of high value to Laotians. Many Laotian Americans live in close proximity to their extended families. Children are generally expected to respect their parents; grown children take care of their elders. Buddhism has a particularly important influence on Laotian life in many ways. Laotian American communities have built Buddhist temples in the United States, known as *wats*. Many of them are located in California. Prominent temples include among others Wat Lao Buddhavong near Washington, D.C.; Wat Lao Buddharam of San Diego, California; Wat Lao of S. Farmington in Minnesota; Wat Lao Buddhamamakaram of Columbus, Ohio; and Wat Lao Mixayaram and Wat Lao Dhammacetiyaram of Seattle, Washington. Besides religious practices, Buddhist teaching also affects everyday life, holidays, and festivals in Laotian American communities. The Pha Vet is an important festival to commemorate the life of the Buddha in the fourth month of the lunar calendar. Another important festival, the Boon Bang Fay, celebrates the Buddha in the sixth month of the lunar calendar.

Laotian Americans have established various community-based organizations to help one another and to represent the interests of their communities. Located in Washington State, the Coalition of Lao Mutual Assistance coordinates efforts and activities of 10 Laotian organizations and provides counseling, tutoring, and other services to the community. Founded in 1996, the Lao American Organization of Elgin (LAOE) strives to grow and advance the Lao community in the area. The LAOE organizes various events to celebrate the Lao culture and provide financial assistance, health and other services, and education programs to adults and youths in the community.

The National Association for the Education and Advancement of Cambodian, Laotian, and Vietnamese Americans (NAFEA) serves Southeast Asian professionals in education, social services, and community development. Its mission is to promote and support the advancement of Southeast Asians, including Laotian Americans, through education, advocacy, networking, and cross-cultural exchange. The NAFEA sponsors conferences, publishes the journal *Journal of Southeast Asian American Education and Advancement,* and provides scholarships, other services, and resources to community members. The Lao Human Rights Council (LHRC) is a nonprofit, nonpartisan, nongovernmental refugee and human rights organization. It has chapters in Colorado, Wisconsin, and Minnesota. The LHRC conducts research and provides information regarding the struggles of Laotian and Hmong refugees. Based in Washington, D.C., Lao Veterans of America is a Laotian and Hmong American veterans' organization.

Founded in 2007 in San Diego, *Lao Roots Magazine* was the national Laotian American publication. Published in English, this magazine mainly targets younger generations of Laotian Americans. Since 2009 the *Lao American Magazine,* an independent online journal based in northern California, has featured stories about Laotian American history, experience, and culture.

Directed by Ellen Kuras (1959–) and Thavisouk Phrasavath (1964–), the documentary film *The Betrayal* (2008) presents the story of a family forced to leave Laos during the Vietnam War. The film won a Spectrum Award for the Fall Frame Documentary Film Festival and was nominated for an Oscar for best documentary.

Bryan Thao Worra (1973–) is a Laotian American poet, fiction writer, and playwright. His books include *On the Other Side of the Eye* (2007), *Touching Detonations* (2003), *Winter Ink* (2008), *Barrow* (2009), and *The Tuk Tuk Diaries: My Dinner with Cluster Bombs* (2003). He is the first Laotian American to receive a fellowship in literature from the National Endowment for the Arts. He received the Asian Pacific Leadership Award from the State Council on Asian Pacific Minnesotans for Leadership in the Arts in 2009 and the Science Fiction Poetry Association Elgin Award for Book of the Year in 2014. He was a cultural Olympian representing Laos during the 2012 London Summer Olympics.

Khan (Bob) Malaythong (1981–) is an American badminton player. He was born in Laos and moved to the United States at the age of eight. He qualified for the U.S. badminton team, playing doubles with Howard Bach (1979–) at the 2008 Summer Olympics.

Jujubee, born Airline Inthyrath in 1984, is an American drag queen and reality television personality of Lao heritage. He was a contestant on *RuPaul's Drag Race* (season 2) and *RuPaul's All Stars Drag Race*. Jujubee has performed throughout the United States with *RuPaul's Drag Race Tour* and has appeared in music videos.

Lan Dong

See also: Buddhism; Theravada Buddhism

Further Reading

Bankston, Carl L., III, and Danielle Antoinette Hidalgo. "Southeast Asia: Laos, Cambodia, Thailand." In *The New Americans: A Guide to Immigration since 1965,* edited by Mary C. Waters, Reed Ueda, and Helen B. Marrow, 625–640. Cambridge, MA: Harvard University Press, 2007.

Hoeffel, Elizabeth M., Sonya Rastogi, Myoung Ouk Kim, and Hasan Shahid. "The Asian Population: 2010." U.S. Census Bureau, March 2012, http://www.census.gov/prod/cen2010/briefs/c2010br-11.pdf.

Proudfoot, Robert. *Even the Birds Don't Sound the Same Here: The Laotian Refugees Search for Heart in American Culture.* New York: Peter Lang, 1990.

Rantala, Judy Austin. *Laos: Caught in the Web; The Vietnam War Years.* Bangkok, Thailand: Orchid, 2004.

Shah, Bindi V. *Laotian Daughters: Working toward Community, Belonging, and Environmental Justice.* Philadelphia: Temple University Press, 2012.

Zasloff, Joseph J., and Leonard Unger, eds. *Laos: Beyond the Revolution.* New York: St. Martin's, 1991.

LGBTQ ASIAN AMERICANS

The construction of sexual and racial identities possesses a comparatively recent history that we can trace along lines that follow those in other hyphenated American communities. Immigrant communities in the United States have sometimes resorted to fictionalizing the reality of their homelands, even going

George Takei (1937–)

George Takei has become one of the boldest and most recognized spokespersons for gay rights and Asian American history via effective use of social media. Well known for his iconic role as Mr. Sulu on the original television series *Star Trek,* Takei became one of the most visible symbols and spokespersons for both gay rights and the historical significance of Japanese American internment. During the cult science fiction show's run from 1966 to 1969, the role of Mr. Sulu was notable for both its visibility and intentional avoidance of stereotypes, all presented in a setting that promised a more diverse and egalitarian future. Together with most of the original cast, he reprised the role in the *Star Trek* films 1 through 6 (1979–1991). After California governor Arnold Schwarzenegger vetoed the state bill granting gays and lesbians the right to marry in 2005, Takei came out in the media as gay.

Takei and husband Brad Altman (now Brad Takei) were married in 2008 in the Japanese American National Museum in Los Angeles, an institution for which Takei served on its board of trustees. Fellow *Star Trek* actors Walter Koenig and Nichelle Nichols served as best man and matron of honor in their wedding party. Since 2011, Takei has become one of the most popular celebrity commentators online, using social media to promote messages of social justice as well as his recent projects such as *Allegiance,* a musical about a family's experience with Japanese American internment. When speaking publicly about the Broadway-bound project, Takei has said that being Asian American in post–World War II America meant that you were automatically suspect and forced into the isolated contradictory category of enemy nonaliens. Aside from his online presence, Takei continues to do voice acting for popular animated shows such as *The Simpsons* and *Adventure Time.*

as far as denying the authenticity or existence of sexual difference among Asians. This denial feeds into larger misperceptions of Asian Americans. Lesbian, gay, bisexual, transgender, intersexed, and queer Asian Americans, like all those who inhabit multiple and overlapping identities, can face challenges of contradictory allegiances and oppressions within these intersections. Rather than remaining invisible, queer Asian Americans have asserted their importance in connection with a larger Asian American political framework, forming both within and running parallel to other activist movements.

Mirroring the development of LGBT activism and legitimization of sexual identities, queer Asian Americans formed coalitions for numerous purposes. Early Asian American LGBTQ groups had multiple origins, some independently formed as local means of mutual support within specific ethnic communities, others in connection with larger national-level LGBTQ and Asian American organizations. Similarly, some Asian American clubs originated on college campuses in connection with larger campus groups. In the 1980s and 1990s, initiatives were started to combat the AIDS crisis more broadly within specific Asian communities. These organizations faced similar challenges and splintering that occurred in other political action groups, criticisms that included explicit and implicit exclusion of marginalized groups and women and neglecting issues outside the bounds of white male experience.

However, many early activists did not capitulate to divided loyalties and worked for social change in multiple arenas: civil rights, feminism, environmentalism, antiwar, and antipoverty. In 1977, librarian and activist Dan C. Tsang wrote a mobilizing essay titled "Gay Awareness" in the early national Asian American publication *The Bridge*. In it Tsang recounted how he first identified as gay at the 1974 Third World People's Solidarity Conference in Ann Arbor, Michigan, standing together with a multiracial group of people dismayed at a speaker's homophobic remarks. At the first gay March on Washington in 1979, lesbian poet and activist Michiyo Fukaya (also known as Michiyo Cornell) gave a speech about her struggles as a single mother of color and an Asian American lesbian, calling for collective action to combat the oppressions faced by those whose difficulties go unnoticed. Writer Merle Woo was a pioneer of Asian American studies and along with poet Kitty Tsui was active in a number of foundational Asian American feminist, socialist, and LGBTQ groups and actions, also speaking often about the need for economic justice and the rights of immigrants and workers. Civil rights and AIDS activist Kiyoshi Kuromiya had participated in Congress of Racial Equality actions in the 1960s as well as Martin Luther King Jr.'s 1963 March on Washington. Kuromiya served as a delegate from Philadelphia's Gay Liberation Front, of which he was a founder, to the Black Panther's People's Revolutionary Constitutional Convention at Temple University in 1970. Kuromiya continued his efforts at unifying different groups during his work in AIDS activism in the 1980s and 1990s. In 1989 he founded the Critical Path Project, an important health information resource that utilized new technologies to freely share needed information between people with HIV/AIDS, researchers, and outreach activists.

Protest rallies held in response to the 1990 Broadway run of *Miss Saigon* both brought together and highlighted internal conflict. Charges of racist and sexist portrayals of Asian women and men as well as the casting of white actors performing in yellowface caused an organized response from groups such as the Asian Lesbians of the East Coast, Gay Asian and Pacific Islander Men of New York, ACT UP, and Gay Men of African Descent. Two prominent New York City LGBTQ organizations—the Lambda Legal Defense and Education

Fund and the Lesbian & Gay Community Services Center—chose to feature this production as part of fund-raising campaigns. While this controversy may not have been resolved satisfactorily, it exposed a need for improved dialogue and the possibility of effective alliances.

Successful coalition building requires that attention be paid to the diversity of experiences and priorities that exist within and between the communities involved. The differences of self-identification and homophobia that exist in different traditions cannot be easily erased. Some Asian cultures contain religious practices that explicitly condemn homosexuality, such as with Christianity in certain Korean and Filipino congregations or with Islam in some South and Southeast Asian groups. Other Asian cultures also contain elements of conservatism, conformity, and shame that create barriers to acceptance. At the same time, taboos vary widely in different contexts, and queer presence can be even more visible than in American mainstream culture in certain locations. In historical texts and artwork, homosexual life is depicted readily, particularly in Japanese and Chinese literature. Legal restrictions were generally lenient, at least for those in privileged social classes.

Historical representation of queer life in Asian cultures often conflates homosexuality and performative drag in theatrical contexts. This association with role-playing also involved obligatory identification with gender binaries in relationships (i.e., tops/bottoms, butch/femme). While this arrangement allowed for a measure of freedom, it kept within policed limitations and permitted participants a mimicry of heteronormative relations. The traditional form of Japanese theater, kabuki, while originally permitting female and young male performers, was restricted to adult male performers in the 17th century. Many of the performers who specialized in female roles rose to great prominence, and the tradition continues into contemporary times. An equivalent Japanese female-only theatrical troupe called the Takarazuka Revue began in 1914. In the United States, Asian American drag queens are most visible in Asian-themed cabarets and on reality television shows such as *RuPaul's Drag Race*.

The Chinese Exclusion Act of 1882 and related laws that barred immigration and naturalization to Chinese migrants after the first waves of immigration during the California Gold Rush and the building projects of the transcontinental railroads resulted in laborer communities where men greatly outnumbered women. Historians refer to the resulting social structure in Chinatowns as bachelor societies, characterized by male communal living arrangements and female prostitutes with the suggestion that some sexual stereotypes of Asians originate in the perceptions of asexual, hardworking, emasculated males and sexualized, objectified, servile females. In a work often referred to in Asian American studies, David Henry Hwang's 1988 Tony Award–winning play *M. Butterfly* addresses Western ideas of the feminized Asian male.

The experience of queer Asian Americans prior to the start of the gay rights movement is difficult to discuss without speculation and conjecture, such as with rumors surrounding early Hollywood actress Anna May Wong. Dr. Margaret Chung, born in Santa Barbara, California, in 1889, became in 1916 the first known Chinese American woman to earn a medical degree. Her personal correspondence and personal life choices lend weight to suggestion that she was one of the earliest known lesbian Asian American public figures. The adversities that Chung faced due to a compounded mix of sexism, racism, and homophobia in all the communities that she inhabited make her story valuable to the time line of LGBTQ personal histories. Her rejection of a conventional gender performance and presentation caused some difficulties with the home community she sought to support, but she took on a political role by supporting American troops overseas after the Japanese attack on Manchuria. Chung took on the public persona of "Mom Chung" who wrote letters to over 1,000 "sons" in the military.

Visibility of queer or straight Asian Americans has been very limited in American media. Anna May Wong was typecast as being either a villainous dragon lady or a pathetic victim. In 1951, Wong starred in a short-lived television show called *The Gallery of Madame Liu-Tsong* in which she played a detective. In another short-lived and problematic attempt years later in 1994, comedian Margaret Cho starred in a family sitcom about a Korean American family titled *All-American Girl.* Cho continued with a successful stand-up career afterward but frequently referred to how Asian stereotypes plagued the show's production. Cho has also been an active supporter of LGBTQ rights, winning her awards from the advocacy groups GLAAD (Gay & Lesbian Alliance against Defamation) and Lamda Legal. Another comedian, Alex Mapa, has performed shows titled *America's Gaysian Sweetheart* as well as worked with political action groups such as the Human Rights Campaign and the Matthew Shepard Foundation.

So far there have been a few small films that have successfully depicted queer Asian stories. In Nisha Ganatra's 1999 film *Chutney Popcorn,* an Indian American lesbian becomes a surrogate mother for her sister. In 2004's *Saving Face,* director Alice Wu tells the story of a Chinese American lesbian surgeon, her girlfriend, and the surgeon's single mother. Patrick Wang's 2011 film *In the Family* more interestingly presents a story about a southern Asian American man who is fighting for custody of his white boyfriend's son. Ang Lee's 1993 film *The Wedding Banquet* depicts an interracial gay couple, Wai-Tung and Simon, living in New York who concoct a fake marriage with an illegal immigrant woman to satisfy the demands of Wai-Tung's Taiwanese parents. While this comedic film is an uncritical fantasy, it serves as a novel presentation of certain aspects of Asian American and gay life in contrast to what is presented as traditional cultural expectations. The typical culture clashes do not play out as the film resolves familial acceptance and reconciliation.

In contrast, Gregg Araki took an antiassimilationist approach in his 1992 film *The Living End*, one of the first films that established the New Queer Cinema genre. Arthur Dong's documentaries examine the history of homophobia, gay bashing, and Asian American representation as well as the experience of Chinese immigrants in America. His 1995 film *Out Rage '69*, part of the series *The Question of Equality*, provides an important history of the gay liberation movement. For further analysis, video artist and academic Hoang Tan Nguyen writes about Asian male sexuality in American and European film and pornography.

Numerous writers and poets follow in the activist footsteps of Michiyo Fukaya, Kitty Tsui, and Merle Woo. Poet and artist Staceyann Chin performs and writes about growing up Chinese and Jamaican and coming out as a lesbian. Poet Justin Chin's work involves issues such as sticky rice and rice queens in gay male dating circles, terms that refer to intra- and interracial sexual preferences. Irshad Manji, human rights activist and director of New York University's Moral Courage Project, writes about the need for progressive reform in Islamic cultures. Lawyer and activist Urvashi Vaid's 1995 book *Virtual Equality: The Mainstreaming of Gay and Lesbian Liberation* advocated a pragmatic approach balancing inclusion with political strategy.

In politics, a few firsts had been accomplished by the start of the 21st century. In 2006, Kim Coco Iwamoto became the first transgendered state official when she won a seat on Hawai'i's Board of Education. Christopher Cabaldon was elected as mayor of West Sacramento, California, in 2004; he was reelected in 2006, 2008, and 2010. In 2012, Pamela Ki Mai Chen became the first Asian American lesbian federal judge. Mark Takano was elected U.S. representative for California's 41st Congressional District, becoming the first nonwhite openly gay member of Congress in 2012.

Gay Marriage

The 1982 murder of Vincent Chin, a young Chinese American who was beaten to death in Detroit by two angry unemployed auto workers who believed that the Japanese auto industry was taking away American jobs, served as a rallying call to Asian American activists and also served as a common cause to further cement a coalition between different Asian American organizations. Journalist Helen Zia led the protests that followed the light sentencing of the murderers and called national attention to the problem of violence against Asians. Zia's efforts led to the establishment of hate crime laws to be applied in similar cases.

Zia has since spoken out against the Proposition 8 proposal to ban same-sex/gay marriage in California. Zia married her wife in 2004 and again in 2008 as allowed by changes in the law.

The debate surrounding the legalization of gay marriage has mobilized queer celebrities and activists to speak out publicly in support of the movement. In 2009 and 2010 Iraq War veteran Dan Choi, who was discharged from the army because of the "Don't Ask, Don't Tell" policy in effect from 1993 to 2011, became a visible spokesperson on behalf of the movement opposing it. The actor George Takei has become one of the boldest and most recognizable spokespersons for gay rights and Asian American history via effective use of social media. Takei, well known for his iconic role as Mr. Sulu on the original television series *Star Trek*, became one of the most visible symbols and spokespersons for both gay rights and the historical significance of Japanese American internment. After California governor Arnold Schwarzenegger

An advocate for LGBTQ rights, George Takei waves to the crowd as the official Celebrity Grand Marshal of the Seattle Pride Parade on June 29, 2014. (James Anderson/iStockPhoto.com)

vetoed the state bill granting gays and lesbians the right to marry in 2005, Takei came out in the media as gay. Takei and husband Brad Altman (now Brad Takei) were married in 2008. Since 2011, George Takei has become one of the most popular celebrity commentators online, using social media to promote messages of social justice.

Ann Matsuuchi

See also: Popular Culture, Asian Americans and

Further Reading

Eng, David L., and Alice Y. Hom. *Q & A: Queer in Asian America.* Philadelphia: Temple University Press, 1998.

Kumashiro, Kevin K. *Restoried Selves: Autobiographies of Queer Asian/Pacific American Activists.* New York: Harrington Park Press, 2004.

Leong, Russell. *Asian American Sexualities: Dimensions of the Gay and Lesbian Experience.* New York and London: Routledge, 1996.

Out Rage '69 [*The Question of Equality, Part 1*]. Directed by Arthur Dong. KQED, 1995. VHS.

Shah, Nayan. *Contagious Divides: Epidemics and Race in San Francisco's Chinatown.* Berkeley: University of California Press, 2001.

Ting, Jennifer. "Bachelor Society: Deviant Heterosexuality and Asian American Historiography." In *Privileging Positions: The Sites of Asian American Studies,* edited by Gary Y. Okihiro et al., 271–279. Pullman: Washington State University Press, 1995.

Tsang, Daniel C. "Gay Awareness." *Bridge: An Asian American Perspective* 3–4 (February 1975): 44–45.

Vaid, Urvashi. *Virtual Equality: The Mainstreaming of Gay and Lesbian Liberation.* New York: Anchor Books, 1995.

Zia, Helen. *Asian American Dreams: The Emergence of an American People.* New York: Farrar, Straus, and Giroux, 2000.

LINSANITY

The term "Linsanity" refers to the euphoric craze and culture surrounding National Basketball Association (NBA) player Jeremy Lin. Linsanity also refers to Lin's seven-game winning streak with the New York Knicks in February 2012. Lin began as a bench player and quickly became a starting point guard for the Knicks due to his breakout game against the New Jersey Nets. Lin is the first American basketball player of Chinese and Taiwanese descent to play in the NBA. He is also the first NBA player to graduate from Harvard in almost 60 years. In his first five career starts, Lin scored 136 points—the most by any player since the NBA and the American Basketball Association merger in 1976. He averaged 25.0 points, 9.9 assists, and 2.2 steals in his first nine starts, which has not been done by an NBA player in 65 years.

History and Origins

Jeremy Shu-How Lin was born in Los Angeles, California, on August 23, 1988, and was raised in Palo Alto, California. He is six feet three inches tall and weighs 200 pounds. Lin's grandparents are from China; his parents are from Taiwan. Lin started playing basketball in the Amateur Athletic Union when he was 10 years old. Appointed team captain in his final year at Palo Alto, Lin helped lead the Vikings to win the state championship.

New York Knicks' Jeremy Lin driving to the basket during the second quarter of an NBA basketball game at Madison Square Garden in New York City, February 4, 2012. (AP Photo/Bill Kostroun)

Lin was named the Northern California Division II Player of the Year as a senior. He applied to 11 colleges but was not awarded any Division I athletic scholarships and chose to attend Harvard University because he was guaranteed to play on the basketball team. At Harvard, Lin had a 3.1 grade point average with an economics major and a minor in sociology. He "was the first player in the history of the league to record over 1,450 points (he finished with 1,483), 450 rebounds (487), 400 assists (406), and 200 steals (225)" (Dalrymple 2012, 117–118). Lin went undrafted and played for the Dallas Mavericks in their summer league team. He signed with the Golden State Warriors on July 21, 2010.

During his rookie season with the Warriors, Lin went three times to the NBA Developmental League, a minor league basketball organization. In his first NBA season, the Warriors waived Lin on December 9, 2011, to clear roster space, and Lin signed with the Houston Rockets within 48 hours. He was with the Rockets for 12 days; they cut him on Christmas morning of 2011. Lin then signed with the New York Knicks on December 27 as third-string point guard. Lin's two-year contract was about to expire. If the Knicks were to waive Lin, it would most likely end his NBA career.

Linsanity

The Knicks had an 8–15 record and lost 11 of their last 13 games. The Nets was the Knicks' final game of three games in three nights. On February 4, 2012, Lin came off the bench and played considerable minutes in the Nets game because of teammates' injuries. In desperation the coach, Mike D'Antoni, allowed Lin to play. Lin scored 25 points, seven assists, and five rebounds. He had career highs in every category.

Lin was granted starting point guard in the next home game against the Utah Jazz on February 6, 2012. In this game, the Knicks were without their leaders: forward Amar'e Stoudemire, forward Carmelo Anthony, and starting point guard Baron Davis. In his first career start, Lin finished with career highs: 28 points and 8 assists. In the following away game against the Washington Wizards on February 8, 2012, Lin scored 23 points with 10 assists and had two turnovers against 2010 NBA top draft pick John Wall. The day before, the Knicks guaranteed Lin's contract.

The Los Angeles Lakers played at Madison Square Garden (MSG) on February 10, 2012. Lin had a career high in points, 38, and seven assists. Lin's 38 points outscored Kobe Bryant's 34 points, one of the most distinguished NBA guards. In the last three games Lin scored 89 points, the most points by a NBA player in the first three starts in the modern era. The Lakers game was a key moment in Linsanity because the game was played in MSG in front of a national audience on ESPN and against the world's most famous basketball team. On February 11, 2012, the Knicks played an away game against the Minnesota Timberwolves. Lin scored 20 points, eight assists, and six rebounds. He totaled 106 points after his first four career starts, which was unprecedented in the NBA.

On February 14, 2012, the Knicks had an away game against the Toronto Raptors. In the final minutes of the fourth quarter, the game was tied 87–87. Lin had the ball in the last seconds and won the game by drilling a 3-pointer with 2.2 seconds left on the clock. He had 27 points and 11 assists. In the last game of the seven-game winning stretch, the Knicks had a home game against the Sacramento Kings on February 15, 2012. Lin finished with 10 points and 13 career-high assists. He accrued 146 points in his first six career starts—5 more than Michael Jordan. Lin scored 136 points in his first five career starts, breaking Shaquille O'Neal's record of 129 points. Lin totaled 200 points and 76 assists after his first eight starts.

Throughout this seven-game winning streak in two weeks, Lin became an instant global phenomenon. From February 4 to 12, Lin's jersey #17 was the top seller at NBAStore.com, shipping to 22 countries around the world. MSG's stock value increased 10 percent. There was a 70 percent increase in television ratings for the Knicks games. His social media following skyrocketed, and he appeared on the cover of numerous magazines. According to Global Language Monitor, "Linsanity" was acknowledged as an English-language word by February 24, 2012. In April, Lin made *Time* magazine's 2012 "Top 100 Most Influential People in the World." In July 2012, ESPN awarded Lin with the ESPY Award (Excellence in Sports Performance Yearly Award) for "Breakthrough Athlete of the Year."

There was high praise during Linsanity, but there was also negative criticism and racial commentary on Lin. A writer was fired because he used a Chinese racial slur in his headline "Chink in the Armor," posted on ESPN Mobile. The MSG regional cable television network showed an image of Lin's face emerging from a broken fortune cookie. Some concentrated on Lin's weaknesses, such as his high turnover rate.

Lin's story attracts people of all different categories because he is an Asian American, an evangelical Christian, a Harvard graduate, and an underdog. Being one of the first Asian Americans to play basketball in the NBA and the only current Asian American NBA player, Lin is a trailblazer. He redefines the images of Asian American masculinity particularly in American media. Linsanity is inspiring for many because of the underdog aspect of his story. Some have overlooked and disregarded Lin's capabilities, but he persevered and continued to move forward with his willpower and confidence to conquer his dream of playing in the NBA.

The Knicks clinched a playoff spot in the 2012 Eastern Conference. Lin tore his meniscus in March and did not play for the remainder of the season. He became a free agent in the summer of 2012. On July 2012 Lin signed a three-year $25 million contract with the Rockets—his only offer. In May 2012, the U.S. Patent and Trademark Office granted Lin the trademark for "Linsanity." On January 20, 2013, *Linsanity*, a documentary film about Lin's story directed by Evan Leong, was released at the Sundance Film Festival. In the summer of 2015, Lin became a free agent after playing for two years with the Houston Rockets and for a year with the Los Angeles Lakers.

Lilly Catherine Chen

See also: Sports, Asian Americans in

Further Reading

Amira, Dan. "Jeremy Lin Is Now Bigger Than Jesus Christ." *New York Magazine*, February 13, 2012, http://nymag.com/daily/intelligencer/2012/02/jeremy-lin-is-now-bigger-than-jesus-christ.html.

Dalrymple, Timothy. *Jeremy Lin: The Reason for the Linsanity*. New York: Center Street, 2012.

"David Stern Fascinated by Jeremy Lin." ESPN New York, February 24, 2012, http://espn.go.com/new-york/nba/story/_/id/7608874/david-stern-says-never-seen-anything-jeremy-lin-frenzy.

Goldman, Tom. "Will Life after 'Lin' Change NBA Recruiting?" NPR, February 21, 2012, http://www.npr.org/2012/02/21/147217237/will-life-after-lin-change-nba-recruiting.

Helin, Kurt. "Jeremy Lin Now Owns Trademark for 'Linsanity.'" NBC Sports, May 31, 2012, http://probasketballtalk.nbcsports.com/2012/05/31/jeremy-lin-now-owns-trademark-for-linsanity/.

"Jeremy Lin." Men's Basketball, Harvard University, http://www.gocrimson.com/sports/mbkb/2009–10/bios/Jeremy_Lin_Bio.

"The Jeremy Lin Phenomenon: 'Linsanity' by the Numbers." The Week, February 16, 2012, http://theweek.com/article/index/224492/the-jeremy-lin-phenomenon-linsanity-by-the-numbers.

Leitch, Will. "According to Sports Illustrated, Jeremy Lin Is the Second Most Famous Knick of All-Time." *New York Magazine*, February 22, 2012, http://nymag.com/daily/sports/2012/02/jeremy-lin-is-the-second-most-famous-knick-ever.html.

Linsanity. Written by Aaron Strongoni, directed by Evan Leong. Ketchup Entertainment, 2013. DVD.

"Lin-sanity Accepted into English Lexicon . . . Lin-ough Already!?" The Global Language Monitor, February 24, 2012, http://www.languagemonitor.com/sports/lin-sanity-accepted-into-english-lexicon-lin-ough-already/.

LITERATURE, ASIAN AMERICAN

Published in 1974 and edited by Jeffery Paul Chan, Frank Chin, Lawson Inada, and Shawn Wong, *Aiiieeeee! An Anthology of Asian-American Writers* is one of the first definitive attempts to explore literature of, by, and for Asian Americans. There were only 14 authors included in the volume, but it inspired generations of self-identified Asian American writers and sparked critical poetic and political questions such as the following: What is Asian American literature? Is it only by Asian Americans? If so, who counts as an Asian American? Or is Asian American literature simply any creative writing that deals with the Asian immigrant experience in the United States? What role does literature even play

Sui Sin Far (Edith Maude Eaton, 1865–1914)

Born in 1865 and writing under the pen name Sui Sin Far, Edith Maude Eaton is recognized as the first writer of Asian descent to publish in the United States. Her father, Edward Eaton, was an English merchant who traded frequently in China. It was in Shanghai where he met Grace "Lotus Blossom" Trefusis, the adopted Chinese daughter of English missionaries. Despite the period's taboos against interracial relationships, the two got married and had 14 children. Edith Eaton was the eldest and known in her family by her nickname Sui Sin Far (Water Lily). The Eaton family lived in England until the early 1870s before immigrating to New York and then Montreal, Canada. At the age of 18, Eaton began her writing career as a typesetter for a local newspaper. In 1888 she started publishing short stories and newspaper articles. Though Eaton was biracial, she never attempted to pass as white and openly identified herself as Chinese American to her readers.

During the 1890s, Eaton traveled from Canada to the Caribbean and eventually settled in Seattle and then San Francisco. During her travels, she produced several short stories and articles that featured complex Chinese American female characters who challenged racist and sexist stereotypes of the time. In 1909 she moved to Boston, where she compiled her stories into a collection titled *Mrs. Spring Fragrance*. In some of these stories she explores the challenges and fulfillment that comes from interracial relationships, the complexity of bicultural identities, and the toll of racism suffered by Asians in the United States. In 1913 and in poor health, Eaton returned to Montreal, where she died a year later. Her writings languished in anonymity until 1995, when a new version of *Mrs. Spring Fragrance* was published and Eaton was lauded as a matriarch of Asian American literature.

in those experiences? And ultimately, what is the relationship between the aesthetics of such literature and its sociohistorical contexts?

In the first critical study of Asian American literature published in 1982, Elaine Kim powerfully shows that Asian American literature "elucidates the social history of Asians in the United States" (Kim 1982, xv). The very emergence of the concept of Asian American literature can be traced to the yellow power movement of the 1960s as Asian immigrant communities fought anti-Asian policies, de facto segregation, and outright violations of their civil rights. The embrace of a Pan-Asian coalitional identity despite the undeniable differences between Asian ethnic groups was necessary to combat the representation and treatment of all Asians as perpetual foreigners and inscrutable "Orientals." Asian American literature thus began as a collective attempt to tell the stories of these immigrants on their own terms in response to their treatment in the United States and as a way of intervening in those social conditions. This literature can thus be divided into an initial period from the mid-1800s to 1965 and from 1965 to today, with each period defined by prevailing themes. Throughout both periods, however, Asian American literature proves itself to be a complex and dynamic cultural tool used by authors to represent Asian American identities in response to and intervention in larger sociopolitical contexts in the United States and their homelands.

History and Origins

Asian immigrant communities began forming in the United States in the latter half of the 19th century and were shaped by the workings of colonialism and capitalist expansion in the Asia-Pacific region. From the close of the 1800s up to the geopolitical transformations of the Cold War, this literature has thus been characterized by predominant themes of imperialism in the Asia-Pacific region, immigration to the United States, and racialization of Asian immigrants as cheap labor.

Western penetration of the East in pursuit of new markets, raw materials, and political dominance has resulted in uneven political, social, and economic relationships between the two hemispheres, creating the conditions for Asian immigration into the United States. From Britain's Opium Wars to Commodore Matthew Perry's gunboat diplomacy in Japan, aggressive imperial policies have destabilized local Asian economies and societies. Simultaneously, developing Western industries have actively recruited Asian immigrants to serve as low-wage labor, taking advantage of their noncitizenship status and pitting them against American workers. In particular, upon annexation of Hawai'i in 1898, Chinese, Japanese, Korean, and Filipino labor was fundamentally necessary to lucrative sugar cultivation. The majority of Asian immigrants in this period either settled in or entered the United States through Hawai'i, and texts by writers such as Haunani Kay Trask, Lois-Ann Yamanaka, and R. Zamora Linmark explore the effects of this plantation legacy and settler colonialism in Hawai'i.

Once in the United States, these immigrants had to reckon with racist perceptions of Asian inferiority and daily social marginalization. Because of antimiscegenation acts and the 1875 Page Act's ban on Asian female immigration, these early communities were predominantly bachelor societies concentrated in ethnic enclaves. An economic downturn in the 1880s exacerbated nativist fears over hordes of Chinese immigrants competing with white labor; as a result, Congress passed the 1882 Chinese Exclusion Act. Writer Sui Sin Far, also known as Edith Maude Eaton, published several short stories almost a decade later that explored the humanity of Chinatown inhabitants and the effects of anti-Asian laws. The motifs of Chinatown and the legacy of racist perceptions of "Chinamen" came to define 20th-century texts by Chinese American authors. Frank Chin's 1972 play *Chickencoop Chinaman*, for example, aims to debunk emasculating stereotypes of Chinese men born from their historical de facto segregation into bachelor societies. In contrast, authors such as Jade Snow Wong, Maxine Hong Kingston, and Fae Myenne Ng have importantly explored the experiences of Chinese American women and how they respond to the pressures of domestic racism as well as patriarchy in their own communities.

With the prohibition of Chinese immigration, Japanese sojourners were the next major wave of Asians to arrive. However, the Japanese government attempted to avoid racist treatment of its citizens and took an active role in screening migrants and encouraging women to travel, as they could serve as a "moralizing" presence and the foundation of respectable Japanese American communities. It was actually the issue of Japanese American children that ultimately caused the exclusion of Japanese immigrants. In 1908, San Francisco schools attempted to segregate Japanese American students. The Japanese government intervened, and in exchange for the schools abandoning segregationist policies, Japan agreed to limit the migration of its citizens. Enough Japanese immigrants had come to the United States by then, however, so that by the 1940s there were vibrant Japanese American communities concentrated in Hawai'i and on the West Coast. The bombing of Pearl Harbor on December 7, 1941, and the subsequent internment of 110,000 Japanese Americans, the majority of whom were citizens, have become dramatic central issues in the literature of this community. John Okada's *No-No Boy* (1957), Miné Okubo's *Citizen 13660* (1946), and Jeanne Wakatsuki Houston and

James D. Houston's *Farewell to Manzanar* (1973) powerfully critique the failure of U.S. democracy and the perceptions of Asians as inevitable racial Others.

The specter of Japanese villainy paradoxically improved the social visibility of other Asian ethnic groups in America. Until World War II, for example, U.S. policy had been to treat Korean immigrants as Japanese subjects; the low numbers of Korean immigrants in the early 20th century was due to the limitation of their immigration as part of Japan's policy of imperial control. The first novel published by a Korean author in the United States, though, was Younghill Kang's *The Grass Roof* (1931), which fictionalized the author's life in Korea and his rejection of service in the anti-Japanese resistance in favor of immigration to America. With the opening of World War II's Pacific theater, however, the United States came to denounce Japanese repression of Korean struggles for independence.

Moreover, in an attempt to combat Japanese attempts to form the Greater East Asian Co-Prosperity Sphere, the United States extended citizenship to Chinese living in the United States and actively recruited Filipino immigrants into military campaigns to liberate their homeland from Japanese occupation. Filipinos had been immigrating since the early 1900s, after the United States took possession of the islands following the Spanish-American War. This meant that Filipinos were considered U.S. nationals and were exempt from anti-Asian immigration policies, thus distinguishing their experiences from the Chinese and Japanese before them; it also ensured that Filipinos had already been exposed to American culture and society in their homeland before even embarking.

Early Filipino American literature, epitomized by the writings of Carlos Bulosan and Bienvenido Santos, critically explores the contradictions to U.S. depictions of itself as the land of equality in light of its colonial control of the islands and the domestic racism experienced on its shores. With recognition of Philippine independence, however, the national status of Filipinos was revoked, and they were subject to an immigration quota of just 50 per year. The end of World War II saw the close of American borders to immigration from the Asia-Pacific region. It would not be until the 1960s that new waves of immigrants would come and with them transformations to Asian America and its literature.

Contemporary Forms

Contemporaneous with the civil rights era, the Asian American movement was a conscientious attempt by Asian immigrant communities to call attention to their histories and insist that U.S. race relations were not just defined by a black-white paradigm. The legislative victories won in the name of this pan-ethnic identity revolutionized the nature of these communities, ironically challenging its unity. Following the Civil Rights Act, the 1965 Immigration Act revoked racist national quotas; as new immigrants from Southeast and South Asia entered the country throughout the 20th century, a shift in the recurring themes of Asian American literature occurred. The figures of the refugee and the model minority appeared in conjunction with previous representations of Asian immigrants as a Yellow Peril, while issues of labor and imperialism were complicated by the heterogeneity of new immigrants and their persisting transnationalism.

It is the emergence of writings by Southeast Asian Americans that is the most visible change in the post-1965 period, as these communities did not even exist before the Cold War. With the fall of Saigon, however, primarily Vietnamese refugees and so-called boat people were resettled all throughout the United States. With the assistance of charitable organizations, the government pursued a policy of geographic dispersal to ensure that no single American community received too large an influx of refugees. Receiving government assistance, these Southeast Asian communities sprung up in locations such as Louisiana that had never had any historical Asian presence. The writings of Vietnamese American authors such as Le Ly Hayslip, Andrew X. Pham, Aimee Phan, and le thi diem thuy explore the trauma of fleeing Vietnam, the challenges of the resettlement process, and the struggle to negotiate the legacies of the war and create a sense of Vietnamese American identity.

The experience and socioeconomic positions of Vietnamese refugees contrast with that of the majority of immigrants entering the United States post-1965. While the Immigration Act did away with the quota system, it also replaced the system with preference categories that prioritized visas for those reuniting with immediate family and who practiced professions suffering shortages in the United States. The result was an exponential increase in the number of Asian immigrants who had previously been underrepresented in earlier waves, leading to an explosion in Korean and South Asian communities. Moreover, whereas early 20th-century Asian immigration had been dominated by agricultural labor, highly skilled workers were needed to keep the United States economically and technologically competitive with socialist Russia and China. The influx of well-educated and professional Asian immigrants, some sponsored by immediate family members and joining already established communities, gave rise to the model minority myth.

The image of the successful Asian American as medical professional, college student, and entrepreneur seemingly proved the lack of racism in U.S. society and celebrated Asians for their work ethic and family values. Used in this way to keep more militant ethnic groups in check, "model minority" became a recurring trope in 21st-century Asian American literature as authors resisted how the myth erased the complexity of Asian American experience. Writers such as Chang-Rae Lee explored the toll of Asian Americans' position as racial middlemen, particularly after the 1991 Los Angeles Riots that resulted in the looting and destruction of the city's Koreatown.

The 1990s also saw the rise of our contemporary moment of globalization as U.S. manufacturing relocated to developing countries with cheaper production costs. The increased flows of information, products, capital, and culture have had contradictory effects. On one hand, linear narratives of immigration, settlement, and assimilation into the United States—whether ideally achieved or critically frustrated—have been complicated by recognition of persisting transnational ties between immigrants and their homelands. Asian migrants shuttle back and forth between countries; some follow elite cosmopolitan circuits enabled by international business, while others are vulnerable to flexible conditions of labor and work in service industries of global cities.

Both cases reveal the hybrid nature of Asian American identity that cannot be neatly confined to a single national space. The novel *Dogeaters* (1990) by Jessica Hagedorn opens and ends with letters from the United States to the Philippines and traces the travels and travails of Manila denizens who are nonetheless connected to those in the diaspora through the sharing of gossip, drama, and American pop culture. Jhumpa Lahiri's 1999 short story collection *The Interpreter of Maladies* focuses on the movements of her various characters back and forth between the United States and India and ultimately explores the desire for understanding that connects us all regardless of location.

The interconnectivity and transnationalism brought on by globalization have their consequences. In a post-9/11 world, such crossings and exchanges are violently policed in the name of the war on terror, and while President Barack Obama may be the "first Asian American president" because of his Hawai'ian and Indonesian homes in childhood and young adulthood, this is not to say that we are in a postracist society. For example, Alex Gilvarry's 2012 novel *Memoirs of a Non-Enemy Combatant* details the story of a Filipino American swept up on suspicion of terrorism in New York and held in a Guantánamo-like cell. Alluding to Japanese American internment, exploring how the Philippines (and Asia in general) was already transnational in earlier periods of imperialism, and playing with the protagonist's faith in the virtues of his new country, the novel suggests new directions in Asian American literature grounded in earlier histories of racialization and yet offering new explorations of Asian American identity in the age of globalization.

Amanda Solomon Amorao

See also: Autobiographies, Asian American; Fiction, Asian American

Further Reading

Chin, Frank, Jeffery Paul Chan, Lawson Fusao Inada, and Shawn Wong, eds. *Aiiieeeee! An Anthology of Asian-American Writers.* Washington, DC: Howard University Press, 1974.

Kim, Elaine. *Asian American Literature: An Introduction to the Writings and Their Social Context.* Philadelphia: Temple University Press, 1982.

Lee, Rachel. *The Americas of Asian American Literature: Gendered Fictions of Nation and Transnation.* Princeton, NJ: Princeton University Press, 1999.

Lowe, Lisa. *Immigrant Acts: On Asian American Cultural Politics.* Durham, NC: Duke University Press, 1996.

Lye, Coleen. *America's Asia: Racial Form and American Literature, 1893–1945.* Princeton, NJ: Princeton University Press, 2005.

Wong, Sau-Ling Cynthia. *Reading Asian American Literature: From Necessity to Extravagance.* Princeton, NJ: Princeton University Press, 1993.

LITTLE MANILAS

Little Manilas, also called Manilatowns or Historic Filipinotowns, refer to designated neighborhoods or areas that contain a significant number of Filipino or Filipino Americans who live alongside a largely non-Filipino population. In the United States, Little Manilas are often situated within or around densely populated urban regions and increasingly less so within rural areas.

Unlike traditional Chinatowns or Japantowns, which are usually defined as ethnic enclaves that support an economy focused on servicing a particular

Filipino Settlement across the United States

Filipinos today constitute a diverse group of Asian immigrants, and the complexities of their differences are largely reflected in the geography of their settlement. Contemporary "Little Manilas" are largely characterized by suburban settlement, particularly in California and New Jersey. The families living in these communities, especially among the first generation, reflect relatively high levels of household income and educational attainment. Yet in places such as Hawai'i, throughout waning communities in cities such as Stockton, California, and in inner-city neighborhoods such as the one in the South of Market district of San Francisco, Filipinos continue to struggle with poverty and obstacles to educational achievement.

ethnic population, Little Manilas are not always distinguished by Filipino-owned businesses with the exception of the Woodside neighborhood in New York and Waipahu in Oahu, Hawai'i. Due to the labor markets produced by previous immigration policies, local statutes, and exclusionary practices, Filipino immigrants were historically relegated to specific types of labor and continue to be underrepresented in business ownership throughout the United States compared to their Asian American counterparts.

Rather, the communal identity of Little Manilas is usually shaped by hometown organizations maintained by Filipino residents who share common regional origins in their homeland or are centered around Catholic churches. These institutions provide mutual aid and social services to support the continuous influx of new Filipino immigrants who continue to settle in large numbers throughout the United States.

History and Origins

The earliest record of a Filipino settlement in America describes a group of Filipino seafarers who fled a Spanish galleon trade ship docked at a port in Morro Bay, California, on October 18, 1587. As colonial subjects of Spain and gifted sailors, indigenous inhabitants from Luzon were used as deck hands and interpreters to help navigate the treacherous Manila-Acapulco galleon trade routes. The trade ships, which set sail only once or twice a year, connected Spain's colonies in the Americas between Mexico, Guam and the Marianas to the Philippines from 1565 to 1815.

Large groups of Filipino seafarers, called "Manila men," jumped ship and resettled outside of major ports in the United States and Mexico. The earliest community formed by Manila men was discovered on the outskirts of New Orleans, Louisiana, in St. Malo. An article published in an 1883 edition of *Harper's Weekly* revealed the presence of this discreet community of Filipinos who had lived along the bayou in stilt houses since 1763.

The First and Second Waves

The first systemic wave of Filipino settlement in the United States was initiated after the Philippines had become an official colony of the United States in 1898. Fleeing impoverished conditions in their home provinces particularly in the Luzon and Visayan regions, the majority of early Filipino immigrants were recruited to work as temporary laborers on plantations in Hawai'i. Once their contract terms were reached, many Filipinos chose to forfeit their return tickets and stayed in Hawai'i or elected to migrate to cities on the West Coast instead.

This group of early migrants constituted the manong (and manang) generation, an honorary title derived from the Visayan dialect that means older brother (or sister). The majority of these labor migrants settled in or nearby Los Angeles and San Francisco, while others eventually found work in the service or naval industries in cities such as Chicago, Detroit, New York, and Philadelphia. Between 1920 and 1930, 60 percent of Filipinos in the United States worked in agriculture. These laborers would go on to form Little Manilas in farming towns such as Stockton and smaller settlements around California's Central Valley region, Oregon, and Washington State. These seasonal labor patterns connected Filipinos between cities along the West Coast and in the Pacific Northwest and eventually formed a labor circuit that led to Filipinos establishing a substantial community in Alaska, centered mostly around the fish-cannery industry.

While there were Filipino women who migrated as students or as married partners accompanying their husbands, most of the early Filipino migrants were young single men. For instance, between 1920 and 1929, only 7 percent of the Filipino immigrants arriving in Los Angeles and San Francisco were female. However, the limited and steady number of Filipino women migrating mainly as nursing students would become significant to establishing communities in the United States, especially once immigration from the Philippines was halted by the Tydings-McDuffie Act of 1934. Filipinos who directly assisted or worked in the U.S. Navy during World War II were exempt from the law, including Filipina nurses. This group was the second wave of Filipino migration. Many of these students, educated in American-established nursing schools in the Philippines beginning in 1906, migrated to cities such as New York and San Francisco and were integral to creating early Filipino American communities particularly on the East Coast.

Contemporary Forms

Once restrictions on Filipino immigration were lifted in 1946 with the Asian Exclusion Repeal Acts, Filipinos took full advantage of the Hart-Celler Act of 1965. Filipinos were the largest group to immigrate to the United States through this legislation. By 1970, there were 343,060 Filipinos in the United States. In 1980, however, that number swelled to 782,895, and in 1990 it increased further to 1,406,770. Immigration preferences designated by the act privileged educated and skilled migrants, precipitating a migration cohort that was distinctly different from the previous manong generation. These select immigrants and the family members who accompanied them would form new Little Manilas in suburban neighborhoods such as Daly City and Union City in California and Jersey City and Bergenfield in New Jersey.

Filipinos today constitute a diverse group of Asian immigrants, and the complexities of their differences are largely reflected in the geography of their settlement. Contemporary Little Manilas are largely characterized by suburban settlement, particularly in California and New Jersey. The families living in these communities, especially among the first generation, reflect relatively high levels of household income and educational attainment. Yet in places such as Hawai'i, throughout waning communities in cities such as Stockton, and in inner-city neighborhoods such as the one in the South of Market district in San Francisco, Filipinos continue to struggle with poverty and obstacles to educational achievement.

The largest population of Filipinos can be found in California, where an estimated 1,195,580 Filipinos constitute 3.2 percent of the total population. According to the 2010 census, this number is followed by Hawai'i (197,497), Illinois (114,724), New Jersey (110,650), New York (104,287), Texas (103,074), Nevada (98,351), Washington (91,367), Florida (90,223), Virginia (66,963), Maryland (43,923), and Arizona (35,013).

Eric J. Pido

See also: Filipino American Folklore; Filipino American Food; Filipino American Immigration

Further Reading

Bonus, Rick. *Locating Filipino Americans: Ethnicity and the Cultural Politics of Space.* Philadelphia: Temple University Press, 2000.

Fujita-Rony, Dorothy B. *American Workers, Colonial Power Philippine Seattle and the Transpacific West, 1919–1941.* Berkeley: University of California Press, 2003.

Hoeffel, Elizabeth M., Sonya Rastogi, Myoung Ouk Kim, and Hasan Shahid. "The Asian Population: 2010." U.S. Census Bureau, March 2012, http://www.census .gov/prod/cen2010/briefs/c2010br-11.pdf.

Mabalon, Dawn Buhulano. *Little Manila Is in the Heart: The Making of the Filipina/o American Community in Stockton, California.* Durham, NC: Duke University Press, 2013.

Vergara, Benito. *Pinoy Capital: The Filipino Nation in Daly City.* Philadelphia: Temple University Press, 2008.

LITTLE SAIGONS

The term "Little Saigon" refers to an ethnic enclave of Vietnamese immigrants outside Vietnam. Sometimes it is also known as Little Vietnam and Little Hanoi. These enclaves vary in size and population; some are well established and large, while others are little more than small Vietnamese commercial districts.

Some Vietnamese American stores and restaurants are located in Chinatowns. Generally speaking, Little Saigons not only provide space for business development but also serve as centers for Vietnamese American communities.

The oldest and largest Little Saigon is in Orange County, California, where a large number of Vietnamese Americans live. Little Saigon first appeared in Westminster in the late 1970s and then expanded to Garden Grove. According to the 2011 American Community Survey, these two cities have the highest concentration of Vietnamese Americans among all cities in the United States: 37.1 and 31.1 percent, respectively. Nowadays, Little Saigon in Orange County is a large community, spreading from Westminster and Garden Grove to Stanton, Fountain Valley, Anaheim, and Santa Ana. There are Vietnamese-language television stations, radio stations, newspapers, and music recording studios as well as a variety of businesses. The annual Vietnamese Lunar New Year Festival is held at Garden Grove Park and hosted by the Union of Vietnamese Student Association Southern California.

Another area with a concentrated Vietnamese American population in southern California is San Gabriel Valley, with Rosemead as its center. In northern California, residents in San Jose have easy access to Vietnamese-

The Trai Cay Ngon fruit and flower store in Little Saigon, Westminster, California, June 17, 2011. Westminster has the oldest and largest Little Saigon in the country. (AP Photo/Damian Dovarganes)

language television stations, radio stations, newspapers, and magazines. Their business district includes many Vietnamese stores, salons, restaurants, and other businesses. The Viet Museum in Kelley Park near the City Historic Museum was opened in August 2007. In Sacramento, the stretch on Stockton Boulevard between Florin and Fruitridge Roads is known as Little Saigon, where the Vietnamese American population has been growing since the 1980s. San Francisco officially designated the portion of Larkin Street between Eddy and O'Farrell Streets as Little Saigon in 2004. Many of the residents in this area are ethnic Chinese from Vietnam. In addition, Oakland and San Diego also have business districts and residential areas with sizable Vietnamese Americans.

The Vietnamese American business district in Seattle, Washington, is around 12th Avenue and Jackson Street, adjacent to the city's Chinatown. Since the 1940s, this area has been known as the International District. In Tacoma, the Lincoln International District has predominantly Vietnamese restaurants, grocery stores, and other shops.

Whether or not officially designated as Little Saigons, Vietnamese American business districts also exist in other states, including Colorado, Florida, New York, Massachusetts, Michigan, and Illinois, among others.

Lan Dong

See also: Chinatown (New York City); Chinatown (San Francisco); Koreatowns; Little Manilas; Little Tokyo (Los Angeles); Vietnamese American Immigration

Further Reading

"American Community Survey." U.S. Census Bureau, 2011, https://www.census.gov /acs/www/.

Hoeffel, Elizabeth M., Sonya Rastogi, Myoung Ouk Kim, and Hasan Shahid. "The Asian Population: 2010." U.S. Census Bureau, March 2012, http://www.census .gov/prod/cen2010/briefs/c2010br-11.pdf.

Kibria, Nazli. *Family Tightrope: The Changing Lives of Vietnamese Americans.* Princeton, NJ: Princeton University Press, 1993.

Rutledge, Paul J. *The Vietnamese Experience in America.* Bloomington: Indiana University Press, 1992.

Tseng, Winston. *Immigrant Community Services in Chinese and Vietnamese Enclaves.* New York: LFB Scholarly Publication, 2007.

LITTLE TOKYO (LOS ANGELES)

The terms "Little Tokyo" and "Japantown" refer to Japanese communities outside of Japan. These ethnic enclaves are usually located in large cities. There are three official Japantowns in the United States, all in California: Los Angeles, San

Francisco, and San Jose. The best known is Little Tokyo in Los Angeles. Also known as the Little Tokyo Historic District, Little Tokyo is a Japanese American district in downtown Los Angeles. It serves as the cultural, religious, and business center of the largest Japanese American population in North America. It was officially declared a National Historic Landmark District in June 1995. The National Historic Landmarks Program states that Little Tokyo in Los Angeles "illustrates the historical development of the major Japanese American community on the U.S. mainland and symbolizes the hardships and obstacles that this ethnic group has overcome" ("Little Tokyo Historic District"), highlighting its historical significance and its service to Japanese American communities.

At the beginning of the 20th century, the area of the current Little Tokyo attracted Japanese immigrants until the Exclusion Act of 1924 curtailed immigration from Asia. At the time, there were a number of shops and markets run by Japanese Americans around the area. During World War II, Little Tokyo became empty briefly as a result of Japanese American internment before other people took residence. After the war, many Japanese Americans moved back to Los Angeles and into neighborhoods near the downtown area. In the late 1970s redevelopment led to the construction of new buildings and shopping centers, although some of the old buildings and restaurants remained.

Declared a National Historic Landmark District in 1995, Little Tokyo (shown in this November 12, 2014 photo) is a Japanese American district in downtown Los Angeles, California. Its annual Nisei Week Festival features many cultural events and celebrations. (Supannee Hickman/Dreamstime.com)

There are many restaurants in Little Tokyo that specialize in Japanese food such as *manjū*, a traditional Japanese confection with many varieties commonly made with flour, rice powder, and buckwheat and filled with red bean paste. This district also has numerous shops selling Japanese videos, games, electronics, manga, anime, magazines, and other merchandise. Some karaoke clubs, cafés, and bookstores are also located in Little Tokyo. In addition, there are Buddhist temples in the area, including the Zenshuji Soto Mission, the first Soto Zen temple established in the United States, and the Koyasan Buddhist Temple, the first Shingon temple founded in the United States as well as Christian churches. Soto Zen is the largest of the three traditional sects of Zen in Japanese Buddhism. It has become popular in North America. Shingon Buddhism is one of the major schools of Japanese Buddhism, with its origin tracing to India and China.

Little Tokyo is home to many arts and cultural centers and organizations. Founded in 1971, the Japanese American Cultural and Community Center (JACCC) is one of the largest Japanese American arts and cultural centers in the country. With a mission "to present, perpetuate, transmit and promote Japanese and Japanese American arts and culture to diverse audiences, and to provide a center to enhance community program," the JACCC has facilitated theater performances, hosted annual New Year's celebrations, featured exhibitions, and organized community engagement programs during the past few decades. It has played and continues to play a vital role in promoting Japanese and Japanese American arts and culture to a wide range of audiences of Japanese heritage and otherwise.

East West Players (EWP), a premiere Asian American theater company, specializes in live theater performances written and performed by Asian American artists. Since its establishment in 1965, the EWP has premiered over 100 plays and musicals about the Asian Pacific American experience and has hosted more than 1,000 readings and workshops. In addition, the EWP organizes play competitions, offers youth arts education programs, and provides professional enrichment opportunities to artists.

The Japanese American National Museum (JANM) is also located in Little Tokyo. In order to promote "understanding and appreciation of America's ethnic and cultural diversity," JANM commissions exhibitions, film screenings, and other cultural events and projects regularly. As the largest museum in the United States specifically dedicated to educating audiences about Japanese American history and experience, JANM also offers educational programs for adults and children.

Founded in 1970, Visual Communications (VC) is dedicated to connecting communities and promoting intercultural understanding through media arts. The organization features a variety of programs supporting the production, education, presentation, and preservation of Asian Pacific American films, videos, and media projects. Today, the VC's programs include the annual Los Angeles Asian Pacific

Film Festival and quarterly community film screenings, the Armed with a Camera Fellowship for emerging media artists, and media education programs for youths, nonprofit organizations, and senior citizens and adult learners. The VC provides production services for nonprofit organizations and serves as a fiscal sponsor for independent productions. The VC is also home to one of the largest photographic and moving image archives of the Asian Pacific experience in America.

Many organizations host various cultural events and celebrations in Little Tokyo. For instance, the Nisei Week Festival is an annual event in August. This festival usually includes a parade, a pageant, a car show, artistic and cultural exhibitions, athletic events, and the Japanese Festival Street Fair. The first Nisei Week in 1934 lasted seven days. Other attractions in Little Tokyo include parks, sculptures, monuments, and other architecture in the area. The monument for astronaut Ellison S. Onizuka (1946–1986) is one such example. Onizuka was a Japanese American from Hawai'i. He was a mission specialist on the space shuttle Challenger when it disintegrated during takeoff in 1986.

Lan Dong

See also: Chinatown (New York City); Chinatown (San Francisco); Japanese American Immigration; Koreatowns; Little Manilas; Little Saigons

Further Reading

"American Community Survey." U.S. Census Bureau, 2011, https://www.census.gov/acs/www/.

Levine, Gene N., and Colbert Rhodes. *The Japanese American Community: A Three-Generation Study.* New York: Praeger, 1981.

"Little Tokyo Historic District." National Historic Landmarks Program, http://tps.cr.nps.gov/nhl/detail.cfm?ResourceId=1961&ResourceType=District.

Lyman, Stanford Morris. *Chinatown and Little Tokyo: Power, Conflict, and Community among Chinese and Japanese Immigrants to America.* Port Washington, NY: Associated Faculty Press, 1986.

Murase, Ichiro Mike. *Little Tokyo: One Hundred Years in Pictures.* Los Angeles: Visual Communications/Asian American Studies Central, 1983.

LUNAR NEW YEAR

History and Origins

The Lunar New Year (in some cases known as the Spring Festival) forms an important part of Asian Americans' social life. It also marks the beginning of the New Year for some communities of Asian Americans. The Lunar New Year

Chinese Lantern Festival

The Chinese Lantern Festival is a celebration on the last day of the Chinese Lunar New Year. The lanterns are shining globe-shaped objects that traditionally are red in color with a candle burning inside. Made of paper, silk, or glass, they are suspended on the doorways of residential quarters and shops. In parades, Chinese Americans carry these lanterns amid fireworks and loud music from drums and cymbals. The festival originated from the western Han dynasty (206 BCE–25 CE) and continues in China as well as places of Chinese diaspora. Chinese immigrants flock together to celebrate the onset of spring. This is accompanied by watching lanterns, a display of fireworks, and eating *yuanxiao* (glutinous rice flour dumplings served in soup). Marking the end of the two-week lunar New Year celebration, Chinese Americans visualize a full moon, gleaming and round. In cities such as San Francisco, the festival has a long history tracing back to the 1860s.

is a gala event for Chinese, Korean, and Vietnamese Americans. The Chinese New Year is widely known globally, which is not surprising due to Chinese being the numerically largest ethnic group globally. The New Year celebrations are based on the traditional Chinese lunisolar calendar (occurring in late January or February) and take place in the period between the winter solstice and the vernal equinox. The New Year for people of Cambodia, Laos, and Sri Lank is in the month of April. Honoring and appeasing ancestors has been a hallmark of Asian civilization. The Lunar New Year festival is no exception.

Chun Jie or Chinese New Year (also known as the Spring Festival), based on the Chinese lunar calendar began in prehistoric times. Originating in the Shang dynasty period (1766–1122 BCE), it has continued through successive periods. Historical legends and mythologies are numerous in tracing the origin of the festival. A mythical dragon called Nian emerges on New Year's Eve with evil intentions of destruction. As the dragon is afraid of fire, loud sounds, and the color red, people launch fireworks and hang lanterns and red decorations to ward off the beast. Lunar New Year falls between January 21 and February 19. It may be a different date each year. The month starts with a new moon, and the New Year begins with the first day of the lunar calendar's first month. Each year is named for one of the 12 zodiac animals.

Tet Nguyen Dan, the Vietnamese New Year, began about 2,000 years ago. The word *tet* means the "beginning of a period of the year." Originating from Daoism, it emphasizes harmonious living with nature and people. Vietnam,

Chinese New Year parade in Chinatown, San Francisco, California, February 23, 2013. Chinatowns and Chinese American communities across the country celebrate Lunar New Year. (Mariusz Jurgielewicz/Dreamstime.com)

which was under Chinese occupation for more than 1,000 years, might have been influenced by the colonizer's culture and tradition, but there are differences. For example, the ox, rabbit, and sheep in the Chinese calendar have been replaced by the buffalo, cat, and goat, respectively, in the Vietnamese calendar. The origin of the Seollal, the Korean Lunar New Year, is obscure. Traditional Chinese literature such as the *Book of Sui* and the *Old Book of Tang* contain references to Seollal. During the period of the Three Kingdoms, Koreans adopted the lunar calendar. The government functionaries exchanged New Year greetings.

Contemporary Forms and Practices in the United States

Although Asian Americans participate in a wide variety of festivals with fellow Americans, the Lunar New Year festivals are unique for Chinese, Vietnamese, and Korean Americans, as it asserts their cultural heritage and transnational identities. Within the Chinese diaspora globally, the dates of the celebration are in tune with mainland China. Earlier it was confined to the Chinatown enclaves of American cities. But with many immigrants living in mixed popula-tion areas and suburbs, the festival has no spatial dimension. It is in California and New York that Chun Jie is celebrated in a bigger way and with gusto. The majority of Chinese Americans reside in cities such as New York, Los Angeles, and San Francisco. It is even a public holiday in San Francisco. Not only will the festival bring prosperity for the Chinese, but also ancestral spirits will receive due homage. The festival, lasting for 15 days, consists of a wide range of activities. The house is cleaned, renovated, bedecked with flowers, and decorated. Food is offered to the kitchen god, who communicates with the Jade Emperor about good as well as bad deeds of the family. Red dresses are put on, and children receive money in red envelopes, called *hong bao*. The food taken has special meaning, such as togetherness (coconut), large family (lotus seeds), longevity (peanuts), and others. Dragon and lion dances are essential components of the festival. People carry floats of dragons and lions to the accompaniment of sounds of drum beating and cymbals. There is bursting of firecrackers. In New York City, firecrackers were prohibited until 2007. The city's Chatham Square witnesses deafening sound and light works produced by firecrackers. The parade in San Francisco, the largest in the United States, is followed by a spectacular fireworks display. On the penultimate day, the lantern festival begins with the hanging of paper lanterns at doorways and shops. It is broadcast live in San Francisco, where the festival began in 1860s.

One of the important cultural occasions for Vietnamese Americans is the Tet Nguyen Dan festival, which has sundry folkloric religious practices. Nature, human beings, cultural traits, care of living relations, and worship to departed souls are all harmoniously balanced and integrated in the festival. The festival starts on the first day of the first month of the lunar calendar and continues for three to seven days. Dwellings are cleaned and whitewashed and decorated with flowers, and *thu phap* (calligraphy pictures) as well as *dong ho* paintings (Vietnamese folk paintings) are suspended. On the festival days, there are get-togethers of friends and relatives. In the home altar, offerings are given to ancestors, and the kitchen god Ong Tao is invoked. Similar to the Chinese New Year, festivities include putting on new dresses, offering lucky money to younger people in red envelopes, performing dragon and lion dances, and feasting on delicious dishes such as *mut* (candied fruit), *banh chung* (steamed sticky rice cake), and *keo dua* (coconut candy). For the aging generation, the Xong Dat is an occasion to share memories of the original homeland with the younger generation. The *tet* is celebrated by the Vietnamese community in the United States by inviting non–Asian Americans as well as Asian Americans. In California, home to the majority of Vietnamese Americans, the *tet* is organized by the Vietnamese Community of Southern California. The Union of Vietnamese Student Associations also organizes the festival.

Korean Americans celebrate Seollal, which is embedded in their culture. Taking place on the first day of each new lunar year, it is celebrated on the same days as the Chinese New Year. Like their Vietnamese counterparts, the Seollal honors family members, departed ancestral spirits, and divinities watching over the family. The Korean immigrants put on *hanbok* (traditional clothes) after an early morning bath, pray and sing hymns, and follow ancestral rites connected with the festival. Elders bless the youngsters, children show respect to elder family members, and participants consume traditional *ddukguk* (soup made with rice cakes, meat, and egg). The popular folk game in the festival is *yut-nori*, a board game played with wooden sticks and markers. Traditionally men may fly *yeon* (rectangle kites), whereas women may prefer a game played with five little *gonggis* made of small stones or small plastic stones (similar to the game of jacks). The festival is an occasion to interact with other immigrants and Americans, who are invited to join in the Lunar New Year festival. Korean Americans join with the Chinese New Year parades in Chinatown areas of Flushing and Queens in New York City. The separate identity of Koreans is asserted in blending elements of traditional culture with contemporary living in the Seollal.

Patit Paban Mishra

See also: Festivals and Holidays, Asian American; Religions and Beliefs, Asian American

Further Reading

"Chinese Lantern Festival." China Highlights, 1998, http://www.chinahighlights.com/festivals/lantern-festival.htm.

Dice, Elizabeth A. *Western and Chinese New Year's Celebrations.* New York: Chelsea House, 2009.

Kaplan, Leslie C. *Chinese New Year.* New York: Power Kids, 2004.

MacMillan, Diane M. *Tet: Vietnamese New Year.* Berkeley Heights, NJ: Enslow Publishers, 1994.

Morrill, Ann. *Religious New Year's Celebrations.* New York: Chelsea House, 2009.

Ngoc, Huru, and Barbara Cohen. *Tet, the Vietnamese Lunar New Year.* Hanoi, Vietnam: Gioi, 1997.

"Seollal: Origins and Traditions of Korean Lunar New Year." Beyond Hallyu, August 2, 2013. http://beyondhallyu.com/culture/seollal-lunar-new-year/.

"Tet: The Biggest Festival in Vietnam." Vietnam Institute, 2010, http://vietnam.missouri.edu/CultureCorner.html.

Underwood, Gary. *Harmony and Understanding: Happy Lunar New Year! An Asian Festival.* Clayton South, Australia: Blake Education, 2006.

Wang, L. Ling-Chi. "Chinese Americans." Advameg, 2014, http://www.everyculture
.com/multi/Bu-Dr/Chinese-Americans.html.

Welch, Patricia W. *Chinese New Year (Images of Asia)*. Oxford and New York: Oxford
University Press, 1997.

Yi, I-Hwa, et al. *Korea's Pastimes and Customs: A Social History*. Paramus, NJ: Homa and
Sekey Books, 2006.

M

MALAYSIAN AMERICAN CULTURE

Malaysian Americans, as naturalized citizens and permanent residents, make up a small percentage of the burgeoning Asian population of nearly 19 million in the United States. In 2013, 1,169 Malaysians became American citizens, which was less than half a percent of the 275,700 Asians who became American citizens that year. In addition, 2,477 Malaysians obtained permanent resident status in 2013 out of a total of 400,548 Asians. Malaysian statistics indicate that in 2013, a total of 308,834 highly trained Malaysians migrated overseas, and 12.2 percent of them moved to the United States, the United Kingdom, and Canada. But these numbers do not distinguish between those who obtained permanent residency or citizenship and those on work permits or student visas. It is therefore more helpful to understand the Malaysian American community as broader than just permanent residents and naturalized citizens. International and exchange students as well as working professionals on temporary or long-term work permits are also integral members of this community. These students and professionals are vibrant contributors to the cities they live in, especially through community and student organizations that have become hubs for Malaysian Americans in the United States.

As a minority within a minority, Malaysian Americans are significantly understudied, despite the fact that Malaysia and the United States have enjoyed a long history of economic and political partnerships. Following Malaysia's independence from British rule in 1957, the country faced rising tensions with Indonesia between 1963 and 1966. During this time, the United States provided economic and military support to Malaysia in addition to petitioning the United Nations on Malaysia's behalf. Under President George W. Bush and following the attacks of 9/11, U.S. ties with Malaysia expanded to include collaboration on counterterrorism efforts. In addition to security ties, the two countries enjoyed significant economic exchange as well. Malaysia is an important economic partner for the United States in Southeast Asia. According to the Office of the United States Trade Representative, Malaysia was America's 20th-largest goods trading partner in 2013, with $40.3 billion in export and import goods trade combined. In 2014 Malaysia was one of four countries President Barack Obama visited as part of his Asia tour, which aimed at establishing the Trans-Pacific Partnership with 12 countries in the region.

Economic and political developments such as these are important factors influencing Malaysian migration to the United States. Following the Malaysian race riots of 1969 and the establishment of the New Economic Policy (a form of affirmative action that attempted to address economic disparities through special programs for the Malay-Muslim community), cities such as Chicago saw an increasing number of Malaysian immigrants, particularly students and working professionals. From the 1970s onward, Malaysian American communities were established along the East and West Coasts as well as the Midwest. A significant number of Malaysian Americans in the Midwest can be found in Chicago, where a 2001 estimate suggested that there were approximately 600–700 Malaysians residing in the city (Steffes 2005). New York and the West Coast are believed to be home to a fairly large number of Malaysian Americans. In cities such as Washington, D.C., the Malaysian American community includes former diplomats, students, and scholars affiliated with various institutions such as the East-West Center, the Johns Hopkins School of Advanced International Studies, the World Bank, the International Monetary Fund, and the US-ASEAN Business Council, according to the Washington, D.C.–based Malaysia-America Society's website. It is important to note that official statistics and the profiles of community organizations such as the Malaysia-America Society may not reflect the presence and contributions of Malaysian Americans who might occupy lower socioeconomic positions within the United States.

Malaysian student and community organizations serve as important venues for preserving, practicing, and developing Malaysian American culture. Prominent student groups include the Malaysian Students Association (MASA) at Ohio State University, the Malaysian Student Association at the University of Michigan, and the Malaysian Students Association at the University of Wisconsin–Madison. In addition to organizing and sponsoring a wide range of cultural events, these student groups also enjoy a significant following on Facebook (300–500 likes per page). Malaysian American community organizations include the Malaysian Club of Chicago (MCC), the aforementioned Malaysia-America Society, the New York Malaysian Association, the Malaysian Association of Georgia, and the Malaysian American Association of Southern California.

These organizations articulate very similar goals: to create forums for political, educational, and cultural exchange and foster a sense of community within the United States. For example, MASA at Ohio State University aims to "promote and share our unique Malaysian culture and diversity; and to contribute to increasing the awareness of a diverse student body through our Malaysian identity." The Malaysia-America Society describes itself as being "dedicated to promoting understanding and friendship between America(ns) and Malaysia(ns)." Similarly, MCC aims to "promote the personal and professional development of the Malaysian American community" and to "sponsor and support activities that enhance the cultural awareness and perception of Malaysian Americans." The activities fostered by these organizations serve not only as a means of cultural exchange but also as a system for building relationships among Malaysian Americans across the United States. Much of this networking takes place on social media platforms such as Facebook and through events that are cosponsored by a variety of organizations and institutions. For example, the Malaysian Association of Georgia's Facebook page features an announcement for a Malaysian restaurant in Cincinnati run by Malaysian Chef Paul Liew. Similarly, the Facebook page for the New York Malaysian Association showcases a rags-to-riches story, first published by the Malaysian newspaper the *Malay Mail*, of a Malaysian chef now based in San Francisco as well as posts by the Malaysia Agriculture Office of Washington, D.C. Malaysian American students across the United States also connect through the Malaysia Midwest Games (MMG), hosted in 2015 by the University of Michigan at Ann Arbor. This annual event is sponsored each year by a different Midwestern university and is attended by a variety of Malaysian student organizations from institutions across the United States. The MMG features Malaysian food and cultural events as well as an extensive range of sporting events popular in Malaysia, such as badminton, *sepak takraw,* and *caroms.*

Many Malaysian American associations also foster ties with other Asian American communities by participating in Pan-Asian food festivals, musical events, and celebrations of the Lunar New Year hosted within their respective cities. Organizations such as the Malaysian Association of Georgia and the New York Association of Malaysia also celebrate festivals tied to Malaysia's distinct ethnic and religious communities, such as Hari Raya celebrated by Malay Muslims, Deepavali celebrated by Indian Hindus, and Christmas celebrated by Christians who have various ethnic backgrounds. As is the custom in Malaysia, Malaysian Americans of different faiths often participate in each other's celebrations. These events thus serve as avenues through which to reinforce and complicate ethnic and religious boundaries in the United States, as they often are in Malaysia.

Organizations such as the Malaysian Club of Chicago also seek to foster prominent ties with their cities through public events such as Hari Merdeka (celebrating Malaysian independence from Britain). The City of Chicago formally recognizes the day with a ceremony that includes the raising of the

Malaysian and American flags and the singing of both countries' national anthems. Similar organizations in New York, Georgia, and southern California also host events celebrating holidays popular in the United States, including Thanksgiving, the Fourth of July, and St. Patrick's Day.

In addition, a variety of Malaysian American associations aim to build and maintain strong connections to Malaysia. For example, MASA hosted the Malaysian Cultural Night at Ohio State University in March 2014, cosponsored by Malaysia's tourism office. The Malaysia-America Society of Washington, D.C., offers a variety of lectures annually on U.S.-Malaysian relations and Malaysian economic and political developments. These sessions have featured prominent Malaysians, including Dató Sri Dr. Jamaluddin Jarjis (1951–), ambassador to the United States, and Malaysian prime minister Dató Sri Najib Tun Razak (1953–). The New York Malaysian Association has sponsored vigils and donation drives for the families of passengers on Malaysian Airlines Flight 17, shot down over Ukraine in 2014. The association has also featured the philanthropic work of the Nasi Lemak Project, a Malaysian organization that provides food, supplies, and educational support to the homeless and impoverished in the city of Kuala Lumpur in Malaysia.

While these organizations offer valuable insights into the large-scale cultural practices of Malaysian Americans, the experiences of individuals and families are much harder to track and far too diverse to catalog. However, it might be useful to note some of the complexities involved in how Malaysian Americans position themselves within the United States. First, like many other immigrant groups, Malaysian Americans do not constitute a monolithic group. Instead, they represent a diverse range of ethnic and religious identities that are linked in various ways to sociopolitical divisions within Malaysia. Malaysian Americans, like Malaysian citizens, may be ethnically Chinese, Malay, Indian, Orang Asli (Malaysia's indigenous people), or some combination of these. They may identify themselves as Muslim, Hindu, Christian, Buddhist, or Confucian. As Daniel P. S. Goh and Philip Holden have noted, "the official categories of Chinese, Malay, Indian and Others (CMIO) [in Malaysia were] inherited from the British colonial administration" (2009, 3). This and the fact that Malaysians still reflexively pair their ethnic heritage with national citizenship make it difficult "to shake the hardened CMIO racializations and their ideological figurations" (8).

These ethnic and religious divisions may be replicated among Malaysian American communities to varying degrees, just as the term "Malaysian American" itself may be interpreted and applied quite differently. Shirley Geok-lin Lim (1944–), a prominent author and academic living in the United States, identifies herself as both Chinese Malaysian and Asian American. Conversations with a

Malaysian American family based in Washington, D.C., suggest a level of discomfort with the term "Malaysian American." Based in the United States for some 30 years, the parents of this family of three, now in their 60s and 70s, do not describe themselves as Malaysian American. They feel that the term does not represent their specific ethnic and religious backgrounds, which they explain in more detail when asked. While they identify as Asian American on formal documents and surveys, they have attempted to instill a sense of Malaysian heritage in their children through frequent visits to Malaysia, food and family stories, and books on Malaysian culture and history. Their daughter, who is now in her early 30s, is married to an American, and has two children of her own, does not self-identify as Malaysian American either. While she sees how the term might serve to articulate both her former Malaysian citizenship and her current American citizenship, she prefers to separate ethnicity from citizenship. Having been raised and educated in the United States, she views herself as an individual who is largely Americanized and identifies predominantly with American culture. At the same time, she enjoys celebrating certain Malaysian holidays and festivals with her parents, cooking Malaysian food, and using a smattering of Malay words that she has picked up over time.

While these anecdotal insights illuminate some dimensions of how Malaysian Americans see themselves, there is more depth and nuance than the label might convey at first glance. In that respect, it shares the inadequacies of other categories of immigrant identity. Many of these labels fall short in capturing the complexities of race, religion, and culture, particularly as communities cross borders and assimilate to or resist the cultures they encounter.

Sheela Jane Menon

See also: Burmese (Myanmar) American Culture; Indonesian American Culture; Singaporean American Culture; Thai American Culture

Further Reading

Department of Homeland Security. *2013 Yearbook of Immigration Statistics.* Washington, DC: U.S. Department of Homeland Security, 2014, http://www.dhs.gov/yearbook-immigration-statistics.

Goh, Daniel P. S., and Philip Holden. "Introduction: Postcoloniality, Race, and Multiculturalism." In *Race and Multiculturalism in Malaysia and Singapore,* 1–16. New York and London: Routledge, 2009.

"In San Francisco, a Penang 'Mamak's' Tale of Rags to Riches." Malay Mail Online, July 6, 2014, http://www.themalaymailonline.com/malaysia/article/in-san-francisco-a-penang-mamaks-tale-of-rags-to-riches-video.

"Malaysia: Office of the United State Trade Representative," http://www.ustr.gov/countries-regions/southeast-asia-pacific/malaysia.

Malaysia America Society, https://sites.google.com/site/malaysiaamericasocietydc /who-we-are.

Malaysia Midwest Games, http://www.malaysiamidwestgames.com/.

Malaysian Club of Chicago, http://www.malaysianclubchicago.com/.

Malaysian Students Association at Ohio State University, http://masa.osu.edu/.

Mattingly, Phil, and Margaret Talev. "Obama Backs Malaysian Plane Probe as Countries Push Trade Pact." Bloomberg News, April 28, 2014, http://www .bloomberg.com/news/2014-04-27/obama-backs-malaysian-plane-probe-as -countries-push-trade-talks.html.

Sodhy, Pamela. "Malaysian-American Relations during Indonesia's Confrontation against Malaysia, 1963–66." *Journal of Southeast Asian Studies* 19(1) (1998): 111–136.

Sodhy, Pamela. "US-Malaysian Relations during the Bush Administration: The Political, Economic, and Security Aspects." *Contemporary Southeast Asia* 25(3) (2003): 363–386.

Steffes, Tracy. "Malaysians." Encyclopedia of Chicago, http://www.encyclopedia .chicagohistory.org/pages/781.html.

U.S. Census Bureau. "Asians Fastest Growing Race or Ethnic Group in 2012, Census Bureau Reports." U.S. Census Bureau Public Information Office, June 13, 2013, http://www.census.gov/newsroom/releases/archives/population/cb13-112.html.

Zeng, Minhao. "The Intricacies of Cosmopolitanism: Shirley Geok-lin Lim's *Among the Whitemoonfaces.*" *Mosaic* 46(1) (2013): 77–93.

MODEL MINORITY

History and Origins

Asians in the United States, regardless of their economic, social, political, and cultural statuses, are imagined as a model minority. This imagination exerts a wholesale, totalizing image of Asians living in America, an image that conjures up hardworking immigrants who cherish the educational opportunities not available in their homelands to become successful in the land of equal opportunity. It is an image that is deeply ingrained in American popular cultures and reinforced by popular media. Although Asian American studies scholars and activists have critiqued the model minority image as a racialized stereotype that fuels ethnic antagonism, the statistical data that measures success, such as median family income and postbaccalaureate professional degrees indicates that this so-called stereotype might indeed bear witness to truth. It is important to discuss the historical development of the model minority image, as it foregrounds the discourse, both negative and positive, surrounding the stereotype.

"The Rise of Asian Americans"

Despite the widespread scholarship to correct faulty practices regarding the model minority stereotype, in 2012, the Pew Research Center used the U.S. census data from 2010 and made the same misrepresentations in its evaluation of Asian Americans as model minorities in its report titled "The Rise of Asian Americans." The Pew report upset Asian American communities and organizations. The Association for Asian American Studies (AAAS) was one of many associations that wrote responses expressing their disappointment of the generalizations and misrepresentations that were made about the ascension of Asian American communities. One of the many concerns that the AAAS addressed is public policy makers using this report to cut back on necessary resources for vulnerable Asian American subgroups. Another apprehension that was expressed in the AAAS letter was the fear that during challenging economic times in the United States, anti-Asian sentiments and violence will be incited because of the perceived unfair advantage of Asian Americans over other minority groups.

The image of model minority was conjured by sociologist William Petersen on January 9, 1966, when he published "Success Story, Japanese-American Style" in the *New York Times Magazine.* This article is one of the most influential articles about an Asian American group. Petersen did not employ the phrase "model minority," but his article alluded to it. He documented the Japanese American experience after World War II, when anti-Asian and particularly anti-Japanese sentiments were still strong. During World War II, Japanese Americans were interned and lost most of their livelihood. Petersen was concerned that the history of racial and ethnic discrimination and prejudice experienced by Japanese Americans would result in them becoming a "problem minority" like the African American communities. "Problem minority" refers to a community of people, minorities, whose socioeconomic indicators of success are low, such as generally having "poor health," "poor education," "low income," "high crime rates," "unstable family patterns," and so on. Instead of finding a community that reflects the indicators of being a "problem minority" Petersen observed that Japanese Americans of that period challenged their historical experiences. He stated that "the history of Japanese Americans, however, challenges every such generalization about ethnic minorities." More important, "even in a country whose patron saint is the Horatio Alger hero, there is no parallel to this success story" (1966, 31). According to Petersen, the key to Japanese American success lies in its "traditional culture." He argued that Japanese immigrants brought with them a strong "work ethic" and an ethic of "frugality" similar to the white Protestant work ethic, which was associated with their success even in the face of racial, political, economic, and social adversities.

Eleven months after the publication of Petersen's article, a similar article was published in *U.S. News and World Report* on December 26, 1966, "Success Story of One Minority Group in the U.S." Supporting Petersen's claims with empirical data, this article described the nation's 300,000 upwardly mobile Chinese Americans. It compared Chinese Americans to African Americans who needed "uplifting" and "support" by the government. The article employed census data and made a conclusion that surprised the general public, who did not expect Chinese Americans to have higher educational attainment and a higher percentage of representation in professional fields than the national average, even higher than white Americans. It argued that like Japanese Americans, Chinese Americans faced and experienced violent racism and prejudice but were able to "pull" themselves up from the hardship and discrimination to become a "model" of self-respect and personal achievement. The phrase "model minority" was not used, but the article considered Chinese Americans a "model" of achievement in American society. Furthermore, its anonymous author suggested that African Americans can learn something from Chinese Americans, as their community represented an example of the true American way. Such a conclusion flamed and fed American resentment for African American communities and placed the blame for all their "failures" on African Americans and their cultural values (or lack thereof).

Similar to Petersen's article, "Success Story of One Minority Group in the U.S." (1966) concluded that Chinese cultural values are key to Chinese Americans' success. In explaining how the "Chinese get ahead," it argued that Chinese immigrants brought with them "the traditional virtues of hard work, thrift, and morality" (74). Moreover, the article suggests that Chinese culture has strong family values, so strong that the streets of New York City's Chinatown are the safest streets around. Both articles, one documenting Japanese American success and the other documenting Chinese American success, argued that both communities historically faced racism and discrimination but were able to overcome these obstacles. According to the article, this proves that American society is a land of equal opportunity, which leads to a belief among many that success is therefore only available and attainable if one's cultural values reflect and mirror that of white American mainstream values. Critics of these attitudes have pointed out that this belief then leads to the dishonest and wrong conclusion that failure, poverty, and literacy are indicators of some cultural pathology within the community, not historical by-products or indicators of institutional inequality. "Success Story of One Minority Group in the U.S." does acknowledge the prejudice and bigotry that Asian Americans had faced in the United States but in doing so ignores the history of slavery and severe prejudice that faced the "Negro":

> It must be recognized that the Chinese and other Orientals in California were faced with even more prejudice than faces the Negro today. We haven't stuck Negroes in concentration camps, for instance, as we did the Japanese during World War II. The Orientals came back, and today they have established themselves as strong contributors to the health of the whole community. (76)

Popular media consumed the success stories of the Japanese and Chinese Americans wholeheartedly. These two case studies affirmed that America is a land of opportunity. Otherwise, as shown by the beliefs in the 1960s' articles and by some whites even today, how could Japanese Americans and Chinese Americans attain success in a relatively short period of time after World War II? How would they have been able to pull themselves up by their bootstraps, out of the slums and out of poverty, over racial prejudice and do so without government support (i.e., welfare)? Chinese American went from being "coolies" to "engineers, doctors, and research scientists." Throughout the 1990s the image of Asian Americans as a model minority flourished, especially due to conservatives who wanted to cut government social programs and affirmative action policies and held them up as examples.

Contemporary Forms and Impact

Conservatives were quick to employ the model minority stereotype to argue against the progress of the civil rights movement, as it critiqued the demands of the black, brown, red, and yellow power movements by arguing that American society and institutions are in fact equal. The model minority stereotype was employed to fuel the flames of ethnic antagonism whereby minority groups fight each other instead of the structures and historical conditions that limit their access to resources. By the 1980s, the model minority image had spread to include Koreans, Asian Indians, and new refugees from Vietnam, Cambodia, and Laos. This period also witnessed an increasing number of publications documenting Asian Americans as a model minority, as seen in *Scientific American*'s "Indochinese Refugee Families and Academic Achievement" (February 1992), Dennis Williams's "Formula for Success" in *Newsweek* (April 23, 1984), and David Brand's article "The New Whiz Kids" in *Time* (August

31, 1987). These popular media accounts document young Asian Americans' academic drive and achievements from elementary school to college; all conclude that their cultural work ethics and value of schooling are key to their success.

One way to evaluate a racial or ethnic group's social welfare is to examine U.S. census data for its socioeconomic status (i.e., family income, educational attainment, and employment status) in comparison to other groups. For example, according to 2010 U.S. census data, Asian Americans have the highest median family income of any racial group, at $76,736 compared to non-Hispanic white families at $64,818 and the total population at $60,609. The median family income for Latino families was $41,102 and for African American families was $39,900. These monetary gaps are being used to support the hypothesis that Asian Americans are a model minority.

However, after the College of Ethnic Studies was established in 1969 at San Francisco State University, scholarship emerged in the 1970s and continues in the present, debunking and demystifying claims that Asian Americans are model minorities. Some scholars critically examined the data collection practices of the U.S. census and found that when the statistics of Asian Americans and Pacific Islanders are disaggregated by ethnic group, some groups substantially fall below the poverty line, such as Samoan Americans, Hmong Americans, and Cambodian Americans. Another critique of the census is related to how income and education are evaluated. The claim that Asian Americans have high economic attainment does not take into account that there are dual and sometimes even multiple income earners in the home in comparison to the single income earner in white middle-class families. Furthermore, many Asian Americans tend to have large families, which means that their resources are being spread among a number of people.

Other scholars who have refuted Asian Americans as model minorities have examined immigration patterns in the United States to reveal a more complete depiction that is not accounted for in U.S. census data. Bill Ong Hing's scholarship on U.S. immigration policy discloses that the H-1B category created in the 1990s to admit South Asians into the United States to fill high-skilled job positions skewed the numbers in the census because past studies did not differentiate between foreign- and American-born Asians. The South Asians who entered the United States under the H-1B category tended to be educated and were placed in high-paying jobs, in comparison to earlier Asian immigrants and the later Southeast Asian refugees.

Another argument that has been made to explain Asian American success is the Asian cultural value that emphasizes the importance of education because it leads to upward social mobility. Proponents of the Confucian values as an explanation for Asian Americans' high educational attainment have referred to the U.S. census and statistics from Ivy League campuses as support of their arguments. As Mary Yu Danico and Franklin Ng note, at the Massachusetts Institute of Technology (MIT) there is such a high representation of Asian Americans that the acronym "MIT" has been informally referred to as "Made in Taiwan," and a similar case has occurred at the University of California, Los Angeles (UCLA), in which its acronym "UCLA" has been labeled "United Caucasians Living among Asians."

This inflated image of Asian Americans as achieving academic excellence has adversely affected impoverished subgroups from gaining access to affirmative action programs. The assumption is that all Asian ethnic groups are the same. When scholars disaggregated the statistical data, they found a huge disparity among the various ethnic Asian groups. For example, in *Southeast Asian American Statistical Profile* (2004), Max Niedwiecki and T. C. Duong show how aggregated data from the 2000 census harms Asian American subgroups. The statistics for educational attainment on the total population consists of 80.4 percent high school graduates, 24.4 percent bachelor degrees or higher, and 1.0 percent PhDs, whereas the statistics for Asian Americans consist of 80.6 percent high school graduates, 42.7 percent bachelor degrees or higher, and 2.7 percent PhDs. Asian Americans have higher ratings than the total population on all three levels of educational attainment. However, when the authors disaggregated the data, Southeast Asian Americans trailed far behind the model minority image. While the Asian Indian population consists of 60.9 percent bachelor degrees or higher, only 19.5 percent of Vietnamese Americans, 9.1 percent of Cambodian Americans, and 7.4 percent of Hmong Americans obtained bachelor degree or higher (15). As Danico and Ng have stated, there are stories behind these numbers; Asian American students have high self-reports of depression, poor self-image, and hostility directed at them from peers in other racial groups and feel racially targeted for discrimination (2004, 33). As shown in these previous examples, aggregated statistical data do not show a complete picture but instead skew it.

Regardless of the widespread scholarship on the model minority stereotype's inaccuracy and its negative impacts, new and contemporary forms emerge. Amy Chua's *Battle Hymn of the Tiger Mother* is a contemporary form of the model minority type. She is a self-proclaimed "tiger mother," a title used to describe her stern parenting style. When her memoir was published in 2011, it evoked debates over what practices could be deemed effective parenting. Chua firmly posits that strict parenting yields the best results because it can mold children into successful citizens, which mirrors that of the model minority type. In one instance, she retells a piano-playing scene with her youngest daughter,

Lulu, who was seven years old at the time and forced to play "Little White Donkey" through dinnertime and into the night without water or bathroom breaks until she was able to play it correctly. Appearing on many morning talk shows and interviews, Chua publicly justifies this harsh treatment by asserting that she is instilling good values of hard work and discipline in order for her two daughters to succeed, alluding to the idea of the model minority. She treats childhood as a training ground for her daughters' future achievements and criticizes the American parenting style by contending that American parents are too lax in allowing their children to waste many hours on social media and computer games without preparing them for success in the real world.

Conclusion

The model minority stereotype has been cast upon Asian Americans as hardworking, persevering overachievers. This stereotype posits that good work ethics determine the success of most Asian American ethnic groups. Upholding this concept is the belief that other racial groups can also reach high academic attainment leading to upward social mobility if only they would simply emulate Asian Americans' Confucian ethics. Underlying this premise is that other racial groups are not succeeding because they are lazy, unmotivated, or culturally deficient. This viewpoint has been asserted to refute systemic racism and discrimination in the United States and places the responsibility fully on the individual and racial group(s). The model minority stereotype is significant to Asian Americans because it has denied public assistance to other ethnic Asian American groups in need, such as Hmong, Cambodian, and Vietnamese. Furthermore, the model minority myth creates a racial hierarchy with whites on top, followed by Asian Americans and the remainder of the racial groups in the United States at the lower rungs of society. This hierarchy creates interracial tensions between Asian Americans and other racial groups (which have often led to anti-Asian violence) while maintaining white supremacy.

Mary Thi Pham and Jonathan H. X. Lee

See also: Chinese Americans and Education; Discrimination against Asian Americans; Japanese Americans and Education; Tiger Mom

Further Reading

Caplan, Nathan, Marcella H. Choy, and John K. Whitmore. "Indochinese Refugee Families and Academic Achievement." *Scientific America* 266(2) (1992): 36–42.

Chou, Rosalind S., and Joe R. Feagin. *The Myth of the Model Minority: Asian Americans Facing Racism.* Boulder, CO: Paradigm Publishers, 2008.

Danico, Mary Yu, and Franklin Ng. "Asian Americans: A Model Minority?" In *Asian American Issues: Contemporary American Ethnic Issues,* edited by Ronald H. Bayor, 23–41. Westport, CT: Greenwood, 2004.

Hing, Bill Ong. "Shaping the Vietnamese American Community: Refugee Law and Policy." In *Making and Remaking Asian America Through Immigration Policy, 1850–1990,* 121–138. Stanford, CA: Stanford University Press, 1993.

Niedwiecki, Max, and T. C. Duong. *Southeast Asian American Statistical Profile.* Washington, DC: Southeast Asia Resource Action Center, 2004.

Petersen, William. "Success Story: Japanese American Style." *New York Times,* January 9, 1966.

Pew Research Center. "The Rise of Asian Americans." Pew Research Center Social and Demographic Trends, released June 19, 2012, and revised July 12, 2012, http://www.pewsocialtrends.org/2012/06/19/the-rise-of-asian-americans/.

"Success Story of One Minority Group in U.S." *U.S. News & World Report,* December 26, 1966, 73.

"2010 American Community Survey 1-Year Estimates." U.S. Census Bureau, 2010, http://www.census.gov/.

"2010 Census Data." U.S. Census Bureau, 2010, http://www.census.gov/2010census/data/.

MONGOLIAN AMERICAN CULTURE

Before the 1990s, Mongolian American culture existed primarily in several small communities of Kalmyk Mongolians in central New Jersey and eastern Pennsylvania. These Kalmyks were descendants of groups who had moved in the 17th century from western Mongolia and Dzungaria to Kalmykia in southern Russia and then to Europe after World War II. As war refugees from the Nazi invasion of their homeland, 571 Kalmyks immigrated to the United States between December 1951 and March 1952, thanks to the efforts of several religious and social service organizations as well as the U.S. government, which regarded the Kalmyks as political refugees from the Soviet Union. The Freewood Acres section of Howell Township, New Jersey, attracted the largest number of Kalmyk Mongolians; that community numbered close to 3,000 in 2010.

Formal diplomatic relations between the United States and the People's Republic of Mongolia began in 1987. With the shift toward a democratic Mongolia between 1990 and 1992, the number of immigrants from Mongolia to the United States increased significantly, especially among students seeking to further their education. Since the early 1990s, an estimated 25,000 Mongolians have settled in the United States. The five largest centers of population are the Oakland–San Francisco Bay area (roughly 5,000); the Washington, D.C., metropolitan area, especially Arlington County, Virginia (roughly 5,000); the Chicago metropolitan area (roughly 5,000); the Denver metropolitan area (roughly 3,000); and central New Jersey (roughly 3,000). Smaller communities live in Arizona, Florida, Indiana, New Mexico, New York, Texas, and West Virginia.

Of the five major centers of Mongolian Americans in the United States, the one most resembling their ancestral homeland is Denver—known as the Mile-High City because its elevation is 5,280 feet above sea level. Similarly, the average elevation in Mongolia is roughly 5,180 feet, and almost exactly like Colorado, Mongolia's topography ranges from snow-topped peaks of 14,000 feet to rolling grasslands and alpine forests. Nevertheless, the contemporary practices and traditions of Mongolian Americans show less regional variety than consistency and cultural continuity across the country.

Almost all Mongolian Americans are first- or second-generation immigrants who seek to retain their Mongolian identity, heritage, and cultural traditions as (relatively) new Americans. As a result, they emphasize family, food, hospitality, cultural organizations, and religion as the key elements that define their Mongolian heritage and culture. Particularly important is maintaining the multigenerational family unit along with the associated values of mutual support, togetherness, and respect for all age groups. Grandparents live nearby if not in the same household as other family members. The raising and education of children is paramount, especially to teach them Mongolian language and traditions.

Mongolian Americans take much pride in their hospitality, maintaining the tradition of welcoming visitors at any time and serving generous portions of food and drink to their guests. Given the wide variety of foods found in the United States, Mongolian Americans have been able to re-create many of their traditional dishes in their new communities. For instance, the meat-filled dumplings known as *buuz* remain popular in the United States, although it is made from beef rather than the mutton that is more typical of the dish in Mongolia. Also commonly consumed in the United States are *khurag* (a combination of fried meat with rice or dough, carrots or potatoes, and onions) and *tsuvan* (a combination of meat with steamed dough or noodles and assorted vegetables). Often served during traditional holidays is *boortsog* (dough that is deep-fried, sometimes with mutton fat). The most ubiquitous beverage is *suutei tsai* (salty milk tea).

These types of traditional dishes are found not only in nearly every Mongolian American home but also at the festivals and celebration where Mongolian Americans gather. One of the most important is Tsagaan Sar (White Moon), which marks the first day of the lunar new year. In the United States as in Mongolia, this is a time to spend with family members—no matter how distant they may be—or alternately to be with neighbors and friends. Second in importance is Nadaam, which is the summer festival originally linked to the lunar calendar but now begins annually on July 11, the date when Mongolia declared its independence from China in 1921. Mongolians celebrate Nadaam with archery, wrestling, and horse racing, though children's foot races have replaced the racing of horses in many American communities. The traditional Ovoo ceremony (a mountain and sky worshipping ceremony often taking place at the end of summer) was commonly held for many years among the Kalmyk Mongols but ended with the passing of the older generations. Nevertheless, there are some efforts being made to revive this traditional practice along with the traditional fire ceremony.

The practice of religion was officially discouraged during Mongolia's communist period but has rebounded not only in democratic Mongolia but also among Mongolian Americans. The Kalmyk Mongolians in the 1950s were one of the first groups to practice Tibetan-style Buddhism in the United States, especially following the founding of the Tashi Lhunpo Buddhist Temple in Howell, New Jersey, in 1955. Other major religious centers in the United States include the Oakland

Yak dancer performing at the Mongolian Festival, a celebration of Mongolian culture in Bloomington, Indiana, October 26, 2007. (blickwinkel/Alamy Stock Photo)

Branch of the Tibetan Center for Compassion and Wisdom, which opened in 2002; the Mongolian Christian Church in Los Angeles, which was founded by a Korean missionary to Mongolia; the Mongolian Gandan Temple in Denver; and the Tibetan Mongolian Buddhist Cultural Center in Bloomington, Indiana.

Another effective method among Mongolian Americans for maintaining their identity and heritage is the creation of Mongolian cultural and philanthropic organizations in the United States. Among the most prominent are the Mongol-American Cultural Association in New Brunswick, New Jersey; the Kalmyk-American Cultural Association in Howell, New Jersey; the Bay Area Mongolian Association; the Mongolian Community Association of Colorado; the Washington, D.C., area Mongolian Community Association and Mongolian School of the National Capital Area in northern Virginia; and the Mongolia Society in Bloomington, Indiana, which is the oldest organization in the United States relating to Mongolia that was founded in 1961 to promote the study of Mongolian history, language, and culture. These organizations help to promote Mongolian-language publications, performances of Mongolian culture such as the Chinggis Khan Ceremony (which memorializes the founder of the Mongol Empire), and various humanitarian activities, such as donating educational materials and clothing to children in Mongolia.

James I. Deutsch

See also: Bhutanese and Nepalese American Culture; Burmese (Myanmar) American Culture; Tibetan American Culture

Further Reading

Baatar, Ts. "Social and Cultural Change in the Mongol-American Community." *Anthropology of East Europe Review* 17(2) (1999): 100–205.

Bahrampour, Tara. "Mongolians Meld Old, New in Making Arlington Home." *Washington Post*, July 3, 2006, http://www.washingtonpost.com/wp-dyn/content /article/2006/07/02/AR2006070200875.html.

Bormanshinov, Arash. "Kalmyks." In *Harvard Encyclopedia of American Ethnic Groups*, edited by Stephan Thernstrom, 599–600. Cambridge: Belknap Press of Harvard University Press, 1980.

Cayton-Holland, Adam. "Among the Mongols: Steppe by Steppe, the Hordes are Descending on Denver." Westword, July 6, 2006, http://www.westword.com/2006 -07-06/news/among-the-mongols/.

Kohn, Michael, Anne M. Henochowicz, Bolortsetseg C. Smith, and Matthew J. Forss. "Mongolian Americans." In *Encyclopedia of Asian American Folklore and Folklife*, edited by Jonathan H. X. Lee and Kathleen M. Nadeau, 811–849. Santa Barbara: ABC-CLIO, 2011.

Rubel, Paula G. *The Kalmyk Mongols: A Study in Continuity and Change*. Bloomington: Indiana University Press, 1967.

MONKEY KING

History and Origin

The Monkey King is a favorite character for children as well as adults in Chinese folklore, literature, and media. Although various cultural elements and sources have enriched his character, the most important text establishing the Monkey King's far-reaching fame is a classic Chinese novel from the 16th century, *Xi you ji* (*The Journey to the West*), commonly attributed to Wu Cheng'en (ca. 1506–ca. 1582). *The Journey to the West* has some loose historical basis in the 17-year pilgrimage of the monk Xuanzang (596–664), also known as Tripitaka or Tang Sanzang, to India in search of Buddhist scriptures from 629 to 645. It is believed that Wu Cheng'en developed Xuanzang's story into a colorful novel, most likely based on previous versions, both written and oral. In this novel, the disciples who accompany Xuanzang on his journey are Sun Wukong, Zhu Wuneng, and Sha Wujing (commonly known as Monkey, Pigsy, and Sandy, respectively).

The novel begins with the monkey's miraculous birth out of a rock on the Flower and Fruit Mountain, where many monkeys reside. The monkey then acquires various skills in martial arts, shape shifting, and other areas, following a Daoist master. After he becomes the king of the monkeys, he seeks a title and recognition from heaven. After being rejected by the gods and goddesses, he

American Born Chinese (2006)

Gene Luen Yang's (1973–) graphic novel *American Born Chinese* (2006) retells the Chinese folk story of the Monkey King in a new light. This graphic novel transforms traditional Chinese folklore and transplants the character of the Monkey King into a contemporary Chinese American context. It converges the story of the Monkey King; Jin Wang, a schoolboy whose parents are immigrants from China; Danny, a seemingly all-American high school student; and cousin Chin-Kee, who represents numerous racial stereotypes of Chinese immigrants and Chinese Americans.

The book enjoyed stunning success shortly after its publication. In addition to winning the favor of general readers, this work has been praised by numerous book reviewers, critics, and scholars. It won the American Library Association's Michael L. Printz Award for Excellence in Young Adult Literature and was a National Book Award finalist in the young people's literature category.

wreaks havoc in heaven and labels himself the Monkey King. As a result, the Buddha confines him under a mountain of rocks with a seal for 500 years. When the bodhisattva Guanyin appoints Xuanzang for the pilgrimage to India, Xuanzang frees the Monkey King and takes him as a disciple to protect and assist him. On their long and dangerous journey to the West, the Monkey King, together with Pigsy and Sandy and sometimes with the guidance or assistance of the bodhisatvva Guanyin, fight against various demons, monsters, humans, wild creatures, and other forces threatening Xuangzang's life. In the end, the Monkey King achieves enlightenment.

The colorful elements in this novel provide an important basis for the Monkey King's characterization, which later versions and adaptations have built on, expanded, and rewritten. Through its many variations and incarnations, the story of the Monkey King has been a favorite for millions of Chinese children and adults and has become known to English-speaking readers as well through translation and media adaptations.

Contemporary Representations in Literature and Media

The Monkey King's tale has become known to English-speaking readers through translation, media adaptations, and literary works that retell his story or draw inspiration from it. English translations of *The Journey to the West* include Arthur Waley's (1889–1966) abridged translation, *Monkey: Folk Novel of China* (1943) and Anthony C. Yu's (1938–) four-volume translation *The Journey to the West* (1977).

The United States has seen several media productions related to the Monkey King's story in recent years. For example, the television miniseries *The Monkey King* (also known as *The Lost Empire*) was produced by NBC and the SciFi Channel in 2001. Directed by Rob Minkoff (1962–), the feature film *The Forbidden Kingdom* (2008) is another contemporary spin-off of this popular character. It reconfigures the character and legend of the Monkey King in an action-packed martial arts film starring both Jackie Chan (1954–) and Jet Li (1963–). In 2014, a fantasy 3D film *The Monkey King*, directed by Pou-soi Cheang (1972–), was released in Hong Kong and mainland China. It is scheduled to be released in the United States in selected theaters. The film stars Donnie Yen (1963–) as the Monkey King and Chow Yun-Fat (1955–) as the Jade Emperor.

Many Asian American literary works have drawn inspiration from the Monkey King and his tale, such as Timothy Mo's *The Monkey King* (1987), Gerald Robert Vizenor's *Griever: An American Monkey King in China* (1987), Maxine Hong Kingston's *Tripmaster Monkey: His Fake Book* (1989), and Patricia Chao's *Monkey King* (1997). All these writers have adapted or alluded to the

Yulin Fang is dressed as the Monkey King during a celebration of the Chinese New Year in Chinatown, New York City, January 17, 2004. (Linda Rosier/NY Daily News Archive via Getty Images)

story of the Monkey King and altered his character as well as the story line for their respective political and critical agendas. The Monkey King has also attracted attention from authors of children's literature and has been adapted into a number of picture books. Some recent examples include Grania Davis's *The Monkey King: Legend of a Wise and Brave Leader* (1998), Ed Young's *Monkey King* (2001), Debby Chen and Wenhai Ma's *Monkey King Wreaks Havoc in Heaven* (2001) and *Tang Monk Disciples Monkey King* (2005). These works generally adapt the Chinese folk story for child readers and their parents.

Lan Dong

See also: Buddhism; Children's and Young Adult Literature, Asian American; Chinese American Folklore; Comics and Graphic Narratives, Asian American; Confucianism; Daoism

Further Reading

Lai, Whalen. "From Protean Ape to Handsome Saint: The Monkey King." *Asian Folklore Studies* 53(1) (1994): 29–65.

Lutgendorf, Philip. *Hanuman's Tale: The Messages of a Divine Monkey.* Oxford and New York: Oxford University Press, 2007.

Pearson, J. Stephen. "The Monkey King in the American Canon: Patricia Chao and Gerald Vizenor's Use of an Iconic Chinese Character." *Comparative Literature Studies* 43(3) (2006): 355–374.

Sims, Cecilia Ann. "The Rebirth of Indian and Chinese Mythology in Gerald Vizenor's *Griever: An American Monkey King in China.*" *Bestia: Yearbook of the Beast Fable Society* 3 (1991): 48–55.

Zhao, Vincent. *The Monkey King: 72 Transformations of the Mythical Hero.* San Rafael, CA: Insight Editions, 2012.

MUSICAL THEATER, ASIAN AMERICAN

History and Origins

Asian American musical theater, defined here as musically dramatic performance that involves artists, audiences, and characters of Asian descent in the United States, has significantly contributed to U.S. culture and popular conceptions. The histories and conventions of this musical tradition reside in earlier productions and genres, specifically opera from China and from Europe. In 1852 the Tong Hook Tong Dramatic Company began to present Cantonese opera in San Francisco; this was the first time traditional Chinese opera was

Flower Drum Song (1958)

Based on the novel by C. Y. Lee (Chin Yang Lee), *Flower Drum Song* was an Asian American musical on Broadway. The musical debuted in 1958 with music by Richard Rodgers and lyrics and libretto by Oscar Hammerstein II. For the musical plot, Hammerstein simplified Lee's story by focusing on the romances of newly emigrated from China Mei-Li and assimilated Asian American Wang-Ta as well as the Asian American nightclub performer Linda Low and owner Sammy Fong. For the score, Rodgers and Hammerstein composed many popular numbers such as "I Enjoy Being a Girl" and "Grant Avenue." The musical is perhaps best remembered for its 1961 film version in which nearly all of the actors were Asian American. It is performed infrequently due in part to the criticism of the stereotypical portrayals of the Asian characters and women. In 2001, David Henry Hwang penned a revised libretto that was critically lauded after its premiere in Los Angeles but poorly received on Broadway. Hwang rearranged the order of songs and integrated them into the new story. His revamped narrative introduced more complexities about immigration, assimilation, and representation, resulting in a rich if contradictory text.

Miss Saigon (1989)

A megamusical about the Vietnam War, *Miss Saigon* aroused momentous controversy over its casting and portrayal of Asians. Based on the opera *Madama Butterfly* (1903) by Giacomo Puccini, which was based on David Belasco's play and stories by John Luther Long and Pierre Loti, the musical debuted on the West End in London in 1989. The score was written and composed by Claude-Michel Schönberg, Alain Boublil, and Richard Maltby Jr. and produced by Cameron Mackintosh. The story follows a white U.S. soldier named Chris who falls in love with Kim, a young Vietnamese sex worker. A Eurasian pimp, known as The Engineer, presides over the brothel. In the evacuation of Saigon, during which a spectacular helicopter effect regales the audience, Chris leaves behind a pregnant Kim. Ultimately he marries another woman and returns to find Kim, who kills herself so that her child might have a brighter future in the United States. When Mackintosh declared that the musical would come to Broadway with Jonathan Pryce, a white actor, in the role of The Engineer, Asian American artists and activists called upon the Actors' Equity to bar this yellowface casting. Some also condemned the Orientalist and abject depictions of Asians as weak, poor, feminized, and sexualized. Despite these critiques, major presses touted Pryce's talents and box office value, and the Actors' Equity ultimately agreed with Mackintosh's arguments about freedom of expression and prejudice against white actors. *Miss Saigon* played on Broadway from 1991 to 2001. Revivals of the musical have again provoked protests, though the 2014 West End production has broken records by grossing more than twice as much as any other show in its first day of ticket sales.

performed in the United States. The troupe was popular among Chinese immigrants who had come to California to mine for gold. When the company performed in New York, however, its aesthetics were misunderstood and poorly received because the East Coast audience was more familiar with Western images of Chinese culture. European operas strongly influenced U.S. interpretations of Asians. Giacomo Puccini's *Madama Butterfly* (1903), with its pentatonic scales, primitive melodies, and plaintive, more Western-sounding arias for sympathetic characters, contributed to an Orientalist musical taxonomy. Operetta, a genre related to opera but typically with more comic and fantastical overtones, has also shaped the soundscape of Asian and Asian American characters, stories, and settings. W. S. Gilbert and Arthur Sullivan's *The Mikado* (1885), which on the one hand incorporates the Japanese military song "Miya Sama" and on the other hand invents Orientalist musical dispositions, is frequently produced today, often still with all-white casts.

Earlier Western lenses of Asians profoundly influenced musical theater into the 20th century, though they also became increasingly multidimensional. U.S. musicals come from a variety of performance traditions, among them opera, operetta, minstrelsy, vaudeville, burlesque, and extravaganza. Comic Asian characters, sometimes played by Asian actors and at other times by white actors, appeared in many musicals. For example, the popular musical *Anything Goes* (1934), composed by Cole Porter, includes Ching and Ling, stereotyped gamblers and Christian converts, as well as leading white protagonists who impersonate Chinese characters toward the end of the musical. Meanwhile Chinatowns, most famously in San Francisco, opened nightclubs that provided many opportunities for Asian American performers to showcase their talents for largely white audiences. Richard Rodgers and Oscar Hammerstein II dramatized such a nightclub in *Flower Drum Song* (1958). Rodgers and Hammerstein are the legendary Jewish American duo often celebrated for their refinement of the integrated book musical beginning with *Oklahoma!* in 1943 through their other Asian-themed musicals, *South Pacific* (1949) and *The King and I* (1951). Building upon Rodgers's dramatic, largely European-inspired music, Hammerstein penned libretti and lyrics to explore racial, ethnic, and national tensions between East and West, often advocating for tolerance and mutual understanding yet replicating stereotypes of Asian-descended characters as feminized and childish. In *Pacific Overtures* (1976), librettist John Weidman and composer Stephen Sondheim dramatized the Westernization of Japan during the second half of the 19th century. Harold Prince directed this production using an all-male and all-Asian cast among other kabuki techniques, and Sondheim incorporated Japanese and Western musical traditions to illustrate changes in Japan.

Contemporary Forms

More recently, Asian Americans have been writing their own musicals. In 1979, Philip Kan Gotanda wrote the playful musical *The Avocado Kid or Zen in the Art of Guacamole,* inspired by the Japanese children's tale about Momotaro the Peach Boy. David Henry Hwang has also become an important part of the operatic and musical worlds. In the 1980s Hwang began to collaborate with Philip Glass, writing several operas such as *The Voyage* (1992) and *The Sound of a Voice* (2003), the latter of which was based on Hwang's plays. Hwang is the most frequently produced living librettist. In addition, he penned the books for the Disney Broadway musicals *Aida* (2000) and *Tarzan* (2006). When he wrote a revised libretto for Rodgers and Hammerstein's *Flower Drum Song* in 2001, the production became the first musical by and about Asian Americans to reach Broadway.

Asian representation in musical theater continues to earn both approbation and condemnation. In 1991 *Miss Saigon* opened on Broadway, triggering criticism of its Orientalist casting, characters, and plot as well as defense of its aesthetic integrity and freedom. *The Nightingale*, based on the Hans Christian Andersen tale set in feudal China, similarly aroused controversy at La Jolla Playhouse in 2012 when the cast consisted almost entirely of non-Asian performers. Other new Broadway musicals have created well-rounded Asian American characters with psychological depth, such as the high-achieving Catholic girl named Marcy Park in *The 25th Annual Putnam County Spelling Bee* (2005), with score by William Finn and based on the book by Rachel Sheinkin.

Several Asian American musicals were in recent development. In 2014 David Henry Hwang's *Kung Fu*, a dramatic piece about Bruce Lee told through

Since the musical *Miss Saigon*'s record-breaking run at London's Theatre Royal, Drury Lane, more than two decades ago, it has played in 300 cities in 15 different languages, winning awards around the world. It has also caused controversies and protests over its casting and portrayals of Asians. This photo is from a performance at West End Live, London, United Kingdom, June 21, 2014. (Dave Evans/ Demotix/Corbis)

music and dance, premiered at the Signature Theater in New York City, where Hwang has a playwright residency. *Allegiance,* which explores a Japanese American family's experiences of World War II internment, came to Broadway in the fall of 2015 after breaking box office records at the Old Globe in San Diego in 2012. The musical boasts many key Asian American artists including director Stafford Arima, writer and composer Jay Kuo, and actor George Takei, who was interned as a child and inspired Kuo. In the popular world of musical theater, Asian Americans in the past few decades have increasingly told and appeared in their own stories.

Donatella Galella

See also: Asian Indian American Performing Arts and Artists; Cambodian American Performing Arts and Artists; Dance, Asian American; Theater, Asian American

Further Reading

Bacalzo, Dan. "A Different Drum: David Henry Hwang's Musical 'Revisal' of *Flower Drum Song.*" *Journal of American Drama and Theatre* 15(2) (2003): 71–83.

Lee, Esther Kim. *A History of Asian American Theatre.* New York and Cambridge: Cambridge University Press, 2006.

Lee, Josephine. *The Japan of Pure Invention: Gilbert and Sullivan's* The Mikado. Minneapolis: University of Minnesota Press, 2010.

Locke, Ralph P. "Reflections on Orientalism in Opera and Musical Theater." *Opera Quarterly* 10(1) (1993): 48–64.

McConachie, Bruce A. "The 'Oriental' Musicals of Rodgers and Hammerstein and the U.S. War in Southeast Asia." *Theatre Journal* 46(3) (1994): 385–398.

Most, Andrea. "'You've Got to Be Carefully Taught': The Politics of Race in Rodgers and Hammerstein's *South Pacific.*" *Theatre Journal* 52(2–3) (2000): 307–337.

MUSIC AND MUSICIANS, ASIAN AMERICAN

History and Origins

Asian American music dates back to the early Asian immigrants who settled in the United States during the 1700s and 1800s. There is a plethora of different types of Asian American music ranging from the variety of countries and cultures the immigrants came from. As Asian immigrants adapted to their new home, they ventured into different genres of music, including jazz, classical orchestra, pop, and R&B, while also acculturating traditional Asian instruments such as *taiko* drums and *kulintang* (Filipino gongs and drums).

Despite the use of Asian instruments to perform and create Asian American music, the formal term "Asian American" was not created until the late 1960s by

Yo-Yo Ma (1955–)

Yo-Yo Ma, a prominent and world-famous cellist, was born into a musical family. His mother was a singer, and his father was a violinist. With this musical background, he became a child prodigy by the age of five. Ma attended the renowned Juilliard School for his musical talents. He has 75 albums, and 15 of them have received Grammy Awards. In addition, he received the Avery Fisher Prize in 1978, which is an award given to an American for his or her accomplishments in classical music. In 2011 Ma received the Presidential Medal of Freedom, the highest civilian award in the United States.

Some of Ma's notable playing was featured in films scores, including *The Untouchables* (1987), *Seven Years in Tibet* (1997), *Crouching Tiger, Hidden Dragon* (2000), *Master and Commander: The Far Side of the World* (2003), and *Memoirs of a Geisha* (2005). Ma and his music were featured on numerous television shows as well, including *Arthur, The West Wing, Sesame Street,* and *Mister Rogers' Neighborhood.*

Currently among other ventures, Ma is involved with the Silk Road Ensemble, which brings together an array of artists with various backgrounds from around the world. The Silk Road Ensemble attempts to combine traditional and contemporary forms of music while performing at numerous venues worldwide.

Yuji Ichioka to serve as a political expression in order to unite people from different Asian ethnic groups, including Japanese Americans, Chinese Americans, Filipino Americans, and Korean Americans. An Asian American musician can be loosely defined as a person who identifies as an Asian American producing, playing, or singing music or any person who is not necessarily of Asian American descent but associates himself or herself by playing an Asian instrument.

The first album that is widely recognized as Asian American music is *A Grain of Sand: Music for the Struggle of Asians in America,* released in 1973 by the group Yellow Pearl. The members included Chris Iijima (1948–2005), Joanne Nobuko Miyamoto, and Charlie Chin. They produced and sang songs to deliver an activist message, which they hoped would resonate with people. The ultimate goal of the group was to provide a message to help change the culture for Asian Americans. Yellow Pearl's iconic song was "We Are the Children." Some of the lyrics include "We are the children of the migrant worker . . . we are the offspring of the concentration camp . . . Sons and daughters of the railroad builder . . . who will leave their stamp on America." Based on the lyrics, the group set out to describe Asian Americans and how they will be a part of American history. Ultimately, this paved the way for future Asian American musicians.

Practices and Traditions

When early Asian immigrants came to the United States in the 1700s and 1800s, they kept many traditional cultures and practices from their homeland to pass down to future generations, including various traditional instruments. Even though these instruments were brought over more than 200 years ago, they are still played by many and used in various cultural ceremonies in the diverse Asian American community.

There are many festivals that contain traditional music and musical instruments. One example is using *taiko* drums for Bon Odori (Bon dance) during Obon festivals, the Japanese Buddhist ceremony that honors the spirits of deceased ancestors. Another example is using *dagu* drums, *bo* cymbals, and *luo* gongs during Chinese festivals, especially together with the lion dance for Chinese New Year. Another example is using the *kulintang* (gongs/drums) for dances in a *debut* (coming-of-age party for young Filipinas).

As stated earlier, the Yellow Pearl musical group is widely regarded as the first Asian American group to produce Asian American music. Their music was a form of resistance and recognition; there were political undertones associated with the lyrics of the songs. Emerging out of the political activism by Yellow Pearl, Asian Americans started to embrace the genre of jazz music. Jazz has been widely associated with race and regarded as a form of resistance throughout the history of the United States. There have been numerous Asian American jazz musicians. For example, pioneering jazz musicians Glenn Horiuchi (1955–2000) and Mark Izu (1954–) are widely known around San Francisco and in the Bay Area. Horiuchi is famous for playing the piano and the *shamisen* (a three-stringed traditional Japanese instrument) and also composing his own music. Izu is known for playing a double bass as well as composing his own music. Another famous pioneering jazz musician from the East Coast was Fred Ho (1957–2014). Ho was famous for playing a baritone saxophone along with composing his own music.

Asian Americans have been widely associated with classical musical instruments such as the violin, cello, and viola. There have been three Asian Americans who have won the Avery Fisher Prize for outstanding achievement in classical music. Yo-Yo Ma (1955–) is a cellist and was the first Asian American to win the Avery Fisher Prize in 1978. Violinists Sarah Chang (1980–) and Midori Goto (1971–) won the Avery Fisher Prize in 1999 and 2001, respectively.

Contemporary Forms

There have been many contemporary Asian American musicians who have garnered mainstream attention. Arguably, the most notable Asian American

Cellist Yo-Yo Ma performing during inauguration ceremonies for Boston mayor-elect Marty Walsh in Conte Forum at Boston College in Boston, Massachusetts, January 6, 2014. A renowned musician with worldwide fame, Ma is a recipient of the Presidential Medal of Freedom. (AP Photo/Michael Dwyer)

group is Far East Movement, consisting of four Asian American men and based out of Los Angeles. The group was formed in 2006. The members are Kevin Nishimura (1984–), James Roh (1984–), Jae Choung (1972–), and Virman Coquia. Far East Movement broke into mainstream media with its song "Round Round," which was featured in *The Fast and the Furious: Tokyo Drift* (2006). Since then, the group has had numerous hit songs including "Girls on the Dance Floor," "Like a G6," and "Rocketeer" featuring Ryan Tedder (1979–), lead vocalist of the group OneRepublic. Most notably, Far East Movement is the first Asian American group to earn a number one hit on the *Billboard* Hot 100 in the United States for its song "Like a G6."

Another mainstream Asian American musical artist is Peter Hernandez (1985–), better known by his stage name Bruno Mars. Mars, part Filipino, started his career by being featured in two popular songs: "Nothin' on You" by B.o.B and "Billionaire" by Travie McCoy (1981–). Amassing so much attention from the previously mentioned songs, Mars began his solo career by releasing his album *Doo-Wops and Hooligans* in 2010. The album produced numerous world-renowned songs, including "Grenade," "Just the Way You Are," and "The Lazy Song." In 2012 Mars released his second album, titled *Unorthodox Jukebox*. The album was a hit success and includes the songs "Locked Out of Heaven," "Treasure," and "When I Was Your Man." Since the release of his first album, Mars has accumulated two Grammy Awards, one for best pop vocal performance for his song "Just the Way You Are" and the other for best pop vocal album for *Unorthodox Jukebox*.

Nicole Scherzinger (1978–) is arguably the most famous Asian American female vocalist. Part Filipino and part native Hawai'ian, she was the lead singer for the all-female group the Pussycat Dolls. The group is famous for songs such as "Buttons," "Don't Cha," "Stickwitu," and "When I Grow Up." The Pussycat Dolls eventually disbanded, and Scherzinger pursued a less successful solo career. Despite her relatively unsuccessful solo career, she appeared as a judge on the first season of the U.S. version of *The X Factor* in 2011. After being let go from the American version of the show, she was a judge on the United Kingdom's *The X Factor* for two years (2012–2013).

Even though there are a few Asian Americans who have broken through to mainstream popular music, there are still an ample amount of Asian American artists hoping to become recognized. These artists have turned to the popular video-sharing website YouTube. A majority of these artists do covers of songs, which is when the YouTube artist takes a song already made famous from someone else and adds his or her original identity to the song. Some of these artists include Jason Chen, Cathy Nguyen, and Joseph Vincent. Each artist has over 300,000 people subscribed to his or her YouTube channel, where the artist uploads music videos or covers of himself or herself. After establishing a strong fan base, a couple of the artists released original songs. Jason Chen released many original singles, but his most popular video is "AutoTune," which has amassed over 3.2 million views on YouTube. Similarly, Joseph Vincent has uploaded multiple original songs, with his most popular single being "If You Stay," which has more than 6.3 million views on his YouTube channel. Not only have the two artists released covers and original songs individually, but they also have collaborated and done a variety of covers that became very popular. A couple of these covers include "Just a Dream" by Nelly and "Hold my Hand" by Michael Jackson featuring Akon. These covers have become widely popular and accumulated 8.3 and 3.7 million views, respectively.

Ryan Hata

See also: Dance, Asian American; Festivals and Holidays, Asian American; Filipino Folk Music; Musical Theater, Asian American

Further Reading

Asai, Susan M. "Cultural Politics: The African American Connection in Asian American Jazz-Based Music." *Asian Music* 36(1) (2005): 87–108.

Bacalzo, Dan. "A Different Drum: David Henry Hwang's Musical 'Revisal' of *Flower Drum Song*." *Journal of American Drama and Theatre* 15(2) (2003): 71–83.

Lam, Joseph Sui Ching. "Embracing 'Asian American Music' as an Heuristic Device." *Journal of Asian American Studies* 2(1) (1999): 29–60.

Pao, Angela. *No Safe Spaces: Re-Casting Race, Ethnicity, and Nationality in American Theater.* Ann Arbor: University of Michigan Press, 2010.

Phillips, Gary. "Dancing between the Notes: Music and Asian American Panethnicity." Color Lines, June 1998, http://www.colorlines.com/archives/1998/06/dancing_between_the_notes_music_and_asian_american_panethnicity.html.

P

PAKISTANI AMERICAN CULTURE

History and Origins

The nation of Pakistan (Land of the Pure) was established on August 14, 1947, after a determined struggle by the All India Muslim League and its leader Muhammad Ali Jinnah (1876–1948). Pakistanis migrated to the United States long before 1947 from the present region of Pakistan during the colonial period but in fewer numbers than in later periods and primarily as laborers. The immigration process was accelerated in the latter part of the 20th century. The lack of opportunity for economic advancement in Pakistan, a high unemployment rate, and prospects of success abroad are major factors for Pakistani migration. With the passage of the Immigration and Nationality Act of 1965, the migration process accelerated. In the last two decades, migration has increased. The

Muhammad Ali Jinnah (1876–1948)

Muhammad Ali Jinnah, a prominent Muslim leader of British India, an architect of Pakistan, and first governor-general, has been revered by Pakistani Americans. Various Pakistani American associations celebrate his birthday. It is Jinnah or the Quaid-e-Azam (Great Leader) who has created an identity for Muslims living in the land that became Pakistan after the partition of India in 1947. He was close with leaders of the Indian National Congress (INC) and joined the organization in 1905. Jinnah was hailed as ambassador of the Hindu-Muslim unity. But he felt marginalized in the INC and endeavored toward a separate nation-state for the Muslims. The Pakistan Resolution was adopted on March 23, 1940. Jinnah spelled out the two-nation theory, highlighting the social, political, economic, and cultural differences between Hindus and Muslims. His efforts paid dividends, and demand for a separate nation for Muslims gathered momentum. In April 1946, Jinnah reiterated demand for Pakistan consisting of Muslim majority areas of Bengal and Assam in the east and the Punjab, North-West Frontier Province, Sind, and Baluchistan in the west. Jinnah's dream materialized, and the Islamic Republic of Pakistan was born on August 14, 1947.

number of Pakistani immigrants was 9,415 in 2003, according to the records of the Homeland Security Office. But the number of people obtaining permanent legal status increased to 14,740 in 2012. Most of the Pakistani migrants are concentrated in the states of New York, New Jersey, California, and Illinois. In the American metropolitan areas, they are found in New York City, Houston, Los Angeles, Philadelphia, and Detroit. Along with top-class professionals, there are more low-paid wage earners such as taxi drivers, bellboys, hawkers, and vendors. Coming from the Islamic Republic of Pakistan, a Muslim state, the immigrants are almost all followers of Islam. With the values, cultural norms, and lifestyles of their home country, the immigrants have endeavored to adapt their culture in the United States. Muslim identity created some problems for Pakistani Americans after the 9/11 terrorist attacks on the United States.

Contemporary Forms and Practices

Pakistani Americans follow a cultural pattern that makes a harmonious balance between their religion and the lifestyle in their original homeland with the environment of their new country. In this way, their identity as Pakistani Americans is preserved. Another problem facing these immigrants is the grouping of Pakistanis with other immigrants from the Middle East in popular perceptions. Grouping them together with Indians, Bangladeshis, Nepalese, and Sri Lankans in a broad South Asian category is also not appreciated by many Pakistani Americans. Pakistani heritage is preserved in language, literature, cuisine, dress, music, dance, festivals, and organizations as well as associations, legends, and popular beliefs.

Believing in the basic tenets of Islam, Pakistani Americans offer prayer five times a day, observe fasting in Ramadan, and celebrate Islamic festivals such as the birth of Prophet Muhammad and Eid. But expression of a unique Pakistani culture and identity is reflected in secular festivals. August 14, the independence day of Pakistan, is marked by parades, dancing, music, and speeches in enclaves where Pakistani Americans are in preponderance. Kite flying is witnessed in the *basant* (advent of spring) festival. The immigrants also participate in typical American holidays such as the Fourth of July, Thanksgiving, New Year, and Halloween. Dance and music are essential features of Pakistani American culture. These cultural expressions are found in weddings and festivals. The *luddi* is a folk dance performed by women moving in circles along with the clapping of hands. The *bhangra,* a popular dance in the Punjab region of the Indian subcontinent, is marked by fast movements with the loud beating of drums. In diaspora *bhangra* is mixed with hip-hop and other Western styles. In night clubs and functions of university campuses, it is performed by the younger generation. The *qawwali,* tracing its origin to Sufi devotional music, is performed in cultural centers, during religious gatherings, and on festive occasions. Nusrat Fateh Ali Khan's troupe is the most popular *qawwali* music. The *harmonium, tabla, sarangi,* and *dholak* are common musical instruments. The lyrical verses of *ghazal* are popular in gatherings of *mushayara* (poetry recital). The music from Pakistani and Bollywood movies is popular. A combination of Western pop with traditional Urdu lyrics is catching on with the new generation. Nadia Ali (1980–) is a famous diaspora singer, and her album *Embers* (2009) has been much appreciated. Detroit's Rasheed Khan and Junoon, a New York rock band, have become popular.

Pakistani American cuisine with its spicy ingredients and aromatic richness is a significant component of culture. The long tradition of Indian cuisine coupled with Central Asian influence has been brought to the United States. Pakistani and Indian cuisine sometimes become presented together and is available in the same restaurants. Visits to Pakistani food outlets and grocery stores tie the immigrants with a Pakistani heritage. Spices, including *garam masala* (usually a combination of cinnamon, nutmeg, cloves, cardamom, mace, peppercorns, coriander, and cumin) or those spices separately, along with turmeric and chili powder, are essential ingredients in Pakistani American cooking. The meat dishes must be *halal* due to religious factors that govern slaughtering requirements. Pork is prohibited in Islam. Some of the delicious dishes in the Pakistani American kitchen are *pulao* (an aromatic rice dish sprinkled with vegetables), *biriyani* (rice marinated with meat or vegetables), *kebab* (spicy meat marinated with spices and lemon juice), Mughlai chicken, *naan* (bread), and spinach. The desserts include *ladu, jalebi, ras malai,* and *kheer.* Keeping with the Indian subcontinent tradition, a meal is sometimes followed by betel chewing (a kind of leaf wrapped around an areca nut). Pakistani American women may enjoy jewelry such as bangles, necklaces, earrings, and rings made of gold, which are studded with precious stones. On festive occasions there is the application of *mehendi* (henna paste), with its delicate and exquisite designs, by women. The traditional dress for them is *salwaar kameez.*

There are newspapers and journals such as *Jung* (New Jersey), *Minaret* (New York), *New York Crescent* (New York), and *Pakistan News* (Washington, D.C.) that highlight issues pertinent to Pakistani Americans. The TV Asia network beamed from New Jersey shows Pakistani movies, soap operas, and plays along with Asian Indian programs. The organizations and associations headquartered in cities with Pakistani American populations look after the interests of particular groups as well as the immigrants as a whole, offering a platform for bringing them together to discuss common issues affecting them. Some of the notable associations are the Association of Pakistani Americans for Community Organization (New Jersey), the Association of Pakistani Physicians (Westmont, Illinois), the Pakistan League of America (Snellville, Georgia), the U.S.-Pakistan Economic Council (New York), and the American Institute of Pakistan Studies (Philadelphia, Pennsylvania).

There are notable personalities held in high esteem by Pakistani Americans, such as Muhammad Ali Jinnah, the founder of Pakistan; cricketer Imran Khan (1952–); Muhammad Iqbal (1877–1938), the poet and inspirer of Pakistan; singers Noor Jahan (1926–2000) and Nusraat Fathe Ali (1948–1997); and of course film stars of the Indian subcontinent. The younger generation of Pakistani Americans might be Americanized in some form with exposure to pop culture and television, but their quintessential culture often remains Pakistani.

Patit Paban Mishra

See also: Festivals and Holidays, Asian American; Popular Culture, Asian Americans and

Further Reading

Alba, Richard, et al., eds. *Immigration and Religion in America: Comparative and Historical Perspectives.* New York: New York University Press, 2008.

Jaffrelot, Christophe. *A History of Pakistan and Its Origins.* London: Anthem Press, 2002.

Malik, Iftikhar Haider. *Pakistanis in Michigan: A Study of Third Culture and Acculturation.* New York: AMS Press, 1989.

McCloud, Aminah Beverly. *Transnational Muslims in American Society.* Gainesville: University Press of Florida, 2006.

Narayan, Anjana, and Bandana Purkayastha. *Living Religions: Hindu and Muslim South Asian-American Women Narrate Their Experiences.* Sterling, VA: Kumarian, 2009.

Pavri, Tinaz. "Pakistani Americans." Advameg, 2014, http://www.everyculture.com /multi/Le-Pa/Pakistani-Americans.html.

Taus, Stacy-Bolstad. *Pakistanis in America.* Minneapolis: Lerner Publications, 2006.

PAKISTANI AMERICAN RELIGIONS AND BELIEFS

History and Origin

The present territory of Pakistan was Islamized in a significant manner in the beginning of the 13th century. Following this, the majority of the population began to profess Islam. With the creation of Pakistan as a nation-state on

Eid al-Fitr

Eid al-Fitr (Festival of Breaking the Fast), is an important festival for Pakistani Americans. It marks the end of the holy month of Ramadan. The first date of Eid al-Fitr is determined by looking at *eid ka chand* (crescent moon). Therefore, the dates may differ from East Coast to West Coast. On the first day, Pakistani Americans offer collective prayers in mosques and exchange Eid greetings. Visits are paid to friends and relatives. The food is special, with delicious dishes and soft drinks. In this three-day festival, people are supposed to give charity for those in need. On the penultimate day, Pakistani Americans participate in parties hosted by Islamic institutions or wealthy persons. A proverb has originated from this festival: if a person is not available for some days, he or she is addressed as *eid ka chand* (rarely to be seen), like the crescent moon of Eid.

August 14, 1947, Islam became the state religion, with about 95 percent of the population following it. The emigrants from the Islamic Republic of Pakistan adhere to the basic tenets of Islam in their religious beliefs and practices. The majority of them belong to the Sunni sect, and they bring with them a strong sense of Islamic tradition to the United States. There is also Shia representation and a small number of individuals belonging to Hinduism, Buddhism, and Christianity. In the areas where there is a concentration of Pakistani Americans, mosques, madrassas, and Islamic centers are constructed. A small number of immigrants are also attracted to the esoteric practices of Sufism emphasizing meditation and spiritualism.

Religious Traditions and Practices

As devout Muslims, Pakistani Americans pray five times a day, read the Quran, learn the five pillars of Islam, and follow Islamic laws. Friday afternoons are kept for visits to mosques. Men and women pray in separate rooms designated for them in mosques. Children are encouraged by parents to strictly follow the principles of Islam. Hajj, or pilgrimage to Mecca, once in a lifetime is a cherished goal. Pakistani Americans follow the ritual of fasting in the month of Ramadan. Except for children, sick persons, and pregnant women, all others do not take food and water from dawn to sunset. The blessing of Allah is sought, and assistance is provided to the needy. In rites to passages, death rituals, and eating habits, Islamic practices must be strictly followed. The birth ceremonies and marriage rituals conform to Islamic faith. Male babies are circumcised. Female

Pakistani American Muslims praying during Eid al-Fitr (Festival of Breaking the Fast) morning services, marking the end of the Muslim holy month of Ramadan in Bridgeview, Illinois, September 10, 2010. Many Muslims in the United States offer Eid prayers at Islamic centers, mosques, and community halls. (AP Photo/M. Spencer Green)

sexuality is very much reserved. Sex before marriage is prohibited for both males and females. The wedding ceremony is performed in a traditional manner with pomp and grandeur. A *maulvi* (priest) officiates in the *nikaah* (marital agreement). Both bride and groom give consent and accept each other in matrimony. In the United States, both sexes join the funeral procession. After the body is washed, it is wrapped in a cloth and buried in a graveyard after the *salat al-janazah* (funeral prayer) as per Islamic rites. Halal food must be consumed. Orthodox persons even avoid food cooked by non-Muslims.

Religious festivals play a significant role in the immigrant community. Eid al-Fitr (Festival of Sacrifice), marking the end of the holy month of Ramadan, is a three-day celebration. After putting on new clothes, people go to mosques. Eid-ul Adha commemorates the sacrifice of Prophet Ibrahim, when he sacrificed his own son in obedience to God. As a symbol of Ibrahim's deeds, an animal (camel, cow, goat, or sheep free from disease) may be sacrificed by a Muslim family; others may pay for halal butchering and give the food away or donate money for meat that will be properly sacrificed. The festival is also known as Bakri-Eid. Maulidun-Nabi is a great festive occasion for celebrating the birthday of Prophet Muhammad. Also known as Id-I-Milad, it is on the 12th day of

Rabi-uh-Awwal, which is the third month of the Muslim calendar. His death anniversary is also on the same date. Apart from going to mosques to pray and listen to the teachings of the Prophet, there is a street parade with hymns in praise of Muhammad. There is decoration of mosques as well as houses. Falling on the 14th day of Shaban, the eighth month of the Muslim calendar, the Shab-I-Barat festival is marked by registering of humankind's fortune in heaven during the night for the coming year. Pakistani Americans recite *fatiha* (blessings) in the name of the Prophet, his daughter Fatima, and her husband Ali. The meal generally consists of *nan* (unleavened bread) and *halwa* (a kind of sweet dish). Muharram, the first month of the Muslim year, is observed on the 10th day to mark the martyrdom of Imam Husain, the grandson of the Prophet. For nine days mourning is observed, recounting the great sacrifice. On the penultimate day, there are barefoot processions with persons carrying banners and *tazias* (replica of Husain's tombs). Pakistani Americans professing Christianity observe Christmas and Easter. Hindus take part in religious festivals of their religion. Baisakhi Purnima, the birthday of Buddha, is observed by followers of Buddhism.

Pakistani Americans usually keep religious activity confined to mosques and homes. They endeavor to adhere to American secular norms in the public sphere. However, all Pakistani Americans cannot be narrowly defined as far as their perception toward religion and religious beliefs are concerned. Some persons follow a blending of South Asian rituals with general tenets of Islam. Even non-Islamic beliefs such as superstition, ghosts, and spirits have crept into the mind-set of the immigrants. Some young Pakistani Americans while observing religious holidays do not adhere to Islamic practices such as praying five times a day and undertaking pilgrimage. There are Pakistani Americans belonging to the above age group who tend toward another direction and identify themselves deeply with Islam. The males of this group place emphasis on wearing traditional dress, keeping a beard, and putting on skull caps. The females cover their faces or at least put on a head scarf. Muslim student associations are formed on college campuses. Muslims from the Middle East, South Asia, and Southeast Asia as well as converted American Muslims also become members of these associations or participate in activities. It is to be seen in the future which type of religion and religious beliefs within the framework of Islam are followed by Pakistani Americans.

Patit Paban Mishra

See also: Festivals and Holidays, Asian American; Religions and Beliefs, Asian American

Further Reading

Alba, Richard, et al., eds. *Immigration and Religion in America: Comparative and Historical Perspectives.* New York: New York University Press, 2008.

Haddad, Yvonne Y. *Muslims in America: From Sojourners to Citizens.* Oxford and New York: Oxford University Press, 2002.

Malik, Iftikhar Haider. *Pakistanis in Michigan: A Study of Third Culture and Acculturation.* New York: AMS Press, 1989.

McCloud, Aminah Beverly. *Transnational Muslims in American Society.* Gainesville: University Press of Florida, 2006.

Mohammad-Arif, Aminah. *Salaam America: South Asian Muslims in New York.* London: Antem, 2002.

Narayan, Anjana, and Bandana Purkayastha. *Living Religions: Hindu and Muslim South Asian-American Women Narrate Their Experiences.* Sterling, VA: Kumarian, 2009.

Williams, Raymond B. *Religions of Immigrants from India and Pakistan: New Threads in the American Tapestry.* New York and Cambridge: Cambridge University Press, 1988.

PHO

History and Origins

Pho is a Vietnamese dish that combines meat, noodles, vegetables, herbs, and spices in a clear beef broth. In English, the word is pronounced "fuh" with a rising inflection. The origins of *pho* are a bit murky, although at the very least the dish can be traced back to the northern part of Vietnam during French colonial rule. One apocryphal story links *pho* to the Mongol invasion of the 14th century, when the invading warriors carried with them lightweight rice noodles to combine in soups with what they could find. It is true that the dish is based upon whatever ingredients are handy, although most commonly it has combined both Vietnamese and Chinese spices with beef, added largely to appeal to the French (cows were too valuable as labor animals to be eaten on a regular basis prior to French colonization). *Pho* is thus a multicultural dish truly international in its makeup. Following World War II and with increased migration from North to South during the Indochina War and the subsequent Vietnam War, the dish increased in popularity and continued to evolve to appeal to new taste palettes and in response to which ingredients were easier or more difficult to obtain.

Although unknown, there is speculation that the word *pho* derived from the French term *pot au feu* (pot on the fire), a form of French beef stew. The practice of charring the onion and ginger used to spice the broth during the simmering process is very similar to a practice employed in making *pot au feu* and unlike

The Vietnamese Diaspora

Toward the end of and particularly following the Vietnam War, numerous residents of South Vietnam fled the country. At least initially, many chose to emigrate for political reasons, although as Vietnam began to move forward into its communist future, emigration was as much for economic reasons due to unemployment and starvation. Although these emigrants ended up in numerous countries, the most common destination was the United States. For many immigrants, their first home was a military installation such as Camp Pendleton, the U.S. Marine Corps base near San Diego, that hosted families until jobs and permanent housing could be secured. Although the postwar diaspora spread to different regions of the United States, the largest number of immigrants settled in southern California, in particular parts of Orange and Los Angeles Counties. According to the 2010 U.S. census, the number of Americans living in Orange County who identify themselves as Vietnamese American is approaching 200,000. The main cluster of this community is in Westminster and has acquired the colloquial name "Little Saigon." This community and others like it around the United States have introduced the mainstream to various aspects of Vietnamese culture, including its unique cuisine, most notably the popular soup-based dish *pho*.

---

any other practice in Vietnamese cooking. Another story has the word deriving from *phan*, the Vietnamese word for Cantonese rice vermicelli. Regardless of its specific origin, *pho* was sold by street vendors in Nam Dimh Province near Hanoi as early as the 1880s; by the 1920s, it was established fare in more formal restaurants. The soup caught on quickly largely because it was adaptable as a food item. During times of privation, whatever was on hand could be used to augment the broth. Today, *pho* has largely lost its associations as a poverty dish and is often thought of as comfort food, much like menudo in Mexico and chicken noodle soup in the United States. *Pho* is also noted for its curative effects, with ingredients high in folic acid, calcium, and vitamin C conducive for alleviating cold symptoms.

Regional Practices and Traditions

Practices vary, although historically *pho* broth has been made by simmering beef bones and oxtails in water for several hours, seasoned by adding ginger, onion, anise, coriander, fennel, clove, and/or cinnamon. Early on before the dish began to migrate south, flank steak was by far the most common cut of

A bowl of Vietnamese *pho* (noodle soup with beef tendon, tripe, and brisket served with onions, scallions, and cilantro). Since the 1970s, *pho* has become a popular Vietnamese dish in the United States (Ronnie Chua/Dreamstime.com)

meat added to the base, although tendon and tripe were also traditional. In Vietnam, there is a distinct regional variation notable in how *pho* is prepared. Historically, the northern part of the country was more poverty-stricken, explaining the general lack of garnish items. Meat is used sparingly, and only ginger, lime, and chili peppers are added. This spartan variety is known as *pho bac* and is difficult to find anywhere outside of the northern part of Vietnam. In the south, however, and in locations across the globe where it is popular, *pho* tends to be a much more complex dish known as *pho nam*. The meat is a central feature of the dish, with bean sprouts, basil, onions, and herbs joining ginger, lime, and chili peppers as additional garnish items.

Contemporary Forms

During the 1970s and 1980s waves of political refugees fleeing Vietnam arrived in the United States, bringing with them aspects of their cuisine. At this time,

Asian cuisine as ingrained in the American mainstream was largely limited to Chinese food and Japanese sushi, although slowly but surely other national cuisines, such as Thai, were beginning to make inroads. As a whole, Vietnamese food has yet to follow such a trajectory, but *pho* has caught on in the American mainstream, although it is variety heavy in meat and noodles that has drifted somewhat from the poverty dish of its origins. Today there are over 2,000 Vietnamese restaurants in North America, many of them employing the word *pho* in their name. To appeal to American palates accustomed to higher meat and starch content, the style of *pho* most often encountered at such restaurants is *pho nam*. The vegetables and herbs are most often brought to diners on a plate, allowing them to in essence construct their own soup by picking and choosing which garnish items and in what amounts to add to the soup. Restaurants often provide a choice of different meats—including nonbeef options such as chicken or pork—and bowls can be ordered in several different sizes. Two condiments often available to add to the bowl are sweet and salty hoisin sauce and chili sauce, often *sriracha* (rooster sauce) at West Coast restaurants. Some restaurants also have options that contain no monosodium glutamate as well as vegan options, the latter of which would feature a broth prepared without the use of beef bones.

The Vietnamese diaspora following the full communist takeover of the country resulted in over 2 million people of Vietnamese origin making their home in diverse places spread across five continents. Although the contemporary forms of the soup mentioned above are North American, due to the shear breadth of the diaspora *pho* has been introduced to a number of other palates, evolving to combine the dictates of these taste publics with more traditional elements of the dish in creating new versions. Although it had been in English usage long before, first appearing in an English-language cookbook in 1935, the term *pho* was added to the *Oxford English Dictionary* in 2007. Due to the Vietnamese diaspora and increased focus in the West on multicultural experiences, *pho* has become a global dish. Furthermore, in owing not only in the ingredients used but also phonetically and culturally to multiple regions around the world, *pho* exists as a cultural object, illustrating the very possibilities of global culture.

Andrew Howe

See also: Chop Suey; Kimchi; Sushi; Thai American Food; Vietnamese American Food; Vietnamese American Immigration

Further Reading
"The History and Evolution of Pho: A Hundred Years' Journey." Loving Pho, April 2009, www.lovingpho.com/pho-opinion-editorial/history-and-evolution-of -vietnamese-pho/.

"The History of Pho." Trongtien88, January 2012, http://trongtien88.hubpages.com/hub/The-History-of-Pho.

"History of Pho Noodle Soup." Viet World Kitchen, October 2008, www.vietworld kitchen.com/blog/2008/10/the-evolution-of-pho.html.

PICTURE BRIDE

History and Origin

Similar to early Chinese immigration into the United States, Japanese immigrants were predominantly male in the 19th century. As a result of the antimiscegenation laws and regulations at the time, they could not marry white American women. Most of them arrived in Hawai'i to work on the sugarcane plantations; some came to the West Coast, particularly after the 1882 Exclusion Act barred Chinese laborers from entering the country.

The 1907 Gentlemen's Agreement between the United States and Japan allowed wives to join their husbands in the United States, creating an opportunity for Japanese immigrants to look for spouses in Japan and bring them to America. While Japanese women make up the majority of picture brides, Korean women also traveled to the United States as a part of this practice. Japan occupied Korea as its protectorate after the Russo-Japanese War of 1904–1905 and officially annexed the country in 1910. As a result Koreans became Japanese subjects, and thus the Gentlemen's Agreement could be applied to them.

The common practice follows the traditional arranged marriages. Immigrant men working in the United States send photographs back home in order to look for potential wives. Their families and relatives, usually with the help of go-betweens, search for prospective brides on their behalf, considering family background, health, and other factors. Once the bride's name is added to her husband's family registry, she can obtain travel documents to join her husband in the United States. It is not uncommon for mass wedding ceremonies to be held at the dock or a nearby location upon the brides' arrival in America.

Many factors contributed to Japanese women's decisions to travel across the Pacific Ocean and marry men they had never met. Some women, usually coming from impoverished families, became picture brides for economic reasons. They hoped for prosperity in the new land. Some were filial daughters and obeyed their parents' arrangements for marriages. Others came to the United States in hopes of gaining freedom away from the patriarchal society of their homeland. Many women were surprised by the difficult reality in their new life. A large gap in age was common for the husband and his picture bride. Sometimes grooms-to-be sent photos of their younger selves or those of good-looking friends or

Four Japanese picture brides in Los Angeles, California, February 2, 1931. The 1907 Gentlemen's Agreement between Japan and the United States allowed wives to join their husbands in the U.S. The arrival of these picture brides changed the gender ratio of the Japanese American community dramatically. (Bettmann/Corbis)

photos of themselves in borrowed clothes posing with other people's houses and cars. The living and working conditions on the plantations were also harsh. Despite many challenges, most picture brides eventually settled down in a life with their husbands, with a few exceptions.

The Japanese government stopped issuing passports to picture brides in 1920. Picture brides' arrival in America changed the structure of the Japanese American community and to a lesser degree the Korean American community. The gender ratio changed dramatically by the 1920s.

Contemporary Representations in Literature and Media

Cathy Song's (1955–) debut collection, *Picture Bride* (1983), won the Yale Series of Younger Poets Award in 1982 and was nominated for the National

Book Critics Circle Award. Born and raised in Hawaiʻi, Song is of Korean and Chinese descent. Her cultural heritage and her personal experience provide inspirations for her poetry. Using rich imagery, the speaker of the title poem envisions her grandmother's journey as a picture bride from Korea to a foreign land with an uncertain future and a husband she will meet for the first time.

Yoshiko Uchida's (1921–1992) novel *Picture Bride* (1987) is another literary representation of picture brides' experiences. The protagonist Hana Omiyah arrived at Angel Island in 1917 to marry Taro Takida. After their wedding, Hana helped with Taro's shop but developed feelings for Kiyoshi Yamaka, who later died of influenza. The novel reflects her experiences through the anti-Japanese sentiment in the 1920s, the Great Depression in the 1930s, and Japanese American internment during World War II. At the end of the novel, Taro dies in the internment camp in Topaz. While centered on Hana's life as a picture bride and Japanese immigrant in California, Uchida's novel addresses historical, political, and social issues about Japanese immigration and sheds light on the rarely documented women's experience.

Directed by Kayo Hatta (1958–2005) and produced by Diane Mark and Lisa Onodera, *Picture Bride* (1995) is an independent feature film. The main character, Riyo (played by Youki Kudoh, 1971–), is a young Japanese woman who arrived in Hawaiʻi as a picture bride in 1918. Getting married to Matsuji (played by Akira Takayama) right after her arrival, Riyo started working on the sugarcane plantation and became acquainted with Kana (played by Tamlyn Tomita, 1969–), a picture bride who came to Hawaiʻi a few years earlier. Refusing to accept her husband, who is much older, and her new life on the plantation that is drastically different from what she imagined, Riyo began doing laundry for others in hopes of saving up money for her journey back to Japan. During harvest season, the workers set sugarcane fields on fire to burn off the leaves. Realizing that her daughter had wandered into the fields, Kana rushed into the burning fields. The film ends with Riyo, Matsuji, and fellow workers dancing at the Bon Festival. A rare representation of Japanese picture brides' experience in Hawaiʻi, the film successfully presents a touching narrative with lyric cinematography. The film premiered at the 1995 Sundance Film Festival and won the Audience Award for narrative feature film. It has won critical claims from various film reviewers, critics, and scholars. Miramax Films released a DVD version in 2004 that includes a special feature, *The Picture Bride Journey*, a documentary on the filmmaking process, casting, historical archives, and behind-the-scenes clips.

Additional works that touch upon the topic of picture brides include Alan Brennert's (1954–) novel *Honolulu* (2009) and Julie Otsuka's (1962–) novel *The*

Buddha in the Attic (2011), among others. Compiled by Nam-su Pak, *Sajin Sinbu* (*Picture Bride*) was published in the Korean language in 2003. This book provides a historical overview of Korean picture brides and addresses related poetry, fiction, and essays. It was compiled for the Korean centennial celebrating the 100-year anniversary of the first known Korean immigrant arriving in the United States in 1903.

Lan Dong

See also: Japanese American Immigration; Japanese American Women; Korean American Women

Further Reading

Brennert, Alan. *Honolulu.* New York: St. Martin's, 2009.

Makabe, Tomoko. *Picture Brides: Japanese Women in Canada.* Translated by Kathleen Chisato Merken. Ontario: Multicultural History Society of Ontario, 1995.

Nakano, Mei T. *Japanese American Women: Three Generations, 1890–1990.* Berkeley, CA: Mina, 1990.

Otsuka, Julie. *The Buddha in the Attic.* New York: Knopf, 2011.

Pak, Nam-su. *Sajin Sinbu: Chaeomi Taep'yo Chakka Munhaksŏn* [Picture Bride]. Washington, DC: Miju Hanin Imin 100-chunyŏn Kinyŏm Saŏphoe Wŏsingt'on, 2003.

Picture Bride. Directed by Kayo Hata. Miramax, 1995.

Sherman, Mark, George Katagiri, and Lawson Fusao Inada, eds. *Touching the Stones: Tracing One Hundred Years of Japanese American History.* Portland: Oregon Nikkei Endowment, 1994.

Song, Cathy. *Picture Bride.* New Haven, CT: Yale University Press, 1983.

Uchida, Yoshiko. *Picture Bride.* Flagstaff, AZ: Northland Press, 1987.

Uchida, Yoshiko, et al. *Picture Bride and Related Readings.* Evanston, IL: McDougal Littell, 1997.

Yamamoto, Traise. *Masking Selves, Making Subjects: Japanese American Women, Identity, and the Body.* Berkeley: University of California Press, 1999.

POLITICS, ASIAN AMERICANS IN

Asian Americans are a growing section of the electorate, with a large number of first-time voters and foreign-born naturalized U.S. citizens. About two-thirds of all Asian Americans who are registered to vote are Democrats, but the Asian American community is not a monolithic group. This includes differences in terms of ethnicity, age, educational attainment, income, English proficiency, and political views.

Daniel Inouye (1924–2012)

Daniel Inouye has been the highest-ranking Asian American politician in U.S. history. A senator since 1963, Inouye was the most senior U.S. senator at the time of his death. He is the second longest-serving U.S. senator in history after Robert Byrd from West Virginia. Inouye continuously represented Hawai'i in the Congress since it became the 50th American state in 1959 until the time of his death, serving as Hawai'i's first congressman and later a senator. Inouye was the first Japanese American to serve in the House of Representatives and the first in the Senate. He never lost an election in 58 years as an elected official. In June 2010, Inouye became president pro tempore of the Senate. Prior to his death, he announced that he planned to run for a record 10th term in 2016, when he would have been 92 years old.

Inouye is also remembered for his remarkable military service. He served as a medical volunteer during the Japanese attack on Pearl Harbor in 1941 and lost his right arm in 1945 when fighting against Germans in central Italy.

Politicians and Policies

Asian Americans have quite recently arisen as a crucial force in American politics. In 1996, more than 300 Asian Americans were elected to federal and local offices; today more than 2,500 hold positions in government.

A total of 52 Asian Americans have served in the U.S. Congress since 1900: 6 senators (4 have also been in the House of Representatives), 26 representatives (including the 4 who served in the Senate), 11 territorial delegates, and 13 resident commissioners from the Philippine Islands. Asian Americans served in a total of 56 seats. Of the 39 Asian Americans who were not resident commissioners, 26 were Democrats, 12 were Republicans, and 1 was an Independent.

In the 113th Congress, 11 Asian Americans were elected to Congress: 1 senator and 10 representatives. Of these 11 members, 5 new Asian Americans were elected to the House: Ami Bera (D-CA), Tammy Duckworth (D-IL), Tulsi Gabbard (D-HI), Grace Meng (D-NY), and Mark Takano (D-CA). Mazie K. Hirono (D-HI), who had previously served in the House, is the first Asian American woman to be elected to the Senate. Also reelected to the 113th Congress were Judy Chu (D-CA), Colleen Hanabusa (D-HI), Michael Honda (D-CA), Doris Matsui (D-CA), and Robert "Bobby" Scott (D-VA), an African American with Filipino ancestry.

Daniel Inouye of Hawai'i (who served from 1959 until his death in 2012) was the president pro tempore of the Senate and the highest-ranking Asian American in congressional history. The first mainland Asian American to become a member of the U.S. House of Representatives was Dalip Singh Saund from California. The first mainland senator was the conservative S. I. Hayakawa, also from California. Patsy Mink (served 1965–1977 and 1990–2002) was the first Asian American woman to serve in Congress.

At state level, George Ariyoshi (governor of Hawai'i, 1974–1986) was the first Asian American to be elected state governor. Gary Locke served as governor of Washington from 1997 to 2005, becoming the first Asian American governor in the continental United States. Bobby Jindal (elected in Louisiana in 2007) is the second Asian American governor on the mainland. Nikki Haley is the current governor of South Carolina.

At cabinet level, Norman Mineta became the first Asian American to be appointed in a presidential administration, initially working as secretary of commerce in 2000. Elaine Chao (secretary of labor, 2001–2009) was the first Asian American woman to serve in a U.S. cabinet. Gary Locke was appointed secretary of commerce in 2009. He joined Secretary of Energy Steven Chu and Secretary of Veterans' Affairs Eric Shinseki in the first Barack Obama administration, the most Asian American cabinet in any administration in U.S. history.

Nowadays as the size of the Asian American segment of the population continues to grow, so does the number of Asian Americans entering the political arena. On the national level, several Asian American organizations have recently formed a coalition to develop a comprehensive policy platform. Their goal is to encourage political leaders to treat Asian Americans with the same level of attention and respect that they do other racial constituents.

Asian American voices have been prominent in policy debates over such matters as education, race relations, and immigration reform. Although polls show that immigration is not a top concern for Asian Americans, candidates who are seen as anti-immigration are often disqualified from consideration.

Voting Trends and the Electorate

The fastest-growing U.S. demographic group is highly educated, quite affluent, and increasingly Democratic. In 2012 they voted almost three to one for President Obama, according to the exit polls. However, the results reflected the diversity of the community: Asian Americans vary in political beliefs and on policies across ethnic lines. Asian Americans are a diverse community with varying social, political, and economic backgrounds.

The percentages of Asian Americans who voted for Obama by ethnic group are as follows (from highest to lowest): Bangladeshi American (96 percent), Pakistani American (91 percent), Indian American (84 percent), Chinese American (81 percent), Korean American (78 percent), Filipino American (65 percent), and Vietnamese American (44 percent).

Not many people know that language assistance and bilingual ballots are crucial for Asian Americans to preserve their access to the vote. More than one-third (37 percent) of Asian American voters were limited in English proficiency, defined as speaking English "less than very well." Only one out of five (18 percent) identified English as their native language.

Asian Americans as a whole now tend to vote for Democrats, but this trend has been cited as being very recent. During the Cold War many Asian Americans were anticommunist refugees, and many had ties to conservative organizations. As late as 1992, incumbent Republican George H. W. Bush received 55 percent of the Asian American vote compared to 31 percent for Bill Clinton. Asian Americans voted Republican and were the only racial group more conservative than whites in the 1990s. The Asian American vote has slowly shifted since then, with Democrat John Kerry winning 56 percent of the Asian American vote in the 2004 presidential election.

Marco Morini

See also: Activism, Asian American

Further Reading

Aoki, Andrew, and Okiyoshi Takeda. *Asian American Politics.* New York: Polity, 2008.

Cho, Wendy K. Tam. "Tapping Motives and Dynamics behind Campaign Contributions: Insights from the Asian American Case." *American Politics Research* 30(4) (2002): 347–383.

Dodge, Andrew R. *Biographical Directory of the United States Congress, 1774–2005.* Washington, DC: U.S. Government Printing Office, 2005.

Edwards, Tom. "Voter Turnout Increases by 5 Million in 2008 Presidential Election." U.S. Census Bureau News, October 29, 2013, https://www.census.gov/.

Le, C. N. "Participating in Politics." Asian-Nation: The Landscape of Asian America, November 6, 2013, http://www.asian-nation.org/politics.shtml.

Risjord, Norman K. *Giants in Their Time: Representative Americans from the Jazz Age to the Cold War.* New York: Rowman and Littlefield, 2006.

Tong, Lorraine H. "Asian Pacific Americans in the United States Congress." Congressional Research Service, July 7, 2010, http://apaics.org/backups/EE/images/uploads/files/APAsCongress97–398.pdf.

POPULAR CULTURE, ASIAN AMERICANS AND

History

Since Asian sojourners and immigrants entered the United States in the 19th century, images of Asian Americans have circulated in American popular culture. Many of these images result from what scholar Edward Said defines as Orientalism, which constructs the synonymous relationship between Asianness and foreignness. Orientalism aids the construction of the East as a mythical and exotic place. In other words, the East is defined as exotic and heathen in comparison to the pure and civilized West.

Yellowface in Entertainment Media

Capitalizing Orientalist perceptions of Asianness, yellowface is a form of minstrelsy that relies on racist stereotypes of Asian Americans. Common elements of yellowface include buckteeth, straw coolie hats, slanted eyes, and the Chinese queue hairstyle of a long ponytail. Yellowface was a tool deployed by popular culture to frame Asian Americans as outsiders and foreigners. A racist complement to blackface, yellowface was employed in the film industry to allow white actors to play Asian characters. One of the earliest forms of yellowface appears in the 1915 silent film *Madame Butterfly* in which actress Mary Pickford stars as Cio-Cio San. The use of yellowface became popular as a result of the Motion Picture Production Code, often referred to as the Hayes Code (1930–1968), that forbade portrayals of miscegenation. To circumvent the Hayes Code, directors, producers, and studios would utilize white actors in roles marked as Asian. For example, in the film adaptation of Pearl S. Buck's novel *The Good Earth* (1937), Anna May Wong was not considered a viable actress because the lead actor was Caucasian. One of the most notorious cases of yellowface is Mickey Rooney starring as Mr. Yunioshi, Holly Golightly's (Audrey Hepburn) bucktoothed Japanese neighbor in *Breakfast at Tiffany's* (1961).

Modern-day usage of yellowface suggests the erasure of Asian American characters in the film industry. For example, the movie *21* (2008) features a majority white cast to portray the MIT blackjack team whose real-life members were predominately Asian American. The casting of *The Last Airbender* (2010) sparked outcry, for the main leads were given to Caucasian actors even though the film was based on a television show about Eastern religion and Asian culture. Actors of Asian descent play secondary characters or villains in the film. In the film *Cloud Atlas* (2012) some of the Asian characters were played by Caucasian actors who wore makeup and eye enhancements to appear Asian.

Due to the pervasiveness of Orientalism in shaping American understandings of Asians, Asians and Asian Americans encountered racial stereotypes. Such stereotypes resulted from Asians and Asian Americans being constructed as forever foreigners. As part of this characterization, Asians and Asian Americans were seen as sneaky, devilish, and mischievous as part of the so-called Yellow Peril. The modern Yellow Peril originated during the mid-1800s, when tensions between white and Chinese laborers in the mining and railroad industries rose as a result of the belief that Chinese laborers were depressing wages. This tension escalated to anti-Chinese violence inflicted on Chinese communities. A similar rhetoric was used against South Asian immigrants and their descendants in the Pacific Northwest.

Fear of Asian Americans continued into the 20th century with the rise of anti-Japanese sentiment during World War II and anti-Chinese sentiment during the Cold War. For example, the December 22, 1941, issue of *Life* magazine included an article titled "How to Tell Japs from the Chinese: Angry Citizens Victimize Allies with Emotional Outburst at Enemy," while *Time* magazine included an article titled "How to Tell Your Friends from the Japs." Similar imagery and rhetoric have been used against South Asian Americans since 9/11. For instance, the August 7, 2012, issue of the *Chicago Tribune*'s magazine *RedEye* published the "Turban Primer" that distinguished between turbans worn by the following groups: Sikh men, Iranian leaders, Taliban members, Indian men, and Muslim religious elders.

Anti-Asian sentiment persisted following the end of the Cold War as a result of the economic success of the so-called Asian Tigers (Hong Kong, Singapore, Taiwan, and South Korea) as well as Japan and the People's Republic of China. For example, Asian Americans faced animosity in the late 1970s and early 1980s as the American automotive industry declined against rising competition from Japanese automakers. As a result, Japanese Americans or any Asian Americans perceived as Japanese were the target of violence. The death of Vincent Chin (1955–1982), a Chinese American, in Detroit, Michigan, was an example.

Moreover, the rise of anti-Chinese rhetoric from the 2010 U.S. election to the 2012 election was demonstrated in television advertisements. The myth of the forever foreigner Yellow Peril entered the American mainstream directly in a campaign advertisement by Michigan Senate candidate Pete Hoekstra (1953–) in January 2012. The negative advertisement implies that Senator Debbie Stabenow (1950–) aided China's economic success by increasing the national debt. The Asian American actress speaks in broken English while riding a bike through rice paddies to stereotypical Chinese traditional music. Such political advertisements stoke fears of the demise of the American empire and the rise of China in the 21st century. This is particularly seen in the 2010 and

2012 advertisements from the third-party group Citizens against Government Waste, which depicts a 2030 university classroom in Beijing, China, and a Chinese professor discussing the demise of the United States with pleasure.

As the myth of the Yellow Peril circulated in popular culture, by the mid-20th century the notion of Asians and Asian Americans as the model minority arose across the United States. The model minority myth promotes the existing stereotype of Asians and Asian Americans as hardworking, passive, and smart. Two seminal articles projecting the model minority stereotype onto Asian Americans were written in 1966, appearing in the *New York Times* and *U.S. News and World Report*. The *New York Times* article on January 9, 1966, by William Petersen highlighted Japanese Americans' ability to overcome internment and integrate themselves into mainstream society, while the December 26, 1966, *U.S. News and World Report* article touted Chinese Americans as a successful minority group. In addition, the perceived success of Japanese Americans after World War II provided conservatives the opportunity to contend that structural and institutional racism and economic inequity did not hinder the ability for minorities to attain the American Dream. The concept of the model minority garnered Asian Americans the characterization of "honorary white" because of their perceived success climbing the American economic ladder.

The model minority myth reappeared in the mainstream as Asian nations gained economic prominence and success. The August 31, 1987, *Time* magazine cover featured the tagline "Asian American Whiz Kids" with a photo of Asian American youths. Rhetoric concerning the academic prowess of Asian Americans continues into the 21st century. Most recently, the Asian American community organized against the 2012 Pew Research Center report "The Rise of Asian Americans." Such generalizations rely on stereotypes of Asian Americans as high achieving and overlook the widening gaps between Asian Americans, where income and educational attainment levels vary.

Stereotypes of Asians in American Popular Culture

Even though the archetypes of the forever foreigner and model minority pervade American society, popular culture also witnessed the development and growth of gendered representations of Asians and Asian Americans. Asian masculinity became defined by the characters of Fu Manchu and Charlie Chan. Created in 1913 by British author Sax Rohmer (1883–1959), Fu Manchu became the archetype of the Yellow Peril. Charlie Chan, created by Earl Derr Biggers (1884–1933) in 1925, shaped contemporary understandings of Asian males as sexless and eunuch-like. Chan is the devoted servant, eager to please, and embodies the model minority.

Derivatives of Fu Manchu and Charlie Chan continue to haunt modern-day depictions of Asian American males as villains or the sexless sidekick. Even as Bruce Lee (1940–1973) rose to transpacific stardom in the 1970s and 1980s, his martial arts skills never allowed him to move past a caricature of Asian masculinity. His success was a result of his appearance to mainstream American viewers as Kato, the hapless, funny Charlie Chan–type sidekick in *The Green Hornet*. As the predecessor to skilled martial artists such as Jet Li (1963–) and Jackie Chan (1954–), Lee usually played the role of the asexual Asian male. Consequently, regardless of their physical prowess, American popular culture limited Asian martial artists as sexually ambiguous kung fu masters.

The concept of the sexless Asian male is best embodied by the character of Long Duk Dong (Gedde Watanabe) from *Sixteen Candles* (1984). The bumbling limited-English foreign exchange student, Dong's slapstick humor was garnered in part by director John Hughes's reliance on Asian stereotypes. For a generation of Asian American men, Long Duk Dong provided new fodder for merciless racist mocking.

Historical media and cultural images of the dragon lady and the lotus blossom perpetuated popular perceptions of Asian American women as exotic and sexual. The dragon lady caricature depicts Asian and Asian American women as overly aggressive, devious, hypersexualized, and manipulative. The lotus blossom stereotype characterizes Asian and Asian American women as the sexually pleasing geisha or China doll and exacerbates the notion that Asian women are exotic, submissive, and polite. Anna May Wong (1905–1961) played the lotus blossom and dragon lady types of characters in a number of films in the early 20th century. While Wong may be seen as complicit in perpetuating Asian American stereotypes, recent scholarship underscores how in Hollywood, limited roles were available to Wong in the 1920s. These limitations for Asian American actresses persisted throughout the 20th century. Nancy Kwan's (1939–) films *The World of Suzie Wong* (1960) and *Flower Drum Song* (1961) secured her success in mainstream cinema. Yet her cinematic achievements came at a cost, for her role as Suzie Wong, a prostitute, fueled recurring images concerning the promiscuous nature of Asian women. The portrayal of the submissive and hypersexual Asian American woman continued to circulate in later films, including *Full Metal Jacket* (1987), and in theater musicals such as *Miss Saigon* (1992).

Contemporary Forms

By late 20th century, Asian American actors and artists began to challenge the racial and gender stereotypes of Asian Americans in popular culture. The

Center for Asian American Media (formerly the National Asian American Telecommunications Association) was founded in 1980 and is dedicated to the growth of Asian American independent media. Directors Ang Lee and Wayne Wang have become notable Hollywood filmmakers. Asian Americans also began to make inroads in theater. Playwright David Henry Hwang garnered attention for his Tony Award–winning play *M. Butterfly* (1988), a critique of and commentary on Puccini's opera *Madame Butterfly*.

As Asian American independent productions provided a space to challenge mainstream portrayals of Asian Americans, comedian Margaret Cho's series *All American Girl* (1994) provided American viewers with the first Asian American family on TV. Even though the series only lasted one season, Cho served as a role model for young Asian American women. Her series provided an alternative portrayal of Asian American femininity. A year earlier, the film adaptation *The Joy Luck Club* (1993) introduced the lives of four pairs of Asian American mothers and daughters to the American mainstream and was criticized by Asian American scholars for its reliance on racial stereotypes.

By the beginning of the 21st century, American popular culture saw various representations of Asian Americans. Actresses such as Tia Carerre (*Wayne's World* and *Wayne's World 2*) and Lucy Liu (*Ally McBeal, Charlie's Angels,* and *Elementary*) find themselves faced with characters who may reify stereotypes of Asian American women even as they seek to cultivate multidimensional Asian American characters. Television stars Ming-Na (*ER*) and Grace Park (*Hawaii Five-0*) also present an alternative Asian American femininity to viewers. Moreover, television channels aimed at children and adolescents provide new avenues for Asian American actresses that are not bounded by stereotypes. Keiko Agena found success on *Gilmore Girls* as the Korean American best friend of the lead character Rory Gilmore (Alexis Blendel). Ashley Argota and Brenda Song launched careers through their work on children's programs on Nickelodeon and the Disney Channel, respectively.

Similar new roles also became available for Asian American men to create a more nuanced masculinity. Justin Lin's independent film *Better Luck Tomorrow* (2002) features an all–Asian American cast. Following four high school friends, Lin's film breaks down stereotypes of the model minority and examines the facade of Asian Americans' academic triumphs. The film's success garnered Lin fame in Hollywood, leading to the opportunity to direct *The Fast and the Furious: Tokyo Drift* as well as *Fast and Furious* and *Fast Five*. The film *Better Luck Tomorrow* also launched the careers of actors Sung Kang and John Cho. In many ways, this film highlights the marketability of Asian American male leads as seen in *Harold and Kumar Go to White Castle,* featuring John Cho and Kal Penn in 2004.

While Asian Americans continue to see success in film and television, Asian American comedians are encountering an upsurge of recent success. As a member of the television comedy series *Parks and Recreation*, Aziz Ansari gained mainstream popularity after a thriving career as a stand-up comedian. The efforts of Indian American actress, writer, and comedian Mindy Kaling came to fruition with the comedy series *The Mindy Project*, premiering in 2012. Kaling previously served as a writer for the successful television show *The Office* and played small roles in films including *The 40-Year-Old Virgin*. Korean American doctor and comedian Ken Jeong gained mainstream notice following his portrayal of Mr. Chow in the three *The Hangover* films and is currently in the comedy television series *Dr. Ken*.

Complementing the increase of Asian Americans on-screen is the rise of Asian Americans in the music and entertainment industry. Kollaboration is an

Mindy Kaling at the 14th Annual Screen Actors Guild Awards at the Shrine Auditorium in Los Angeles, California, January 27, 2008. She is best known for her television comedy series *The Mindy Project*. (Featureflash/Dreamstime.com)

arts and entertainment nonprofit organization dedicated to highlighting the talents of young Asian and Pacific Islander Americans. Founded in 2000, Kollaboration currently produces 15 shows in 14 cities in North America. In the past decade Asian American entertainers achieved success in the mainstream market. The hip-hop quartet Far East Movement entered the mainstream with its 2010 *Billboard* hit "Like a G6." The group's music has also been featured on *The Fast and the Furious: Tokyo Drift* soundtrack and television shows including *CSI: Miami, Gossip Girl,* and *Lie to Me.* Stars from Asia continue to find crossover success in the United States as well: Filipina singer Charice joined the cast of *Glee* for its second season as Sunshine Corazon, and Korean pop star PSY became the first person to receive 1 billion hits on YouTube with his song "Gangnam Style."

The ability for Asian artists to enter the American music market illustrates the ways in which YouTube and the Internet provide a platform for Asian American artists to gain popularity and challenge racial stereotypes. Due to the popularity of her YouTube channel, musician Clara Chung became a YouTube celebrity and was the winner of the 2010 Kollaboration Los Angeles award. KevJumba (Kevin Wu) gained prominence as a YouTube celebrity as well. Together with his father, KevJumba appeared in the 17th season of CBS's *The Amazing Race.* He has worked with Wong Fu Productions, which produces videos and films on topics related to Asian Americans.

Even as Asian Americans continue to influence the ways in which they are portrayed in popular culture, the persistence of racial and gender stereotypes continues into the 21st century. In Android mobile phones' Google application store, users may download the app "Make Me Asian." Promoting yellowface, the user may add features such as a Fu Manchu mustache, a rice paddy hat, and slanted eyes to their uploaded photo. News outlets and an online petition circulated through the end of 2012 to highlight the racist nature of this app. As Asian Americans break down racial barriers, it is clear that the historical stereotypes continue to circulate in popular culture.

Kimberly McKee

See also: Fashion, Asian Americans and; Television, Asian Americans on

Further Reading

Danico, Mary Yu, and Franklin Ng. *Asian American Issues.* Westport, CT: Greenwood, 2004.

Lee, Robert G. *Orientals: Asian Americans in Popular Culture.* Philadelphia: Temple University Press, 1999.

Okihiro, Gary. *Margins and Mainstreams: Asians in American History and Culture.* Seattle: University of Washington Press, 1994.

Petersen, William. "Success, Japanese-American Style." *New York Times* January 9, 1966.

Shimizu, Celine Parreñas. *The Hypersexuality of Race: Performing Asian/American Women on Screen and Scene.* Durham, NC: Duke University Press, 2007.

Shimizu, Celine Parreñas. *Straitjacket Sexualities: Unbinding Asian American Manhoods in the Movies.* Stanford, CA: Stanford University Press, 2012.

"Success Story of One Minority Group in the U.S." *U.S. News & World Report,* December 26, 1966, 73–76.

Tajima, Renee E. "Lotus Blossoms Don't Bleed Images of Asian Women." In *Making Waves: An Anthology of Writings by and about Asian American Women,* edited by Asian Women United of California, 308–317. Boston: Beacon, 1989.

PROPOSITION 209 (1996)

Proposition 209, also known as the California Civil Rights Initiative (CCRI), is a ballot proposition in the state of California that amended the state constitution to prohibit state government institutions from considering race, sex, or ethnicity in the areas of public employment, public contracting, and public education. Private colleges, universities, and employers are not subject to the CCRI. Authored by Glynn Custred and Tom Wood, it was modeled after the Civil Rights Act of 1964. With over 54 percent of the vote, it was approved on November 5, 1996. It is considered the first electoral test of affirmative action policies in the history of the United States.

According to Proposition 209, "The state shall not discriminate against, or grant preferential treatment to, any individual or group on the basis of race, sex, color, ethnicity, or national origin in the operation of public employment, public education, or public contracting" (California State Office of Outreach 2002, 16). Proposition 209 has met with strong support as well as opposition. Supporters of the initiative are in favor of its protection of an individual's rights not to be discriminated against or granted preference based on his or her race, sex, or ethnicity. The Sacramento-based American Civil Rights Institute, a conservative think tank devoted to issues of race and ethnicity, as well as the Center for Equal Opportunity and the Pacific Legal Foundation are among the organizations supporting Proposition 209. Opponents of Proposition 209 argue that the initiative is against affirmative action policies and practices. There were demonstrations and protests after it was voted into law. Organizations in opposition include the ACLU of Southern California, the Feminist Majority Foundation, and California Votes NO! on 209, among others. Since its approval, there have been multiple lawsuits challenging Proposition 209's constitutionality. So far, it has withstood legal scrutiny.

A number of scholars in various disciplines have collected data and conducted studies of the impact of Proposition 209. For instance, based on his three-year research and assessment, Richard H. Sander of the University of California, Los Angeles, finds that Proposition 209 has had a positive impact on the education of African American and Hispanic students in California. Not only has their freshman enrollment rate increased, but their graduation percentage has gone up as well since 1998. Comparing data from applicants and employees within the University of California system before and after Proposition 209, Peter Arcidiacono, Esteban Aucejo, Patrick Coate, and V. Joseph Hotz (2011) address the initiative's notable positive effects on minority students' college enrollment and graduation rates. The Thelton E. Henderson Center for Justice at the University of California–Berkeley School of Law released a report in 2008 on an investigation of trends in public employment since the 1990s and analyzes the impact of Proposition 209 on workforce diversity in the public section. This study suggests that Proposition 209 may have limited workforce diversity for people of color and women in California. Generally speaking, California has provided employment opportunities for people of color and women. However, racial and gender disparity still exists.

Lan Dong

See also: Chinese Americans and Education; Japanese Americans and Education; Model Minority; Tiger Mom

Further Reading

Arcidiacono, Peter, Esteban Aucejo, Patrick Coate, and V. Joseph Hotz. "The Effects of Proposition 209 on College Enrollment and Graduation Rates in California." Duke University, December 2011, http://public.econ.duke.edu/~psarcidi/prop209.pdf.

California State Office of Outreach. "Proposition 209 and the Courts: A Legal History." January 2002, http://sor.govoffice3.com/vertical/Sites/%7B3BDD1595 -792B-4D20-8D44-626EF05648C7%7D/uploads/%7B9B228323-7833-4431 -91F0-1617AFA60A8E%7D.PDF.

Chávez, Lydia. *The Color Bind: California's Battle to End Affirmative Action.* Berkeley: University of California Press, 1998.

Grodsky, Eric, and Michal Kurlaender, eds. *Equal Opportunity in Higher Education: The Past and Future of California's Proposition 209.* Cambridge, MA: Harvard Education Press, 2010.

Ong, Paul M., ed. *Impacts of Affirmative Action: Policies and Consequences in California.* Walnut Creek, CA: AltaMira, 1999.

"Proposition 209 and Public Employment in California: Trends in Workforce Diversity." Thelton E. Henderson Center for Justice, September 2008, http://www.law .berkeley.edu/files/September_2008_Proposition_209_and_Public_Emplo yment_-_Workforce_Diversity.pdf.

Sander, Richard H. "An Analysis of the Effects of Proposition 209 Upon the University of California." Project SAEPHE, http://www.seaphe.org/pdf/analysisoftheeffect sofproposition209.pdf.

White, Cody. "Rising from the Ashes: The Impact of Proposition 13 on Public Libraries in California." *Libraries & the Cultural Record: Exploring the History of Collections of Recorded Knowledge* 46(4) (2011): 345–359.

R

RELIGIONS AND BELIEFS, ASIAN AMERICAN

The term "Asian American" was used by Yuji Ichioka for the first time in the late 1960s. This ended the use of adjectives such as Oriental and Asiatic for people of Asian origin living in America. Asian Americans comprise almost 6 percent of the total U.S. population, according to the 2010 U.S. census. Since Asia is a continent with innumerable ethnic, cultural, and historical indicators, it is very difficult to determine a common trajectory in the culture of Asian Americans. In 2012, the Pew Research Center completed a comprehensive survey of Asian Americans and religious beliefs and found that Christians are the largest religious group among U.S. Asian adults (42 percent), with those who are unaffiliated second (26 percent). The report noted that "Buddhists are third, accounting for about one-in-seven Asian Americans (14%), followed by Hindus (10%), Muslims (4%) and Sikhs (1%). Followers of other religions make up 2% of U.S. Asians" ("Asian Americans: A Mosaic of Faiths," 2012).

For practical purposes, the demographics of Asian Americans can be broken into three subcategories: Asian Americans from South Asia, Asian Americans from East Asia, and Asian Americans from Southeast Asia. All of these sub-categories of Asian Americans represent a vast religious diversity ranging from atheism to different old and new religions such as Hinduism, Sikhism, Jainism, Islam, Buddhism, Christianity, Confucianism, Taoism, Shintoism, and others.

East Asian Americans, who include Chinese, Korean, and Japanese Americans, come from these religious backgrounds: Mahayana Buddhism, Shintoism, Taoism, and Confucianism. However, many, especially Koreans, immigrated to America as Christians, primarily Protestants. Filipino Americans are predominantly Catholic, and Southeast Asian Americans from Laos, Cambodia, Thailand, and Myanmar (Burma) are mainly responsible for bringing Theravada Buddhism to America. Vietnamese Americans as well as Southeast Asians are more similar to their East Asian cousins in religion, but as with all groups within the larger umbrella of Asian Americans, the Vietnamese have a complex background of religion, including not only Catholicism and Protestantism but also Confucianism, Daoism, and Buddhism. In addition, there are some Muslims of ethnic Cham ancestry or Malay ancestry who lived in Vietnam as well as in Cambodia. South Asian Americans from the Indian subcontinent are often

Hindu but also include Sikhs, Orthodox Christians, Buddhists, Zoroastrians, and Jains. Pakistani Americans draw from a Muslim heritage. Pacific Islanders are predominantly Christian or Mormon but have blended indigenous practices into their faith.

Hindus believe in Vishnu, Shiva, and Shakti as godly figures. They believe in *punarjanma* (reincarnation), karma theory (one's action liable for the status of birth and living in the next life), and the Varna system (four broad ranks dividing traditional Hindu society). Hindu sacred scriptures are the Vedas, the *Gita,* and the *Ramayan.* About 330,000 deities are found in Hindu culture. The mythology enlists 360 million deities.

Sikhism is an Indian religion, founded in the 16th century by Guru Nanak. It is based on the teachings of Guru Nanak and that of the nine gurus after him. They believe in one God and the equality of human beings and focus on doing good work rather than merely performing rituals. *Guru Granth Sahib* is their holy book. The followers of Sikhism reached the United States during the 19th century. Major Sikh populations live in Detroit, Chicago, and Austin and along the East and West Coasts.

Jainism is also an Indian religion. Jains believe in the welfare of each and every being in the universe. They also believe that every animal, plant, and human being has a living soul, so everything should be treated with respect and compassion. They remain vegetarian. Jains arrived in the United States in small numbers in the 20th century, particularly in the early 1970s.

Islam is a monotheist and Abrahamic religion that believes in the unity of Allah, that is, God. Allah has deputed from time to time many prophets to spread Islamic teachings. Adam, Noah, Jesus, Moses, and Abraham are also the prophets of God. Muslims believe that Islam existed in the world from the beginning of time, but the migration of Muhammad from Medina to Mecca is considered the beginning of this religion for practical purposes.

Buddhism is another popular Asian American religion. It was started by Gautama Buddha in India. After Buddha's demise there arose many disagreements and schisms within Buddhism that led to the division of Buddhism into 18 sects. The *Tripitaka* is the sacred religious text of Buddhists. They believe in the four Noble Truths, the Eightfold Path (the eight codes of conduct), and karma. Nirvana is the ultimate aim of the soul in Buddhism. In the state of nirvana, the passions of the soul extinguish, and it is liberated from the troublesome cycle of birth, illness, age, and death.

Daoism is a polytheist religion. In a way, Daoism is not a systematic airtight religion; rather, like many Oriental religions, it is a way of life. Many subsects and schools of Daoism have varied practices. In ancient China, Daoism flourished as a lifestyle with the objective of making life simple, spontaneous, and easygoing. The schools and sects of Daoism have so many overlapping and diverting tendencies that it is difficult to have a clarified version of the subdivisions. The traditional Dao practices of magic, folk medicine, detachment from desires, divination, and methods of longevity, ecstatic wanderings, exorcism, and naturalism associate it with the ancient folk traditions in China. Many Asian Americans practice the virtues of Daoism in their personal lives.

Confucianism is a commandment of certain ethical and philosophical patterns of living with values and mutual respect in public life. Confucius (551–479 BCE), a Chinese philosopher, advocated a set of patterns and principles for ethical and all-inclusive living in human society that came to be known as Confucianism. Initially it was popularized as ethical-sociopolitical teaching. Confucianism in a way is humanism, and in popular practices it overlaps with Buddhism and Daoism. Confucianism believes in the piety and goodness of human life, giving importance to family life. Confucian thought neither extols divine will and higher laws nor shows belief in gods or the afterlife, and it believes in good habits in human life. It is enshrined in the cultivation of virtue and maintenance of ethics in personal and public life. Under its principles every person has the scope to be taught and to be improved, and every human being can reach the state of perfection by his or her own efforts associated with the efforts of society.

Shintoism (*kami-no-michi*), practiced by some Asian Americans, is a Japanese religion. *Kakiji* and *Nikong* are two sacred religious texts of Shintoism. The followers of Shintoism believe in animism and eternal sacredness in the universe, which should be followed by human beings. Animism believes that even non-human entities such as animals, plants, and inanimate beings have spirit, and spirit exists in every aspect of nature. Initially anthropologists used the term "animism" for certain belief systems related to cosmology prevalent among the first nations in certain ethnic belts. The term totally has an anthropological origin, because no indigenous language has a term like this.

Whatever their cultural and religious beliefs, many Asian Americans undertake a sense of utter spirituality. Asian Americans are often highly religious in domestic life but secular on the public front. Asian Americans try to maintain their religious beliefs and identity with a genuine purpose of making a healthy adjustment in the new land. Many who are members of a diaspora in the United States choose to frame a glocal identity, which keeps them ready to manage potential upheavals in the process of adjustment. Their religious beliefs and culture form many subcultures and ultimately turn into mutual cooperation.

Ravindra Pratap Singh

See also: Buddhism; Cambodian American Religions and Beliefs; Confucianism; Daoism; Hinduism; Hmong American Religions and Beliefs; Islam; Pakistani American Religions and Beliefs; Shamanism; Theravada Buddhism; Traditional Polytheistic Religions; Vietnamese American Religions and Beliefs

Further Reading

"Asian Americans: A Mosaic of Faiths." Pew Research Center, Religion and Public Life, July 19, 2012, http://www.pewforum.org/2012/07/19/asian-americans-a-mosaic-of-faiths-overview/.

Hoeffel, Elizabeth M., Sonya Rastogi, Myoung Ouk Kim, and Hasan Shahid. "The Asian Population: 2010." U.S. Census Bureau, March 2012, http://www.census.gov/prod/cen2010/briefs/c2010br-11.pdf.

Iwamura, Jane Naomi. "Asian American Religions." In *Religion and American Cultures: Tradition, Diversity, and Popular Expression,* edited by Gary Laderman and Luis León, 25–30. Santa Barbara, CA: ABC-CLIO, 2003.

Lawrence, Bruce B. *New Faiths, Old Fears: Muslims and Other Asian Immigrants in American Religious Life.* New York: Columbia University Press, 2002.

Min, Pyong Gap, and Jung Ha Kim, eds. *Religions in Asian America: Building Faith Communities.* Walnut Creek, CA: AltaMira, 2002.

Yoo, David K. *New Spiritual Homes: Religion and Asian Americans.* Honolulu: University of Hawai'i Press, 1999.

S

SCIENTISTS, ASIAN AMERICAN

Asian Americans held prominent positions and made outstanding contributions to American scientific advancement throughout the 20th century. The most notable achievements in the sciences by Asian Americans have been in the fields of mathematics, physics, chemistry, biomedical research, engineering, and the computer sciences. For their research and discoveries, Asian American scientists are globally acknowledged and have received the Nobel Prize in a range of disciplines as well as the Fields Medal, the Wolf Prize, and the Turing Award. Yet despite their contributions to American scientific inquiry and the disproportionately high number of Asian Americans in government and academic labs as well as public research centers, few have managed to break through the so-called bamboo ceiling into advanced positions in the scientific community and academia. As a result, since the mid-1990s questions have begun to be raised about the ongoing stereotypes of Asian Americans as the model minority and the influence that such perceptions have had on institutional discrimination and career advancement in the sciences.

Since World War II, Asian Americans have formed one of the most highly recognized and distinguished groups of researchers within the American scientific community. Asian American researchers have been awarded the Nobel Prize in scientific fields, including Chen Ning Yang and Tsung-Dao Lee (1957), Samuel Ting (1976), Steven Chu (1997), Daniel Tsui (1998), Yoichiro Nambu (2008), and Charles Kao (2009) in physics; Yuan Lee (1986), Charles Pedersen (1987), and Roger Tsien (2008) in chemistry; and Har Gobind Khorana in medicine (1968). In addition, Shing-Tung Yau (1982) and Terence Tao (2006) won the Fields Medal for outstanding discoveries in mathematics, Shiing-Shen Chern (1983) for mathematics and Ching Tang (2011) for chemistry were awarded the Wolf Prize, and Andrew Yao (2000) received the Turing Award for his work in the computer sciences. Other notable Asian American scientists include physicist Amar Bose, AIDS researcher David Ho, nuclear scientist Wen Ho Lee, and American astronauts Ellison Onizuka, Taylor Gun-Jin Wang, Leroy Chiao, Ed Lu, Franklin Chang-Diaz, Eugene Trinh, Mark Polansky, and Kalpana Chawla.

Wen Ho Lee (1939–)

A Taiwanese scientist, Wen Ho Lee came to America in 1965 and received his doctorate in mechanical engineering from Texas A&M. Lee eventually became an American citizen and in 1978 was employed as a nuclear scientist at the Los Alamos National Laboratory in New Mexico. Lee was fired on March 8, 1999, following an article in the *New York Times* about the sale of American nuclear secrets to China and the release of the government's Cox Report, which alleged that China had built a nuclear arsenal similar in design to U.S. technology. Lee was accused of stealing U.S. nuclear data for having downloaded classified information and endangering national security. In December 1999 he was indicted and spent nine months in jail, where he was prohibited from speaking Chinese, was kept in solitary confinement for 278 days, and had limited access to his family and attorneys. Federal investigators failed to provide evidence of espionage or Lee's intent to sell secrets but charged him with improper handling of restricted data, for which he pleaded guilty. The unfair treatment Lee received compared to similar cases involving non-Asians and the lack of evidence presented led to suggestions of racial profiling. In June 2006 Lee received $1.6 million from the federal government and five media organizations as settlement.

Unfortunately, their achievements in the sciences have often contributed to stereotypes of Asian Americans as model minorities who are publically viewed as quiet, hardworking, self-reliant, efficient, well-educated, nonconfrontational, and submissive. While in the workforce many of these attributes may initially be seen as positive, they also perpetuate several negative stereotypes about Asian Americans and impede their long-term career advancement. Such negative stereotypes include the presumption that Asians don't want to be leaders, that they are not outgoing enough, and that their lack of language skills, which has led them to excel in the maths and sciences, would also make them inappropriate candidates for administrative or executive positions. Due to these stereotypes, both employers and many in American society frequently ignore the varied nature of Asian Americans and their communities, place higher and often unreasonable expectations upon Asian researchers, and presume that because of their successes Asians are not subject to racial discrimination. The consequences of these stereotypes and the situations that follow from them have become known as the bamboo ceiling, a term used to describe and often facilitate institutional discrimination, limiting the progress of Asian Americans in the sciences and academia.

David Ho speaking during a news conference on the SARS virus in Hong Kong on May 11, 2003. Born in Taiwan, Ho is a pioneer in the understanding and treatment of HIV infection. He received the 2001 Presidential Citizens Medal. (Reuters/Corbis)

As a result of these rising concerns in the 1990s, a study into the lack of Asian Americans in senior management positions at the National Institutes of Health concluded that despite the disproportionately high number of Asian Americans employed in government and private-sector science and research facilities, there was an unequal and inconsistently low number promoted to the level of senior scientists and administrators. Indeed, further employment statistics of the sciences reiterate these findings, indicating that while Asian Americans comprise a majority of the scientific, research, engineering, and laboratory personnel, very few are engaged in senior administration roles. A review of the employment status of Asian American scientists in academia revealed that they are similarly subject to the limitations of the bamboo ceiling. This review revealed that while as a group they comprise approximately 6 percent of science faculty, they hold just over 2 percent of administrative positions.

While these situations are of concern to the Asian American community, professional scientists' employers have asserted that despite the evident statistics, race and cultural heritage have little to do with promotions in research facilities and academia. Instead, administrators have tentatively suggested that perhaps traditional Asian qualities such as being self-effacing and deferential are values that do not translate into leadership potential. Following this argument, the suggestion is that as a result of these values Asian American scientists are often passed over for promotions and career recognition because they fail to build strong career networks, do not engage in self-promotion, and do not present themselves as leaders despite their exemplary research findings, publications, and job performance.

Concerns regarding institutional discrimination were further highlighted in 1999 when Wen Ho Lee, a senior nuclear scientist in Los Alamos laboratories, lost his position and was later indicted for espionage. While eventually only found guilty of the mishandling of government information, the lack of evidence and the use of racial profiling to target Lee as well as the unusually harsh treatment he received have heightened both public and scholarly discourse regarding the role and achievements of Asian Americans in the scientific community throughout America.

While the debate as to whether the race and heritage of Asian American scientists has influenced their rate of promotion into senior positions is ongoing, the situation has nonetheless prompted a number of questions. The consideration of the bamboo ceiling has led to inquiries regarding institutional discrimination in research labs and academia, opened discussions as to whether the achievements of all individuals are equally recognized, and has made many Asian Americans reassess their career expectations in the sciences. In addition to the public and scholarly debates this issue has opened, many in the political forum in America have highlighted the importance of Asian Americans to the country's achievements, scientific research, economic development, and national defense, thereby reiterating that limiting the achievements of Asian American scientists would only undermine the nation's own progress.

Sean Morton

See also: Activism, Asian American; Demographics, Asian American; Discrimination against Asian Americans

Further Reading

Hyun, Jane. *Breaking the Bamboo Ceiling: Career Strategies for Asians.* New York: HarperCollins, 2005.

Mervis, Jeffery. "A Glass Ceiling for Asian Scientists?" *Science* 310(5748) (2005): 606–607.

Williams, Cyrell. *Workplace Barriers for Asian-Americans in Management: Do Aversive Racism and Shifting Standards Explain the Glass Ceiling?* Los Angeles: Alliant International University, 2008.

SHAMANISM

History and Origins

Shamanism is the practice of reaching an altered state of consciousness with the goal of interacting with spirits through an intermediary known as a shaman who has the ability to connect to the spirit world through intense dreams or omens or by the inherited right of ancestry. Shamans are usually chosen by their community with the goal of maintaining relationships between the human world and the spiritual realm. Most shamans are male, but they can be female. The term "shaman," meaning "he who knows," originates from the Tungus language, with anthropological evidence recorded on oracle bones dated back to the Shang dynasty around 1600 BCE.

The purpose of the shamanic rituals is multifaceted but usually for the good of the community by regulating positive relationships with his people, his environment, and the spirit world. The belief is that spiritual forces affect the lives of the living; therefore, a mediator is needed to connect the two worlds together in order to communicate and dwell in harmony with each other. In order for this to occur, the shaman must place himself in a trance in which a part of his soul can leave his physical body and travel to the spirit world. This is accomplished through a spirit guide, who leads the shaman through the spirit world. A spirit guide is a benevolent essence who leads the shaman toward his intended goal. The trance is accomplished through autohypnosis produced by the consistent and rhythmic beat of a drum, although the shaman is still aware of his physical environment. The drum's top portion is painted to represent the heavens, while the bottom portion is symbolic of images of the underworld in which the shaman is to travel. The use of rocks, believed to have special powers, and hallucinogenic plants are smoked and strained into a tea to aid in the metaphysical process needed to transition into an altered state of consciousness. Objects are often used, such as a sword for protection against malevolent spirits, gongs clanged to announce his arrival, and a wooden table where he perches his body to symbolize a horse galloping into the spirit world. A rooster is sometimes held as a way to make the shaman appear invisible to evil entities during his travel by masking his own soul with the spirit of the fowl.

It is believed that by communing with spirits, the shaman can regulate favorable weather conditions, whether seeking rain during drought or a lighter snowfall for safer travels, expelling harmful spirits looking to bring financial or agricultural misfortune, reading the future, increasing fertility in the women of the community, or healing the sick. For example, in most Asian cultures, it is believed that a person's soul, known as the *khwan*, has 32 distinct parts to the whole. During a mental or physical illness, it is believed that a piece of the soul has traveled outside the body and has become lost in the spirit world or was abducted by a malevolent spirit. In order to heal the ailing person, the shaman puts himself into a trance through various modes during a Sukhwan ceremony, traveling to entice the spirit world to return the captured piece of the soul or to retrieve it if lost. In order to accomplish this goal, the shaman must offer gifts to the spirits, such as wine or food. Animals sacrificed during the ceremony, such as a chicken, rooster, dog, pig, or goat, are viewed as sacred and are believed to have their spirits elevated to a higher level in which they will be reincarnated to a life of luxury in exchange for allowing the spirits to exchange their souls for the soul of the ailing human for 12 months. At the conclusion of the 12 months, the animal's spirit is released and blessed. It is considered a great honor for the animal to serve mankind in this aspect. Once the soul is retrieved, the shaman's goal is to mend the soul by returning it to the ailing human body, thereby creating balance and eliminating physical sickness. To ensure that the soul remains whole inside the body, a white string is tied on the wrist to be worn for at least three days. The Sukhwan ceremony still takes place today, especially during joyous occasions such as the birth of a new baby, weddings, and for families wishing for prosperity and good health.

Regional Practices and Contemporary Forms

The role of the shaman varies, depending on the culture and regional practices of the people whom he or she serves, yet a shared expression of spirit unifies various Asian cultures. Shamans are considered healers in some traditions such as the Hmong culture, while others from Central Asia, Siberia, and Japan would go to the shaman for a connection between earth, sky, and spirit as a method to show reverence to nature and to ask for agricultural blessings. Korean shamans are usually lower-class women who are fortune tellers and foresee financial and marital outcomes.

After the Vietnam War, people of various Asian descent migrated to North America at a faster rate, bringing shamanistic beliefs with them called *ua neeb*. In the United States today, shamanism is practiced and often blended into Christian and Catholic faiths incorporating traditions and ceremonies from the roots of their culture. It is also being used by licensed medical practitioners called *txiv neeb* in hospitals as a form of homeopathic healing, especially in states such as California. This blending of Western with Eastern forms of healing, often referred to as the neoshamanic movement, is created through blending the shamanic spiritual focus into American society and has become more and more accepted in regard to natural healing of the unified body and spirit.

Brittany Spurlock

See also: Hmong American Culture; Korean American Folklore; Religions and Beliefs, Asian American; Traditional Healing and Medicine, Asian American

Further Reading

Baldick, Julian. *Animal and Shaman: Ancient Religions of Central Asia.* New York: New York University Press, 2000.

Fadiman, Anne. *The Spirit Catches You and You Fall Down: A Hmong Child, Her American Doctors, and the Collision of Two Cultures.* New York: Farrar, Straus and Giroux, 1997.

Maxfield, Melinda. "The Journey of the Drum." *ReVision* 16(4) (1994): 157–163.

Sonhsath, Jandee. "The Spirits, Soul, and Ceremonies." California State University, 2008, http://www.csuchico.edu.

SINGAPOREAN AMERICAN CULTURE

Singaporean Americans make up one of the smallest Asian American communities in North America. According to the U.S. Census Bureau, the Singaporean American population numbers about 15,000, with fewer than 3,000 naturalized citizens between 1997 and 2006. In Canada, there are over 1,300 Singaporeans according to the 2006 ethnic origins census report. One reason for the low numbers may be that Singaporean presence is difficult to track

Singapore Day

Singapore Day is an event organized by the Singaporean government for the purpose of bringing together Singaporeans living outside of Singapore. Though the event is meant to be limited to Singaporeans (everyone must register and prove to be either a citizen or a permanent resident of Singapore), attendees are permitted to bring non-Singaporean guests to the event. Since its opening in 2007, Singapore Day has been held in a different city every year. It has been held twice in the United States: Manhattan, New York, in 2007 and Brooklyn, New York, in 2012, with over 5,000 attendees in each instance. Each year the event is themed, and in 2012 it was "Our Home, Our Future." One of the favorite aspects of Singapore Day is the free food—local hawkers are flown in to serve their signature dishes at Singapore Day. Other notable components of Singapore Day include the entertainment, which has included Singaporean musicians, comedians, and actors. Since the event is put together for state purposes, a large part of the event is the experiential showcase, with interactive booths displaying information about the latest social and infrastructural developments in Singapore.

because of the tendency to categorize identity by broad categories of race and ethnicity rather than nationality. Singapore is a multicultural and multilingual nation consisting of three main ethnic groups: Chinese (74 percent), Malay (13 percent), and Indian (9 percent). Singaporean citizens are required to mark their ethnic group for Singaporean state bureaucratic purposes. It is common that Singaporeans mark their ethnic identities on North American census forms rather than nationality and tend toward Chinese, Malay, or South Asian diasporic communities when migrating to the United States rather than Singaporean ones. Moreover, any Singaporean immigrants who arrived in the United States prior to Singapore's independence in 1965 may have identified as Malaysian because Singapore and Malaysia were formerly part of the same country.

These elements make Singaporean American culture both difficult to track and challenging to identify. Though there are no firm statistics on Singaporean American demographics, one can assume based on Singapore's status as a relatively wealthy and modernized nation that Singaporean Americans are highly educated and professionalized. Many Singaporeans go to the United States to pursue higher education as international students. In 2013, over

Visitors taking part in Singapore Day at Central Park in New York City, April 21, 2007. Organized by the Singaporean government to bring together overseas Singaporeans, Singapore Day has been held in the United States twice: once in Manhattan in 2007, and the other in Brooklyn in 2012. (Eric Thayer/Reuters/Corbis)

4,500 Singaporeans were studying at American universities. There are, however, formalized spaces in which Singaporean communities gather, including student clubs at universities and on Singapore Day, an event organized by the Singaporean government that has taken place in the United States twice since its inception in 2006. Conversely, if we are to consider Singaporean American culture as a transnational formation, one might then look to the American expatriate community in Singapore. Although the American community in Singapore is not entirely an Asian American community—in the sense that it is not a racial formation—there are institutions and organizations such as the Singapore American School, the American Club, and the American Association of Singapore that we might loosely define as Singaporean American.

The city-state of Singapore is on a small island less than one-fourth the size of Rhode Island located off the tip of the Malaysian peninsula in Southeast Asia. Though at first a Malay fishing village, Singapore eventually became a busy trading port for the British Empire in 1819, chosen for its convenient location in the Southeast Asian straits. Singapore was briefly taken over by the Japanese Imperial Army at the end of World War II. After it was returned to the British Empire, Singapore made moves toward independent rule under the direction of Lee Kuan Yew and the People's Action Party in 1959. Singapore first gained independence from Britain upon a merger between Malaysia, Sarawak, and North Borneo to form the Federation of Malaya. Following racial tensions between the Chinese immigrants and Malay Muslims, however, Singapore was expelled from the federation, which led to its complete independence on August 9, 1965. Since its independence, Singapore has rapidly developed and modernized. It continues to be one of the busiest trading ports in the world, and its location has helped it become a financial, biotechnological, and corporate hub. Much like its days as a British trade outpost that attracted migrant labor from East and South Asia to supplement the labor provided by the indigenous Malay population, Singapore is multicultural and continues to draw in professional and service labor from throughout the region. English is widely spoken in the island nation not only because of its status as a former British colony but also because all Singaporeans attending government-run schools are required to learn two languages, one of which must be English.

Like many immigrant nations, ethnic traditions remain strong in Singapore, the diversity of which is evident through its holidays and language. Singapore celebrates as public holidays Chinese New Year, Hari Raya (Muslim New Year), Vesak Day (Buddhist holy day), and Deepavali (Hindu autumn festival). Besides these public holidays, other ethnic traditions such as the Hungry Ghost Festival and Thaipusam are also celebrated. English, Tamil, and Mandarin are Singapore's official languages, while Malay is its national language. Many

Chinese families speak dialects such as Hokkien, Cantonese, Teochew, and Hainanese at home or in casual everyday conversation.

Although within Singapore cultural traditions and practices tend to divide according to ethnicity, religion, and language, there are hybrid cultural formations that draw from the many different communities in Singapore. One example is its cuisine, which is unique to the island. Singaporean street hawker food draws influence and ingredients from throughout the Southeast Asian region. Singapore's multilingual population is also reflected in its creole language known as Singlish, which draws from English, Malay, Tamil, and Chinese dialects such as Hokkien.

Because of the small population of the Singaporean American community, cultural practices and traditions are less established. Singaporeans in the United States have found each other through university student clubs and Internet forums such as Meetup.com. Of course, what social activities these Singaporean communities choose to do vary. Besides celebrating ethnic traditions, Singaporeans may come together for National Day on August 9, or Singapore's day of independence. In Singapore independence is commemorated with the National Day Parade, which in recent years has been made readily available to viewers online. Singaporean communities have been growing in the United States since the Singaporean government established the Overseas Singaporean Unit in 2006, an agency that sustains friendly relations with Singaporeans who have left the country and provides funds and infrastructure for Singaporeans living abroad to find and maintain ties with each other.

A number of Singaporean literary artists have immigrated to the United States. Among them are Fiona Cheong, a novelist and English professor in Pittsburgh; Lydia Kwa, a novelist and poet who has written three novels and two books of poetry; Shirley Geok-lin Lim, an English professor in Santa Barbara who is Malaysian but identifies a strong connection with Singapore in her writing; Vyvyane Loh, a medical doctor and choreographer who is also a novelist based in Boston; Wena Poon, a lawyer based in the United States who has written about diasporic Singaporean Chinese; Hwee Hwee Tan, a writer who was living in New York City for a number of years; and Chay Yew, a Singaporean playwright and stage director based in Chicago.

Singapore's probusiness environment and its friendly trade ties with the United States have brought many American families to Singapore. A number of U.S.-based religious groups such as Mormons have also established their presence in Singapore. American expatriates in Singapore mostly follow American cultural traditions. For example, many families celebrate holidays such as Thanksgiving, and at the Singaporean American School students practice American sports such as football and cheerleading.

Cheryl Narumi Naruse

See also: Burmese (Myanmar) American Culture; Laotian American Culture; Malaysian American Culture; Thai American Culture

Further Reading

Baker, Jim. *The Eagle in the Lion City: America, Americans and Singapore*. Singapore: Select Books, 2005.

"Ethnic Origins, 2006 Counts, for Canada, Provinces and Territories." Statistics Canada, 2013, http://www12.statcan.gc.ca.

Hoeffel, Elizabeth M., Sonya Rastogi, Myoung Ouk Kim, and Hasan Shahid. "The Asian Population: 2010." United States Census Bureau, March 2012, http://www.census.gov/2010census/.

"International Student Totals by Place of Origin, 2011/12–2012/13." Institute of International Education, 2013, http://www.iie.org/opendoors.

"Singapore Day." Overseas Singaporean Unit, 2013, http://www.singaporeday.sg.

SPORTS, ASIAN AMERICANS IN

Although the visibility and recognition of Asian Americans in sports may not be quite as extensive as that of African Americans and Latinos, athletes of various Asian and Pacific heritages have nonetheless had a profound impact on a range of sports in the United States, particularly baseball, basketball, boxing, martial arts, and figure skating. The number of Asian and Pacific American athletes in professional U.S. sports has increased dramatically in recent years as a result of sizable growth in the Asian/Pacific American population and the globalization of several different sports, which has expanded the popularity of U.S. athletics in Asia and the Pacific Rim.

Michelle Kwan (1980–)

California native Michelle Kwan is the most decorated American figure skater in the sport's history. The daughter of immigrants from Hong Kong, Kwan won the silver and bronze medals in women's singles competition at the 1998 and 2002 Winter Olympics, respectively. Over the course of her professional career, Kwan has captured dozens of medals, including five world championships and nine U.S. championships. She began skating at five years old and quickly developed a passion for the sport. In addition to her impressive athletic accomplishments, Kwan also earned a bachelor's degree in international studies from the University of Denver and graduated from Tufts University with a master's degree in international relations in 2011.

Basketball and Baseball

Basketball and baseball represent two of the most popular sports in the United States, and each of these sports has witnessed a growing number of Asian American athletes. The Houston Rockets of the National Basketball Association (NBA) made history in 2002 when they selected 7′6″ center Yao Ming (1980–), a native of Shanghai, China, as the first pick in that year's NBA draft. Yao went on to play eight seasons with the Rockets before injuries forced him into early retirement in 2011. Nevertheless, Yao was selected to the NBA All-Star Game each of his eight seasons, and the 2004 documentary *The Year of the Yao* chronicles his cultural transition to life in the United States during his NBA rookie year.

More recently, Taiwanese American NBA point guard Jeremy Lin (1988–) generated intense media buzz with his outstanding performance as a member of the New York Knicks in February–March 2012. Born in Los Angeles to Taiwanese immigrant parents, Lin is the first American of Taiwanese heritage to play in the NBA. Despite the Knicks harboring one of the league's worst records, during his second year in the league Lin rose to superstardom status when he worked his way into the team's starting lineup and turned the Knicks' fortunes around by leading them on an improbable winning streak. Over this stretch, Lin guided the Knicks to several unlikely victories over more talented teams, scored 38 points on the Los Angeles Lakers' Kobe Bryant (considered one of the league's best players), and scored a game-winning 3-point shot against the Toronto Raptors. Lin's unlikely rise to stardom and the instant fan gravitation toward him led the press to dub these phenomena "Linsanity." Before joining the NBA, Lin had a stellar collegiate basketball career at Harvard, where he became the first Ivy League player to ever score 1,450 points, 400 rebounds, and 200 steals as well as earning a bachelor's degree in economics.

The success of Yao and Lin notwithstanding, the first Asian player in NBA history was Wat Misaka (1923–), whom the New York Knicks drafted in 1947. Actually, Misaka was the NBA's first nonwhite player of any racial background. The son of Japanese immigrants, Misaka was born and raised in Utah and led the Utah Utes to an upset victory over the heavily favored Kentucky Wildcats in the 1947 NCAA championship game.

In 1995, Hideo Nomo (1968–) became the second Japanese player in the major leagues (the first was Masanori Murakami [1944–], who briefly played for the San Francisco Giants in 1964–1965) when he debuted for the Los Angeles Dodgers. A native of Osaka, Japan, Nomo achieved immediate success as he produced a 13-6 record with a 2.54 ERA during his rookie season. He also led the National League in strikeouts, surpassing Sandy Koufax's single-season Dodgers record. Nomo was selected as the starting pitcher for the National

League in the 1995 All-Star Game and earned National League Rookie of the Year honors. His success was in part attributed to his unique pitching style, nicknamed "the tornado," in which he fully extended both arms overhead while twisting his body in a corkscrew fashion during his delivery. Aside from his on-field accomplishments, Nomo cultivated a memorable legacy by attracting a large Japanese and Japanese American fan base, a social phenomenon that sports journalists dubbed "Nomo-mania." Fittingly, Nomo's rookie year occurred while he played in Los Angeles, home of the nation's largest Japanese American community and its historic "Little Tokyo" ethnic enclave. Baseball experts credit Nomo's popularity and success with opening up new opportunities for Asian players in the United States by shattering the once-common stereotype that Asians were too small and slender to excel in Major League Baseball (MLB). In striking out that stereotype, Nomo threw two no-hitters during his career against the Colorado Rockies and Baltimore Orioles; he is still the only player ever to have pitched a no-hitter at Coors Field or Camden Yards.

Since 1995, more than 50 players from Japan and South Korea have competed in the major leagues. One of the most successful has been Ichiro Suzuki (1973–) of the Seattle Mariners, who was voted to 10 MLB All-Star Games from 2001 to 2010. Ichiro set the MLB record for most base hits in a season (262) in 2004 and was named the American League's Most Valuable Player and Rookie of the Year in 2001 while also leading the league in stolen bases.

Football

Relatively fewer players of East and Southeast Asian descent have achieved prominence in collegiate and professional football in the United States, although numerous players from the South Pacific/Oceania have achieved notoriety in the National Football League (NFL). The best-known Asian American NFL star is Hines Ward (1976–), an outstanding wide receiver who played 14 seasons with the Pittsburgh Steelers. Born in Seoul, South Korea, to a Korean mother and an African American father serving in the U.S. military, Ward grew up in Georgia and attended the University of Georgia before being drafted by the Steelers in 1998. Ward's career highlights include winning two Super Bowls, being named Most Valuable Player of Super Bowl XL, and breaking the Steelers all-time records for receptions, receiving yards, and receiving touchdowns. He currently serves as an analyst for NBC's Sunday night coverage of NFL games. Ward has also become an outspoken advocate for the acceptance of mixed-race children in Korean society and has been featured on the cover of *KoreAm*, a monthly magazine that covers issues of importance to the Korean American community.

Another notable Korean American professional football player is offensive lineman Eugene Chung (1969–), who was the 13th player selected in the 1993 NFL draft. Chung was selected by the New England Patriots and became the first player of Korean descent to be drafted in the first round. He played six seasons with the Patriots, the Jacksonville Jaguars, and the Indianapolis Colts. He currently serves as the assistant offensive line coach for the Kansas City Chiefs after spending three seasons as an assistant coach with the Philadelphia Eagles.

Dat Nguyen (1975–) became the NFL's first player of Vietnamese descent when the Dallas Cowboys selected him in the third round of the 1999 draft. Nguyen, who was born in a refugee center in Arkansas, played seven seasons with the Cowboys as a middle linebacker until he retired due to a neck injury. He was named All-Pro for the 2003 season. Nguyen also won the Chuck Bednarik Award, given to the best defensive player in college football, in 1998 when he played for the Texas A&M Aggies.

Dozens of athletes of South Pacific and Polynesian descent have played in the NCAA and the NFL since the 1970s. Arguably the most famous is Troy Polamalu (1981–) of Samoan heritage who, like Ward, was drafted by the Pittsburgh Steelers. Polamalu plays strong safety and is regarded as one of the top defensive backs and hardest hitters in football, having been named to the NFL's All-Decade Team for the 2000s. Known for his trademark long hair, Polamalu is an eight-time Pro Bowler and was named NFL Defensive Player of the Year for the 2010 season. He was also featured on the cover of the video game *Madden NFL 10*.

Figure Skating

Two Asian American figure skaters, Kristi Yamaguchi (1971–) and Michelle Kwan (1980–), rose to the elite ranks of their sport in the late 20th and early 21st centuries, respectively. Yamaguchi, a fourth-generation Japanese American from northern California's East Bay, won the gold medal in figure skating at the 1992 Winter Olympics in Albertville, France. She also captured the gold medal at the Women's World Figure Skating Championships in 1991 and 1992. Kwan, the daughter of immigrants from Hong Kong, grew up in southern California and took up figure skating during her childhood. Over the course of her career, Kwan won more medals in national and international competitions than any other U.S. figure skater in history. She won the silver and bronze medals at the 1998 and 2002 Winter Olympics, respectively, and captured five gold medals at the Women's World Figure Skating Championships. Kwan also won nine U.S. Figure Skating titles between 1996 and 2005.

Michelle Kwan, a decorated figure skater, waving an American flag after winning the gold medal at the World Figure Skating Championships in Washington, D.C., March 29, 2003. (AP Photo/Roberto Borea)

In 1999, the Chinese American Museum honored Kwan by awarding her its Outstanding Achievement in Sports accolade.

Combat Sports: Martial Arts and Boxing

The best-known and most influential martial artist of all time was Bruce Lee (1940–1973). Born Lee Jun Fan in San Francisco's Chinatown, Lee remains the most significant martial arts cultural icon in American society more than 40 years after his untimely death. The son of immigrants from Hong Kong, Lee spent much of his childhood and adolescence in Hong Kong, where he began studying the Chinese martial art *wing chun*. Upon returning to the United States in 1959, he enrolled at the University of Washington, where he studied philosophy and opened his own martial arts academies in Seattle, Oakland, and

Los Angeles. Lee created his own martial arts style, *jeet kune do*, that blended physical training techniques with his own personal philosophical principles. He later ventured into acting, landing the role of Kato in the 1960s TV series *The Green Hornet* and starring in films such as *Fists of Fury* (1971) and *Enter the Dragon* (1972). These roles enabled Lee to expose millions of Americans to Asian martial arts, although he tragically died unexpectedly of an allergic reaction in Hong Kong in July 1973 shortly before *Enter the Dragon* premiered on the silver screen.

Manny "Pac-Man" Pacquiao (1978–) has emerged as one of the most dominant boxers of recent years. A native of the Philippines, Pacquiao has captured 10 world titles in eight weight divisions during his professional career. No other fighter in boxing history has won titles in as many different weight divisions, and the Filipino star has been regarded by boxing experts as one of the best pound-for-pound fighters in the sport for nearly his entire career. Elected to the Philippine Congress in 2010, Pacquiao splits his time between Manila and Los Angeles and has accumulated a professional boxing record of 55 wins, 5 losses, 2 draws, and 38 knockouts. Currently competing in boxing's welterweight division, he remains perhaps the most popular athlete of Asian heritage in the United States. On May 2, 2015, however, Pacquiao lost a world welterweight championship match in Las Vegas to Floyd Mayweather in what was billed the "Fight of the Century," and some of those who placed heavy bets in Pacquaio's favor filed suit against him for failing to disclose an earlier shoulder injury.

Two other younger Filipino American fighters have followed in Pacquiao's footsteps and have made a name for themselves in professional boxing. Nonito Donaire (1982–), nicknamed "The Filipino Flash," captured the International Boxing Federation's flyweight championship in 2007 and the World Boxing Council's bantamweight title in 2011. Brian Viloria (1980–), also known as "The Hawaiian Punch," has amassed a professional record of 34 victories and 4 defeats and has won world titles in the flyweight and superflyweight divisions.

Justin D. García

See also: Linsanity; Popular Culture, Asian Americans and

Further Reading

Franks, Joel. *Asian Pacific Americans and Baseball: A History.* Jefferson, NC: McFarland, 2008.

Gonzalez, Joaquin Jay, III, and Angelo Michael F. Merino. *From Pancho to Pacquiao: Philippine Boxing in and out of the Ring.* Minneapolis: Mill City Press, 2012.

How Bruce Lee Changed the World. Directed by Steve Webb. A&E Home Video, 2009. DVD.

Pacquiao, Manny. *Pacman: My Story of Hope, Resilience, and Never-Say-Never Determination.* Nashville: Dunham, 2010.

Rafiq, Fiaz. *Bruce Lee: Conversations.* London: HNL Publishing/Publishers Group UK, 2010.

The Year of the Yao. Directed by Adam Del Deo and James D. Stern. York: NBA Home Entertainment Video, 2004. DVD.

Yep, Kathleen. *Outside the Paint: When Basketball Ruled at the Chinese Playground.* Philadelphia: Temple University Press, 2009.

SRI LANKAN AMERICAN CULTURE

Even though there are records from the U.S. Census Bureau showing that Sri Lankans arrived in America in the early days, the most significant arrival of Sri Lankans happened in the mid-1950s due to the Official Language Act of 1955 in Sri Lanka. The early immigrants were mostly English educated and from well-to-do families, and most of them belonged to the ethnic groups of Burghers (Sri Lankans with Portuguese or Dutch ancestry) or Tamils. While the Burghers migrated mainly in search of jobs, most of the Tamil and Sinhalese immigrants in the early days entered America as students. Sri Lankans in America were categorized as other Asians before 1975; Sri Lankans were

Sinhala Hindu New Year Celebrations

The Sinhala Hindu New Year is celebrated in accordance with the Hindu astrological calendar every year in April when the sun travels from the last house Pisces to the first house Aries, completing a full cycle. The exact date is calculated by the astrologers in Sri Lanka. In recent years, the auspicious time to cook the first meal, the time to partake of the first meal, and other auspicious times are calculated for the diaspora's benefit too in accordance with the different time zones. Sri Lankan Americans come together to celebrate the New Year in private or community gatherings. Most homes strive to comply with the auspicious times for different activities to mark the beginning of the New Year, and both Sinhalese and Tamils from Sri Lanka take part in religious activities to usher in good luck and prosperity. The cultural activities, organized by the Sri Lankan Associations in different states, take place on a weekend or a holiday, thus enabling the participation of most community members. The celebrations include traditional games, beauty pageants, and traditional food throughout the day. The events of the day usually are concluded with Sri Lankan songs and music.

classified as a separate category for the first time in 1975. The second significant wave of immigration from Sri Lanka to America took place in the mid-1980s after the July Riots in 1983. The migration continued until the early 2000s because of the Sri Lankan Civil War that displaced many people. They migrated to Western countries in search of political asylum and peaceful environments.

Sri Lankan Americans have strived to maintain their distinct ethnic variances while being united as Sri Lankans, distinguishing themselves from other immigrant groups from South Asia. Many Sri Lankans prefer to settle in large urban areas that already have large Sri Lankan communities, such as New York City, Los Angeles, and San Francisco. Little Sri Lanka, in the Tompkinsville neighborhood of the borough of Staten Island in New York City, is one of the largest Sri Lankan American communities.

Ethno-Religious Groups and Cultural Practices

There are three distinct ethno-religious groups among Sri Lankans in America: Sinhalese, Tamil, and Muslim. The Sinhalese, who constitute the largest ethnic group in Sri Lanka—74.88 percent according to the 2011 census—congregate mainly in urban areas in the United States and are listed as 12,000 Sinhalese in the 2010 census. Tamils, who are the second-largest ethnic group in Sri Lanka—11.2 percent according to the 2011 census—are the largest diasporic group in America. The Muslims and Burghers make up a small number of Sri Lankans in America.

All the different ethno-religious groups share the same cultural values: strong family ties, extended family support (when possible), and deep community bonds. All the Sri Lankan groups continue to practice the patriarchal family structure in America with an emphasis on the mother's role in the well-being of the family. There is also a strong emphasis on education and being a good citizen, which translates to most Sri Lankans living above the poverty line in America. Second-generation Sri Lankan Americans are encouraged to learn Sri Lankan traditions through various state and regional Sri Lankan associations. Buddhists and Hindus also rely on their temples to educate younger generations about traditional culture. Sri Lankan associations in America organize the Independence Day celebrations (February 4) and Sri Lanka Day (variously in July or August) to celebrate Sri Lankan music, traditions, and general collective feeling among Sri Lankan Americans.

Cricket is the national pastime for Sri Lankans and unites Sri Lankans all over the world. Sri Lankan Americans share the same passion despite America's lack of a cricket culture and gather to watch different International Cricket matches at various private venues. Supporting Sri Lanka unites them, and these cricket gatherings usually feature many popular food items for Sri Lankans

Kaushalya and Sitara Wijeratne, leading the way for the Sri Lanka contingent at the Gala Parade of Nations, celebrating Los Angeles County's 150th birthday in 2000. Sri Lankan immigrants began to arrive in the United States in significant numbers in the 1950s. (Clarence Williams/Los Angeles Times via Getty Images)

such as chicken curry, string hoppers (rice flour pressed into noodle form and then steamed), and other savory snacks made of meat or boiled and tempered pulses called "bites" as an accompaniment to drinks.

Sri Lankan music, classical and popular, is a main cultural identity of Sri Lankans in America. Various groups in America sponsor musicians and music bands from Sri Lanka to raise funds for charities in Sri Lanka and to gather Sri Lankans in America. These musicians range from established classical maestros of Sinhalese music to popular young musicians and bands ranging from modern music to *baila*. A popular folk music form originally from the kaffirs (people of Portuguese, African, and native Sinhalese heritage), *baila* was appropriated into Sri Lankan popular culture in the 1960s. Sri Lankan Americans and Sri Lankan diaspora all over the world in general are nostalgic about the *baila* music from the 1960s to the 1980s, and music bands are encouraged to perform *baila* music at various cultural events in America.

Sri Lankan food is a key part of Sri Lankan culture in America. Despite their ethno-religious differences, Sri Lankans in America rejoice over *kottu roti* (a typical street food made with flat wheat bread cut into pieces and mixed with vegetables, meat, eggs, and other spices over a hot wok) at cultural events, such as Sri Lanka Day. Other Sri Lankan food items such as hoppers (pancakes made with fermented rice batter), *katta sambol* (ground red chilis, onions, and maldive fish with lime and salt), coconut *sambol* (same as *katta sambol* with the addition of grated coconut), string hoppers, chicken curry, yellow rice (rice with saffron and raisins), and sweet dishes such as *watalappan* (coconut custard pudding made with jaggery) and cream caramel pudding are also popular among Sri Lankans in America. These food items have varied origins but have been appropriated to Sri Lankan taste, thus carrying an essentially Sri Lankan identity in taste and spices. Sri Lankan gatherings, large or small, always feature some of these food items. Traditional Sri Lankan sweetmeats such as *kevum* (oil cakes), *aasmi* (rice flour pressed into noodle form and deep-fried and decorated with sugar syrup), *kokis* (deep-fried sweet dish made with rice flour), *aluwa* (sweet made with rice flour and sugar or treacle), *dodol* (sweet toffee-like concoction with rice flour, coconut milk, and treacle), and *undu walalu* (sweet made from *urad dhal* flour, deep-fried and infused with treacle) are important parts of the traditional New Year's celebration in April. Food is an essential part of the Sri Lankan culture in America, and there are ethnic food stores that supply Sri Lankan ingredients and food items for the diasporic Sri Lankan communities living in large urban areas.

Notable Sri Lankan Americans

Fiction writers such as Mary Anne Mohanraj, V. V. Ganeshananthan, Ru Freeman, and Karen Roberts are notable Sri Lankan Americans. Indran Amirthanayagam is a notable poet and a U.S. diplomat of Sri Lankan origin. There are many Sri Lankan Americans noted for their contributions to a variety of fields in academia, business, and music. Second-generation singer and rapper Dilan Jayasinha (DeLon) is the first Sri Lankan artist to earn a place on U.S. *Billboard* charts.

Shashikala Muthumal Assella

See also: Bangladeshi American Culture; Pakistani American Culture; Singaporean American Culture

Further Reading

"A Community of Contrasts: Asian Americans in the United States: 2011." Asian American Center for Advancing Justice, http://www.advancingjustice-aajc.org /sites/aajc/files/Community_of_Contrast.pdf.

De Silva, Chandra Richard. *Sri Lanka: A History.* New Delhi: Vikas, 1987.

Holt, John Clifford, ed. *Sri Lanka Reader: History, Culture, Politics.* Durham, NC: Duke University Press, 2011.

"Population by Ethnic Group according to Districts, 2012." Sri Lankan Department of Census and Statistics, http://www.statistics.gov.lk/PopHouSat/CPH2011/Pages/Activities/Reports/cph2011Pub/pop42.pdf.

Ross, Russell R. *Sri Lanka: A Country Study.* Washington, DC: Library of Congress Federal Research Division, 1990.

SUSHI

History and Origins

Sushi, literally translated as "seasoned rice," is a type of Japanese cuisine with worldwide popularity. Modern sushi consists of cooked rice and vinegar. It is topped or rolled with a variety of fish, vegetables, and/or egg. The term "sushi" dates back to a fourth-century Chinese dictionary reference of a fermented fish in cooked rice. Fish preservation had been done as early as 500 BCE, originating in Southeast Asia. Fish would quickly decompose unless salted until it was discovered that it could be preserved in cooked rice. The cleaned fish and rice would then be pressed, usually under a heavy stone, in a vessel or barrel for a few weeks.

Sushi was introduced to Japan in the ninth century as a way to prepare, store, and preserve fish. Rice's natural fermentation process produces lactic acid that pickles the fish. It would be ready to eat in a few months to a year. Only the fish would be consumed and the rice discarded. This type of cooked rice and fermented fish was referred to as *nare-zushi* (aged sushi).

Bluefin Tuna

Bluefin tuna is the most widely used fish in preparing sushi. The largest of the tuna species, bluefin is desired for its fatty cuts and tender red meat. Bluefin tuna is also the backbone of the global sushi market, as cuts are priced as they are prized. In 2012, a 593-pound bluefin tuna sold for over $736,000 in Tokyo. From the late 1970s, coastal fishing regulations and environmental protection groups slowed Japan's fishing fleets. This made Japan dependent on global imports, such as commercial fisheries in New England, to supply their demand. From 1984 to 1993, bluefin tuna imports in Japan increased over 60 percent. Unfortunately, due to overfishing, lack of government regulations on fishing quotas, and the demand for bluefin tuna, it is now on the endangered species list. The 18th Special Meeting of the International Commission for the Conservation of Atlantic Tunas, an intergovernmental body of fishing countries, put in place strict new quota regulations for the farming of bluefin tuna.

Religion and geography also affected the development of sushi. Imperial decrees by Emperor Temmu prohibited the consumption of cattle, horses, dogs, monkeys, and chickens in the year 675. These decrees were based on Buddhist principles and the Shinto taboo of animal consumption. Fish were excluded. Japan's placement as an island as well as the numerous inlets and shallow bays made it conducive to fishing. Its vast array of marine animals such as urchins, herrings, bonito, and salmon were harvested for sushi.

Regional Practices and Traditions

In the Shiga prefecture, *funa-zushi* was first prepared over 1,000 years ago using the funa karp. This particular species was indigenous to Lake Bawa. Fish would be caught and salted, soaked in water, then placed in cooked rice. The fish and rice would be placed under pressure, with the fish eaten after 18 months of fermentation. *Nama-zushi* (raw sushi) would involve a faster fermentation period of only a month. This would be later introduced in the 15th and 16th centuries.

In the 17th century, sushi practitioners in Edo (Tokyo) would add vinegar to hasten the fermentation process. This new type of fermentation spurred a boom in sushi shops in Edo. Nori, an important ingredient in sushi, was cultivated in the later part of the 17th century, contributing to its modern incarnation.

In the 1820s, *nigiri-zushi* was invented by Hanaya Yohei (1799–1858) in Edo. It consists of rice vinegar and salt added to freshly cooked rice. This is then rolled by hand into a ball with a piece of fish, raw or cooked, placed on top. This sushi is not placed under pressure and is eaten immediately after preparation. This appealed to casual eaters, as it could be quickly made and consumed. Portable sushi stalls were set up to accommodate this newly invented fast food.

In 1958 *kaitenzushi*, or conveyor-belt sushi, originated in Higashi, Osaka. This transformed sushi from a high-class cuisine to a popular and accessible food to the masses. Invented by Yoshiaki Shiraishi after seeing the conveyor-belt lines of the Asahi brewing company, Shiraishi developed this to keep prices available to the largely working-class clientele of his restaurant. *Kaitenzushi* continues to be popular today, integrating a touch-panel computer system that accurately tracks orders. Currently there are over 3,000 *kaitenzushi*-type restaurants throughout Japan.

Chirashizushi, or scattered sushi, consists of a bowl of rice topped with assorted types of ingredients. This dish varies from region to region. For instance, *edomae chirashizushi*, or Edo-style *chirashizushi*, consists of uncooked ingredients on top of spread rice, whereas *gomokuzushi*, or Kasai-style sushi, may use cooked and uncooked ingredients. *Oshizushi* is another type of sushi originating from Osaka. This sushi consists of rice and toppings, which is then placed under a wooden block, or *oshibako,* and retains a block shape.

Contemporary Forms

Today's sushi consists of cooked or raw fish on top of a bed of rice and vinegar with wasabi and pickled ginger. A wide variety of both cooked vegetables and seafood is used in modern sushi. This includes shrimp, sea urchin, roe, and shellfish, with tuna as the most widely used in the cuisine. The dish also consists of nori, which may be wrapped around the fish and rice to create a roll. Expert sushi chefs, or *shokunin,* roll and cut sushi by hand. Today's sushi also shares characteristics of Yohei's *nigiri-zushi* and may consist of raw fish, salmon eggs, cooked shrimp, or a sliced egg on top of a ball of rice.

Maki-zushi, or rolled sushi, comes in various forms. The most basic form consists of rice rolled with nori that is filled with vegetables, cooked or raw fish, and other fillings. The *maki* is then chopped into several bite-size pieces. *Te-maki,* or hand-rolled sushi, is rolled into cone shapes of nori and consists of larger vegetables or smoked salmon. *Futomaki,* or large, fat roll, is typically vegetarian and consists of a few ingredients and rice. Conversely, *hosomaki* is smaller cylindrical rolls a few centimeters apiece. These rolls consist of a single ingredient, usually cucumber or carrots. *Uramaki* refers to sushi rolls with the rice on the outside and nori on the inside. Sesame seeds or roe are sometimes added as an outer coating of *uramaki.* Related to *maki* is *gunkanmaki,* for which a ball of rice is formed by hand, then topped with ingredients such as roe or sea urchin. A wrap of nori is then placed around the rice and topping. This prevents the topping from falling off of the rice.

Another type of sushi that is typically eaten includes *inari-zushi* and *temari-zushi. Inari* consists of a piece of deep-fried tofu, which is flattened and folded over to form a pocket. Rice and other ingredients are then placed inside the pocket. *Temarizushi,* or ball sushi, is sushi that consists of a ball of rice with a fish topping.

There are a number of utensils used in the creation of sushi. A *hangiri* is a small tub used for the cooling of rice. An *uchiwa* is a handheld fan also used to cool rice. A *shamoji* is a flat spatula used to spread rice. *Makisu* is a mat used to roll the rice. These utensils are usually constructed out of wood or bamboo.

Sushi in the United States

Japanese food has been available in Japanese diasporas such as Hawai'i and America's West Coast since the early 1920s. In the second half of the 20th century, sushi became more widespread in North America and among non-Japanese. Prince Akihito of Japan formally introduced the cuisine to the United States during a dinner hosted by the Japanese embassy in 1953.

Sushi restaurants in America began to take hold in the 1960s and 1970s, with the globalization of sushi starting soon after. Japan's growth as an economic force, the 1960s counterculture movement, and the rise of health and organic foods had stimulated the food's popularity. The *New York Times* had a special front-page feature on the opening of a sushi bar at the Harvard Club of New York City, signifying a sense of sophistication and class around the cuisine. From the late 1980s to the late 1990s, sushi eateries in the United States quintupled and continue to grow. Take-out establishments and supermarkets had further increased the accessibility of sushi even more.

Sushi practitioners in California had become noteworthy for their use of vegetarian sushi dishes, utilizing spices not found in Japan and using local seafood and vegetables. For instance, the California Roll, or *unamaki*, is aptly named, as it was created in Los Angeles by a Japanese chef. This type of *maki-zushi* contains avocado, crab, and cucumber wrapped in nori or rice. The roll was made to be more palatable for Western tastes or to hide the nori traditionally wrapped around the roll.

The globalization of sushi has even made a reverse import of sorts. Sushi has been exported to the West, modified, and returned and remarketed to Japan. There are sushi restaurants that specialize in American sushi. This fusion food is marketed as American chic, using nontraditional fillings and emphasizing New York and California styles of the cuisine. These *maki* rolls differ from their Japanese counterparts by utilizing ingredients such as cream cheese (Philadelphia Roll), smoked salmon, chicken, beef, and fruits such as mangoes or bananas.

Junior Tidal

See also: Chop Suey; Filipino American Food; Japanese American Immigration; Japanese Tea Ceremony; Kimchi; *Pho;* Thai American Food

Further Reading

Allen, Matthew, and Rumi Sakamoto. "Sushi Reverses Course: Consuming American Sushi in Tokyo." *Asia-Pacific Journal: Japan Focus* (January 2011): 1–16.

Bestor, Theodore C. "How Sushi Went Global." In *The Cultural Politics of Food and Eating: A Reader,* edited by James L. Watson and Melissa L. Caldwell, 13–20. Malden, MA: Blackwell Publishing, 2005.

Issenberg, Sasha. *The Sushi Economy: Globalization and the Making of a Modern Delicacy.* New York: Gotham Books, 2007.

Mouritsen, Ole G. *Sushi: Food for the Eye, the Body & the Soul.* New York: Springer, 2009.

T

TAE KWON DO

Originating in Korea, tae kwon do (taekwon-do, taekwondo, or tae-kwon-do) is a form of martial arts that combines defensive and offensive techniques. It was developed in Korea in the mid-20th century. According to the International Taekwon-Do Federation, General Choi Hong Hi (1918–2002) developed a form of martial arts incorporating elements of the ancient Korean martial art of taek kyon and shotokan karate that he had learned in Japan and adopted the name "taekwon-do" in 1955. He later wrote the 15-volume *Encyclopedia of Taekwon-Do* to explain its rules and practices. Since then tae kwon do has gained popularity among children and adults in many countries, including the United States.

A number of organizations have been formed to promote the teaching and practice of tae kwon do and to organize competitions at various levels. General Choi Hong Hi founded the International Taekwon-Do Federation (ITF) in 1966. In 1969, the ITF organized the first Asian Tournament in Hong Kong. Over the years, the ITF has expanded substantially, with affiliated organizations in many countries.

Established in 1973, the World Taekwondo Federation (WTF) is an international organization governing the sport of tae kwon do and a member of the Association of Summer Olympic International Federations. Founded in Korea, the WTF includes over 200 member national associations.

Eternal Grand Master Haeng Ung Lee (1936–2000) founded the American Taekwondo Association (ATA) in 1962, with its headquarters in Little Rock, Arkansas. The ATA held closed tournaments for members and trained instructors. In the late 1980s, Master Lee introduced 18 Songahm forms as part of an integrated curriculum through which to reinforce everything a student learns in tae kwon do. Songahm tae kwon do emphasizes personal development of the mind and body and facilitates the progression from one rank to the next. The ranks are correlated with the belts. Ranking from beginner to advanced levels, the ATA Songahm tae kwon do belts include white belt, orange belt, yellow belt, camouflage (camo) belt, green belt, purple belt, blue belt, brown belt, red belt, red/black belt, and black belt. Today the ATA and its affiliated organizations have over 300,000 members worldwide.

Founded in 1978, USA Taekwondo (USAT) is the national governing body of tae kwon do for the United States Olympic Committee. The USAT selects U.S. national junior and senior teams for World Taekwondo Federation events, including the Summer Olympic Games tae kwon do competition event.

As an evolving form of martial art, tae kwon do is practiced as a sport and as an exercise in and outside Korea. Its emphasis on high kicks and hand techniques helps practitioners develop strength, speed, balance, and flexibility. A student usually wears a uniform, often white, with a belt. Traditionally tae kwon do is practiced with bare feet, although there is particular footwear for practicing tae kwon do as well. Students in the junior ranks usually wear colored belts and sometimes have stripes on their belts. Those in the senior ranks typically wear black belts. Generally speaking, students have to complete promotion tests before they can advance from one rank to another. When practicing tae kwon do, commands are usually in Korean. The ranking systems and titles vary among different organizations. Besides physical techniques and strength, tae kwon do

Dressed in a Taekwon-Do uniform, a girl demonstrates her high kick at the 2013 Korean Festival at Kapi'olani Park, Oahu, Hawai'i. Taekwon-Do became an official Olympic event in 2000. (Rico Leffanta/Dreamstime.com)

also highlights discipline and philosophy of life. In the United States, many schools and organizations offer tae kwon do classes for adults and children, both in metropolitan areas where there are sizable Korean American populations and in small towns where the number of Korean American residents is rather small. Tae kwon do was an Olympic Games Demonstration Sport for the 1998 Seoul Olympic Games and the 1992 Barcelona Olympic Games and became an official Olympic Sport for the 2000 Sydney Olympic Games.

Lan Dong

See also: Judo; Karate; Tai Chi

Further Reading

American Taekwondo Association, http://ataonline.com/.

Coelho, Rebeca Cardozo, Lev Kreft, and Teresa Lacerda. "The Aesthetic Experience of Taekwondo Athlete." *Ars & Humanitas: Revija Za Umetnost in Humanistiko* 6(1) (2012): 107–115.

International Taekwon-Do Federation, http://www.itftkd.org/.

Kyung, H. Min. "Taekwondo Past, Present and Future: An American Perspective." *Koreana: Korean Art and Culture* 14(4) (2000): 16–19.

Lee, Kyong-myong. "Taekwondo on the World Stage." *Koreana: Korean Art and Culture* 14(4) (2000): 20–23.

Little, John R., and Curtis F. Wong, eds. *Ultimate Guide to Tae Kwon Do.* Lincolnwood, IL: Contemporary Books, 2000.

Magnan Park, Aaron Han Joon. "Technologized Tae Kwon Do Millenialism: Robot Taekwon V and the Assertion of a Triumphant South Korean National Identity." *Journal of Japanese and Korean Cinema* 2(2) (2010): 109–130.

USA Taekwondo, http://www.teamusa.org/usa-taekwondo.

Wood, Alix. *Tae Kwon Do.* New York: PowerKids, 2013.

TAI CHI

Often spelled variously as *taiji* or *t'ai chi*, tai chi is a concept originating from Chinese philosophy, a Chinese cosmological term for the "Supreme Ultimate" or the "Great Ultimate." The tai chi diagram representing the Supreme Ultimate is composed of a white half circle and a black half circle with an S-shaped flowing line in between so that the two halves do not appear to be separated from each other but instead appear to grow out of each other and/or into each other, forming a whole. Each half contains a small circle of the opposite color. It emphasizes the interdependence of all things—even things that seem to be opposites contain within themselves the seed of their contrary nature. The diagram is also known as "yin-yang fishes": each half of the diagram resembles a fish and represents yin and yang, respectively. The diagram together holds the meaning that tai chi creates yin and yang, which produce all things. As night follows day, yin and yang circle eternally. Balance between the two halves represents the harmony of the primal energy.

The term "tai chi" is most commonly used to refer to *tai chi chuan*, alternatively spelled *t'ai chi ch'uan* or *taijiquan*, a Chinese internal martial art based on the principles of yin and yang and Daoist philosophy. It was founded by ancient Chinese martial arts experts who developed it from the philosophy of tai chi. By adding the term *chuan* (the fist), the martial art is distinguished from the philosophy that forms its foundations. But the practice of *tai chi chuan* is meant to be in harmony with the tai chi philosophy. The art of *tai chi chuan* is a series of flowing circular movements that physically illustrate the balance and energy of the human body. All movement in *tai chi chuan* forms emphasize circular motion. Practiced with a high degree of mental concentration, these movements seek to establish balance within the individual and harmony in the way of nature, or Dao.

The first documented use of the name *tai chi chuan* dates from the 17th century and is attributed to Chen Wangting (1580–1660) at the time of transition between the Ming and Qing dynasties. The art of *tai chi chuan*

A group of elderly individuals practicing tai chi. A form of martial arts with a connection to Daoist philosophy, tai chi is practiced by many for health benefits. (Kanjanee Chaisin/Dreamstime.com)

for a few hundred years was closely guarded as esoteric and taught only to members of the Chen family. During the 19th century the first nonfamily member, Yang Luchan (1799–1872), learned the art from Chen Changxing (1771–1853).

Yang later developed his own variations and created the yang style, with an emphasis on health and health maintenance. Since the early 20th century, *tai chi chuan*'s health benefits have become more noticed by the world, and people with little or no interest in martial training have begun to practice tai chi for its benefits to health. Today *tai chi chuan* is represented by five family styles: chen, yang, wu (hao), sun, and wu. They all share a common heritage and basic principles. Medical studies of tai chi support its effectiveness as an alternative exercise and a form of martial arts therapy.

Zheng Manqing (Cheng Man-ch'ing, 1902–1975), a student of the yang-style tai chi master Yang Chengfu (1883–1936), is one of the pioneers who openly taught tai chi in the United States. Manqing founded and taught at the Shr Jung T'ai Chi school after he moved to New York in 1964. He revised the yang long-form tai chi and created a short form he called the "Yang-style tai chi in 37 Postures." His shortened form became extremely popular in Taiwan, Malaysia, and the United States. He has taught many students who have continued to spread his form around the world.

Tai chi chuan as a form of martial arts or exercise frequently appears in film, fiction, games, etc. In Asian American literature and cinema, it plays the role of a cultural icon, representing the situation of traditional Chinese culture in the United States. In Ang Lee's 1992 film *Pushing Hands*, the lead character Old Chu is a tai chi martial artist from mainland China moving to New York to live with his son Alex and American daughter-in-law Martha. Old Chu practices tai chi, calligraphy, and qigong daily at home, while Martha works at home writing. With no communication between the two owing to the language barrier, Martha constantly feels stressed by Chu's presence, showing no understanding of his lifestyle and the value of his practice. Chu later chooses to leave his son's home and starts out on his own, and his skills become known to people, bringing him both Asian and American students. "Pushing hands," an important tai chi training, appears repeatedly in the film as a theme about Chinese tradition in the context of American culture and functions as a pivotal point in the plot of the film. Instead of meeting force directly with force, tai chi and pushing hands emphasize resolving force and conflict by redirecting and regenerating and in this sense suggest a solution for cultural coexistence. The ending scene shows Alex teaching Martha pushing hands. Martha finally gets to understand and learn from tai chi, interpreting the art of balance keeping in pushing hands as "like marriage."

Man of Tai Chi, a 2013 film directed by Keanu Reeves and starring Reeves and Tiger Chen, illustrates another way that popular culture uses tai chi as cultural capital. Tiger Chen, the sole descendant of an old master's secret tai chi martial art, has yet to learn and understand the philosophical meaning of tai chi and is involved in a secret fight club through which he becomes a ruthless fighter. Martial arts, fighting scenes, and tai chi as an ancient martial art form as well as exotic Asian clothing and ambience are produced to be consumed as commodities on-screen. Although Tiger Chen in the end does learn the meaning of tai chi, this process is not so important because the film primarily focuses on the brutal fighting scenes that prevail throughout the film.

Hongmei Sun

See also: Daoism

Further Reading

"Choy Kam Man—Yang Tai Chi in the 70's." Best Tai Chi Videos Online, September 20, 2012, http://taichivideos.org/choy-kam-man-yang-tai-chi-in-the-70s.

Kohn, Livia, ed. *Daoist Body Cultivation: Traditional Models and Contemporary Practices.* Magdalena, NM: Three Pines, 2006.

Wen, Haiming. *Chinese Philosophy.* New York and Cambridge: Cambridge University Press, 2012.

TELEVISION, ASIAN AMERICANS ON

History

Asian Americans have been underrepresented on television and have been portrayed in roles that are one-dimensional and stereotypical. In the 1950s, the earliest Asian American movie stars made TV appearances. Anna May Wong (1905–1961) became the first Asian American to star in a U.S. television series, *The Gallery of Madame Liu-Tsong* (1951). Sessue Hayakawa (1889–1973) made numerous guest appearances, as did Keye Luke (1904–1991), who first appeared on TV in 1949 on *The Milton Berle Show* (1948–1967) and later starred in shows such as *Anna and the King* (1972), *Kung Fu* (1972–1975), and *Sidekicks* (1986–1987). Character actors Philip Ahn (1905–1978) and Richard Loo (1903–1983) also played roles in many popular TV series.

One of the earliest Asian American character types to emerge on TV was the servile, desexualized male Chinese houseboy, such as Peter Tong (Sammee Tong) on *Bachelor Father* (1957–1962), Hey Boy (Kam Tong) on *Have Gun—Will Travel* (1957–1963), and Hop Sing (Victor Sen Yung) on *Bonanza*

Connie Chung (1946–)

An Emmy- and Peabody Award–winning Chinese American journalist, Connie Chung was born on August 20, 1946, in Washington, D.C. She graduated from the University of Maryland with a degree in journalism in 1969. Chung worked at WTTG in the District of Columbia before becoming a news correspondent for the *CBS Evening News with Walter Cronkite.*

From 1976 to 1983, Chung was a news anchor at KNXT in Los Angeles. From 1983 to 1986, she was the anchor of *NBC News at Sunrise.* She married TV host Maury Povich and later adopted a son. In 1989, she returned to CBS to anchor *Saturday Night with Connie Chung.* From 1993 to 1995, she was coanchor of the *CBS Evening News with Dan Rather,* the first Asian American and second woman to coanchor a major U.S. network news show. She was also hosting *Eye to Eye with Connie Chung* at the time. Chung cohosted ABC's *20/20* from 1998 to 2002 and later hosted shows on CNN and MSNBC that were quickly canceled. She went on to a teaching fellowship at the Harvard Kennedy School. Chung is often credited with creating the stereotype of the female Asian American newscaster, known as the Connie Chung syndrome.

(1959–1973). Asian American women were also cast as domestics. One of the earliest leading roles for a Japanese American was housekeeper Mrs. Livingston (Miyoshi Umeki) on *The Courtship of Eddie's Father* (1969–1972). Another popular Asian American character type was the Asian martial arts expert who served as the mentor or sidekick to the lead white male character. Bruce Lee played Kato, the valet and sidekick on *The Green Hornet* (1966–1967). On *Kung Fu* (1972–1975), blind Master Po (Keye Luke) and Master Kan (Philip Ahn) trained Kwai Chang Caine (David Carradine, in yellowface).

Asian Americans had minor roles even on shows set in Hawai'i and Asia, notably *M*A*S*H* (1972–1983), set in South Korea during the Korean War. Though there were a few Asian American guest appearances, most were played by Japanese, Chinese, or Vietnamese American actors. Asian American actors were and still are cast interchangeably regardless of ethnicity. The only regular Asian American character was Nurse Kellye (Kellye Nakahara). Soon-Lee (Rosalind Chao) appeared as Corporal Maxwell Klinger's war bride at the end of *M*A*S*H* and in the short-lived spin-off *AfterMASH* (1983–1984).

Asian Americans were also often cast as villains who perpetuated the Yellow Peril stereotype. Cold War–era spy programs such as *The Man from U.N.C.L.E.* (1964–1968) and even spoofs of the spy genre such as *Get Smart* (1965–1970) featured Asian villains. Asian Americans were frequently cast in roles that portrayed them as perpetual foreigners. Pat Morita played several such characters, including diner owner Matsuo "Arnold" Takahashi on *Happy Days* (1974–1984) and a Japanese inventor on *Mr. T and Tina* (1976), the first U.S. sitcom centered on an Asian character. A few Asian Americans on TV in the 1960s and 1970s were not portrayed as foreign or inscrutable. George Takei played Hikaru Sulu on *Star Trek* (1966–1969). Jack Soo played Sgt. Nick Yemana on *Barney Miller* (1974–1982). Johnny Yune appeared on *The Tonight Show with Johnny Carson* over 30 times during the 1970s and 1980s, among the most appearances by any comedian and a first for an Asian American.

Toward the end of the 20th century, Asian Americans on TV continued to be portrayed as unassimilable, inscrutable foreigners. On *Gung Ho* (1986–1987), Gedde Watanabe played Japanese plant manager Kaz Kazuhiro. Pat Morita starred in *Ohara* (1987–1988), about a police lieutenant who solved crimes with spiritual techniques and martial arts and spoke in Charlie Chan–like epigrams. The Asian martial artist type also persisted in shows such as *Sidekicks* (1986–1987) and *Martial Law* (1998–2000).

East Asian Americans made some progress on TV in the 1980s and 1990s. Rosalind Chao played Keiko O'Brien on *Star Trek: The Next Generation* (1987–1994) and *Star Trek: Deep Space Nine* (1993–1999). On shows for younger audiences, Thuy Trang played the original Yellow Ranger on *Mighty Morphin Power Rangers* (1993–1996), and Jennie Kwan played Sam Woo on *California Dreams* (1992–1997). A few Asian American comedians also had brief success on television. Steve Park was a 1991–1992 cast member of the sketch show *In Living Color.* Margaret Cho starred in a short-lived sitcom loosely based on her stand-up routine, *All-American Girl* (1994–1995), the first U.S. TV show about an Asian American family and only the second sitcom centered around a character of Asian descent. It also starred Amy Hill, Jodi Long, Clyde Kusatsu, BD Wong, and J. B. Quon.

Southeast Asian American representation—characters of Filipino, Cambodian, Laotian, Thai, Malaysian, and Indonesian descent, for example—was almost entirely absent from television in the 1980s and 1990s. Limited Vietnamese American portrayals at this time had to do with the Vietnam War, as in *Tour of Duty* (1987–1990) and *China Beach* (1988–1991). One of the few complex Vietnamese American TV characters was Harry Truman "H. T." Ioki (Dustin Nguyen) on the teen cop show *21 Jump Street* (1987–1991).

South Asian American representation on TV was also severely limited. Jawaharlal Choudhury (Joher Coleman) was an Indian exchange student on *Head of the Class* (1986–1990). The most famous South Asian American TV character was Kwik-E-Mart owner Apu Nahasapeemapetilon (voiced by white actor Hank Azaria) on *The Simpsons* (1989–).

Asian American women continued to be exoticized and hypersexualized, portrayed as submissive lotus blossoms or as femme fatale dragon ladies. Even when not playing prostitutes or mail-order brides, Asian American female characters often embodied these stereotypes. The most famous example of the hypersexualized dragon lady on TV was Ling Woo (Lucy Liu) on *Ally McBeal* (1997–2002).

Asian American women did gain visibility on television as news correspondents and anchors, with the success of journalists such as Connie Chung, Tritia Toyota, and Ann Curry. This is in stark contrast to the near absence of Asian American men on TV news.

Contemporary Forms

In the 21st century though Asian Americans are still underrepresented, there has been increased visibility and diversity of roles for Asian Americans on television. This is in part the result of advocacy by organizations such as the Media Action Network for Asian Americans (MANAA), which monitors the media's portrayal of Asian Americans and works with networks to increase diversity in their programming. TV channels have also been created to target Asian American audiences, such as AZN Television, ImaginAsianTV (iaTV), and, most successfully, Myx TV, which was launched in 2007 and is available in over 15 million households in major U.S. cities.

Public television has also been an important outlet for Asian Americans. PBS has broadcast documentary films and series such as *Nisei Soldier* (1984), *The Color of Honor* (1987), *The Story of Vinh* (1990), *Ancestors in the Americas* (1996, 1998) and *Searching for Asian America* (2003). The PBS series *POV* (1988–) and *Independent Lens* (1999–) have also featured numerous Asian American documentaries.

In television for children and teens, Keiko Agena played Lane Kim on *Gilmore Girls* (2000–2007), and Brenda Song starred in Disney Channel productions such as *The Suite Life of Zack and Cody* (2005–2008), *The Suite Life on Deck* (2008–2011), and *Wendy Wu: Homecoming Warrior* (2006). The hit musical series *Glee* (2009–2015) has several regular Asian American characters, including Tina Cohen-Chang (Jenna Ushkowitz), Mike Chang (Harry Shum Jr.), and Blaine Anderson (Darren Criss), though the show has sometimes made jokes at their expense.

Asian Americans have also been featured on reality TV. MTV's *The Real World* has starred a handful of Asian Americans. Tila Nguyen starred in *A Shot at Love with Tila Tequila* (2007–2008). Asian Americans have won several reality competition series, including Yul Kwon on *Survivor: Cook Islands* in 2006,

Chloe Dao on *Project Runway* in 2006 and Anya Ayoung-Chee in 2011, Tammy and Victor Jih on *The Amazing Race* in 2008, and *America's Best Dance Crew* winners Jabbawockeez, Quest Crew, and Poreotics. On the singing-competition show *American Idol,* the most famous Asian American contestant to date is William Hung, who auditioned in 2004 and was mocked as a foreign, talentless buffoon in the media. Ming Tsai was one of the first Asian American TV chefs. Padma Lakshmi hosts the cooking competition show *Top Chef* (2006–), which has had Asian American winners Hung Huynh, Paul Qui, and Kristen Kish.

Asian American comedians have had continued success on television. Bobby Lee was a cast member on the sketch show *MADtv* from 2001 to 2009. Margaret Cho returned to TV in her own reality sitcom, *The Cho Show* (2008); competed on *Dancing with the Stars* in 2010; was nominated for a 2012 Emmy for Outstanding Guest Actress in a Comedy Series for her role as Kim Jong-il on *30 Rock* (2006–2013); and is currently a series regular on *Drop Dead Diva* (2009–). Steve Byrne cocreated and starred in *Sullivan & Son* (2012–2014), also starring Jodi Long and Vivian Bang. *Fresh Off the Boat* (2015–) is a sitcom inspired by chef and former stand-up comic Eddie Huang's memoir of the same title, about a Taiwanese American family living in Orlando, Florida. Starring Constance Wu, Randall Park, Hudson Yang, Forrest Wheeler, and Ian Chen, the show is the first network sitcom to feature an Asian American family in 20 years, since *All-American Girl,* and has been renewed for a second season.

There has been increasing representation of South Asian Americans on TV. *Outsourced* (2010–2011) was the first U.S. TV series set in India and featured a largely South Asian ensemble cast. Mindy Kaling wrote for and starred as Kelly Kapoor in *The Office* (2005–2013) before going on to create and star in *The Mindy Project* (2012–), the first TV show to have a South Asian American lead. Other popular shows have featured South Asian Americans, such as Jonathan (Maulik Pancholy) on *30 Rock* (2006–2013), Rajesh Koothrappali (Kunal Nayyar) on *The Big Bang Theory* (2007–), and Tom Haverford (Aziz Ansari) on *Parks and Recreation* (2009–2015).

Many TV shows continue to perpetuate stereotypes of Asian Americans. Asian Americans are still cast as the Yellow Peril, evidenced by the countless procedural shows that have episodes about triads, tongs, the yakuza, or other Asian criminals. Asian Americans are also stereotyped as the model minority, especially in roles as medical professionals, such as Dr. Deb (Jing-Mei) and Chen (Ming-Na Wen) on *ER* (1994–2009), Dr. George Huang (BD Wong) on *Law & Order: Special Victims Unit* (1999–), Dr. Lawrence Kutner (Kal Penn) and Dr. Chi Park (Charlyne Yi) on *House M.D.* (2004–2012), and Dr. Cristina Yang (Sandra Oh, Canadian Korean) on *Grey's Anatomy* during 2005–2014.

Actor and comedian Aziz Ansari arriving at an Emmy Award screening of his television show *Parks and Recreation* at the Academy of Television Arts and Sciences in Hollywood, California, May 19, 2010. (Carrie Nelson/Dreamstime.com)

Asian American women continue to be hypersexualized, as seen in the controversy over the pilot episode of *Dads* (2013–2014), which jokes about sexualizing Asian women. Asian American men continue to be portrayed as nerdy, effeminate, and sexually repulsive. Examples include Vince Masuka (C. S. Lee) on *Dexter* (2006–2013), Señor Chang (Ken Jeong) on *Community* (2009–), and Han Lee (Matthew Moy) on *2 Broke Girls* (2011–), the immigrant diner owner who is constantly made fun of for his short stature, foreignness, and asexuality.

In contrast to these stereotypical portrayals, many contemporary TV shows feature complex Asian American characters. For instance, there are Asian American LGBT characters such as Camile Wray (Ming-Na Wen) on *Stargate Universe* (2009–2011), the first Asian American lesbian on a prime-time network or basic cable show; Lloyd Lee (Rex Lee) on *Entourage* (2004–2011); and Mulan (Jamie Chung) on *Once Upon a Time* (2011–).

Lost (2004–2010) starred Daniel Dae Kim and Yunjin Kim as Jin and Sun Kwon and had recurring roles for Ken Leung and François Chau. *Heroes* (2006–2010) had three lead Asian and Asian American actors, Masi Oka as Hiro Nakamura, James Kyson Lee as Ando Masahashi, and Sendhil Ramamurthy as Mohinder Suresh. John Cho has starred and guest starred in several shows, including *Sleepy Hollow* (2013–) and *Selfie* (2014). Maggie Q starred in *Nikita* (2010–2013) and *Stalker* (2014–2015). Steven Yeun plays Glenn Rhee in AMC's *The Walking Dead* (2010–). *Hawaii Five-0* (2010–) has three regular Asian American cast members—Daniel Dae Kim, Grace Park of *Battlestar Galactica* (2004–2009), and Masi Oka—as well as recurring roles for Brian Yang, Dennis Chun, Ian Anthony Dale, Will Yun Lee, and other Asian American guest stars. Lucy Liu plays Joan Watson in the Sherlock Holmes adaptation *Elementary* (2012–).

Caroline Kyungah Hong

See also: Comedy and Humor, Asian American; Popular Culture, Asian Americans and

Further Reading

Chin, Christina, Meera E. Deo, Jenny J. Lee, Noriko Milman, and Nancy Wang Yuen. "Asian Pacific Americans in Prime Time: Setting the Stage." Asian American Justice Center, 2006, http://www.advancingjustice-aajc.org/news-media/publications/asian -pacific-americans-prime-time-setting-stage.

Davé, Shilpa S. *Indian Accents: Brown Voice and Racial Performance in American Television and Film.* Urbana: University of Illinois Press, 2013.

Hale, Mike. "Maggie Q and Lucy Liu: Asian-Americans as Leading Ladies." *New York Times,* November 21, 2013, http://www.nytimes.com/2013/11/22/arts/television /maggie-q-and-lucy-liu-asian-americans-as-leading-ladies.html.

Hamamoto, Darrell Y. *Monitored Peril: Asian Americans and the Politics of TV Representation.* Minneapolis: University of Minnesota Press, 1994.

Kim, L. S. "Be the One That You Want: Asian Americans in Television Culture, Onscreen and Beyond." *Amerasia Journal* 30(1) (2004): 125–146.

THAI AMERICAN CULTURE

Thai American culture has been defined by varying economic conditions in Thailand, the educational and financial opportunities available in the United States, American involvement in the Vietnam War, the shifting immigration policy of the United States, and the immigrant experience in the United States. The three periods of Thai immigration reveal changes in ethnicity, class, education, and gender of Thai immigrants coming to America. As a result, these shifting immigrant trends have shaped the Thai American community, making it far less hierarchical than traditional Thai society. Moreover, despite striving to maintain ties to traditional customs, the steady assimilation of Thai immigrants has led to a high rate of Americanization.

The nation of Thailand is located in Southeast Asia and is bordered by Burma (also known as Myanmar), Cambodia, Laos, Malaysia, and the Gulf of Thailand. Known as Siam from the mid-19th century to the outset of World War II, Thailand maintained its independence from regional aggression as well as European colonization. Despite a constitutional monarchy being established in 1932, from the mid-1940s to 1963 Thailand was controlled by General Sarit Thanarat and later ruled by various military officials until 1973. Since 1954 Thailand has become a strong U.S. ally in the region, allowing the United States to establish army bases in order to support American troops, first in Korea and then in Vietnam. Thailand remained both economically impoverished and politically unstable until the 1990s.

There have been three significant periods of Thai immigration to America. The first took place during the 1940s and 1950s in response to the rise of the country's nationalist movement. During this period, political officials, professionals, and students seeking higher education made up the majority of Thai immigration to America. In particular, many of these immigrants were sons from wealthy ethnic Chinese Thai families. During this period, there were few female Thai immigrants coming to America.

By comparison, the second wave of immigration between 1965 and the early 1980s reflects the rising popular dissatisfaction with the Thai government and impoverished regional conditions as well as changes to American immigration policies in 1965 and the increasing U.S. involvement in and eventual withdrawal from Vietnam. During these years, Thai immigrants were primarily women who had married American servicemen during the Vietnam War and sought to return to the United States with their husbands. The majority of these women were ethnically Lao peasants with limited education who had been employed on American bases. Around the same time, a shortage of nurses in America during the 1960s and 1970s led to a large number of trained Thai women immigrating to the United States working as professionals in nursing. Thai immigrants during this period came from a range of ethnicities, regions, and classes in Thailand; as a result, they changed the social dynamic of Thai American culture.

Finally, the third period of immigration during the 1980s and the 1990s resulted from declining economic opportunities in Thailand as well as the potential for academic and professional advancement in the United States. It is worth noting that this period also saw a dramatic rise in Thai immigrants who became undocumented workers in the United States. Overall, Thai immigration to

America began to decline by the late 1990s, as the nation's standard of living and rising regional economic prospects gave people fewer incentives to leave.

The Thai American population reflects a relatively small group of Asian Americans, consisting of ethnic Thai, Lao, and Chinese. Despite their ethnic differences and the traditional social hierarchy, they generally identify themselves as Thai Americans. As a group, Thai Americans have often been confused with Korean, Vietnamese, and Chinese Americans; have endured racism and stereotypes; and have been stigmatized as refugees rather than immigrants.

The largest concentrations of Thai Americans are found in New York City and Los Angeles as well as near military and air force bases throughout the nation. Thai Americans tend to be well educated, with most holding at least a bachelor's degree. Generally speaking, they have a high level of participation in the labor force and a high medium income, being employed as professionals such as college professors, scientists, and business entrepreneurs. However, the Thai American community is divided between professionals with advanced degrees who tend to reside in California and those in the service industry with elementary education who often live on or near military bases.

A group of women representing the Thai American Association preparing food at the Florida Homestead Fruit and Spice Park Asian Culture Festival in 2014. Pad Thai, a noodle dish, has become popular in the United States. (Jeff Greenberg/Alamy Stock Photo)

Regardless of location, Thai American communities maintain close family connections and continue conventional social customs, seeking to keep traditional culture and practices in the United States by establishing Thai-language schools, Buddhist temples, and cultural nonprofit and professional associations. To this end, Thai Americans have striven to maintain strong cultural, economic, and political ties to Thailand. Yet despite the practice of maintaining their traditional customs, Thai Americans also demonstrate a willingness to accept and adapt to American social norms. As a result, Thai American communities and families tend to be highly assimilated into American culture. Perhaps the largest influence on Thai communities in the United States has been the steady decline in the size of immediate and extended families. In addition, the practice of arranged marriages and the limitation of unions between families of equal social and economic status have slowly ceased.

The vast majority of Thai Americans are Buddhists, with smaller minorities practicing Muslim and Christian faiths. The construction of Buddhist temples and the relatively high numbers of monks in the United States reiterate the importance of Buddhism in the Thai American community. Temples often serve as the center of the Thai American community and a place for contemplation, socialization, and community support. In Thai American culture both traditional and Western holidays are celebrated, with many Thai Americans observing common public holidays, dates of national commemoration, and the important events in the life of Buddha. Thai holidays include New Year's Day, Chinese New Year, Magha Puja in February, Chakri Day on April 6, Songkran or the Thai New Year in April, Coronation Day on May 5, Visakha Puja (also known as Buddha Day), the Queen's Birthday on August 12, the King's Birthday on December 5, and Christmas.

Sean Morton

See also: Buddhism; Thai American Food

Further Reading

Baker, Christopher John, and Pasuk Phongpaichit. *A History of Thailand*. 3rd. ed. New York and Cambridge: Cambridge University Press, 2014.

Fong, Timothy P. *The Contemporary Asian American Experience: Beyond the Model Minority*. Englewood Cliffs, NJ: Prentice Hall, 1998.

Lai, Eric Yo Ping, and Dennis Arguelles, eds. *The New Face of Asian Pacific America: Numbers, Diversity & Change in the 21st Century*. San Francisco: AsianWeek with UCLA's Asian American Studies Center Press, in cooperation with the Organization of Chinese Americans and the National Coalition for Asian Pacific American Community Development, 2003.

Wyatt, David K. *Thailand: A Short History*. New Haven, CT: Yale University Press, 1984.

THAI AMERICAN FOOD

History and Origins

Although Thai Americans are a relatively new immigrant and a small ethnic group, Thai cuisine has become one of the most popular foods in the United States, influencing even non-Asian restaurants. Nowadays, Thai restaurants can be found in almost every urban area in the United States, with the acceptance of Thai food evident by the plethora of Thai restaurants nationally.

Since the 1980s Thai restaurants have begun to proliferate in the United States, starting with cities in which large Thai communities have thrived. Thai restaurant owners regarded Chinese restaurants as their nearest competition in terms of menu prices and comparable cuisine. Thai cuisine became known for its spiciness and affordability.

Some Thai restaurants in the United States promote themselves as serving authentic Thai cuisine that uses traditional ingredients, methods, and seasonings found in Bangkok, the capital of Thailand. Other Thai restaurants differentiate themselves by focusing on regional cuisine. Shaped by hillside tribal dining in the mountains, northeastern (*isaan*) Thai food restaurants exist in larger cities

Restaurants with Authentic Thai Taste

Based on their expectations of clientele, some restaurants may be geared toward more of an authentically Thai taste rather than a more Americanized version of Thai cuisine. In addition, Thai restaurants across the United States vary in their access to Thai ingredients. How do we judge the authenticity of Thai American restaurants, especially for diners who desire more "Thai" than "American" in their eating experience?

One way is to analyze the menu for the ingredients used in well-known Thai dishes. For example, *pahd seew* and *lahd na* are both noodle dishes that traditionally use Chinese broccoli (*pahk kha na*). To cater to American tastes, Chinese broccoli has been replaced by American broccoli, altering the taste and texture of both Thai dishes. The presence of *pahk kha na* reflects a Thai clientele.

Another way is to request to see the restaurant's *khruung,* the four traditional Thai seasonings of sugar, fish sauce, vinegar with pickled peppers, and ground, dried red pepper flakes. Often jarred together in a set of four, these flavorings are used to customize each Thai dish. If a Thai restaurant is unable to provide *khruung,* its clientele is most likely not Thai.

in the United States and may be recognized by the presence of sticky rice (instead of jasmine rice) and insects on the menu, such as fried ants and grasshoppers. Restaurants emphasizing southern Thai fare in the United States are rare; influenced by neighboring Malaysia, southern Thai restaurants feature seafood found near the coast and curries infused with coconut milk.

Typical Thai American Food Dishes

Food is an important part of Thai culture. Thais consider eating a communal activity in which several dishes are typically served and shared at the same time with jasmine rice. Eschewing chopsticks, Thais eat with spoons and forks, using the fork in the left hand to push food into the spoon held by the right hand, which in turn acts like a scoop for the food to the mouth. Thai dishes contain bite-sized pieces of protein and vegetables that fit into a spoon easily.

Skewered and grilled, *satay* may consist of chicken or beef. It is commonly served as an appetizer in Thai American restaurants. *Satay* is accompanied by peanut sauce and a vinegar-based salad consisting of cucumbers and red onions.

Noodle dishes in Thai food vary in texture and appearance. Thin, transparent, gluten-free, rice-based noodles are known as bean thread or cellophane noodles and are used in soups and entrées. Wide flour noodles are prominent in entrées such as *pahd seew* and *lahd naa*. *Mee krob* noodles are fried, white, airy, and crispy and are the primary component of the appetizers. The most famous Thai noodle dish is *pahd Thai*, which features stir-fried rice noodles.

Tom yum and *tom kha gai* are Thai soups. *Tom yum* is sour, while *tom kha gai* is more sweet due to the coconut milk in the latter. Thai salads are known as *yum* and are sour, salty, and sweet, derived from lime juice, fish sauce, and palm sugar. *Yum* often contain *prik khi niu*. Termed "little bird chilies," *prik khi niu* peppers are spicy and may be green or red. Fish sauce, or *nahm pla*, is an ingredient used in the preparation of most Thai dishes. *Nahm pla* imparts saltiness from its primary component of fermented fish.

Herbs commonly found in Thai food include lemongrass, mint, cilantro, galangal, and kaffir lime leaves. Lemongrass has little taste but is aromatic. Mint leaves may be found as an ingredient of or garnish to Thai dishes. Shrimp paste, fermented fish, and dried shrimp are rare in American versions of Thai food in the United States, though all three ingredients are found liberally in Thailand.

Thai curries, or *gang*, are famous and may be red, green, or yellow. Red and green curries derive their color from the red or green chilies crushed into the dish. Based on coconut milk, yellow curries are known as *masaman* and derive their characteristic yellow color from turmeric. Thai desserts are sweet but not intensely sweet, though American versions have amplified the sugariness of

Thai desserts. *Khao niew mamuang*, or sticky rice served with sliced mango and coconut milk, is a well-known Thai dessert. In Thailand, meals may end with fresh fruits as desserts, but ripe rambutan, lychee, durian, and jackfruit are not as easily found in the United States.

Contemporary Forms of Thai American Restaurants

With the increase in the popularity of Thai cuisine, more commonly known Thai dishes may now be found outside of Thai restaurants. Thai dishes appear alongside Korean, Chinese, Japanese, and Indian items in Asian fusion and Pan-Asian restaurants. In Asian fusion restaurants, *pahd Thai*, a popular Thai noodle dish, graces the menu as the basis for other culinary collaborations. Similarly, Thai grilled beef dishes, Thai peanut sauces, and *khao niew mamuang* (sticky rice with mango) desserts surface within Pan-Asian restaurant selections.

The focus of restaurants featuring Thai cuisine is changing across the United States. Today's Thai American restaurants are branching out from Thai cuisine. Increasingly, Thai restaurants have combined Thai food with Japanese cuisine because the latter has a higher price point expected by American clientele. Because Japanese cuisine, especially sushi, is acknowledged as more expensive fare, the addition of Japanese offerings to Thai menus raises profits for Thai American restaurant owners.

Thai food itself is undergoing a renovation in the United States. Thai cuisine has slowly transformed from affordable dining in small eateries to expensive experiences in upscale restaurants. No longer limited to prices under $10 for an entrée, new Thai restaurants are elevating expectations in cuisine, service, and costs, diversifying Thai food in the United States across levels of restaurants.

Jenny Ungbha Korn

See also: Chinese American Food; Chop Suey; Fusion Cuisine; Kimchi; *Pho;* Sushi; Thai American Culture

Further Reading

Fine, Gary Alan, and Jenny Ungbha Korn. "Arun's: A Review." *Contexts* 4 (2005): 63–65.

Inness, Sherrie A., ed. *Pilaf, Pozole, and Pad Thai: American Women and Ethnic Food.* Amherst: University of Massachusetts, 2001.

Korn, Jenny Ungbha. "Thai Americans." In *Multicultural America,* edited by Carlos E. Cortes and J. Geoffrey Golson, 2065–2067. Thousand Oaks, CA: Sage, 2013.

Pinsuvana, Malulee. *Cooking Thai Food in American Kitchens.* Bangkok, Thailand: Thai Watana Panich, 1992.

THEATER, ASIAN AMERICAN

History and Origins

Asian American theater encompasses drama and performance by, about, and for Asian-identified peoples in the United States. Although studies of Asian American theater typically spotlight Chinese- and Japanese-related playwrights, this theatrical sphere also comprises South Asian–related artists, among many others. The styles range from proscenium (picture frame) theater vested in realism to avant-garde performance art. This genre also includes performance texts that employ Asian American critiques of the state and nation, exploring issues such as immigration and assimilation. Such an expansive definition is demanded because theater, much like Asian America, is heterogeneous, hybrid, and multiple. Still, this tradition is historically situated, and it must be remembered that "Asian American," as a pan-ethnic term of solidarity, was not

David Henry Hwang (1957–)

David Henry Hwang, the most celebrated contemporary Asian American playwright, has written many award-winning plays and often engages with inter- and intracultural issues. He was born in 1957 in Los Angeles to Chinese immigrant parents. In 1980 his first play, *FOB,* premiered off Broadway at the Public Theater in New York City. *FOB,* slang for "fresh off the boat," deals with Asian American assimilation, class, and gender. The play was well received and won an Obie Award, suggesting the popularity of Hwang's dramatization of Asian America. Hwang received more support from the Public Theater in 1981 when his plays *The Dance and the Railroad* and *Family Devotions* debuted there. The former depicts a struggle between two Chinese men working on the transcontinental railroad—a young idealist seeking "Gold Mountain" and a cynic performing to preserve his opera training. The latter is a somewhat autobiographical farce about a well-off Christian fundamentalist Chinese American family. Hwang's most renowned work is *M. Butterfly,* his critique of the Orientalist butterfly narrative that premiered on Broadway in 1988, making this play the first by an Asian American writer to reach the Great White Way. In 1994 Hwang won acclaim for *Golden Child,* which examines the Westernization of his family in the early 20th century. He again turned to personal experience in 2007 when he wrote the play *Yellow Face,* a meditation on his father's death, the American Dream, and the *Miss Saigon* controversy. *M. Butterfly* and *Yellow Face* were finalists for the Pulitzer Prize for Drama. Hwang continues to write and is regularly produced in New York and across the United States.

widespread in the United States until the civil rights era. Formal Asian American theater companies first appeared in the 1960s, but earlier theatrical depictions of Asians in the United States must be recognized in order to understand later responses to such depictions.

Earlier portrayals and histories of imperialism laid the foundation for Orientalist theater. According to Edward Said (1979), Orientalism is the collection of texts that, from a "Western" perspective, objectify, feminize, exoticize, essentialize, and Otherize the "East," whose glory is relegated to an unchanging past (1). In the United States, this performance tradition began with the first performance of *Orphan of China* by French philosopher Voltaire in 1767. In the 19th century, museums, circuses, side shows, and World's Fairs around the nation presented Chinese people as intriguing exhibits. The most famous performers were Chang and Eng, conjoined twins who prompted the term "Siamese twins." As more Chinese immigrants arrived to work in the mines and on the transcontinental railroad and then chose to stay in the United States, anti-Chinese sentiment rose. Plays such as *The Chinese Must Go* (1879) by Henry Grimm and *Ah Sin!* (1877) by Mark Twain and Bret Harte reinforced negative stereotypes, namely the dumb forever-foreign opium addict as well as the conniving, assimilable monkey. European works such as Giacomo Puccini's *Madama Butterfly* (1903) became popular in the United States and contributed to other stereotypes, especially the butterfly, a delicate Asian woman who sacrifices herself for a Western man. This type serves as the foil to the dragon lady, who deceives, fights, and romances the protagonist. As one example of the popularity of these depictions, Paul Osborn's 1958 Broadway play-turned-film *The World of Suzie Wong*—a world of prostitution—plays upon such tropes. The history of these performances helped to establish and secure yellowface performance, a practice of typically white actors putting on yellow makeup, taping their eyes, taking mincing steps, and speaking in pidgin English, among other racialized acts, in order to appear Asian or, more accurately, an Orientalist vision of Asianness. The growing civil rights and Third World movements of the 1950s and 1960s and later protests of yellowface casting and Orientalist portrayals, such as in *Lovely Ladies, Kind Gentlemen* (based on *The Teahouse of the August Moon*) in the 1970s, helped to organize Asian American theater practitioners. In 1991, *Miss Saigon* became another major site of struggle over Asian representation.

Regional Practices and Traditions

Since the 1960s, many Asian American–specific theater companies have developed across the United States. The first four companies were the East West Players, the Asian American Theater Company, the Northwest Asian

American Theater, and the Pan Asian Repertory Theater. Founded in 1967 in Los Angeles, the East West Players was initially led by artistic director Mako Iwamatsu and executive director Soon-Tek Oh. The company's early vision was to train and showcase Asian American artists for Hollywood projects, produce canonical European plays with Asian American actors and settings, and cultivate new Asian American plays. For instance, one initiative was to host playwriting contests, which helped to launch the careers of playwrights such as Frank Chin.

Chin is frequently considered the father of Asian American theater because his plays *The Chickencoop Chinaman* (1973) and *Year of the Dragon* (1974) were among the first Asian American performance texts to gain national attention. In these lyrical works, Chin typically focuses on the struggles of young Asian American men; the relations between white, black, and Asian Americans; issues of authenticity; and stereotypes. He is perhaps most notorious for his accusations about writers such as David Henry Hwang and Amy Tan of being "fake Asians" who replicate Orientalist images of Asians for white consumers. In 1973, Chin initiated the Asian American Theater Workshop in San Francisco that largely focuses on cultivating Asian American writers. After a few years, he left not only the company but also the world of playwriting.

In Seattle, what was to become the Asian American Theater Workshop originated on the campus of the University of Washington in 1974. The company aspired to end yellowface, show a more accurate picture of Asian American experiences, and provide opportunities for Asian American artists. Finally, in New York the Pan Asian Repertory Theatre had its origins at Ellen Stewart's La MaMa Experimental Theater Company in the 1970s. Tisa Chang, who remains the artistic director of Pan Asian Rep today, has been interested in intercultural storytelling from classic and contemporary Eastern and Western perspectives. One additional example of this interculturalism is the mission of the National Asian American Theatre Company, formed in 1989, to produce plays with all Asian American actors, casts for whom those plays were not originally written.

Asian American playwrights are often categorized in several historical waves. Although Hawaiʻian playwrights such as Gladys Li began writing in the 1920s, later writers of the 1970s such as Frank Chin, Wakako Yamauchi, and Momoko Iko are typically considered the first wave. A Nisei (second-generation Japanese American), Yamauchi is well known for her Depression-era play *And the Soul Shall Dance* (1977) and her engagement with Japanese American internment in *12–1-A* (1982), both of which premiered at East West Players. The 1980s ushered in a second wave of writers, most notably David Henry Hwang and Philip Kan Gotanda. Beginning with *FOB* (1980), Hwang rose to prominence

Playwright David Henry Hwang at the Americans for the Arts National Art Awards in New York City, October 17, 2011. He is known for many productions including the 1988 Broadway show *M. Butterfly*. (BFA/SIPA/Newscom)

on major New York stages and reached Broadway with *M. Butterfly* in 1988, becoming the first Asian American playwright to do so. This production also launched the career of actor BD Wong. Although critics argue about Hwang's representations, politics, and popularity, they can agree on his importance to U.S. theater. Meanwhile, Gotanda was frequently produced at West Coast companies, and his work ranges from culturally specific stories such as *A Song for a Nisei Fisherman* (1980) to critiques of Hollywood Asian stereotypes such as *Yankee Dawg You Die* (1990). Rick Shiomi, another major second-wave writer, parodied noir in the well-received play *Yellow Fever* (1982) and cofounded the Asian-based yet intercultural Theater Mu in Minneapolis in 1992. Ralph Peña, another playwright and artistic director, penned *Flipzoids* (1996) and cofounded the Ma-Yi Theater Company, which was originally devoted to Filipino American–centered work but has expanded its mission to a Pan–Asian American vision.

This trend toward greater complexity and ambivalence over the meanings of Asian American identity is mediated by other second-wave playwrights as well as third-wave playwrights, including Velina Hasu Houston, Genny Lim, Jeannie Barroga, Jessica Hagedorn, Ping Chong, Chay Yew, Naomi Iizuka, and Diana Son. Houston, for instance, is of Japanese, African American, and Native American descent, and she unpacks racial, national, and cultural dynamics in plays such as *Tea* (1987) and has significantly contributed to the publication and analysis of Asian American drama. Lim and Barroga have turned to historical events in *Paper Angels* (1980), about the immigrants held on Angel Island, and in *Walls* (1989), about the Vietnam War Memorial, respectively. Artists such as Hagedorn and Chong have used multimedia in their performance art; the former is best known for *Dogeaters* (1998) about the experience of Filipinos in the United States, while the latter turned to the history of Western imperialism in East Asian nations for his *East/West Quartet* (1990–1999). From the 1970s through the 1990s, avant-garde solo performers such as Winston Tong and Dan Kwong have similarly explored intersectional identity issues, often using their own lives as theatrical material.

Contemporary Forms

In recent years, several South Asian American playwrights have gained wide acclaim. Rajiv Joseph became, after David Henry Hwang, the second Asian American playwright to reach Broadway when his play *Bengal Tiger at the Baghdad Zoo* opened there in 2011. Inspired by actual events during the invasion of Baghdad in 2003, the play uses soldiers, a translator, and an anthropomorphic tiger to deal with the travesties of war. Joseph's other plays often unpack racial and national dynamics, such as *Animals Out of Paper* (2008) and *The North Pool* (2011). In 2013 Ayad Akhtar won the Pulitzer Prize for Drama for *Disgraced*, the first time an Asian American has done so. His play examines four characters from very different positions who argue over religion and politics in the post-9/11 age of Islamophobia.

Korean American playwright, performer, and director Young Jean Lee has become one of the most well-known avant-garde theater makers today. She attests to writing the plays that she least wants to write, and she collaborates significantly with her actors. Her eclectic works range from comical examinations of race, as in *Songs of the Dragons Flying to Heaven* (2006) and *The Shipment* (2008); mortality, as in *We're Gonna Die* (2011); and gender, as in *Untitled Feminist Show* (2012). No Asian American woman has yet had her play produced on Broadway.

In 2011, the Asian American Performers Action Coalition (AAPAC) formed to research and raise awareness about race and casting practices. The AAPAC concluded that from 2006 to 2012, only 2–3 percent of roles on professional New York City stages (Broadway and major off-Broadway nonprofit theater companies) went to Asian-identified actors. Almost all of those roles were specifically marked as Asian, as opposed to roles being open to any race or ethnicity, as they often are in contemporary productions of William Shakespeare's plays. Since releasing these studies, the AAPAC has hosted panels about casting disparities and continued instances of yellowface.

Finally, many major playwrights of earlier waves continue to write on topics that resonate with the present. Since 1992, Ping Chong has been collecting and staging oral histories about cultural issues in *Undesirable Elements,* resulting in dozens of different texts. David Henry Hwang's latest plays include *Chinglish* (2011), another East meets West exploration, this time centered on contemporary language and U.S.-China business relations. The Asian American theater canon is rich with dynamic texts and artists and deserves a brighter spotlight in U.S. history and on U.S. stages.

Donatella Galella

See also: Asian Indian American Performing Arts and Artists; Cambodian American Performing Arts and Artists; Musical Theater, Asian American

Further Reading

Berson, Misha. *Between Worlds: Contemporary Asian-American Plays.* New York: Theatre Communications Group, 1993.

Eng, Alvin, ed. *Tokens? The NYC Asian American Experience on Stage.* Philadelphia: Temple University Press, 2000.

Houston, Velina Hasu, ed. *But Still, Like Air, I'll Rise: New Asian American Plays.* Philadelphia: Temple University Press, 1997.

Kurahashi, Yuko. *Asian American Culture on Stage: The History of the East West Players.* New York and London: Routledge, 1999.

Lee, Esther Kim. *A History of Asian American Theatre.* New York and Cambridge: Cambridge University Press, 2006.

Lee, Josephine. *Performing Asian America: Race and Ethnicity on the Contemporary Stage.* Philadelphia: Temple University Press, 1997.

Lee, Josephine, Donald Eitel, and Rick Shiomi, eds. *Other Spaces of Asian America: Plays for a New Generation.* Philadelphia: Temple University Press, 2011.

Moy, James. *Marginal Sights: Staging the Chinese in America.* Iowa City: University of Iowa Press, 1994.

Nelson, Brian, ed. *Asian American Drama: 9 Plays from the Multiethnic Landscape.* New York: Applause Books, 2000.

Said, Edward. *Orientalism.* New York: Vintage, 1979.

Shimakawa, Karen. *National Abjection: The Asian American Body Onstage.* Durham, NC: Duke University Press, 2002.

Uno, Roberta, ed. *Unbroken Thread: An Anthology of Plays by Asian American Women.* Amherst: University of Massachusetts Press, 1993.

THERAVADA BUDDHISM

The word "Theravada" is derived from the Sanskrit word *sthaviravada,* which connotes "the teaching and practices of the Elders." It is the most ancient surviving sect of Buddhism. Since it believes in the fundamental teachings of Buddha, it is comparatively more conservative than other sects of Buddhism, standing closer to the teachings of Gautam Buddha in comparison to any other existing form of Buddhist tradition. Gautam Buddha used the terms "Dhamma" (doctrine) and "Vinaya" (discipline). With the proliferation of Dhamma in and out of India, after Buddha's demise there arose many disagreements and schisms within the Sangha (association, company, and community) that led to the division of Dhamma into 18 sects of Buddhism. One of these 18 schools proclaimed itself to be the Mahayana, and the others claimed themselves to be the Hinayana. Today Theravada Buddhism is the only sect out of these non-Mahayan denominations in existence. Due to the Theravada school's historical influence in the region of south Asia, it is also known as Southern Buddhism. The followers of Theravada Buddhism are found the world over, especially in Sri Lanka, Cambodia, Laos, Myanmar, Thailand, China, Vietnam, Singapore, Indonesia, and Malaysia. Within the Asian American community, followers of Theravada Buddhism are also found. Separate and lenient practices for a layperson and for a monk are one of the reasons for its popularity and acceptability. The population of Theravada Buddhists across the globe is roughly 150 million.

The origin of Theravada Buddhism goes back to the Second Buddhist Council, where a group persuaded the Sthaviras—a group of elderly members— to modify the Vinaya. In their failure to persuade them, the Hinayans segregated themselves from the Mahāsāmghika—the majority group of the Buddhists. The Theravada school is based on the Vibhajjavāda (doctrine of analysis), a division of the Sthaviravada, and believes in the teachings of awakening. Their scriptural inspiration comes from the Tipitaka, or Pali canon. The canons of Theravada Buddhism were ratified and agreed upon during the Third Buddhist Council (250 BCE) organized during the reign of Indian emperor Ashoka (250 BCE). Originally, Theravada principles were known as Vibhajjavada. With the passage of time, they were split into four subsects—Mahīśāsaka, Kāśyapīya, Dharmaguptaka, and Tāmraparnīya.

Theravada Buddhism views nirvana, or *nibbāna* (salvation), as the ultimate aim of human life. In the state of nirvana, the passions of the soul are extinguished, and it is liberated from the troublesome cycle of birth, illness, age, and death. In the *samsara* (the world), 10 fetters keep human beings enchained. Under the Samyojanapuggala Sutta of the *Angutarra Nikaya,* Gautam Buddha has marked four conditions of life. Only a person in the fourth (Arahant) state attains nirvana. In the line of enlightenment, the four steps are: Stream-Enterers, Once-Returners, Non-Returners, and Arahants. The Stream-Enterers are those people who cut the fetters, including the false view of self, doubt, and clinging to rites and rituals. The Once-Returners destroyed the first three fetters mentioned above and decrease the fetters of lust and hatred. The Non-Returners stand successful in destroying the five lower fetters that bind a human being to the world of the senses. The Arahants remain successful in attaining enlightenment. They extinguish the craving for and attachment to anything, become deathless, and cross the cycle of birth and death. Nirvana can be attained by acquiring knowledge through study and by practicing morality, meditation, and wisdom (*sila, samadhi,* and *panna*). Although the attainment of nirvana is a commandment for the ordained monastic, the layperson can achieve it by bringing happiness into his or her own life and into the lives of others without focusing on nirvana. Under the Theravada system the roles of scholar monks and meditation monks are different, yet both categories of monks serve their community in their own ways, following and practicing Buddhist virtues, morality, and teachings. The scholar monks under the scholastic tradition study and practice Buddhist scriptures such as the *Abhid-hammika* and other works. The meditation monks, also known as forest monks, specialize in the cult of knowledge through meditation. The meditation monks may learn the scriptures through Pali, but they are supposed to learn the religious and spiritual canons through their personal experience in meditation and with their gurus. The monks in the meditation tradition, besides attaining spiritual knowledge, try to gain some supernatural powers as well called *abhiñña*. These *abhiñña* powers are mainly mind reading, seeing and conversing with gods, providing protection from evil spirits, making merit for a future birth remembering the past life, and being capable of associating with many lives. In some Theravada cultures, it is a common practice for young men to be ordained as monks for a fixed period of time. Even being ordained as a monk for a short spell can bring virtues in human personality that make him a discrete leader in his worldly life. In Myanmar and Thailand the short spell of being a monk is practiced, while in Sri Lanka a temporary ordination for a monk is not preferred.

The 19th century saw a greater upsurge in the East-West spiritual confluence. Helena Blavatsky (1831–1891) and Henry Steel Olcott (1832–1907), the founders of the Theosophical Society, have greatly contributed to popularizing Theravada Buddhism in the Western world. The Vipassana movement started in the 1970s. It is in the line of Buddhist modernism and has played a vital role in popularizing Theravada Buddhism in American and European cultures. Followers of Theravada Buddhism have established dozens of monasteries in

Europe and North America. They are spreading a layperson's understanding of Buddhism for the followers and those interested in the teachings of Buddhism through their meditation centers.

Ravindra Pratap Singh

See also: Buddhism; Confucianism; Daoism; Religions and Beliefs, Asian American

Further Reading

Collins, Steven. *Nirvana and Other Buddhist Felicities.* Cambridge: Cambridge University Press, 1998.

Gombrich, Richard. *Theravada Buddhism: A Social History from Ancient Benares to Modern Colombo.* London and New York: Routledge, 1988.

Nyanaponika, Thera, and Hellmuth Hecker. *Great Disciples of the Buddha.* Boston: Wisdom Publications, 1997.

Swearer, Donald. *The Buddhist World of Southeast Asia.* 2nd ed. Albany: State University of New York Press, 2009.

TIBETAN AMERICAN CULTURE

Officially known as the Tibet Autonomous Region of the People's Republic of China, Tibet is located in southwestern China about 14,800 feet above sea level. According to a 1998 census conducted by the Central Tibetan Administration, around 122,000 diaspora Tibetans live in Asia, Oceania, Europe, and North America (MacPherson, Bentz, and Ghoso 2008). Tibetans began to arrive in North America in the 1940s and 1950s, although the number of Tibetan immigrants coming to the United States remained rather small. According to Yosay Wangdi's study, the earliest record of Tibetans in the United States dates back to 1948. A small delegation, led by Tsepon Shakabpa (1907–1989), visited Washington, D.C., on behalf of the Tibetan government in Lhasa. By the mid-1980s, about 500 Tibetans lived in the United States. The Immigration Act of 1990 has a section authorizing 1,000 visas to displaced Tibetans living in India and Nepal. By 1998 the Tibetan American population increased to around 5,500, mainly as a result of family reunification (MacPherson, Bentz, and Ghoso 2008). According to the Office of Tibet's estimation, there are around 9,000 Tibetans currently living in the United States; most of them reside in urban areas such as New York, Minneapolis, and San Francisco, among others. California has the largest Tibetan American population in America. Even though the overall number of Tibetan Americans is small, the issue of Tibet and its relationship with China's central government has captured a lot of attention in the United States.

Many Tibetan Americans keep their cultural tradition while assimilating into American life. One of the Tibetan traditional staples is *tsampa*, made of roasted barley flour. Many of the Tibetan traditions and values are influenced by their Buddhist beliefs. Prayer wheels, bells, and beads are important in practicing Tibetan Buddhism. The chant of monks is considered the music of Tibet. Sometimes chanting is accompanied by traditional musical instruments. Tibetan dance also indicates the connection to their spiritual and religious beliefs. Holiday celebrations and weddings are commonly social events for communities. The Tibetan language bears a resemblance to Sanskrit and Burmese. It is common for Tibetans to incorporate proverbs in everyday conversations.

The primary religion among Tibetans is Tibetan Buddhism. One of the most important teachings in Tibetan Buddhism is Mahayana. Its goal is to achieve the enlightenment of Buddhahood through spiritual development for the purpose of helping other beings. Tibetan Buddhism is most influential in Tibet, Mongolia, Bhutan, parts of Nepal, parts of India, and other Himalayan regions. Tibetan Buddhism has a long history of oral transmission of its teachings. Similar to other Buddhist belief systems, Tibetan Buddhism emphasizes respect and reverence for the teacher, generally known as lama. Tibetan

Tibetan Buddhists greeting the Dalai Lama, the spiritual and political leader of Tibet, outside the Beacon Hotel in New York City, October 17, 2013. (Robert Nickelsberg/ Getty Images)

Buddhist tradition recognizes reincarnation or the reality of Tulkus; believers accept the existence of past and future lives. One of the distinct aspects of Tibetan Buddhism is the incarnate lamas. The most prominent example of the incarnate lamas are the Dalai Lamas who have been the spiritual as well as political leaders of Tibet since the 17th century.

His Holiness the 14th Dalai Lama was born in 1935 in Tibet to a peasant family. At the age of two he was recognized as an incarnation of Avalokiteshvar, the Buddha of Compassion. In addition to the canon of monastic discipline, metaphysics, and other Buddhist subjects, he also studied English, sciences, geography, and mathematics. After the People's Republic of China was founded in 1949, the Dalai Lama had several meetings with the Chinese political leaders. After the Tibetan resistance in 1959, the Dalai Lama and approximately 100,000 Tibetans fled to India seeking political refuge. Since 1960 he has lived in Dharamsala, India, known as "Little Lhasa." He is considered the leader of the Tibetan government in exile. Since then he has traveled around the globe, bringing awareness to the issue of Tibet. He was awarded the Nobel Peace Prize in 1989 and has authored or coauthored over 80 works.

Established in 1964, the Office of Tibet, now in Washington, D.C., is the official agency of His Holiness the 14th Dalai Lama and the Tibetan Administration-in-Exile. Their mission is to raise the issue of Tibet at the United Nations. The organization also looks after the welfare of Tibetans living in North America, supports community efforts to educate younger generations about Tibetan language and culture, coordinates His Holiness the 14th Dalai Lama's visits to North and South America, and helps raise awareness of the issue of Tibet among the general public.

Lan Dong

See also: Buddhism; Theravada Buddhism

Further Reading

Central Tibetan Administration, http://tibet.net/.

Dotson, Brandon. "Complementarity and Opposition in Early Tibetan Ritual." *Journal of the American Oriental Society* 128(1) (2008): 41–67.

H. H. Dalai Lama. *The Buddhism of Tibet.* Translated by Jeffrey Hopkins. Ithaca, NY: Snow Lion Publications, 1987.

Haerens, Margaret, and Lynn M. Zott, eds. *Tibet.* Detroit: Greenhaven, 2014.

MacPherson, Seonaigh, Anne-Sophie Bentz, and Dawa Bhuti Ghoso. "Global Nomads: The Emergence of the Tibetan Diaspora (Part I)." Migration Policy Institute, September 2, 2008, http://www.migrationpolicy.org/article/global-nomads -emergence-tibetan-diaspora-part-i.

The Office of Tibet, http://tibetoffice.org/.

"Reincarnation." The Office of His Holiness the 14th Dalai Lama of Tibet, September 24, 2011, http://www.dalailama.com/messages/statement-of-his-holiness-the-fourteenth-dalai-lama-tenzin-gyatso-on-the-issue-of-his-reincarnation.

Yocum, Glenn, and Janet Gyatso. "Symposium on Donald S. Lopez Jr.'s *Prisoners of Shangri-La: Tibetan Buddhism and the West.*" *Journal of the American Academy of Religion* 69(1) (2001): 163–213.

Wangdi, Yosay. "'Displaced People' Adjusting to New Cultural Vocabulary: Tibetan Immigrants in North America." In *Emerging Voices: Experiences of Underrepresented Asian Americans,* edited by Huping Ling, 71–89. New Brunswick, NJ: Rutgers University Press, 2008.

TIGER MOM

In her memoir *Battle Hymn of the Tiger Mother* (2011), Yale law professor Amy Chua (1962–) reflects upon her own upbringing by immigrant parents as well as her experience raising two biracial daughters. Right before Penguin Press released her book, excerpts from her memoir, provokingly titled "Why Chinese Mothers Are Superior," appeared in the *Wall Street Journal* in January 2011, causing immediate debate over different parenting styles. In her book and article, Chua generalizes Chinese mothers and Western parents and discusses their child-rearing styles as polarized opposites. Self-identified as a strict disciplinarian tiger mother, she listed some of the things her daughters Sophia and Louisa were never allowed to do, such as attending a sleepover, having a playdate, being in a school play, watching television and playing computer games, getting a grade less than an A, not playing the piano or violin, and not being the number one student in every subject at school except for gym and drama, among others. Since then the term "tiger mom" (also known as "tiger mother") has been used as a neologism to describe a strict, tough, disciplinarian parent.

Chua defines the Chinese mother loosely to include Chinese fathers as well as parents of other ethnicities and races who are strict and hold extremely high expectations when it comes to child rearing. Born in Champaign, Illinois, Chua was raised and strongly influenced by her immigrant disciplinarian parents, particularly her father, who graduated from the Massachusetts Institute of Technology with a doctoral degree. According to her, Chinese mothers tend to be demanding and hold their children to high standards. As a result, their children usually realize their potential and thrive at school when they are young and in life when they grow up. She considers Western parenting the complete opposite, in which parents concern themselves too much about their children's self-esteem and therefore fail to prompt them to work hard and try their best to succeed in academic studies and in life.

Battle Hymn of the Tiger Mother documents episodes of Chua's own childhood as well as motherhood. A Harvard graduate, she worked for a Wall Street law firm for a few years before joining academia, first at Duke University in North Carolina and then at Yale University in Connecticut. Her memoir also includes stories about her grandparents, parents, and siblings. Demanding excellence in academic subjects and music, she required her daughters to spend extra time studying and practicing piano and violin on a daily basis even when the family traveled. Her elder daughter Sophia performed in Carnegie Hall as a soloist after winning first prize at an international piano competition in 2007. Her younger daughter Louisa plays violin. Chua is equally invested and strict with Louisa's training and practice, although Louisa has rebelled as a teenager.

Chua's *Wall Street Journal* article and memoir generated a tremendous amount of response and caused much controversy and debate among scholars and the general public. Some supported her parenting style and claims of the sharp differences between Chinese and Western parents; others criticized her generalizations and reinforcement of the model minority myth for Asians. Chua defended herself in multiple interviews, public appearances, and writing. For instance, in a follow-up article, she emphasizes that her book is not a how-to guide. Rather, it is a memoir documenting her family's journey in two cultures and her decision to retreat from the strict Chinese approach after her younger daughter Louisa's rebellion at the age of 13. Her older daughter Sophia Chua-Rubenfeld published an open letter in the *New York Post* in 2011 defending her mother's child-rearing philosophy and methods. Sophia emphasized the important role her tiger mother played in her rite of passage and ended her letter with the statement "If I died tomorrow, I would die feeling I've lived my whole life at 110 percent. And for that, Tiger Mom, thank you" (Chua-Rubenfeld 2011). Sophia started college at Harvard University in 2011.

Chua has appeared on many television programs including *Good Morning America*, *The Today Show*, and *The Colbert Report*, among others. She was named one of *Time* magazine's 100 most influential people in the world in 2011. On March 29, 2011, the *Wall Street Journal* organized an event titled "The Return of Tiger Mom" in the New York Public Library. Chua attended the event together with her husband Jed Rubenfeld, a professor at Yale Law School, and daughter Sophia. Attendees discussed differences in child rearing in a more nuanced manner.

Satires of the term "tiger mom" have appeared in various media. For instance, Bill Holbrook's (1958–) *Kevin and Kell*, an online anthropomorphic comics series, portrayed the tiger mom in 2011 and 2012. Ryan Max Riley's article "Bios for New York's Most Popular Tutors" on the website CollegeHumor in 2013 satirizes Chua's memoir and describes the Asian mom as "the best known teacher" whose students achieve perfect scores on standardized tests. *Battle Hymn of the Tiger Mother* was a *New York Times* best seller and has been translated into dozens of languages, including Chinese. Chua has visited China and appeared in a number of interviews with Chinese reporters and news personnel. Inspired by Chua's book, a Chinese television drama series titled *Tiger Mom* started filming in 2014.

Moret recently, Chua coauthored a book with her husband Jed Rubenfeld, *The Triple Package: How Three Unlikely Traits Explain the Rise and Fall of Cultural Groups in America* (2014). This book was widely reviewed shortly after its release. It has caused a fair amount of debate over racial profiling and stereotypes.

Lan Dong

See also: Chinese American Immigration; Chinese Americans and Education; Chinese American Women; Confucianism; Model Minority

Further Reading

Asian Women United of California, ed. *Making Waves: An Anthology of Writing by and about Asian Women*. Acton, MA: Beacon, 1989.

Chan, Sucheng. *Asian Americans: An Interpretive History*. New York: Twayne, 1991.

Chua, Amy. *Battle Hymn of the Tiger Mother*. New York: Penguin, 2011.

Chua, Amy. "The Tiger Mother Responds to Readers." *Wall Street Journal*, January 13, 2011, http://blogs.wsj.com/ideas-market/2011/01/13/the-tiger-mother-responds-to-readers/.

Chua, Amy. "Why Chinese Mothers Are Superior." *Wall Street Journal*, January 8, 2011, http://online.wsj.com/articles/SB10001424052748704111504576059713528698754.

Chua, Amy, and Jed Rubenfeld. *The Triple Package: How Three Unlikely Traits Explain the Rise and Fall of Cultural Groups in America*. New York: Penguin, 2014.

Chua-Rubenfeld, Sophia. "Why I Love My Strict Chinese Mom." *New York Post*, January 18, 2011, http://nypost.com/2011/01/18/why-i-love-my-strict-chinese-mom/.

Hune, Shirley, and Gail Nomura, eds. *Asian Pacific Islander American Women: A Historical Anthology*. New York: New York University Press, 2003.

Mazamdar, Sucheta. "Through Western Eyes: Discovering Chinese Women in America." In *A New Significance: Re-envisioning the History of the American West*, edited by Clyde A. Milner, 158–168. Oxford and New York: Oxford University Press, 1996.

Yu, Timothy. "Paper Tiger Mother: On Amy Chua." Tympan, Feburary 2, 2011, http://tympan.blogspot.com/2011/02/paper-tiger-mother-on-amy-chua.html.

TRADITIONAL HEALING AND MEDICINE, ASIAN AMERICAN

Most Asian American medical and healing traditions hold holistic views toward health and illness. These traditions have developed integrated systems of personalized health care, usually with conformity with nature as a fundamental way through which a person maintains health and wellness. These views constitute an important part of culture and a way of living and lead to different approaches toward treatment and therapy compared to conventional medicine in Western traditions. Due to the rise in the cost of health care and the increased speed and stress of contemporary life, many people have turned to these alternative medicines for medical care and well-being.

Each ethnic group has its own medical and healing traditions. The Asian Indian medical tradition, for instance, is distinct from the Cambodian, Mongolian, Tibetan, Chinese, and Korean traditions. Some of the widely practiced and influential methods include acupuncture, Ayurveda, yoga, tai chi, and qigong, among others. Aside from being practiced as treatments, these forms of medicine and exercise focus on the prevention of disease as opposed to its cure.

Traditional Chinese treatment is the most popular of all alternative therapies. Since Richard Nixon's (1913–1994) first visit to China, Chinese methods of health enhancement, especially acupuncture, have seen great growth in the United States as well as other Western societies. There are now thousands of professionally trained acupuncture, herbal, and massage practitioners in America, joined by an increasing number of tai chi and qigong masters.

Chinese medicine holds an integrated approach to health, a methodology that takes the patient's whole being, lifestyle, and social situation into account. All parts of traditional Chinese medicine and healing are based on the same Daoist philosophy: Dao, the fundamental way of the universe that all existence follows; qi, the vital force or energy that flows along the meridians of the body and determines the functioning of the body and mind; yin and yang, the two complementary aspects of Dao that alternate in their interaction to form the dynamic system of nature and the body; and the five phases (or five elements), the basis of an extensive correspondence system at the root of diagnosis and treatment, connecting five minor and major stages of yin and yang with five organic substances of the body.

Acupuncture is the most popular Chinese medicine modality; herbal medicine and other healing methods are not considered medicinal by the American medical establishment. Licensed acupuncturists can use many other Chinese medical modalities, such as herbs, moxibustion, and cupping. Acupuncture is a treatment involving insertion of needles into specific meridian points along the

A traditional Chinese pharmacy in New York City's Chinatown, November 21, 2013. Tai chi, herbal medicine, acupuncture, ayurvedic medicine, and other medicines and methods are all part of Asian American traditional healing. (Mirko Vitali/ Dreamstime.com)

body. It can help regulate the flow of qi by either strengthening the normal qi so that diminished function is restored or by promoting the expulsion of pathogenic influences or excess, again to restore normal body function.

Tai chi, a Chinese internal martial art based on the principles of yin and yang and Daoist philosophy, is practiced for its health benefits. It is particularly beneficial for the general health of the elderly. The flowing, circular movements of tai chi that emphasize the balance and flow of energy in the body have been reported as useful in maintaining good health and treating a number of ailments.

Massage in Chinese medicine is considered not only for pain relief and relaxation but also as an effective and comprehensive form of clinical therapy, closely related to acupuncture in its use of the meridian system and diagnosis techniques. Massage seeks to establish a harmonious flow of qi and to encourage the body to heal itself. The classical methods of Chinese massage were adapted in Japan into three major methods: Shiatsu (finger pressure), Jinshendo (way of the compassionate heart), and Reiki (numinous qi).

Qigong includes physical as well as meditation exercises and healing efforts. These qi exercises activate and nourish qi in the body through the application of specific techniques, thereby improving the practitioner's state of health. With proper training, the practitioner might also be able to heal others. There are many styles of qigong, and their techniques for cultivation and healing vary.

Ayurvedic medicine is a system of traditional medicine that is native to the Indian subcontinent. Ayurveda, a Sanskrit term, means "life related to knowledge" and offers a holistic approach to health and well-being. Yoga originally refers to the physical, mental, and spiritual exercises that aim to achieve the union of one's soul with gods and attain a state of permanent peace of mind. It is today one of the most popular treatments of Ayurveda and has found a growing number of followers around the world. Practiced commonly for its health benefits, yoga is found to be useful in alleviating stress, treating health problems, and maintaining a healthy lifestyle.

As an important part of Asian American culture, traditional healing and medicine often appear in literature and popular culture as a major theme. Louis Chu's (1915–1970) novel *Eat a Bowl of Tea* (1961) and Wayne Wang's (1949–) 1989 film of the same title, for instance, seek a solution to the major problems of the story from traditional Chinese medicine, hence the title "eat a bowl of tea" of herbs. Alice Wu's (1970–) film *Saving Face* (2008) tells a story about love and romance of two generations of Chinese Americans and revolves around a theme of traditional medicine and healing. In Wu's film, Dr. Shing and his son are both traditional medical doctors, and the protagonist Wilhelmina's grandfather practices tai chi as a daily exercise.

Hongmei Sun

See also: Acupuncture; Daoism; Tai Chi

Further Reading

Kohn, Livia. *Health and Long Life the Chinese Way.* Magdalena, NM: Three Pines, 2005.

Wainapel, Stanley, and Avital Fast, eds. *Alternative Medicine and Rehabilitation.* New York: Demos, 2003.

TRADITIONAL POLYTHEISTIC RELIGIONS

Polytheistic practices are found in the illustrations of Greek, Roman, Sumerian, and Egyptian gods in the related civilizations. Norse Æsir and Vanir, the Yoruba Orisha, the Aztec gods, and many others also relate to polytheistic order, but they are typically considered mythology today. Polytheism is a religious practice of believing in more than one god or deity. Hinduism, Buddhism, Daoism,

Zoroastrianism, Shintoism (*kami-no-michi*), Paganism, and the Ahl-e Haqq are notable polytheistic religions.

Hinduism began in India around 500 BCE. Hindus believe in Vishnu, Shiva, and Shakti as godly figures. They believe in *punarjanma* (reincarnation), karma theory (one's action dictates the status of birth and living in the next life), and the Varna system. Sacred Hindu scriptures are the Vedas, the *Gita*, and the *Ramayan*. The followers of Hinduism are found in the Indian subcontinent, Fiji, Mauritius, Trinidad, Suriname, Guyana, Bali, Australia, the United Kingdom, the United States, France, Germany, Switzerland, Finland, Sweden, Malaysia, and Southeast Asia. From the point of view of cultural anthropology, about 330,000 deities are found in Hindu culture. The mythology enlists 360 million deities.

Buddhism began in India in 486 BCE. Gautam Buddha was its exponent. Gautam Buddha used the term *dhamma vinaya* (doctrine and discipline) for the faith system he started. With the proliferation of the Dhamma, in and out of India, after Buddha's demise, there arose many disagreements and schisms within the *sangha* (association, community) that led to the division of the Dhamma into 18 sects of Buddhism. The *Tripitaka* is the sacred religious text of Buddhists. They believe in the four Noble Truths, the Eightfold Path or eight codes of conduct, and karma. They believe in nirvana as the ultimate aim of the soul. In the state of nirvana, the passions of the soul extinguish, and it is liberated from the troublesome cycle of birth, illness, age, and death. There are about 18 deities in Buddhism. There are almost 376 million followers of Buddhism, spread over the Indian subcontinent, Sri Lanka, East Asia, Indochina, certain regions of Russia, and the Netherlands.

Daoism is also considered as a polytheist religion. In a way Daoism is not a systematic religion but, like many Asian religions, is instead a way of life. Many subsects and schools of Daoism have different practices. In ancient China, Daoism flourished as a lifestyle in opposition to authority and government, with the objective of making life simple, spontaneous, and easygoing. The schools and sects of Daoism have so many overlapping and diverting tendencies that it is difficult to have a clarified chart of the subdivisions. The history of Daoism may be understood by the fact that certain traces of Daoism are found even in the prehistoric folk religious beliefs in China. The Dao practices of magic, folk medicine, detachment from desires, divination, obtaining longevity, ecstatic wanderings, exorcism, and naturalism associate Daoism with the ancient folk traditions in China.

Zoroastrianism promotes the philosophy and teachings of Prophet Zoroaster (Zarathustra) and was apparently founded earlier than the sixth century BCE in Iran. It is also known as Mazdaism. Ahura Mazda is the supreme divine authority and is worshipped in Zoroastrianism. *Avestan* is the sacred text. Zoroastrianism has Persian cultural tradition, and its followers are sporadically found in small numbers in western India, central Iran, southern Pakistan, and some pockets of Britain, Canada, and the United States. Under the religious beliefs of Zoroastrianism, Azhura Mazda fights for a person to be good. It is the soul that chooses between Azhura Mazda and Ahriman. Zoroastrians believe in the afterlife. If at the time of death evil is finally defeated, the soul will be ultimately reunited with Fravashi (guardian spirit). In a way, Zoroastrianism is a universalist religion with respect to salvation.

Shintoism (*kami-no-michi*) started in Japan in 500 BCE and professes the emperor of Japan as the religious figure. *Kakiji* and *Nikong* are the two sacred religious texts. Shintoism believes in animism and eternal sacredness in the universe, which human beings can become attuned to.

Paganism is another polytheist practice. It believes in many deities. Its followers are found in the Far East, the Americas, Central Asia, and Africa. Paganism counts approximately 100,000 to 500,000 followers.

Ahl-e Haqq (People of Truth), also known as Yârsân, is another polytheistic religion. Sultan Sahak founded this religion in the late 14th century in western Iran. Its followers today are found in Iran and Iraq, mostly among ethnic Kurds and Laks, and are estimated to be around 1 million. Some people from the Luri and Azeri ethnic groups and some other Persian and Arab adherents are also known to be followers of Ahl-e Haqq. The followers of Ahl-e Haqq are also known as Kaka'I in Iraq. Ahl-e Haqq follows Iranian culture and claims to be 1,000–5,000 years old. Its followers believe in 11 holy lineages, or Khándáns (i.e., the clan or dynasty). Each Khándáns is headed by a sayyid, or priest. Followers of Ahl-e Haqq believe in the afterlife, and the nature of their deities is caring. *Gorani* is their primary sacred text. *Burhan al-Haqq* and *Firqan al-Akhbar* are other supplementary texts, all in Kurdish. Ahl-e Haqq believes that the universe is made of two different but related worlds: the internal world and the external world. Human beings are only aware of the outer world, but their lives are governed by the rules of the inner world.

Polytheist practices are popularizing in today's phase of globalization and liberalization. Many lovers of ecology and nature have turned to a certain extent as believers in nature, in a way leading toward polytheist practices. Under American multiculturalism, many Asian Americans practice polytheistic beliefs.

Ravindra Pratap Singh

See also: Buddhism; Confucianism; Daoism; Hinduism; Religions and Beliefs, Asian American; Theravada Buddhism

Further Reading

Boyce, Mary. *Zoroastrians: Their Religious Beliefs and Practices.* 2nd ed. New York and London: Routledge, 2001.

Collins, Steven. *Nirvana and Other Buddhist Felicities.* New York and Cambridge: Cambridge University Press, 1998.

Inoue, Nobutaka, et al. *Shinto: A Short History.* New York and London: Routledge, 2003.

Jain, Pankaj. *Dharma and Ecology of Hindu Communities: Sustenance and Sustainability.* Burlington, VT: Ashgate, 2011.

Pilgrim, Richard, and Robert Ellwood. *Japanese Religion.* Englewood Cliffs, NJ: Prentice Hall, 1985.

Saran, Parmatma. *The Asian Indian Experience in the United States.* Cambridge, MA: Schenkman Publishing, 1985.

Tejomayananda, Swami. *Hindu Culture: An Introduction.* Piercy, CA: Chinmaya Publications, 1993.

TRANSCONTINENTAL RAILROAD

On May 10, 1869, at Promontory Summit, Utah Territory, a Euro-American tycoon and politician drove the last spike into the final baseplate that fixed an iron rail to a wooden railroad tie, thereby joining the Central Pacific to the Union Pacific Railroad in what was to become one of the grandest industrial achievements in the history of North America: the transcontinental railroad. Before that last spike, millions were hammered down by Irish tracklayers concentrating on the Union Pacific line, which began on the east bank of the Missouri River in Council Bluffs, Iowa, and by Chinese laborers who made up 80–90 percent of the workforce that laid 690 miles of track for the Central Pacific that originated in Sacramento, California. The 1,776-mile monumental railway took six years to build at an estimated cost of $100 million (relative value 1860). The large number of Chinese immigrant men who built the railroad for the United States contributed to the beginnings of Asian American culture.

Pick and shovel, hammer and crowbar, saw and ax, wheelbarrow and mule cart, these were the tools of the tracklayer trade. As proprietary stakeholders were busy selling U.S. government–backed bonds to raise money for the venture and seeking buyers for the adjacent land granted to them by the federal government, Irish and Chinese overachievers were cutting, sawing, drilling, digging, tunneling, and hammering away. The railroad manifested the machinery of industry that would make trade and travel within the country less expensive and more rapid and would connect the American West with the rest of the nation. Yet after the railroad was completed and the men of Irish and Chinese descent went on their way, they experienced intense discrimination within the United States. The Irish, though, were eligible to buy cheap land in the West thanks to their European complexion and to the Homestead Act of 1863, which also helped railroad proprietors sell plots to cover their financial obligations. Chinese presence in the United States led to the Chinese Exclusion Act of 1882.

History and Origins

There were few Chinese people living in North America when the earliest steam locomotives started rolling in the United States and when the idea of stretching a railroad track across the continent was conceived. Most of these immigrants were sailors or merchants supporting an incipient U.S.-China maritime trade. At the time, coast-to-coast travel took about two months by stagecoach running night and day, just over one month by steamers plying waters on both sides of the Isthmus of Panama, and six months by sailing ship veering around South America's Cape Horn. Then gold was discovered in the Sierra Nevada of the Territory of California. Four years later, there were more than 20,000 Chinese living on the West Coast. They were mostly poor men from Guangdong Province who spoke Cantonese. Their rush for "Gold Mountain" was hastened by economic, political, and population pressures that made life in their homeland precarious. Some fortune seekers came from Peru, where they worked on coastal plantations and in guano mines as servant-slaves brought in from Portugal's colony in Macau, China. When the opportunity arrived, they would board northbound ships as cooks and servants, jump off at San Francisco—the "Golden City"—and head for the hills to become prospectors. From this ever-expanding pool of immigrants came a significant labor force that would be central to the construction of the transcontinental railroad.

To make sure such an endeavor was feasible, in 1852 the U.S. Department of War authorized the Pacific Railroad surveys. For three years and across 400,000 square miles of the American West, expeditionists collected information on life, land, and people in order to determine the best route for the railroad. The result was an extraordinary multivolume geography, published between 1855 and 1860, that enabled stakeholders and government leaders to build consensus on the kinds of financial instruments and legislative policies necessary to get the trains rolling. By this time the hills were no longer withholding heaps of gold, and many Chinese—50,000 by now and mostly residing in the states of California and Oregon and the Territory of Washington—were finding other work, mainly in kitchens, hand laundries, and mines.

In 1862 the federal government passed the Pacific Railroad Act; construction on the Central Pacific began almost immediately, while the American Civil War (1860–1865) delayed work on the Union Pacific. Initially, recruiting laborers for the lead-off line was difficult. Euro-Americans were engaged in agriculture, mining, and other trades. The Chinese had established their own occupational niches besides mining. Contractors rolled out a vigorous advertising campaign in California with little success. They decided to refocus their efforts on China, paying recruits advances of $25 to $40 for the overseas voyage to San Francisco. In 1865, 3,000 Chinese were on the Central Pacific payroll; that number increased to 12,000 by 1867.

The "Celestials," as the Chinese workers were sometimes called, were small in stature, with an average height of 4 feet 8 inches tall and a weight of 120 pounds. They usually wore traditional clothes: coolie hats, both conical and skull caps (Giap Mao), and the Tang-Zhuang–style shirt, coat, and pajama. Many grew a sinewy ponytail called a *queue*. They ate traditional food, since the necessary ingredients were widely available, and lived in segregated camps along the tracks, and most did not speak English. Their prevailing reputation varied dramatically in regional newspapers: clean, quiet, patient, and industrious concluded some, but foul, sneaky, vicious, and unhealthy noted others. Indeed, the transcontinental construction site was hardly a cultural melting pot so that animosity between ethnic groups was the rule, but the grandness of the enterprise—and the decent wage of one to three dollars a day for most all unskilled laborers—harmonized all efforts and talents.

The upper echelons of the workforce were college educated and/or former Civil War engineers, surveyors, and accountants. On the Central Pacific, some of these men supervised work crews of 20–40 Chinese laborers. Each crew had a cook and a Chinese headman or boss whose grasp of English was sufficient to relay directives from the top. They also passed on salaries and kept members of the crew in line. Besides laying track—at which the Central Pacific crews excelled, even laying a record 10 miles of track in a single day—they built roads and bridges and, perhaps their most grueling achievement, chiseled out 15 tunnels through granite slopes of the Sierra Nevada. With uncanny physical stamina, a few tools, gunpowder, and dynamite, on the best of days they would advance one foot into the rock face. Tunnel Number 6 on Donner Summit is the railroad's longest at 1,660 feet. Of the 100–150 Chinese laborers who lost their lives while building the Central Pacific, several did so in and around the tunnels.

Once the transcontinental railroad was completed, many Chinese employed their skills on the construction of rail lines that fed into the transcontinental railroad, such as the Southern Pacific. A few turned to mining remnants of gold or other ores in various parts of the West. Others settled in local cities and in newly established Chinatowns in San Francisco Bay and Sacramento, where they opened up or toiled in laundries and restaurants for the most part. Still, others moved eastward to escape the discrimination and violence that was creeping into their lives in the West.

Today

From U.S. Interstate Highway 80, one can see original track beds of the Central Pacific; those originating in Sacramento and extending into central Nevada now gird rails that Amtrak's daily California Zephyr uses to haul passengers between the San Francisco Bay Area and Chicago. Also visible are the Chinese walls made of stone and cement that were built on ravines and steep slopes to block sliding snow and earth from disrupting traffic. The highway also leads to the Golden Spike National Historic Site on Promontory Summit, where on display in the museum and sold in the gift shop are copies of the most popular photograph taken at the Golden Spike Ceremony in 1869. In it are two giant locomotives surrounded by a party of men, but none of them are Chinese. To supplement popular history with a dose of truth, a number of the sixth-generation descendents of the so-called Chinese Railroad recently gathered at the junction point of the Central and Union Pacific Railroads and posed for a group picture. Their performance was not lost on the U.S. government, which in 2014 inducted the Chinese railroad workers into the Labor Department's Hall of Honor with a glass plaque.

Ken Whalen

See also: Chinese American Immigration

Further Reading

Ambrose, Stephen E. *Nothing Like It in the World: The Men Who Built the Transcontinental Railroad, 1863–1869.* New York: Simon and Schuster, 2000.

Bain, David Haward. *Empire Express: Building the First Transcontinental Railroad.* New York: Viking Penguin, 1999.

"Central Pacific Railroad Photographic History." Central Pacific Railroad Photographic History Museum, http://CPRR.org.

White, Richard. *Railroaded: The Transcontinentals and the Making of Modern America.* New York: Norton, 2012.

V

VIDEO AND ONLINE GAMES, ASIAN AMERICANS AND

History and Origins

Video games have become an essential part of U.S. culture whereby thousands of American citizens spend countless amounts of money buying new consoles and games. The video game industry has become one of the fastest-growing global industries, expected to be worth nearly $70 billion in the next couple of years. The history of video games is complex, with numerous companies revolutionizing this market. With this revolution, more video game companies are now aiming to please a growing audience of adolescents.

In the 1970s, video games began to grow with the first system, Atari, and the first game, *Pong*, created by Nolan Bushnell and Al Alcorn. These creators launched the first game system at a local bar in California. With the popularity of the game that the two designers created, the video game industry grew as more companies began to buy Atari for entertainment. Atari soon influenced other companies to start developing their own versions of video games, including companies such as Nintendo, which quickly rivaled Atari's creation.

In 1989 Nintendo created a new sensation called Game Boy, a handheld gaming system that took the United States by storm. With consoles such as the Nintendo Entertainment System, Game Boy became a hot new seller for consumers. Japan, one of the biggest contributors and sellers in the video game industry, introduced its products such as the PlayStation in 1994 and PlayStation 2 in 2000. The creation of PlayStation 2 began a new era of video games. Sony had produced a system that could function as a CD and DVD player. As a result, it produced a machine that revolutionized the video game industry. This development pushed other companies such as Nintendo and the computer enterprise Microsoft to join the fray of video game developers and producers. As video games have progressed throughout the years, the competition continues to push companies to develop better and faster consoles and games.

Contemporary Forms

Asian Americans are significant consumers of video games in the United States. In order for gaming companies to tap into this racial market, they have started to use different aspects of Asian culture as a way to represent Asian American characters in these video games. Large Asian video game companies such as Square Enix (creator of the famous *Final Fantasy* series), Nintendo (creator of the well-known game *Super Mario*), Capcom, and others all adapt their video games according to the needs of consumers and the market in order to sell their products to a larger audience. With the video game becoming an important part of the world market, these games will become representative of Asian Americans and their culture.

Ethnicity is a factor that draws people into playing a certain kind of video game. Within each game there is always a hero or a protagonist. In most games, a white heterosexual male usually represents the main hero that must accomplish a great quest or jobs in order to save the world from great evil. With this in mind, characters of color are mostly represented by supportive characters or are seen as the great evil that must be vanquished. Thus, many Asian American children view being white as always right. A large number of video

A group dressed as *Street Fighter* characters attending the E3 Electronic Entertainment Expo in Los Angeles, California, June 18, 2015. (Daniel Boczarski/WireImage/Getty Images)

games target white Americans as potential players. Games such as Call of Duty, a popular first-person shooter game for the PlayStation and Xbox series, focus on the experiences of a white male character as the savior of the world from the forces of evil. Many of the enemies in the game are located in countries in Southeast Asia, East Asia, Africa, or South America, which deters some Asian Americans from playing these games because of the type of racial representation they present. With the enemies primarily being Asians, players may assume that Asians are the primary threats to the world. As a result, Asian Americans will be seen as foreigners and will continue to be viewed as a threat to the United States. Even though this video game is popular among young adults, the game continues to reinforce evil Asian American stereotypes.

Some Asian Americans prefer to play fighting genre games that depict a large number of Asian American characters. For example, games such as *Dynasty Warriors* and *Mortal Kombat* feature Asian American protagonists; however, these games continue to perpetuate the racial stereotype that all Asians can do martial arts. In *Dynasty Warriors* and *Mortal Kombat*, the main characters battle with multiple weapons such as swords and spears, among others. Players are able to pick different characters in ancient China. Since these games emphasize a significant aspect of Asian culture, some players may generalize that all Asian Americans can do martial arts. With the idea of Asian culture and Asian Americans being part of the trend, many video game companies began to sell the idea of different aspects of Asian culture to the major global market.

Asian American women are often portrayed as sexualized individuals. Chun Li is a popular female character throughout the *Street Fighter* series. Chun Li represents a persona that stereotypes many Asian American women as exotic. By endowing characters with physical qualities such as large breasts, the creators of Chun Li and other such video game characters continue to sexualize Asian women. Other video games such as *Tekken*, *Dead or Alive*, *Soul Caliber*, *Mortal Kombat*, and *Ninja Gaiden* stereotype Asian women as sexual commodities for male consumers. Each of these series allows players to objectify Asian women.

Future of Video Games and Asian American Players

Asian Americans and Asian culture contribute to some part of the video game franchise. Throughout the history of video games, companies have slowly started to incorporate different aspects of culture in order to make the games profitable. Video game companies allow these perpetual stereotypes of Asian

Americans to continue to exist, and the players who buy the video games continue to perpetuate these stereotypes.

Even though these game designers have developed video games with fictional characters, these characters reflect on some part of Asian culture. Video games in effect allow people to purchase a culture. As video games become a strong part of U.S. culture, people will start to learn about different cultures more through video games than through classes, such as ethnic studies courses. They will only see the minimal aspects of the culture instead of learning about how these traditions are created. Asian culture will soon be represented through video games, and more Asian Americans may be subjugated to racial stereotyping through video games. Video games will become a stronger source of cultural exposure. As a result, more people only see one side of a person's culture rather than actually wanting to learn from diversity.

Vincent Kwan

See also: The Internet and Asian Americans; Popular Culture, Asian Americans and

Further Reading

Glaubke, Christina R., et al. "Fair Play? Violence, Gender, and Race in Video Games." *Children Now* (December 1, 2001): 2–37.

Kabiling, Maria Cristina Ana. "World War II Popular American Visual Culture: Film and Video Games After 9/11." MA thesis, Georgetown University, 2010.

Nichols, Randall J. "The Games People Play: A Political Economic Analysis of Video Games and Their Production." PhD dissertation, University of Oregon, 2005.

Rishe, Patrick. "Trends in Multi-Billion Dollar Video Game Industry: Q/A with Gaming Champ Fatal1ty." *Forbes,* December, 23, 2011, http://www.forbes.com/sites /prishe/2011/12/23/trends-in-the-multi-billion-dollar-video-game-industry-qa -with-gaming-champ-fatal1ty/.

Saleem, Safwat. "A Brief History of Video Games (Part 1)." TED, http://ed.ted.com /lessons/a-brief-history-of-video-games-part-i-safwat-saleem#review.

Shiu, Anthony S. F. "What Yellowface Hides: Video Games, Whiteness, and the American Racial Order." *Journal of Popular Culture* 39(1) (2006): 109–125.

Williams, Dmitri, et al. "The Virtual Census: Representation of Gender, Race, and Age in Video Games." *New Media Society* 11(5) (2009): 815–834.

VIETNAMESE AMERICAN ARTS AND ARTISTS

History and Origins

Vietnamese American arts and artists have gained increasing visibility since the mass exodus of South Vietnamese after the fall of Saigon in 1975. Because of

Dinh Q. Le (1968–)

Dinh Q. Le was born in Ha Tien, Vietnam, in 1968 and escaped with his family to the United States in 1979. Le received his BA at the University of California, Santa Barbara, and his MFA at the School of Visual Arts in New York. Well known for his photoweaving projects, such as *From Hollywood to Vietnam*, and conceptual work, such as the *Damaged Gene* project, Le's art explores the complex memories and mediations of the Vietnam War. A 2007 exhibition of his oeuvre of works was held at the Bellevue Arts Museum in Washington and cataloged in *A Tapestry of Memories: The Art of Dinh Q. Le*.

the profound effects of the Vietnam War on refugees and later generations, concerns about memory, trauma, community politics, and gender dynamics often emerge in the creation and criticism of Vietnamese American artwork. As scholars have articulated, popular visual depictions have dominated the impressions of both Vietnam and the Vietnam War (1959–1975). Of particular impact are photographs such as *Saigon Execution* (1968), *Massacre at My Lai* (1969), and *Napalm Girl* (1972). These photos worked to amplify the antiwar movements of the time as well as propel ethical discourse about U.S. imperialism and national identity. In the decades following the war, these images problematically constructed memories of the past and elided the experiences of Vietnamese refugees and subsequent generations. By addressing and often moving beyond these mainstream images, Vietnamese American artists reveal the dynamic experiences, concerns, and fissures within the Vietnamese American community.

A number of Vietnamese American artists have transformed the dominant depictions of the war to reflect the perspectives of the Viet Kieu (overseas Vietnamese). Among the most well known are Dinh Q. Le's photo weavings, Binh Danh's chlorophyll-processed prints, and An-My Le's war reenactment photos. Through their innovative materials and techniques, these artists reflect the vexed nature of postwar memory and yet the war's continued resonance within the psychical and physical landscape of Vietnam and its people. In his projects, Dinh Q. Le cuts and recombines popular visual images of the war, anonymous Vietnamese photographs, and personal images into a large tapestry. In his article "Speak of the Dead, Speak of Vietnam," Viet Thanh Nguyen argues that Le's weavings highlight the struggle between the public and private, the U.S. government and the minority, in the memorialization of the war (2006, 23–30). Similarly, Binh Danh through his invention of the chlorophyll-printing

Artist Dinh Q. Le attending the opening reception for the reinstallation of contemporary art from the collection at the Museum of Modern Art in New York City, June 29, 2010. Known for his photoweaving and conceptual projects, Le focuses his work on memories of the Vietnam War. (Charles Eshelman/WireImage/Getty Images)

process records an archive of Vietnam war images onto organic materials such as leaves, while An-My Le depicts embodied memorializations of war through her engagement with and photographs of Vietnam War reenactments staged in South Carolina.

In addition to popular images of the war, dominant conceptions of Vietnamese refugees color postwar discourse. Scholar Yen Le Espiritu (2010) states that "hyperfocus on the refugees' needs and neediness has made 'un-visible' other important facets of Vietnamese personhood: their self-identity, their dreams for themselves, their hopes for their children, and their 'ground of being'" (198). A number of Vietnamese American artists' works reflect Vietnamese personhood through both representational and abstract images. Painter and sculptor Long Nguyen is acclaimed for his *Tales of Yellow Skin* series. Painted in shades of yellow, Nguyen's canvas emulates scarred and burned skin that registers and maps the unsettling and traumatic cartographies of war on the racialized body. Surrealist painter Lien Truong's works conjure cross-generational images of the Vietnamese that move beyond stereotypical representations of the abject refugee. Painter Ann Phong also counteracts the stigma surrounding so-called boat people through her abstract renderings of the ocean, boats, and legs in motion that express the endurance of the spirit. Other notable artists whose works address the rich textures of the Vietnamese American community include Tran T. Kim-Trang's *Blindness Series,* Pipo Nguyen-duy's staged photographs, Dong Phan's *Journey* series, Darlene Nguyen-Ely's symbolic sculptures, Vi Ly's immense and textured paintings, Truong Tran's environmentally conscious mixed media, Lan Hoang Vu's political cartoons, Han Nguyen's minimalist photos, Howard Tran's two-dimensional paintings and sculptures, and Hiep Nguyen's community-based projects.

Contemporary Forms

Since the lifting of the economic embargo between the United States and Vietnam in 1994, heretofore imagined ties to Vietnam have been actualized. These possibilities inflect a number of artists' cultural productions. For example, G. B. Tran's graphic memoir *Vietnamerica* illustrates his first trip to Vietnam with his parents. After publishing the first graphic memoir by a Vietnamese American, Tran has collaborated with artist Thi Bui. Other collaborations have forged transnational art centers, sites, and networks. Founded in 2007 by Dinh Q. Le, Tuan Andrew Nguyen, Phu Nam Thuc Ha, and Tiffany Chung, San Art is an organization located in Ho Chi Minh City that supports and exhibits artwork from Vietnamese and Viet Kieu artists. Cofounder Tuan Andrew Nguyen reflects these transnational dialogues in *Quiet Shiny Words,* an exhibition that illuminates the influences of hip-hop on the Vietnamese subcultural scene. Other transnationally influenced artists include James Truong Nguyen, Gabby Quynh-Anh Miller, and Julie Thi Underhill.

While transnational linkages and movements have been productive for Vietnamese American arts, they are not without controversy. Namely, entrenched anticommunism in Vietnamese diasporic communities has colored the production and reception of various endeavors. The 2009 *F.O.B. II: Art Speaks* exhibit, curated by Lan Duong and Tram Le, received criticism from anticommunist community members because of the fraught North Vietnamese images used by a number of the exhibition's artists. Brian Doan's photograph, which included both the present flag of Vietnam and the image of Ho Chi Minh, received the brunt of the backlash. The protests against the exhibit reveal complicated postwar politics and intracommunity fissures. Issues about race, gender, and sexuality also inflect intracommunity dialogues and are thus central to a number of Vietnamese American visual artists who seek to challenge heteronormative constructions of U.S. national and diasporic Vietnamese identities. Activist artist Hanh Thi Pham's photography draws from her experiences as a refugee from Vietnam and pervasive encounters with discrimination based on her race, gender, and sexuality in the United States. Queer filmmaker Nguyen Tan Hoang's works destabilize heteronormative refugee narratives of exile, longing, and return. In his experimental film *PIRATED!* Nguyen juxtaposes footages of refugee escape, Vietnamese diasporic cultural productions, and campy and erotic pirate movie scenes. This pastiche of images, texts, and sounds demonstrate the ineluctable mediation of memory and identity.

There have been an increasing number of anthologies, catalogs, websites, and articles that provide context for and conversations between Vietnamese American artists and their artwork. Three prominent websites, the Vietnamese American Arts & Letters Association, the Diasporic Vietnamese Artists Network, and diaCRITICS bring together Vietnamese artists from within and outside the United States. These websites provide information about a heterogeneous group of artists including Kim Huynh, Toi Hoang, Tam Van Tran, Quynh Nguyen, Diem Chau, Quyen Troung, Hoang Vu, Hung Viet Nguyen, Kai Hoang, Kevin T. N. Nguyen, Thomas Thuan Dang Vu, Christine Nguyen, and more. Utilizing different mediums, these artists' work vary from direct engagement with racial and ethnic specific concerns to more abstract or universalizing themes. Whether Vietnamese artists directly represent the Vietnamese American experience or not, the continued diversity and richness of works being produced illuminate the contours of what constitutes Vietnamese American art.

Quynh Nhu Le

See also: Arts and Artists (Visual), Asian American; Vietnamese American Films and Filmmakers; Vietnamese American Immigration

Further Reading

diaCRITICS, www.diacritics.org/.

Diasporic Vietnamese Artists Network, www.dvanonline.com.

Duong, Lan, and Isabelle Thuy Pelaud. "Vietnamese American Art and Community Politics." *Journal of Asian American Studies* 15(3) (2012): 241–269.

Espiritu, Yen Le. "Negotiating Memories of War: Arts in Vietnamese American Communities." In *Art in the Lives of Immigrant Communities in the United States*, edited by Paul DiMaggio and Patricia Fernández-Kelly, 197–214. New Brunswick, NJ: Rutgers University Press, 2010.

Le, Viet. "The Art of War: Vietnamese American Visual Artists Dinh Q. Le, Ann Phong, and Nguyen Tan Hoang." *Amerasia Journal* 31(2) (2005): 21–35.

Le, Viet, and Alice Ming Wai Jim, eds. *Charlie Don't Surf: 4 Vietnamese American Artists*. Vancouver: Vancouver International Centre for Contemporary Asian Art, 2005.

Nguyen, Viet Thanh. "Speak of the Dead, Speak of Viet Nam: The Ethics and Aesthetics of Minority Discourse." *New Centennial Review* 6(2) (2006): 7–37.

Vietnamese American Arts & Letters Association, www.vaala.org.

The Vietnamese Artists Collective. *As Is: A Collection of Visual and Literary Works by Vietnamese American Artists.* San Francisco: Vietnamese Artists Collective, 2006.

VIETNAMESE AMERICAN COMMUNITY ORGANIZATIONS

With the arrival of Vietnamese immigrants in the United States, there was an immediate need to form social networks in order to address the refugee crisis, provide language and vocational training, encourage civil involvement, and deal with the proliferation of drug use, violence, and other social problems. Many social organizations that initially aided the community were targeted not specifically at improving the life of Vietnamese but rather refugees and immigrant communities in general, such as the Ameriasian Program (for children of American servicemen) and the Humanitarian Program. By the 1990s Vietnamese also opted for active participation in many nonethnic social organizations, such as the measurably large participation of Vietnamese in Boy Scout and Girl Scout Clubs in northern Virginia.

As time went on, more and more organizations were founded specifically to serve the Vietnamese community. The Vietnamese Chamber of Commerce in Orange County is one such example. This process also led to a proliferation of student/academic and professional organizations as well as civic, political, and even recreational organizations. As academic work on Vietnam and Vietnamese studies progressed in the United States, several heritage and cultural organizations were founded to promote the understanding of Vietnamese culture. The 2003 Directory of Mutual Assistance Associations lists 46 Vietnamese specific organizations, making Vietnamese-led organizations more prevalent than any other Southeast Asian group in California.

Sài Gòn Nh (Little Saigon) refers to Vietnamese American enclaves across the United States. Sài Gòn Nh also refers specifically to the oldest and largest Vietnamese enclave of nearly 200,000 individuals from a neighborhood centered on Bolsa Avenue in Westminster, Orange Country, California, in the suburbs of Los Angeles that began to grow in 1982. As the neighborhood became a commercial and cultural center for Vietnamese immigrants, it has been featured particularly in Vietnamese American literature. "Bolsa," "Westminster," and "Garden Grove" are direct references to this community in English, while and Sài Gòn Nh and *tinh Cam* (Orange County) are references used in Vietnamese.

Political participation of the Vietnamese American community has not followed predictable trends and has still been considered to be at the early stages of development as of the 2000s. Most Vietnamese Americans initially had no wishes whatsoever of returning to Vietnam, which is accompanied by increased political activism. In 1992 Tony Lâm was the first Vietnamese American to be elected to the Westminster City Council. In 1995 Châu Minh Nguyen became the first Vietnamese American councilwoman in Garrett Park, Maryland. Văn Thái Tran was elected to the Westminster City Council in 2000. Lân Quoc Nguyen was first elected to the Board of Education in 2002. In 2004, Kim-Oanh Nguyen-Lâm and Trung Quang Nguyen were elected to the Garden Grove Unified School District, giving the district its first Vietnamese majority. In the same year Văn Thái Tran was raised to the office of assemblyman, becoming one of two in the United States (the other was Hubert Võ of Texas). Nevertheless, there have been two major ways that the Vietnamese have popularly supported social involvement in the United States: through publication and through protest.

Publications were a key aspect of Vietnamese communal organizations, although as of 2008 there was no "long standing, well-indexed Vietnamese language newspaper in the United States" (Như and Meyer 2008, 89). There were 6 Vietnamese language publications in 1975. By the mid-1980s at least 27 Vietnamese newspapers and periodicals were in circulation. By 1985 there were at least 185 publications. However, most did not survive into the 1990s. Nonprofit organizations showed a similar mushroom effect, reaching 420 in 1985. In 1999, American-trained sociologist Hien Đuc Đo produced his own account of Vietnamese Americans in his book *The Vietnamese Americans* that was acclaimed to be one of the best "insider accounts" of the community at the time (Freeman 2001). In a recent collection, Michele Janette argues that Vietnamese American literature can be traced back to 1962. Her book recounted the waves, biographies, and views and pointed out the complexity of Vietnamese American literature as a means of social organization. However, the revival of Vietnamese American literature and communal organizations does not suggest that there are no social conflicts in the Vietnamese community.

From 1998 to 1999, protesters gathered in front of the Hitek video store of Mr. Trương Tran at Bolsa Avenue, Westminster, California, because he displayed a Vietnamese flag and a portrait of Ho Chi Minh. The protesters were almost all Vietnamese Americans and numbered as many as 15,000 at the peak. The protest was a form of social organization, arguing in favor of American values and the values supported by a proposed majority of Vietnamese Americans. It also became a way for individuals to comment on the existing politics in the United States as well as in Vietnam. The protests were different from those of the Vietnam era, during which a "We don't need your racist war!" slogan was used to unite Pan-Asian antiwar sentiment. They were also not the form of protests that had shock-familiarized Americans with Vietnamese culture from the Vietnam War era. Meanwhile, Vietnamese American–led protests were almost nonexistent after 1975 until a spike in 1993 and another spike in the late 1990s. The 1993 spike can be explained through the debate regarding normalization of Vietnamese American relations. Regardless, almost all protests were led by individual communal leaders and held in Westminster, California, and were related to U.S.-Vietnam relations (23 percent) and Vietnamese American politics (33 percent). The grand majority of the protests seem to have been against actions undertaken by members of the Vietnamese American community, and hence it seems that the Vietnamese American community has eliminated the participation of a number of other groups. An example of protests more recently include arts issues regarding the portrayal of Vietnamese identity, such as in the ban of *Miss Saigon* and protests against the portrayal of Vietnamese identity led by many individuals, including poet, author, and activist Bao Phi.

William Brokaw Noseworthy

See also: Little Saigons; Vietnamese American Immigration

Further Reading

Freeman, James M. "Review: *The Vietnamese Americans* by Hien Duc Do." *Journal of American Ethnic History* 20(3) (2001): 177–178.

Như, Ngoc T. Ông, and David S. Meyer. "Protest and Political Incorporation: Vietnamese American Protests in Orange County, California, 1975–2001." *Journal of Vietnamese Studies* 3(1) (2008): 78–107.

Pham, Phương Chi. "Review: *My Viet: Vietnamese American Literature in English, 1962–Present.*" *Journal of Vietnamese Studies* 7(2) (2012): 183–185.

Wood, Joseph. "Vietnamese American Place Making in Northern Virginia." *Geographical Review* 87(1) (1997): 58–72.

VIETNAMESE AMERICAN FILMS AND FILMMAKERS

History and Origins

Like other forms of cultural production in the United States, Vietnamese Americans have been involved in the film industry, both in the United States and abroad, in a variety of capacities including as performers, writers, choreographers, stuntmen, producers, and filmmakers in television and cinema and online.

When Vietnamese immigrants and refugees arrived in large numbers in the United States following the fall of Saigon and the withdrawal of American troops from Vietnam in April 1975, the new immigrants were dispersed across

Tony Bui (1973–)

One of the most influential Vietnamese American filmmakers, Tony Bui is known for his critically acclaimed *Three Seasons* (1999) and *Green Dragon* (2001), the latter done in collaboration with his brother, Timothy Linh Bui. Tony Bui was born in Saigon in 1973. Leaving about one week before the fall of Saigon, he arrived in the United States in 1975 as a refugee with his family.

While a film student at Loyola Marymount University in Los Angeles, Bui directed his first independent short film, *Yellow Lotus* (1995), which later debuted at Sundance and went on to win 15 film festival awards worldwide. He would later write, produce, and direct his first feature film, *Three Seasons,* starring Harvey Keitel, Nguyen Ngoc Hiep, and Don Duong. *Three Seasons* meditates on the recent past of Vietnam, the early days of Doi Moi, and the effects of capitalism in the nation's neoliberalizing economy. It debuted at Sundance and won both the Grand Jury Prize and the Audience Award. *Three Seasons* also holds the distinction of being an American film to be filmed entirely on location in Vietnam and the first to be filmed there after President Bill Clinton normalized relations with Vietnam and lifted the embargo.

Bui later produced and cowrote *Green Dragon* (2001), which his brother directed. The film starred Patrick Swayze and Forest Whitaker as American military personnel involved in the relocation of Vietnamese refugees at Camp Pendleton in San Diego. It premiered at the 2001 Sundance Festival and received the Humanitas Award.

the country, many in places that had no existing significant populations of Asian Americans. It is not surprising, then, that many of these immigrants found themselves migrating again to congregate in places such as Orange County in California, Dallas and Houston in Texas, and New Orleans in Louisiana, where they established what would be called Little Saigons—densely populated ethnic enclaves of immigrant Vietnamese. Integral to this early community formation was the emergence of a media industry by and for Vietnamese Americans, much of which originally used the Vietnamese language and through the end of the 20th century increasingly used English.

Important media outlets, in addition to print journalism and literature, were local public access cable programming, radio shows, and most significantly music media in the form of cassettes in the 1970s and 1980s and later VHS, laser discs, and DVDs. By the late 1980s and early 1990s, original video programming of Vietnamese singers and dancers was being produced and distributed worldwide, with much of it coming primarily from southern California. The most famous of

Viet Kieu Actors

One of the major driving forces in Vietnam's burgeoning film industry since the late 1990s is the influx of Vietnamese diasporic filmmakers and actors. This flow of talent, educated and trained abroad, has brought knowledge, experience, and technical expertise that had previously been lacking in Vietnam's film industry, which until the 1990s had been characterized by low-budget nationalistic films. The most notable figures among returnee actors include Dustin Nguyen and Johnny Tri Nguyen, who have both starred in a new wave of Vietnamese films. Unlike the Vietnamese films that came before, these new features have markedly higher production values, more diverse themes, and varied genres.

Dustin Nguyen, a 1.5-generation Vietnamese American actor, came to the United States when he was 12 years old. In the late 1980s he was a regular on the popular American TV show *21 Jump Street,* where he performed alongside Johnny Depp and Holly Robinson. Since then Nguyen has appeared in numerous television shows and feature films, and by the mid-2000s he was regularly starring in, producing, and directing movies in Vietnam, including historical dramas, horror films, and action thrillers.

Johnny Tri Nguyen came to the United States at the age of eight and made a name for himself in the American film industry as a stunt man, martial artist, and actor. In 2007 he starred in the colonial-era action film *The Rebel* opposite Dustin Nguyen and Thanh Van Ngo and established himself as a full-fledged star and heartthrob in Vietnam.

Along with filmmakers such as Victor Vu and Othello Khanh, these actors have changed the landscape of Vietnamese cultural production. Previously whereas much of the popular media consumed by the Vietnamese was made within the diaspora and flowed into Vietnam, today the trajectory of media moves in multiple directions, with the Vietnamese-produced media consumed in the United States and elsewhere. Much of this is a result of Viet Kieu actors and filmmakers returning and reviving the industry.

these is the *Paris By Night* variety shows by Thuy Nga, which recorded live performances distributed as boxed sets several times a year. *Paris by Night* has served an important function for communal remembering of past traumas and celebrating of Vietnamese and Vietnamese American culture, including dancing, singing, skits, and beauty and cultural pageants.

Vietnamese Americans have also participated in mainstream American media, with Vietnamese American actors appearing in Hollywood television and film since the early 1980s. Jonathan Ke Quan appeared in major Hollywood films, including major roles as a child in *Indiana Jones and the Temple of Doom*

(1984) and *The Goonies* (1985). Dustin Nguyen appeared in the popular television series *21 Jump Street* (1987–1990) following smaller roles in *General Hospital* (1985) and *Magnum P.I.* (1985), and later Thuy Tran would be one of the most recognizable Vietnamese Americans as Trini Kwan/Yellow Ranger in *The Mighty Morphin Power Rangers* (1993). Hiep Thi Le is the most notable Vietnamese American woman to star in a major Hollywood film, playing Le Ly Hayslip opposite Tommy Lee Jones in Oliver Stone's *Heaven and Earth* (1993), an adaptation of Hayslip's biographies. There have also been many notable Vietnamese American news anchors, including Leyna Nguyen in southern California, Betty Nguyen for CNN and CBS, and others.

Since the 1990s, Vietnamese Americans have been increasingly active in the media and film industries, with more Vietnamese Americans both in front of and behind the cameras, in mainstream film, independent and documentary films, and online. Many Vietnamese Americans are also taking their experience and education learned from working in U.S. industries to work in Vietnam, thereby contributing to a burgeoning film and media industry in the homeland that they or their parents fled in the 1970s.

Regional Practices and Traditions

As with literature or any form of cultural production, it is dangerous to generalize the practices of Vietnamese Americans in the film and media industries, especially as the various capacities in which these individuals and groups participate in these industries is so diverse. In general, however, early Vietnamese American media of the 1970s and 1980s originated out of small ethnic enclaves of Vietnamese Americans, was produced by recently displaced and exiled artists, and catered to those with similar experiences of displacement and resettlement. These texts tended to be homegrown, with low production value, and were almost entirely in Vietnamese. Thematically, they were highly critical of the new communist government and nostalgic for a lost and romanticized homeland. Formally, many of the primarily musical performances hearkened back to traditional forms of music that originated in Vietnam, and some experimented with Western musical genres such as tango, disco, rock 'n' roll, and American pop.

By 1983, the growing popularity for the local music industry of Vietnamese Americans carved out a niche for the *Paris by Night* video series, which originated in France by To Van Lai and his wife Thuy Nga—refugees from Saigon who had previously been in the recording industry in Vietnam and eventually moved to the United States. The series was inspired by USO shows, Hong Kong videos, and the then newly popular MTV. Aside from escapist spectacle, the series established a cohesive ethnic community of diasporic Vietnamese providing a space to celebrate ethnic identity, share political concerns, and reimagine a Vietnamese culture outside of Vietnam. The videos feature an array of elaborate song and dance performances, sketch comedy, beauty pageants, interviews, and commemorative media. They also established figures such as MCs Nguyen Cao Ky Duyen and Nguyen Ngoc Ngzn, who have since become recognizable celebrities in Vietnamese diasporic communities. Hugely popular in the diaspora, these videos are largely banned in Vietnam but have a huge viewership estimated at roughly 70 million Vietnamese, who gain access through pirated media available in the country's so-called gray market.

Outside of media such as *Paris by Night*, which are marketed exclusively to the Vietnamese-speaking community in the United States and abroad, Vietnamese Americans were most visible in films from the 1980s and 1990s that depicted or reflected upon the Vietnam War. Such films largely offered narratives that almost exclusively reflected the perspective of American servicemen in Vietnam, with the Vietnamese having marginal roles as unidentified villagers or enemy Viet Cong. Vietnamese Americans slowly began to take on more diverse representations in mainstream media in the 1980s with the presence of child-actor Jonathan Luke Ke Huy Quan, who had supporting roles in *Indiana Jones and the Temple of Doom* (1984) as Dr. Indiana Jones's young sidekick Shortround and in *The Goonies* (1985) as tech geek Richard "Data" Wang, alongside an ensemble cast. In 1987, actor Dustin Nguyen garnered national attention as Officer Harry Truman Ioki, a role he would play for three years in the undercover police procedural drama *21 Jump Street* opposite Johnny Depp and Holly Robinson. Nguyen would go on to do several notable films, including Oliver Stone's Vietnam War drama *Heaven and Earth* (1993) with fellow Vietnamese American actress Hiep Thi Le and the critically acclaimed Australian drama *Little Fish* (2005) opposite Cate Blanchett and Hugo Weaving.

In the 2000s, the United States saw an increasing number of Vietnamese American–helmed film projects that featured narratives written and directed by Vietnamese Americans reflecting the point of view of the Vietnamese who responded to Vietnam War films of earlier decades that were marketed largely for white American audiences. Notable films of this period include *Catfish in Black Bean Sauce* (1999), *Three Seasons* (1999), *Green Dragon* (2001), *Journey from the Fall* (2006), the documentary *A Village Called Versailles* (2009), and *Touch* (2011).

In the 2000s, a growing number of Vietnamese Americans would return to a newly liberalizing and increasingly postsocialist Vietnam to revitalize its cultural industries. Influential actors in this movement included actors such as Dustin Nguyen, Johnny Tri Nguyen, and Kathy Uyen and directors/writers/editors such as Tony Bui, Victor Vu, Ham Tran, Luu Huynh, and Charlie

Nguyen. These individuals would establish important media organizations such as Créa TV, a private multinational production company founded by Othello Khanh that works with American television and film productions such as the CBS reality TV series *The Amazing Race* as well as original films including Vietnamese horror films such as *The House in the Alley* (2012). Major films to come out of this transnational movement of talent include the colonial-era action film *The Rebel* (2007), starring Johnny Tri Nguyen, Dustin Nguyen, and Thanh Van Ngo; *Passport to Love* (2009), directed by Victor Vu and starring Vietnamese actor Binh Minh and American actress Kathy Uyen; *Floating Lives* (2010) and *Once upon a Time in Vietnam* (2013), both written, directed by, and starting Dustin Nguyen; the romantic comedy *Battle of the Brides* (2011) and martial arts fantasy epic *Blood Letter* (2012), directed by Victor Vu; *The White Silk Dress* (2006), written and directed by Luu Huynh; and many others.

The transnational actors and filmmakers have been integral in energizing a film industry that prior to normalization and liberalization had been a state-run mechanism for low-budget nationalist and propaganda media. The influx of American-trained talent brought a surge of higher-quality media that satiated the appetites of Vietnamese audiences who desired Western-quality entertainment that spoke to their national contexts. These films have also been widely popular with Vietnamese audiences in the diaspora, and many are available at low cost through online streaming services and video platforms such as YouTube. These films also reflect a broad range of themes, genres, and styles that draw heavily from diverse influences and source material, the Hong Kong–inspired martial arts films, the American-style romantic comedies, and Japanese- and Korean-like horror movies. The very local tradition of tragedy or drama, so often invoked in traditional poetry and music, is still strong and increasingly shifting toward urban-based narratives to reflect internal migration trends facing much of the population.

Contemporary Forms

Perhaps most significant in contemporary media production is the prominence of Vietnamese Americans and their relative success on Web 2.0 social media platforms such as social networking and video-sharing sites. The most famous and notorious of these figures is Tila Nguyen, better known as Tila Tequila. Although often seen as a controversial attention seeker, Tila Nguyen was notable for her use of the online social network MySpace, which she joined early in 2003. Prior to her MySpace fame, she had been a minor import car model and a Playboy Cyber Girl of the Month, but she quickly learned to negotiate social media to promote herself and launch her career in modeling, acting, and singing and as an entrepreneur. By 2006 at the height of her MySpace fame, she had amassed over 1.5 million friends on the network; had landed an MTV show, *A Shot at Love with Tila Tequila;* and was making small appearances in Hollywood films. That same year she was featured in *Time* magazine, signaling a major shift in the Internet and the social dynamics of Web 2.0.

Tila Tequila's career suffered, and she largely fell out of the media spotlight after several controversies in 2008, but by then she had paved the way for other Vietnamese American women on social media. Of these, the most noteworthy is Internet cosmetic guru Michelle Phan, who launched her career by sharing makeup tutorials on YouTube. Phan posted her first self-made video in 2007 after being active as a vlogger on the early blogging site Xanga, and by the close of 2013 she had 285 videos uploaded and over 5.5 million subscribers to her personal YouTube channel. Her immense social media cache was built upon her popularity on the video-sharing site and led to partnerships with advertisers, other celebrities, and her role as Lancôme's official video makeup artist. She eventually went on to launch her own brand of cosmetics with L'Oreal.

Musicians such as Cathy Nguyen and Thao Nguyen also demonstrate the importance of social media for independent and new musicians. Thao, an Indie folk singer, has been featured on NPR and its various media outlets, while Cathy Nguyen shares videos of her vocal and acoustic covers of pop songs, often in conjunction with fellow musician friends. Cathy Nguyen is a singer performing mostly covers of material by other artists, and her YouTube channel is notable for featuring her crossover collaborations with other Asian American YouTube stars including Chester See, Ryan Higa (who himself has over 11 million YouTube subscribers to his own channel), and the team behind Wong Fu Productions, with whom she has collaborated and starred in comedy video shorts.

Ultimately, Vietnamese Americans have been active in American film and media industries since the 1980s. Because the conventional roles offered to artists, filmmakers, and producers are limited and often required compromise, Vietnamese Americans have found inventive new ways to produce their own content and promote themselves, their work, and their communities by seeking alternate routes either in independent media or transnational contexts or via social media, thus circumventing dominant media industries that are difficult to break into. This broad range of activities reflects the adaptability and persistence in the United States of one of its most recent immigrant groups.

Anne Cong-Huyen

See also: Little Saigons; Vietnamese American Folklore; Vietnamese American Immigration; Vietnamese American Literature

Further Reading

Boudreau, John. "Decades after Fleeing, Vietnamese American Filmmakers Return Changed." *Mercury News,* November 24, 2012, http://www.mercurynews.com/ci _21965098/decades-after-fleeing-vietnamese-american-filmmakers-return -changed.

diaCritics: Covering the Arts, Culture and Politics of the Vietnamese at Home and in the Diaspora, http://diacritics.org/.

Diasporic Vietnamese Artists Network, http://www.dvanonline.com/.

Knibbs, Kate. "How Social Media Created and Destroyed Tila Tequila." Digital Trends, May 11, 2013, http://www.digitaltrends.com/social-media/how-social -media-created-and-destroyed-tila-tequila/.

Lieu, Nhi T. *The American Dream in Vietnamese.* Minneapolis: University of Minnesota Press, 2011.

VIETNAMESE AMERICAN FOLKLORE

Vietnamese American folklore comprises the origin myths, children's tales, heroic legends, oral histories, and other meaningful stories that express the history, identity, and relationships of Vietnamese in the United States. These stories are often retold among family members, in public festivals and events, and through literature and film. In some of the most popular of folklore, themes of separation, rebellion, honor, and sacrifice reveal the history of colonialism, war, exile, and resilience that the Vietnamese American community has experienced.

The Trung Sisters

The Trung sisters were born around 12 CE and died in 43 CE. Accounts of their existence appear in Fan Ye's *Book of the Later Han* (5th century) and Ngo Si Lien's *Complete Annals of Dai Viet* (15th century). While there is a dearth of historical information on the sisters, their presence in the imagination, oral histories, and cultural productions of Vietnamese Americans abound. According to legend, after years of brutal rule by the Chinese, the Trung sisters were able to build an army of 80,000 Vietnamese peasants to drive the colonizers out. After ruling for three years, wherein they continually battled against Chinese incursion, the Trung sisters were finally defeated. Some accounts maintained that the sisters drowned themselves, while other accounts declare that the sisters disappeared into the clouds rather than be captured. These differing accounts reflect the diversity of Vietnamese American oral tradition.

History and Origins

An early Vietnamese folklore narrates the origins of the Vietnamese people. According to a version of the story, the first ancestors of the Vietnamese people were the 100 sons of a dragon named Sung Lam or Lac Long Quan and a princess named Au Co. During his trip to the north to confront the king who has been pillaging Lac Long Quan's land to the south, the sea dragon meets Au Co. The two fall in love and get married. After their union, Au Co gives birth to 100 sons. After a time, Au Co and Lac Long Quan both separate, the former heading back to the mountains and the latter to the sea. They take with them 50 sons each. These sons are the original ancestors of the Vietnamese people. Among these sons is Hung Vuong, who is considered the king of the first ruling dynasty in Vietnam.

Like the emergence story of the Hung dynasty, historical figures have taken on mythic qualities in Vietnamese and Vietnamese American lore. These stories often have the purpose and effect of inspiring generations of Vietnamese and Vietnamese Americans to support particular political and social causes. Among the most popular are heroic figures such as the Trung sisters, Trieu Au, and Le Loi, who all throughout the course of Vietnamese history led rebellions against colonial powers. The Trung sisters, considered the first successful leaders of a revolt against China, ruled between 40 and 43 CE. According to a version of the legend, sisters Trung Trac and Trung Nhi led the charge against the Han dynasty after Trac's husband was murdered. The Trung sisters ruled for two to three years after liberating the 65 provinces of Vietnam from the Chinese. Upon their defeat in 43 CE, the Trung sisters retreated to Hat Giang, a river in which they committed suicide. Another story of rebellion against the corrupt rule of the Chinese centers on Trieu Au. In 248 CE, an unmarried orphan named Trieu Au is fabled to have led the rebellion on an elephant. Accounts of Trieu Au also depict her as having long breasts and wearing a yellow tunic or golden armor into battle. Like the Trung sisters, Trieu Au committed suicide after the Chinese overpowered the uprisings. Another military hero named Le Loi was successful in ending the rule of the Ming dynasty in 1428 CE. His dynasty subsequently ruled for over 300 years. In the folk story, a turtle god named Kim Qui provides Le Loi with a magical sword to lead the rebellion with the stipulation that Le Loi return the sword upon victory. The sword and the turtle are said to be located at the Hoan Kiem Lake in Hanoi. This story was retold in Ham Tram's 2007 film *Journey from the Fall* and worked to highlight aspects of the Viet Kieu experience.

Children's stories communicate the character and traditions of Vietnamese culture to the next generation. *Toad Sues Heaven* teaches children to respect and value the many creatures of the world and explains why toads croak before it rains. The folk story narrates how a toad was able to save the world from a long drought. On his trip to petition the king of heaven to bring rain to Earth, Toad enlists a crab, a tiger, a wasp, and a fox to help. When they get to the king's gates, Toad, with the aid of his cohorts, overcomes multiple attacks from the king's assistants and is finally given the respect and hearing that he demands. After fulfilling Toad's request, the king of heaven tells him to croak the next time he wants it to rain. Another folktale that explains natural phenomena is the story of Cuoi, a woodsman who finds a tree that is able to heal and bring people back from the dead. He takes the tree home with him and plants it. Heeding a warning from an elder about watering the tree with only pure water, Cuoi is able to use the tree to heal others in his village. One day Cuoi's wife forgets that the tree requires special watering and urinates on the ground near it. The tree gets uprooted and floats upward toward the sky. Upon seeing it flying up Cuoi grabs hold of the roots and is all the way to the moon. The story explains why the image of a man under a tree is marked on the moon. This story is often told during the Moon Festival (Tet Trung Thu). Translations of these and other stories have been published in recent years and provide a means to transmit the traditions to subsequent generations of Vietnamese Americans.

Contemporary Forms

Since the mass arrival of South Vietnamese refugees to the United States after the fall of Saigon in 1975, Vietnamese folklore has played a major part in Vietnamese American cultural life. Often, folk stories become reinterpreted in different forms and venues to reflect the experiences and concerns of the present community. The legendary figure of Kieu, for example, has been refashioned in order to address the complex role of women in expressing Vietnamese American identities and ties to homeland. Written by Vietnamese poet Nguyen Du in the early 1800s, *The Tale of Kieu* follows the tragic life of the eponymous legend as Kieu, in order to save her family from imprisonment, breaks her engagement to her first love and marries a man who owns a brothel. After escaping from her life as a prostitute and slave, Kieu finally reunites with and marries her first love in a celibate union. Kieu has often been glorified and allegorized as a female figure who dutifully sacrifices herself for the family and nation. Scholar Viet Nguyen argues that Le Ly Hayslip's autobiography *When Heaven and Earth Changed Places* parallels these themes of female sacrifice and duty. Scholar Lan Duong argues that Trinh T. Minh Ha's films *Tale of Love* (1995) and *Surname Viet, Given Name Nam* (1989) represent the differing interpretations and meanings of Kieu for Vietnamese and diasporic women. Other adaptations of this famous figure include Othello Khanh's 2007 film *Saigon Eclipse* and Vu Thu Ha's 2006 film *Kieu*. These recent films reveal how adaptations of Vietnamese myths, tales, and legends continue to express and shape Vietnamese American refugee experiences, resettlement, and transnational ties.

Quynh Nhu Le

See also: Vietnamese American Immigration; Vietnamese American Literature

Further Reading

Duong, Lan. *Treacherous Subjects: Gender, Culture, and Trans-Vietnamese Feminism.* Philadelphia: Temple University Press, 2012.

Garland, Sherry. *Children of the Dragon: Selected Tales from Vietnam.* Honolulu: University of Hawai'i Press, 2003.

Lee, Jonathan H. X., and Kathleen M. Nadeau, eds. *Encyclopedia of Asian American Folklore and Folklife.* Santa Barbara: ABC-CLIO, 2011.

Nguyen, Viet. *Race and Resistance: Literature and Politics in Asian America.* New York and Oxford: Oxford University Press, 2002.

Taylor, Keith. *The Birth of Vietnam.* Berkeley: University of California Press, 1983.

VIETNAMESE AMERICAN FOOD

Vietnamese American food has made such an impact on American culture that there are at least two food items—*bánh mì* (sandwiches) and *pho* (soup)—that can be described as culinary phenomena. Vietnamese American food as a whole derives from all parts of Vietnam. Viet-Am cuisine is generally seen as being northern or southern, with the term "central" being replaced by a particularly notable blend of noodles and sauces that is generally known by the old imperial capital of Hue. Some dishes are considered to epitomize Vietnamese national identity, such as *bánh xèo* (Vietnamese crepe or Vietnamese Pancake), which is not sweet but served with a variety of savory sauces. Claypot catfish, *cá kho,* is another example, along with *bò kho* and broken pot rice. Vietnamese immigrants are credited with introducing not only Vietnamese cuisine but also 20–30 different plants to the United States in an effort to keep certain recipes authentic. It is important not to separate the study of food from the understanding of Vietnamese culture. From the rice cakes to the best-known Vietnamese holiday, the lunar New Year Tet Nguyên Đán, food has played a central role in Vietnamese culture and has become a strong marker of Vietnamese identity in diaspora.

A number of scholars have studied the connection between food and Vietnamese identity. Nir Avieli (2005) invoked Benedict Anderson's concepts of constructing "imagined communities" to explain how the *bánh Tet* were part of constructing Vietnamese identity. His conception of the *bánh Tet* is linked to the notion of Vietnamese historical identity and the inevitable defeat of foreign powers. Avieli considers food, the *bánh Tet* in particular, as a means to preserve cultural traditions.

In the world of Vietnamese soups, *pho* is the one that has become popular in diaspora. There are a variety of soups in Vietnamese cuisine, including *canh chua* (sour soup) that requires *bac hà* (taro stem). My Liên T. Nguyen (2007) has demonstrated that the Vietnamese term *bac hà* actually shifted in meaning from northern Vietnam, where the term refers to a culinary mint, to southern Vietnam, where the term refers to either *Alocasia odora* or *C. gigantea*. Furthermore, Nguyen argues that this plant is generally not only not a "taro" (Caloscasia esculenta) but also that the parts used in *canh chua* are actually the petioles of the plant. Regardless, it is the southern version of *canh chua* soup, *canh chua cá lóc* (sour snakehead-mullet fish soup), that is the most popular and symbolic of southern Vietnamese cuisine, providing a "balance of sourness, sweetness, spiciness and texture" (Nguyen 2005, 187). The plant *bac hà* was once not even in existence in the United States but is now cultivated in Hawai'i and available throughout the country.

Through further research into the *canh chua cá lóc* cuisine in a comparative framework, Nguyen demonstrated that recipes in the United States and Vietnam are not the same, even though the food was present in 14 out of 15 cookbooks in the United States. Alternatives to sour soup have been sold to accommodate American palates, including Vietnamese fisherman's soup, sweet and sour soup, and hot and sour soup, although all of them use essentially *canh chua* recipes. Some of the recipes have a northern flare, including dill (*Anethum graveolens*), and a southern flare, including certain flowers (*Sesbania grandiflora*). Certain ingredients widely available in Vietnam are replaced by other ingredients available in the United States. Another plant that the Vietnamese community introduced to the United States is the *Limnophila chinensis*, which is ever present in Vietnamese recipes but much less common in the United States. It is one of the species that have been introduced to the United States by the Vietnamese community through the so-called market-garden tradition, a tradition that was carried to Hawai'i, California, New Orleans, and northern Virginia. The introduction of Vietnamese American cuisine in the United States brought new tastes, new flavors, and new species to the United States. Vietnamese recipes are adapted, and new flavors are sold to American markets. It appears that Vietnamese American food is enjoying an ever-increasing era of popularity.

William Brokaw Noseworthy

See also: *Pho;* Vietnamese American Community Organizations; Vietnamese American Immigration; Vietnamese American Literature

Further Reading

Avieli, Nir. "Vietnamese New Year Rice Cakes: Iconic Festive Dishes and Contested National Identity." *Ethnology* 44(2) (2005): 167–187.

Nguyen, My Liên T. "Bac Hà (Colocasia giantea [Blume] Hook. F.) in the Culinary History of Vietnamese-Americans." *Economic Botany* 59(2) (2005): 185–190.

Nguyen, My Liên T. "Community Dynamics and Functional Stability: A Recipe for Cultural Adaptation and Continuity." *Economic Botany* 61(4) (2007): 337–346.

Phillips, Delores B. "Quieting Noisy Bellies: Moving, Eating and Being in the Vietnamese Diaspora." *Cultural Critique* 73 (2009): 47–87.

Wood, Joseph. "Vietnamese American Place Making in Northern Virginia." *Geographical Review* 87(1) (1997): 58–72.

VIETNAMESE AMERICAN IMMIGRATION

Beger and Hein (2001) highlight the most problematic aspect of Vietnamese American immigration in a study of legal cases that they attempted to complete, arguing that the surname "Nguyen" could be used as a common unique marker of Vietnamese identity. There are over 50 ethnic groups from Vietnam who speak Vietnamese. There is no set definition of what "being Vietnamese" means. Even though there are nearly 2 million Vietnamese heritage residents in the United States, Vietnamese Americans are underrepresented in scholarly studies.

History and Origins

It is likely that the first Vietnamese immigrants came to the United States in the late 19th to early 20th centuries. However, both popular perceptions and scholarly studies usually associate Vietnamese American immigrants with Cold War refugees. Đức Đo Hien has pointed out the complexity of the terminology (1996, 61). Immigrants are viewed as having a hand in the decision, while refugees are seen as being forced. Scholarly and popular sources saw Vietnamese immigrants, particularly those arriving in the 1970s, as "representatives of an alien culture and race" (Montero 1979, 625), despite the longer history of Vietnamese relations with the United States. Montero noted that official U.S. reports included five waves of Vietnamese immigration in the 1970s. However, today most scholars agree Vietnamese American immigrations came in at least three waves: first, between 1955 and 1975 before reunification 18,000 individuals, most of whom were wives, students, and academics; second, between 1975

The Vietnam War

The name "Vietnam War" usually refers to the war in Vietnam from 1955 to 1975. However, "Vietnam Wars" may be a better way to describe the process of decolonization in the former colony of Indochina (Vietnam, Cambodia, and Laos), which began with the Vietnamese declaration of independence in 1945 and ended with the fall of Saigon and the collapse of the Republic of Vietnam (South Vietnam) in 1975. The war was exacerbated by American involvement and by the greater context of the Cold War as well as by the American refusal to sign the Geneva Accords in 1954. The conflict involved American, Vietnamese, French, South Korean, Canadian, Australian, Japanese, Cambodian, Philippine, Thai, Lao, and minority forces and personnel mobilized throughout Southeast Asia. Many historians believe that the factors of American exceptionalism and racist preferences for white American lives as well as a false perception that simply eliminating the communist North Vietnamese as a people would lead to a victory resulted in the opposite. The North Vietnamese succeeded in overtaking Saigon and South Vietnam and reunifying the country under communist rule. And there were huge losses: an estimated 225,000 South Vietnamese troops died. An estimate from the Vietnam government in 1993 gave the figure of 1.1 million North Vietnamese military members' deaths. Among civilians, at least 250,000 died. According to the U.S. Archives, Americans lost more than 58,000 U.S. troops who died or were reported missing in action. In addition, other nationalities involved also suffered heavy losses, including Cambodians and Laotians and service members from other countries. Countless villages were destroyed. Twelve million tons of toxic defoliants were dropped, and the destabilization of the region has been linked to ongoing conflicts that persisted in Laos, the genocide in Cambodia, and political instability in Thailand.

and 1993 from reunification to the open-door policy in Vietnam; and third, since the open-door policy in 1993. The largest number of immigrants, around 125,000, came to the United States after the fall of Saigon in 1975; from 1979 to 1982 the number was around 270,000. Each wave of migration has different characteristics associated with it. Earlier waves were generally associated with attempting to make a better life and gain access to education before decolonization created massive forced relocations. Forty percent of the 1975 first wave was Catholic, and 20 percent had university education. The so-called boat people were the second wave, comprising mostly war refugees, and were mostly Viet Hoa, or Chinese Vietnamese. Later migrations may be viewed as economic diasporas created by an imbalance in the global economy.

Boat People

The term "boat people" generally refers to refugees who moved from Vietnam to other countries in Southeast Asia and the United States during the late 1970s and early 1980s. The image comes from the construction of small wooden boats that were used for the initial stretch of migration. The boats were incredibly dangerous, and the waters that they initially sailed through were plagued by pirates. However, the term in Vietnamese is broader, referring to southern Chinese migrations to the Mekong Delta region during the 18th and 19th centuries. Families in the United States may simply identify themselves as "boat people" in English for simplicity's sake, although they may only belong to one or both of the boat people communities, and the distinction is complicated by the large presence of Viet Hoa (Chinese Vietnamese) among the refugees in the late 1970s and early 1980s.

In light of the Vietnam War (1945–1975), major immigration centers were opened in Texas, California, Florida, Virginia, Pennsylvania, Louisiana, and Washington. These centers served not only Vietnamese immigrants but also Southeast Asian American communities at large. Nevertheless, Vietnamese immigrants outnumber almost all other Southeast Asians. Furthermore, the depictions of initial camp life and eventual resettlement into particular urban centers created many negative perceptions regarding the Vietnamese. The camps were in Thailand, the Philippines, Hong Kong, and Malaysia. The common prejudices against Vietnamese immigrants view them as pathetic, downtrodden, immobile, and incapable. Meanwhile, the places where Vietnamese relocated were also seen as having particular characteristics that favored the Vietnamese community. These characteristics could be surface level and relatively noncomplex, such as a warmer climate, or more complex and realistic, such as job and economic opportunities as well as social and psychological support. Communities began to spring up around the industries that they supported. Shrimp farmers became particularly well known in Galveston and other parts of Texas, while meat packers became popular in parts of Kansas. Uptown Chicago became a business hub, as did Bella Vista in Philadelphia and the Washington, D.C., suburbs of northern Virginia. These suburbs were attractive mostly for their economic prospects.

Many of the demographic studies have pointed out the number of Buddhists versus Catholics. Following the Vietnam War, Vietnamese immigrants were predominantly Catholic. There was less consideration of any other forms of

Father Vien The Nguyen (third from left), with volunteers during a luncheon served after Mass at Mary Queen of Vietnam Catholic Church in New Orleans, Louisiana, November 1, 2005. Vietnamese immigrants began to arrive in New Orleans in large numbers in the 1970s; many are Catholics. (AP Photo/Robert F. Bukaty)

Vietnamese religion (for example, Cao Dai'ism, Hoa Hao Buddhism, Theravada Buddhism, and Mahayana Buddhism). One of the most well-known Catholic neighborhoods was Versailles in New Orleans, a neighborhood that was devastated by Hurricane Katrina in 2005. Although American unemployment is low by global comparison, the attitude of American exceptionalism has been used to create prejudice against Vietnamese immigrants. Hence, in the late 1970s and early 1980s when unemployment hit a high of 9 percent (high by American standards), this was used to argue against immigration. However, Vietnamese scholars have played their own critical roles in changing the impressions of Vietnamese American communities and promoting a better understanding of Vietnamese American experience.

Initially, Vietnamese immigrant communities were characterized by disproportionately low employment of women. This trend inverted by the 1980s, since women were more widely employable in low-skill sectors. Shifts in the gender balances that many families considered traditional led to higher rates of abuse, child neglect, and divorce in some cases; in other cases Vietnamese immigrants strengthened their families and adapted to the new value sets that were not necessarily in line with traditional Vietnamese ideas about gender roles.

The 1.5 and second generations of Vietnamese Americans are generally confronted with a new set of challenges. Initially, the Vietnamese immigrant community was characterized by disproportionately low levels of English-language skills, although this trend later began to reverse. For example, in March 1976, 65 percent of Vietnamese immigrants spoke virtually no English one year after leaving Vietnam. While this did not impact employment rates, it did shift the nature of work for many professionals. Furthermore, Vietnamese experienced initial severe discrimination in the job market. Skills could not be transferred across the linguistic and cultural barriers. Blatant prejudice was a factor in barring employment or removing employment statuses for certain individuals. Nevertheless, civil rights litigation appeared much later among the Vietnamese community when compared to other forms of litigation, such as domestic and business complaints. Across economic sectors, former military personnel were left chronically unemployed. Nevertheless, the median income of households was equivalent to that of the broader U.S. population by 1984, and seeking an education was almost always an initial indicator of attempts at greater employment and a reason frequently given for an unemployed status as of 1979.

Contemporary Forms

The drive of Vietnamese to "seek an education" combined with the concept of *tran can cu,* which "combines hard work, patience and tenacity into a relentless drive to survive or be successful," were likely a major factor in the shift toward the recognition of the Vietnamese as the newest "model minority" (Espiritu 2006, 415). However, some scholars have argued that the Vietnamese were explicitly *not* a model minority, since the Vietnamese communities faced problems of gangs, drugs, gambling, and abuse, just as with other communities. Unfortunately, this concept was used to create tensions between the Vietnamese and other long-standing minority communities in the United States. Nevertheless, individuals in all communities fought back against these trends throughout the 1980s and the 1990s. Yen Le Espiritu invokes Linda Trinh Vo to suggest that the incorporation of studies on the Vietnamese into Asian American studies as an academic subject was still underrepresented. It was revealed that the model minority status was a myth, simply used to deny minority status to Asian Americans while being simultaneously capitalized upon in order to demonstrate that the Vietnam War was still a good war in the American mind-set, since the model minority of the Vietnamese was generally seen to be politically conservative, successful, and anticommunist. Yen Le Espiritu is careful to highlight that these new presumptions about the Vietnamese American immigrant community emerged not only out of American constructions but also out of Vietnamese attempts to articulate themselves within those constructions.

William Brokaw Noseworthy

See also: Little Saigons; Vietnamese American Community Organizations; Vietnamese American Women

Further Reading

Beger, Randall R., and Jeremy Hein. "Legal Adaptation among Vietnamese Refugees in the United States: How International Migrants Litigate Civil Grievances during the Resettlement Process." *International Migration Review* 35(2) (2001): 420–448.

Espiritu, Yen Le. "Toward a Critical Refugee Study: The Vietnamese Refugee Subject in US Scholarship." *Journal of Vietnamese Studies* 1(1–2) (2006): 410–433.

Hien, Đuc Đo. "The New Migrants from Asia: Vietnamese in the United States." *OAH Magazine of History* 10(4) (1996): 61–66.

Montero, Darrel. "Vietnamese Refugees in America: Toward a Theory of Spontaneous International Migration." *International Migration Review* 13(4) (1979): 624–648.

Wood, Joseph. "Vietnamese American Place Making in Northern Virginia." *Geographical Review* 87(1) (1997): 58–72.

VIETNAMESE AMERICAN LITERATURE

History and Origins

Coming out of a relatively short span of roughly 40 years, dating from the first major influx of Vietnamese immigrants and refugees to the present, Vietnamese American literature encompasses a wide variety of genres, styles, and forms addressing the diverse communities that make up Vietnamese populations in the diaspora. The authors and the narratives they produce are increasingly varied as they reflect the range of experiences and perspectives that make up the Vietnamese American experience. Although the presence of Vietnamese in the United States is generally attributed to mass migrations following the withdrawal of American troops from the conflict in Vietnam and the fall of Saigon on April 30, 1975, the earliest English-language texts by Vietnamese Americans date between 1962 and 1965.

A good deal of Vietnamese American literature was produced by the first wave of Vietnamese immigrants to the United States following the fall of Saigon in 1975, when the United States saw a massive influx of Vietnamese immigrants and refugees fleeing the communist regime of the newly unified Vietnam. The first wave of such immigrants included about 130,000 Vietnamese who were

Lan Cao (1961–)

Lan Cao is professor of law at Chapman University's Dale E. Fowler School of Law. Cao's novel *Monkey Bridge* (1997) has become a canonical text of Vietnamese American literature and is widely taught in high schools and university courses. The novel traces the story of Mai Nguyen, a 1.5-generation Vietnamese American teenager, and her mother, a Vietnamese refugee who is hospitalized for a stroke. The novel functions as part bildungsroman, following Mai as she copes with her new life in the United States. Much of the novel's conflict for the protagonist revolves around the dangers of mediation: war films that reimagine the war, news footage that remediates the fall of Saigon, oral narratives of the war, and unreliable memories. Unlike many American immigrant narratives, Mai and her mother's story are burdened with traumas of war and forced displacement, and the characters' struggle to make sense of their pasts and the ordeal of recovery and adapting to a new and alien home while still fighting to make sense of a familial and national history shrouded in violence and uncertainty.

The title draws upon the image of skinny bamboo bridges that span rivers and creeks in rural Vietnam and represents the sometimes perilous undertaking of traversing between different shores, time periods, memories, and relationships. The novel functions as a refugee resettlement narrative, a war story, and a mother-daughter drama. Reflective of the aftermath of the Vietnam War, the narrative incorporates various rhetorical devices to reveal the difficulty of recuperating from the trauma of war: flashbacks, history, pop culture references, and changing points of view, among others. The complexity of the novel therefore makes it an ideal text for narrative analysis and historical study.

---

airlifted out of Vietnam. After this initial wave, between 1976 and 1982 there occurred a second wave of migration, a mass exodus of an estimated 2 million people, including ethnic Chinese, who fled Vietnam as "boat people." These refugees were scattered across the United States, even though Vietnamese Americans would later congregate in southern California, Louisiana, and Texas.

The Vietnamese immigrants brought with them the long literary traditions of Vietnam, but more important, the literature affiliated with this era of Vietnamese American writers is characterized by the perspective of a displaced people living in exile, nostalgic for their homeland. Many texts acted as testimonials of the Vietnamese conflict and denounced the communist regime from the perspective of the witness. Others were heavily invested in Vietnamese politics and in remembering a homeland that was lost. The early Vietnamese American authors had difficulty finding American publishers, and much of the

Le Ly Hayslip (1949–)

Perhaps one of the most controversial figures in Vietnamese American culture, Le Ly Hayslip is an author, a businesswoman, and a humanitarian. She is most notable for her post–Vietnam War memoirs *When Heaven and Earth Changed Places: A Vietnamese Woman's Journey from War to Peace* (1989), coauthored with Jay Wurts, and *Child of War, Woman of Peace* (1993), coauthored with her son James Hayslip, both of which were adapted by Oliver Stone into the film *Heaven & Earth* (1993) as the final installment of his Vietnam War trilogy.

Hayslip's books chronicle a somewhat idyllic early life in rural Vietnam and then her collaborations with the local Viet Cong, the traumas of wartime imprisonment, sexual violence, ostracism, and the difficulties of immigration and exile. Over the course of her two memoirs, Hayslip positions her female body as being the site of violence and offers herself as a bridge to reconciliation between the United States and Vietnam. Literary scholars have debated the problematics of such a portrayal and the implications for national as well as racial and gender politics.

Hayslip's language of reconciliation coincides with her early advocacy for normalization of U.S. relations with Vietnam, which angered and sparked protests by Vietnamese Americans. This community vocally objected to her representation of the Vietnamese, particularly her cultural power as the most recognizable voice of Vietnamese Americans, a voice that they felt did not adequately represent the experience of most Vietnamese in America who came to the United States as refugees and who opposed the socialist regime. Many challenged the fact that Hayslip, who came to the United States before the end of the war via marriage, had the right to speak for them. They also argued that her political actions equaled support for the communist regime and was tantamount to forgiveness for North Vietnamese war crimes. Mainstream American audiences, however, largely celebrated her bravery and survival instinct and applauded her transnational humanitarian efforts.

---

literature in this period was written in Vietnamese for Vietnamese American communities who shared similar political views as refugees hailing primarily from South Vietnam. As a result, a robust Vietnamese American literary scene emerged with Vietnamese-language literary magazines, journals, and presses.

By the mid-1980s, English-language Vietnamese American literature was being published by American publishers. To the chagrin of the majority anticommunist Vietnamese American community, these texts frequently reflected the perspective of North Vietnamese rather than that of South Vietnamese allies. These early texts would prime the literary scene for Vietnamese American authors to come with later generations, including the 1.5 generation who re-member Vietnam from childhood memories and second-generation Vietnam-ese American children who write about experiences growing up in the United States with no recollection of Vietnam. Today, the population of ethnic Viet-namese in the United States numbers roughly 1.7 million people of diverse backgrounds across the United States. The literature likewise is increasingly varied and experimental, often garnering much critical acclaim.

Regional Practices and Traditions

Vietnamese American literature spans many different heterogeneous forms and genres, ranging from poetry to prose and including nonfiction memoirs, autobiographies, travelogues, scholarship, and fiction. Many of these corre-spond with specific stages in the short history of Vietnamese Americans in the United States.

The earliest Vietnamese American literature is considered sojourner literature rather than immigrant or refugee literature, as later generations would be. These texts include the personal essay "Electioneering Vietnamese Style" (1962) by Nguyen Thi Tuyet Mai and the novel *No Passenger on the River* (1965) by Tran Van Dinh, both working as students in the United States. Tuyet Mai and Dinh viewed themselves as temporary sojourners who would return to Vietnam; thus, they wrote as Vietnamese visitors in America, and their essays and novels served to educate American audiences about Vietnamese politics, history, and culture in order to bring to light corrupt political contexts of the South Vietnamese regime, at the time bolstered by the United States. For example, Tuyet Mai's essay draws on personal experience to expose the corrupt politics of South Vietnam, and Dinh's *No Passenger on the River*, published the same year American marines would arrive in Vietnam, offers a Vietnamese perspective in critiquing the corruption, brutality, and mismanagement of South Vietnamese president Ngo Dinh Diem's government, thus revealing the flawed basis of U.S. involvement in the civil conflict. Foreshadowing later Vietnamese American texts, these two precursors were thematically focused on critiquing government corruption, disappointment with existing political structures, and conflict between strong patriotism and critique, all themes that would reemerge in later texts.

The subsequent phase of Vietnamese American literature surfaced after the settlement of new Vietnamese refugees after 1975. This literary period saw Vietnamese Americans carving out their own primarily Vietnamese-language cultural enclave when American publishers showed little interest in Vietnamese American textual production. This context allowed for the development of literary magazines, journals, and newspapers. The most notable of these include

Van Hoc Nghe Thuat (Art and Literature), *Van Hoc* (Literary Studies), and *Nhan Chung* (Witness), among others. Like the texts that preceded them in the 1960s, these publications were dedicated to politics in the home nation of Vietnam and can be characterized as exilic texts that long for a lost homeland and past, feelings of marginalization and displacement in the host nation, and confusion ranging from anger, appreciation, resentment, and disappointment toward Americans.

It was not until the mid-1980s that American publishing firms took notice of and began to release English-language texts by Vietnamese Americans, some written in collaboration with white Americans. Texts from this period were often memoirs and operated under an imperative to recount their firsthand stories to educate American audiences, explain what occurred in Vietnam, and offer themselves up as examples of immigrants and refugees who wanted understanding and acceptance. Although the majority of Vietnamese Americans hailed from South Vietnam and authors from this community were heavily invested in the politics and human rights abuses of the new Vietnamese government, mainstream American publishers showed little interest in these texts. Instead, the books that garnered attention tended to reflect upon the experience of the Vietnam War from the perspective of North Vietnamese enemies. Paradigmatic texts of this period include *A Vietcong Memoir* (1985) by Truong Nhu Thang; *When Heaven and Earth Changed Places* (1989) by Le Ly Hayslip in collaboration with Jay Wurts, which would later be adapted to film by Oliver Stone; and the lesser-known *Fallen Leaves* (1989) by Nguyen Thi Thu-Lam. Of these, Hayslip's *When Heaven and Earth Changed Places,* along with her later book *Child of War, Woman of Peace* (1993), is the most well known. It is also the most controversial and drew the most ire from the Vietnamese American community, including scholars. Her linear biography is indicative of much Vietnamese American literature in its didactic tone and argues for reconciliation, here accomplished through a personal narrative that traces her early life in rural central Vietnam to her resettlement in the United States. It has been read as a nationalist argument for reconciliation and normalization that plays out upon her multiply victimized female body. *Fallen Leaves,* on the other hand, revolves around feelings of yearning for a lost home while offering harsh critiques of both communism and hardships encountered in the United States, thematic concerns that proliferate in much of the Vietnamese American literature of this period.

In 1995 the United States normalized relations with Vietnam, lifting a decades-long embargo and marking an important phase in Vietnamese American culture. This period saw a surge of Vietnamese American memoirs, starting with Jade Ngoc Quang Huynh's *South Wind Changing* (1994), Nguyen

Qui Duc's *Where the Ashes Are: The Odyssey of a Family* (1997), and Andrew X. Pham's *Catfish and Mandala: A Two-Wheeled Voyage through the Landscape and Memory of Vietnam* (1999), which offer personal narratives that track an individual's experience in Vietnam, immigration to the United States, and resettlement without concentrating heavily on military conflicts. Often this personal narrative is related to that of the larger family. The emphasis in these texts was on events immediately following the war, especially the hardships faced in reeducation labor camps and refugee camps, the difficulty of carving out a life after immigrating, and the desire to return to the familiar Vietnam. Throughout, a struggle materializes between feelings of hope for the future, grief, regret, and nostalgia and the difficulty of balancing individual desires with the expectations of family.

These concerns—of homeland, migration, resettlement, and homecoming—have remained prominent themes in Vietnamese American literature, even being used as organizing principles in anthologies such as *The Other Side of Heaven: Post-War Fiction by Vietnamese and American Writers* (1995), edited by Wayne Karlin and Le Minh Khue. Subsequent phases of Vietnamese American literary production, coming from 1.5- and second-generation immigrants, would transition from these dominant themes toward the concerns of those growing up Asian American and reflect a different consideration for literary style and aesthetic with less emphasis on the war and its aftermath.

Contemporary Forms

Contemporary Vietnamese American literature diverges from the more recognizable mainstream texts of the 1980s and 1990s in several notable ways. Rather than fixing upon the colonial, wartime, or even postwar periods that have been the preoccupation of Vietnamese American texts, today's literature authored primarily by the 1.5- and second-generation writers tends to be concerned with racialized experience in the United States. More emotionally detached from Vietnam as homeland in a way distinct from early writers, exemplary texts including li thi diem thuy's *The Gangster We Are All Looking For* (2003), Aimee Phan's *We Should Never Meet* (2004), and Lac Su's *I Love Yous Are for White People* (2009), among many others, are frank in representing the struggles of Vietnamese Americans within a hostile and racist American culture. Authors such as Lan Cao, in *Monkey Bridge* (1997), intricately weave hazy fictionalized events of war-torn Vietnam with a gloomy American present fraught with economic, social, and cultural traumas brought on by immigration and the violence of language and unreliable memory. Authors such as Linh Dinh, in his novel *Love Like Hate* (2010), satirically critique the American-Vietnamese relationship after normalization. Dinh importantly deconstructs the American Dream, highlighting an emasculated Vietnamese American male subject opposite a cosmopolitan sexualized Vietnamese female. Dinh's novel, like the texts of Lac Su, reveals the economic and social reality for many Vietnamese Americans who do not neatly fit the myth of the model minority and seek to use their privilege as Viet Kieu (overseas Vietnamese) to return to Vietnam in search of validation through participation in the transnational economies of marriage.

The novelist to have received the most critical acclaim is Monique Truong, whose debut novel *The Book of Salt* (2003) won the PEN/Robert Bingham W. Prize, among others, in 2004. Unique among Vietnamese American fiction, Truong's book is completely removed from the Vietnam War and is set in France between the two world wars. The novel was inspired by *The Alice B. Toklas Cook Book* (1954), by the longtime partner of Gertrude Stein, wherein Toklas references employing two "Indo-Chinese" male cooks while the pair lived in France. Truong brought one such anonymous Indo-Chinese man to life in the fictional character of Binh, a homosexual man who leaves French colonial Vietnam under mysterious circumstances. The novel's delicate exploration of exile, belonging, gender, and sexuality through larger motifs of food and service labor was well received and established Truong as one of the most inventive and skillful Vietnamese American novelists.

Another literary genre of note is Vietnamese American poetry. Linh Dinh, despite the publication of one novel, is known primarily as a poet and translator of Vietnamese poetry. Taking part in a long tradition of Vietnamese poetry, he joins poets such as Nguyen Do in translating Vietnamese poetry for English-speaking audiences while also publishing his own innovative work. Dinh, along with a new generation of young poets, has pushed the boundaries of what is typically expected for Asian American poetry. Rather than adhering to styles and themes associated with ethnic literatures that focus on ethnic experience in the United States, his poetry takes on broader topics, and his verse is contemporary, darkly humorous, and often ridiculous or grotesque. In recent years, there has also been a rise in politically active spoken word performers and slam poets including Bao Phi, Sahra Vang Nguyen, and Fong Tran, who have actively resisted stereotypes of Asian Americans as meek and submissive model minorities.

In 2011, Vietnamese American literature experienced one of its more radical formal shifts with the publication of *Vietnamerica: A Family's Journey* by G. B. Tran. *Vietnamerica* is the first notable graphic novel by a Vietnamese American. It chronicles the story of his family in Vietnam, their flight and resettlement in the United States, and his own personal narrative as a second-generation Vietnamese American returning to Vietnam. The novel made innovative use of both narrative structure and visual devices and went on to critical acclaim, also receiving numerous nominations and awards. As with many instances of Vietnamese American literature, Tran's work of combining American forms of pop culture and art with the diverse thematic concerns of immigrant and refugee Americans provides one example of the many original and hybrid forms of literary production undertaken by Vietnamese Americans.

Anne Cong-Huyen

See also: Vietnamese American Films and Filmmakers; Vietnamese American Folklore; Vietnamese American Immigration

Further Reading

Karlin, Wayne, Le Minh Khue, and Truong Vu, eds. *The Other Side of Heaven: Post-War Fiction by Vietnamese and American Writers.* Willimantic, CT: Curbstone, 1995.

Leong, Russell C., Brandy Lien Worrall, Yen Le Espiritu, and Nguyen Vo Thu-Huong, eds. *"30 Years AfterWARd": Vietnamese Americans and US Empire.* Special issue of *Amerasia Journal* 31(2) (2005).

Michele, Janette. *My Viet: Vietnamese American Literature in English, 1962–Present.* Honolulu: University of Hawai'i Press, 2011.

Thuy Pelaud, Isabelle. *This Is All I Choose to Tell: History and Hybridity in Vietnamese American Literature.* Philadelphia: Temple University Press, 2011.

Tran, Barbara, Monique Truong, and Khoi Truong. *Watermark: Vietnamese American Poetry and Prose.* New York: Asian American Writer's Workshop, 1997.

Truong, Monique. "The Emergence of Voices: Vietnamese American Literature 1975–1990." *Amerasia Jorunal* 19(3) (1993): 27–50.

VIETNAMESE AMERICAN RELIGIONS AND BELIEFS

Given the complexity of Vietnamese ethnicity and the Vietnamese-speaking community, Vietnamese American religions and beliefs encompass a broad range of faiths, including not only Catholicism and Protestantism but also the nativist Vietnamese conceptions of *tâm giáo* (three paths) in which Confucianism, Daoism, and Buddhism are the pillars of a traditional Vietnamese religious life. In addition, there are many Muslims who were originally of Vietnamese nationality but ethnic Austronesian Cham ancestry or Malay ancestry and were relocated to the United States. There are also large numbers of highland peoples, particularly linked to the United Front for the Liberation of Oppressed Races movement, who moved to the United States and may advocate specifically for their own form of religion. This is generally viewed as Dega Protestantism by American Protestants. Furthermore, the trend toward transnational socially engaged Buddhism in the wake of decolonization began to blur the doctrinal lines between Theravadin (mostly ethnic Khmers formerly living in what is now Vietnam) and Mahayana (mostly ethnic Vietnamese) monks who were living in diaspora. Among these monastics, the most notable among them in the United States is Thích Nhat Hanh, although a whole range of Vietnamese monastics were part of the new construction of Vietnamese American religious identity and belief practices.

Catholicism

Vietnamese Catholicism began as an extension of the French Foreign Missions in the 17th century. Even though there were always tensions between Vietnamese royalty and the Catholic parishes, the Catholic population grew. In 1954 there was a mass migration of 1 million North Vietnamese families to the south. It is estimated that between 600,000 and 800,000 individuals were Catholic. Unfortunately for Catholics, the preferential treatment that they received under the Ngo Dinh Diem regime translated into seeming extra repression at the hands of communist leaders. Former archbishop of Saigon Francis Xavier Nguyen Van Thuan spent years in prison from 1975 to 1988 before he fled to the United States. Although Catholics were only 6–8 percent of the population in Vietnam, they made up 25–33 percent of the refugees from Vietnam to the United States in the 1980s. Catholics remained roughly 25 percent of the Vietnamese American population throughout the 1990s, and by the 2000s they made up approximately 30 percent of the Vietnamese American population.

If religion tends to be a factor that causes some communal strife in Vietnam, it remained such a factor in the United States. Catholics nonetheless continued to bond together and found their own social organizations. The National Pastoral Center for the Vietnamese Apostolate in Baton Rouge, Louisiana, and the Federation of Vietnamese Catholics in Philadelphia, Pennsylvania, are examples of such. These overarching organizations serve as a means to support small individual parishes; as Carl Bankston had observed, the major logic behind preserving separate parishes for the Vietnamese was the maintenance of the Vietnamese language. Hence, the parish became a source of Vietnamese communal involvement, contrasting with the perception of the church in Vietnam. Part of the movement toward social organizations was encouraged by family ties. In the community of Versailles, the ties could be traced mostly through two southern Vietnamese settlements, Vung Tau and Phúc Tĩnh, which in turn had been populated by Catholics really only after 1954 migrations from a single North Vietnamese settlement, Bui Chu. These familial ties

Thuong Dinh being baptized by Monsignor Joseph Trinh at Saint Helena Catholic Church in Philadelphia, Pennsylvania, April 4, 2015. Vietnamese Catholicism can be traced back to the 17th century as an extension of the French Foreign Missions. Catholics make up more than a quarter of the Vietnamese American population in the 2000s. (AP Photo/Matt Rourke)

were likely a factor in the centrality of social activism among the community in Versailles. The Dung Lac organization countered the trend of high school dropouts and incorporated youths into community service projects. This was also the case in other major Vietnamese Catholic communities: Little Saigon and San Jose in California; Houston, Dallas–Fort Worth, and Port Arthur in Texas; and Virginia and Washington, D.C. Even outside of these communities, Vietnamese Catholics have generally continued to worship in Catholic parishes. Other Catholic organizations included the Congregation of Mary Co-Redpemptrix (Dong Dong Cong) of Carthage, Missouri, and 20 religious organizations specifically for women, including the Dong Men Thanh Gia (Lovers of the Cross), an organization dating back to 17th-century Vietnam and having maintained links between the diaspora and overseas Catholics. Among these communities, Vietnamese-language papers remained prominent into the 2000s, and celebrations not only included Catholic occasions but also the Vietnamese lunar New Year Tet Nguyên Đán, the fall of Saigon (April 30), and feast of the martyrs of Vietnam (November 24). The social organization became critical in the movement of Vietnamese to rebuild their community in light of the Hurricane Katrina disaster.

Scholars have noted that the model minority myth was used as a major means of explaining the rapid rebuilding of the "Village Called Versailles" after Hurricane Katrina. They argued that this myth was constructed in the 1950s and 1960s in order to explain certain presumptions about various minority communities in the United States. However, seeming to contrast with the views that American society had changed communal activism, Father The Vien Nguyên cited the Catholic tradition as a pillar of society as the major means for the rapid recovery of the Versaille community. Regardless, Airriess, Chen, Keith, Leong, and Li (2007) concluded that even though the model minority was a myth, Catholic communal activism in the case of Versailles was indeed a model of how historical memory could be employed in order to benefit communal structures. This did not, however, mean that there was universal equality that emerged for the Catholic minority. The hire of a Vietnamese American still comes across as a token employment strategy rather than actual real communal equality ensured for Vietnamese Catholics in New Orleans.

Buddhists

Given the diversity of Vietnamese American religion, it seems fair to say that a disproportionate amount of press has focused on Vietnamese American Catholicism when compared to the Buddhist majority. One reason for this is that Buddhist organizations stemming from the 1950s and 1960s, not just in Vietnam but across the world, have tended to form more and more transnational associations of their notions of the *sangha* in order to support ideas of Pan-Asian identity in the process of decolonization and formally international identity in the postcolonial environment. So, even though it could be said that Vietnamese Buddhists are just as likely to support preserving Vietnamese language and culture, the internationalist approach has impacted scholarly and popular visions of Vietnamese American Buddhism. The Mahayana strain of Buddhism makes up 25 percent of American Buddhist organizations, although Vietnamese make up 13.4 percent of American Buddhists. For this reason, one could expect that there would be a trend of assimilation of Vietnamese into the larger Japanese American Buddhist community in certain locations. Nevertheless, given the focus on Japanese American Buddhism, it is safe to say that Vietnamese American Buddhism remains relatively understudied as an academic subject. There are 160 Vietnamese Buddhist organizations in all of North America according to a 2001 survey, making the Vietnamese Buddhist community one of the most widespread on the continent, more so than all Theravada and Chinese Buddhist communities.

William Brokaw Noseworthy

See also: Buddhism; Theravada Buddhism; Vietnamese American Community Organizations; Vietnamese American Immigration; Vietnamese American Literature

Further Reading

Airriess, Christopher A., Angela Chia-Chen Chen, Verna M. Keith, Karen J. Leong, and Wei Li. "Resilient History and the Rebuilding of a Community: The Vietnamese American Community in New Orleans East." *Journal of American History* 94(3) (2007): 770–779.

Bankston, Carl L. "Vietnamese-American Catholicism: Transplanted and Flourishing." *U.S. Catholic Historian* 18(1) (2000): 36–53.

Gregory, Peter N. "Describing the Elephant: Buddhism in America." *Religion and American Culture: A Journal of Interpretation* 11(2) (2001): 233–263.

Phan, Peter C. "Vietnamese Catholics in the United States: Christian Identity between the Old and the New." *U.S. Catholic Historian* 18(1) (2000): 19–35.

Smith, Buster G. "Variety in the Sangha: A Survey of Buddhist Organizations in America." *Review of Religious Research* 48(3) (2007): 308–317.

VIETNAMESE AMERICAN WOMEN

Vietnamese American women and feminism, an identity heavily rooted in Confucianism, exists as a sociohistorical group that had a voice before the introduction of Western feminism or First World feminism. Under Confucian ideals, a "good" Vietnamese woman abides by the *three* obediences: she must obey her father as a daughter, her husband as a wife, and finally her son as a widow. The gender code dictates that women's responsibilities are that of the home—the domestic sphere—under the supervision of men. She also exemplifies the four virtues: diligent work, appearance, proper speech, and morality. The obligations for a virtuous woman require the mastering of domesticated labor (cooking, sewing, child rearing), physical appearance (clean, attractive, presentable), and appropriate speech (polite, soft-spoken, contained) and behavior (honest, loyal, submissive).

Vietnamese women have always played an important role in the Vietnamese nationalist identity development. Vietnamese women's history often glorifies two national narratives: *Hai Bà Trưng* (Trung Sisters) and *Truy n Kieu* (The Tale of Kieu). In 39 CE, Trung Trac and Trung Nhi—the Trung sisters—went to war against and gained independence from China. Though their victory afforded

Trinh T. Minh-Ha (1952–)

First World feminism in the United States habitually privileges upper-middle-class, Euroamerican-centric, and middle-aged women. Vietnamese American feminism struggles to establish its presence in the community and the academy. Trinh T. Minh-Ha, a foremother of Vietnamese American feminism, challenges the definitions of feminism in the United States. Trinh is an avant-garde film-maker, composer, writer, and postcolonial feminist. Born in 1952 in Vietnam, Trinh immigrated to the United States in 1970 to study French literature, music, and ethnomusicology at the University of Illinois, Urbana-Champaign. She was an associate professor of cinema at San Francisco State University and is currently a professor of women's studies and rhetoric at the University of California, Berkeley. Trinh's bodies of critical work—theory, poetry, and film—focus on language and identity. As an essayist, she conflates the definitive boundaries between the author and the reader to question the authenticity of the self. Trinh is one of the first Vietnamese American feminists to theorize Vietnamese American women.

only two years of independence, the Trung sisters became national heroines and the symbol of resistance. Another heroine figure in Vietnamese women's history is the subject of Nguyen Du's epic poem *Truy n Kieu*, a work in the national literary canon with a strong female protagonist. Kieu scarifies herself for her father, her lover, and her society—representing the ideal traditional woman. In modern times, a greater number of first-generation Vietnamese immigrants reinterpret Kieu's narrative as a patriotic obligation to return to a precommunist Vietnam in an unforeseen future. These historical mythologies have taught Vietnamese women to be strong but submissive to their male counterparts.

Predating the mass migration in 1975 to the United States and other Western countries, the Vietnamese Communist Party propagated women's liberation as a major issue to be sought after in the Vietnam War. The Communist Party understood the important roles of women during the war. The war agenda promoted healthy female heroic imagery, relied on women to maintain economic stability on the home front, and employed women as guerrilla soldiers on the battle fronts. Since the war, in postrevolutionary Vietnam, upper-class women have been pushed back into the home to perform domestic labor, while men with strong communist allegiance monopolize state powers. The postwar administration in Vietnam views feminism as a Western phenomenon. Similarly, Vietnamese immigrants in the United States utilize comparable rhetoric against Western feminism as a way of preserving native culture.

The deconstruction of the Vietnamese American family structure is crucial to understanding the diasporic experience. Throughout the three waves of mass migrations, Vietnamese women played an important role in reshaping the familial structures as part of the assimilation process. Based on Confucian gender roles, the male inherits rights to be the head of the household and dictates power over his family. However, the female is responsible for re-creating a familial environment to relieve the pressure of the assimilation process. The importance of cultural retention varies between generations. The older generation—first-generation immigrants—has a fixed identity with a higher value on maintaining the Vietnamese heritage. The younger generation—1.5 and second-generation immigrants—has a fluid identity that flows between the Vietnamese and American cultures while searching for cultural authenticity. There is no distinct age marker for the generational gap. Language barriers serve as a major factor in creating the tensions present in the generational gap.

Language plays a crucial role in the development of the Vietnamese cultural identity in the United States. Vietnamese immigrant parents who lack English-language proficiency often fail to maintain the traditional parental power structure with their children. In a case study of linguistic isolation, the Vietnamese community in comparison to other Asian ethnic groups has a higher preference for speaking Vietnamese over English. Linguistic isolation is observed within a household where no one over the age of 14 fluently speaks English. These cases are examples of Vietnamese American households deliberately retaining the Vietnamese language as a form cultural resistance. Additionally, younger Vietnamese immigrants developed a coping mechanism—code switching—to narrow the cultural barriers in the generational gap. Common in disaporic narratives, one faces a higher risk of persecuted isolation when he or she deviates from or challenges larger cultural narratives.

Redistribution of Resources

Vietnamese elders often equate academic success with professional success. Embedded in Confucian tradition, the highest honorable status is awarded to scholars and philosophers. Unfortunately, due to various factors the Vietnamese American community continues to face challenges within the education system. For example, only about 20 percent of students go on to complete a four-year college degree. Still, Vietnamese American communities regularly reinforce different controlling images of model minority and gender roles. This deduction of reason utilizes the same rhetoric that entraps Asian American identity into a binary of the model minority and the Yellow Peril. The dichotomous representations of Vietnamese Americans equate "a good subject" with those who have succeeded and discount the remainder of the population as "a bad subject." Viet Thanh Nguyen (2002), a Vietnamese American theorist, reapplies the bisectional relationship of model minority and expands on the relationship of the bad subject as those who reject "dominant ideology" (144). This dialectical argument exposes the commodification of ethnic identity as a capitalistic source for racial exploitation. Similar to many patriarchal cultures, the Vietnamese hierarchical system heavily relied on the adult male for economic stability. Due to capitalistic development—in both modern-day Vietnam and the United States—the family places higher values on both male and female children with the intention of yielding greater profits upon marriage by doubling the incomes.

Earning a paycheck creates a sense of independence that was not always accessible in the past for Vietnamese women. The access to financial power did not immediately translate to economic equality for the genders. However, men continue to retain most of the control of the accumulated resources. Men and women experienced the economic power shift differently; it varies depending on age, marital status, and occupational background.

Vietnamese immigrants most often pursue careers in maintenance, repair, personal services, laundry, retail, and factory work (mostly electronic industries) due to the low-skilled requirement. The high demand creates a niche market. Niche markets develop within isolated communities due to various reasons such as low-wage labor, little net profit return, lack of demand, and many other factors. Businesses within the Vietnamese niche market have a high success rate due to strong community support, family-based labor, and the high customer demand for cheaper products and service. Nail salons exemplify one of the strongest stereotypes for the Vietnamese American ethnic niche. Due to the nature of domesticated labor, the presence of male manicurists further creates a unique gender dynamic within the Vietnamese American community.

Vietnamese immigrant women performing low-wage labor as manicurists establish a significant financial freedom. However, Vietnamese immigrant men performing low-wage labor as manicurists further exacerbate the historical stereotypes that feminize Asian American men. Domesticated professions have been undervalued throughout the socioeconomic history. Vietnamese American men often seek jobs in nail salons, unlike previously isolated Chinese American bachelors who were forced into physical, social, and psychological containment through lack of job opportunities and labor laws. Men and women continue to enter the industry due to various reasons ranging from making quick money, having flexible hours, and having extensive leaves of absence.

Vietnamese American women perform a very particular role in the American culture whereby they sometimes represent a war-traumatized, colonized, and exotic figure. Vietnamese American feminism deconstructs the heteropatriarchal hierarchy, rooted in Confucius tradition, to create new narratives in literature and media that account for the complexity of gender, sexuality, class, and transnationality.

Khoi Nguyen

See also: Vietnamese American Immigration; Women, Asian American

Further Reading

Alba, Richard D., and Victor Nee. *Remaking the American Mainstream: Assimilation and Contemporary Immigration.* Cambridge, MA: Harvard University Press, 2003.

Janette, Michele. *My Viet: Vietnamese-American Literature in English, 1962–Present.* Honolulu: University of Hawai'i Press, 2011.

Lowe, Lisa. *Immigrant Acts: On Asian American Cultural Politics.* Durham, NC: Duke University Press Books, 1996.

Kibria, Nazli. *Family Tightrope: The Changing Lives of Vietnamese Americans.* Princeton, NJ: Princeton University Press, 1993.

Mies, Maria. *Patriarchy and Accumulation on a World Scale: Women in the International Division of Labour.* London: Zed Books, 1986.

Nguyen, Viet Thanh. *Race and Resistance: Literature and Politics in Asian America.* New York and Oxford: Oxford University Press, 2002.

W

WAR BRIDES ACT (1945)

The War Brides Act was enacted in 1945 to allow foreign spouses, natural children, and adopted children of U.S. military servicemen to enter the United States. While the War Brides Act exempted spouses and dependents of U.S. soldiers from the quota system set up by the 1924 Immigration Act, the Page Act of 1875 was still in force and excluded Asians from entering the United States. By 1947, the War Brides Act was amended to allow American veterans of Asian descent to marry and bring their wives to the United States. This dramatically changed the preexisting male-dominated bachelor communities of Asian America. Thousands of Filipino wives, for example, accompanied their Filipino American military spouses or joined their husbands who had immigrated earlier. Japanese, Korean, and Filipino women often married non-Asian servicemen. However, many Filipino wives married Filipino servicemen in the U.S. Navy.

Between 1947 and 1952 when the provisions of the amended War Brides Act ended, some 6,000 Chinese wives of American servicemen migrated to the United States. Between 1945 and 1975, 45,000 Japanese wives of American servicemen migrated to the United States. The majority of these women, however, came as a result of the McCarran-Walter Immigration and Nationality Act of 1952, which allowed the naturalization of Korean and Japanese immigrants and provided nonquota visas for the spouses and children of American citizens. During this same period, women were the majority of immigrants into the United States.

Unlike earlier migration flows, Asian immigration during the postwar years was overwhelmingly female. The end of the war and new immigration policies allowed these women to enter the United States. However, despite their nonquota immigration visa status, many, especially during the initial period of this migration wave, were harassed and detained by immigration officials who threatened to deport them. Yen Le Espiritu documented protests and many suicides committed by women who were told by immigration officials that they would be deported. These acts of protest drew negative publicity for the U.S. Immigration Service in the media and the press. As a result of this negative publicity and pressure coming from the American Civil Liberties Union, the

Fong Lai, a war bride, and her children in Chinatown, New York City, December 1950. Enacted in 1945, the War Brides Act allowed foreign spouses and children (natural and adopted) of U.S. military servicemen to enter the country. (Leonard Mccombe/The LIFE Images Collection/Getty Images)

U.S. Immigration Service agreed to stop detainment procedures and to settle immigrants' rights of entry at the point of departure.

Kathleen M. Nadeau

See also: Korean American Immigration

Further Reading

Espiritu, Yen Le. *Asian American Women and Men: Labor, Laws, and Love.* Lanham, MD: Rowman and Littlefield, 2008.

Lee, Robert G. *Orientals: Asian Americans in Popular Culture.* Philadelphia: Temple University Press, 1999.

Shukert, Elfrieda Berthiaume, and Barbara Smith Scibetta. *War Brides of World War II.* Novato, CA: Presidio, 1988.

Zeiger, Susan. *Entangling Alliances: Foreign War Brides and American Soldiers in the Twentieth Century.* New York: New York University Press, 2010.

WOMEN, ASIAN AMERICAN

Historically, U.S. immigration laws have curbed Asian immigration of both genders to the United States in one form or another as a result of xenophobia. The Chinese Exclusion Act of 1882 and the 1917 Immigration Act categorized immigrants on a racial basis, dividing them into whites and nonwhites. Asian American women have faced more discrimination than men in the history of Asian immigration to the United States. The National Origins Act of 1924 did not allow women from China, India, Japan, and Korea to become U.S. citizens. It allowed a small number of Asians to reside in the United States without their wives. The U.S. Supreme Court prohibited entry of Chinese wives of American citizens by the case of *Chang Chan et al. v. John D. Nagle* in 1925. In the 1940s immigration restrictions were relaxed slowly by legislation passed in 1940, 1943, and 1944 affecting Filipinos, Chinese, and Japanese, respectively. As a result of the War Brides Act of 1945, wives and children of U.S. Army personnel were allowed to enter the United States. Following the elimination of national origin quotas by the 1965 Immigration and Nationality Act, the number of Asian immigrants, both men and women, started to increase. Professionals and those with families in the United Sates were given priority. After the end of the Vietnam War, a number of refugees from Laos, Cambodia,

Kalpana Chawla (1961–2003)

Kalpana Chawla, the first Asian American female astronaut, was killed aboard the space shuttle *Columbia* on February 1, 2003, along with six other crew members. Born in Karnal, a town in the Haryana state in India, on July 1, 1961, Chawla received her bachelor's degree in aeronautical engineering from the Punjab Engineering College in 1982. She received her master's of science in aerospace engineering from the University of Texas, Arlington, in 1984. In 1988, she finished her doctoral program at the University of Colorado, Boulder. She joined the National Aeronautics and Space Administration in 1994 and accomplished her various technical assignments. Flying for her was not a profession but a passion. Her first space mission started on November 19, 1997, in the space shuttle *Columbia*'s flight STS-87. Over her career she made 252 orbits around Earth, covering 10.4 million miles. On January 16, 2003, the space shuttle *Columbia* made its ominous journey with seven crew members, including Chawla. *Columbia* broke into pieces while reentering Earth's atmosphere, and all the crew members perished. Chawla was married to a flying instructor, Jean Pierre Harrison. She has been posthumously awarded numerous honors.

and Vietnam came to the United States. Public Law 95-145 of 1977, an amendment to the Indochina Migration and Refugee Assistance Act of 1975, provided the permanent residency status for Indochinese refugees including men, women, and children. These refugees can apply for citizenship five years after their arrival. The relaxation of immigration laws reached its high point when Congress passed the 1990 Immigration Act, giving priority to skilled personnel and reunification of families.

In recent years, professionals from engineering, medicine, finance, and other sectors filled vacancies in the United States. One of the interesting features of the arrival of Asian American women from Japan, Korea, and Southeast Asian countries is advertising for life partners. Picture brides started to migrate to the United States in the early 20th century. Most of them married Japanese and Korean laborers in Hawai'i. In the 1990s, women from poverty-stricken areas in Southeast Asia sought to marry American citizens through matchmaking agencies, hoping for a better life in the United States. They become known as mail-order brides. It is estimated that about 5,000 potential brides entered the country from former Soviet territories and Southeast Asia in the 1990s. The Immigration Marriage Fraud Amendments of 1986 and 1990 require for foreign spouses a mandatory waiting period of two years before they can become citizens. Washington State Senate Bill 6412, passed in 2002, requires a thorough background check for the prospective spouse. The arrival of Asian men and women in large numbers since the 1990s has changed the demographic profile of the United States.

Practices in Employment and Education

Immigrant women are confronted with many challenges in the United States in coping with the changes in the workplace and at home. Living far from their country of origin and starting a new life in a host country results in lots of mental and physical stress. Even for American-born generations, balancing family life with career is not an easy task. The share of Asian Americans in the labor force has been growing. In 2010 it included 7.2 million, 57 percent of whom were women. Most of them are employed in the private sector, and a small percentage work for the government. The percentage of Asian Americans self-employed was 6.3 in 2010. Asian American women made up 3.1 percent of those employed in managerial and professional occupations in 2010. Among women directors, Asian American women are 3.3 percent. South Asian American women have lower participation in the workforce compared to Southeast Asian American women. Asian American women are unrepresented in major employment sectors, such as government, corporate, and education. Many of them have faced discrimination in employment and get paid less compared to their male counterparts and white women. Some women work in family-owned business. It is very unlikely to find a woman having ownership while male family members work as employees. Usually the husband is the manager, and the wife is the cashier.

According to the Bureau of Labor Statistics, compared to median weekly earnings of Asian American men ($1,055) in 2012, Asian American women's earning was $770. Despite the Equal Pay Act of 1963, a woman earns 77 cents to every dollar a man earns in the United States. The gender-based wage gap is stark for women of color, including Asian American women. In terms of wage labor, the garment industry is most manipulative in terms of wages toward Asian American women. Asian American women holding bachelor's degrees do earn $10,840 on average, while white men holding the same degrees earn $11,354. Another form of gender discrimination is the lack of paid sick leave in low-wage working places. The number of Asian American women seeking full-time jobs was 166,000 in March 2013, compared to 19,000 Asian American men. Equity in pay structure is a challenging issue for Asian American women.

Generally speaking, family is the basic unit of Asian American communities. A traditional family consists of husband, wife, children, grandparents, and sometimes dependent relatives. In recent years the nuclear family has become a common practice, although extended families still exist. Family values, loyalty, and honor are important for many Asian American families. A woman's traditional role is to take care of her children and household chores. The influx of younger generations migrating to or born in the United States has transformed the family structure and the division of labor to a considerable extent. Sometimes a wife has to take a paying job to help support the family. A number of Asian American women have taken on the double task of being housewives as well as working women. Maintaining a balance between the two roles becomes crucial for a harmonious family life. Arranged marriages have become scarce, although parental consent is highly respected. Interracial dating and marriages have become more and more common among young generations of Asian Americans.

In American popular culture, Asian American women have traditionally been portrayed as submissive, docile, unassertive, demure, meek, and mild. For instance, a stereotypical perception is that Asian and Asian American women possess exotic sexuality like Japanese geishas. There is also the image of the manipulating dragon lady. Another stereotype is the attractive and good-hearted prostitute Suzie Wong. Asian American women have been targets of harassment and satire. For example, the colored *bindis* (dots) that South Asian women put on have become a subject of caricature. The racists bent on harassment are known as dot busters. Apart from racial discrimination and prejudice at large, some Asian American women are victims of domestic abuse.

According to the U.S. Census Bureau, in 2011 there were approximately 1 million women living in poverty in the United States. From 2002 to 2010, the poverty rate of Asian American women increased by 46 percent. About 12.1 percent of Asian American women lived in poverty in 2010. Approximately 40 percent of Asian American women are not proficient in English. Because of the limits in language skills, they usually have to take up low-wage jobs. Among Asian Pacific Islander Americans, 20.6 percent did not have health insurance at the beginning of the 21st century before the Affordable Care Act was passed. Many of them lack access to health care due to language, cultural, and financial barriers. The leading causes of mortality for Asian Americans in 2010 were cancer, heart disease, and diabetes. Compared to other ethnic groups, Asian American women have the highest average life expectancy at 85.8 years. Women under the age of 18 undergoing Pap tests are lower, at only 68 percent. From 2004 to 2007, the Centers for Disease Control and Prevention reported that compared to other ethnic groups, Asian American women age 65 and older committed a higher number of suicides—6.5 per 100,000 people. Psychological well-being has become a major concern for many Asian American women. Bipolar disorder, schizophrenia, and other types of mental disorders are on the rise among Asian American women. The Community and Mental Health Centers Act of 1963 set up mental health centers throughout the country, providing services such as inpatient care, partial hospitalization, and consultation. Various support groups, human service professionals, and governmental organizations also offer assistance to Asian American women.

Asian American women have excelled in various fields, including literature, science, business, film, beauty contests, fashion and clothing designs, and visual and performing arts. Some have become pioneers in their respective fields. Notable figures in literature include Jhumpa Lahiri, Anita Desai, Kiran Desai, and Bharati Mukherjee, among others. Mira Nair is a well-known filmmaker. Some prominent Asian American actresses are Michelle Yeoh, Isabella Leong, Ming Na, Joan Chen, Yunjin Kim, Brenda Song, Puja Mohindra, Fawzia Mirza, Jamie Chung, Julia Ling, Moon Bloodgood, Lucy Liu, and Vanessa Hudgens. Mohini Bharadwaj won an Olympic medal in gymnastics in Athens in 2004. Amrita Singh and Rachel Roy have become widely known names in the fashion industry. Sarah Chang is a notable violinist. Salma Arastu and Samantha Chundur have exhibited their talents in painting. Angela Oh is a famous attorney and community leader. Chien-Shiung Wu is a winner of the Nobel Prize in Physics. Julia Chang Bloch was appointed as ambassador to Nepal in 1989. Mary K. Chung is president of the National Asian Women's Health Organization. The national director of the National Asian Pacific American Women's Forum is Kiran Ahuja. Indra Nooyi is chief executive officer of

PepsiCo. Kalpana Chawla is the first female astronaut of Asian descent. Elaine Chao was secretary of labor in President George W. Bush's administration. The first Asian American female senator, Mazie Hirono from Hawai'i, was elected in 2013. On September 15, 2013, Nina Davuluri was crowned Miss America.

Patit Paban Mishra

See also: Asian Indian American Children and Family; Autobiographies, Asian American; Cambodian American Women; Chinese American Women; Comfort Women; Dragon Lady and Lotus Blossom; Filipino American Women; Japanese American Women; Korean American Women; Vietnamese American Women; War Brides Act (1945)

Further Reading

"The Asian Population: 2010." U.S. Census Bureau, http://2010.census.gov/news /press-kits/summary-file-1.html.

Bhabha, Jacqueline, et al. *Worlds Apart: Women and Immigration and Nationality Law.* London: Pluto, 1985.

"Labor Force Statistics from the Current Population Survey." Bureau of Labor Statistics, http://www.bls.gov/cps/.

Chin, Jean Lau, ed. *Relationships among Asian American Women.* Washington, DC: American Psychological Association, 2000.

Foo, Laura Jo. *Asian American Women: Issues, Concerns and Responsive Human and Civil Rights Advocacy.* Lincoln, NE: IUniverse, 2002.

Glodava, Mila, and Richard Onizuka. *Mail Order Brides: Women for Sale.* Fort Collins, CO: Alaken, 1994.

Kang, Laura Hyun Yi. *Compositional Subjects: Refiguring Asian/American Women.* Durham, NC: Duke University Press, 2002.

Nemeto, Kumiko. *Racing Romance: Love, Power, and Desire among Asian American/ White Couples.* Rutgers, NJ: Rutgers University Press, 2009.

Smith, Earl, and Angela Hattery. *Interracial Relationships in the 21st Century.* Durham, NC: Carolina Academic, 2009.

Y

YOGA

Yoga began as an ancient school of Indian philosophy that may have originated some 6,000 years ago. The term "yoga" comes from a Sanskrit word that means to yoke, join, or unite. Unlike other schools of philosophy, yoga is also considered a science and a discipline that can govern many areas of life. Within the umbrella of yoga there are different limbs, branches, or types of yoga, including among others karma yoga, the yoga of action; bhakti yoga, the yoga of devotion; jnana yoga, the yoga of knowledge; and hatha yoga, the physical practice of yoga. While hatha yoga is indeed grounded in physical movement, for many yogis it is first and foremost a mental exercise. According to swami Gurumayi Chidvilasananda, "The postures of hatha yoga are a form of physical action, yet they lead to detachment from physical action. Outer movements are taking place, of course—the physical body is becoming stronger and suppler. Yet the whole purpose of hatha yoga is to draw the attention inward."

The yoga asanas (postures) that are known today were created as a way to prepare the body for meditation by calming the mind, body, and spirit. Each yoga style has a different emphasis, but overall hatha yoga remains at its core the practice of calming and strengthening the body while drawing individual attention inward. The three main components of hatha yoga practice are physical postures (or asanas), meditation, and breathing or breath control (pranayama). Within hatha yoga there are many variations, including but not limited to ashtang yoga (power yoga), bikram yoga (hot yoga), integral yoga (with a focus on pranayama), Iyengar yoga (known for precise alignment of postures, using props such as blocks and belts and with teachers who must complete a rigorous Iyengar training program for certification), and Kundalini yoga (a spiritual yoga with emphasis on breathing, meditation, and chanting).

Yoga has firmly entrenched itself in mainstream American popular culture, especially in the past 10 to 15 years. It used to be the case that yoga programs were found primarily only on the West Coast, Hawai'i, and the upper East Coast. There are now yoga programs and studios in every state in the United States. According to Carolyn Gregoire, there are an estimated 20 million yoga practitioners in the United States and thousands of classes across the country, both in dedicated yoga centers or studios as well as offered at YMCAs, health clubs, schools, and retirement facilities. The popularity of physical and meditative yoga practices in the United States is seen as helping those who want to remain fit and flexible throughout life as well as those who seek an antidote to stress, too much technology, and too much busyness.

Although yoga practitioners are primarily women, at approximately 70 percent, more and more men have been joining in recent years. Older people who have been active in sports such as running, cycling, and skiing like yoga for its challenging physical and mental work but less jarring wear on the body. Classes are also popular among young people, and there are even beginning modified classes for children and young adults. Yoga's spirituality is also appealing to many and especially fits well with those Americans who describe themselves as spiritual but not religious. Some yoga centers have connections with India and teach physical and meditative yoga and organize annual yoga tours to India; others teach physical and posture yoga without direct ties to India. Some classes teach the Sanskrit terms for poses or practices; others do not. Among others, Dr. Deepak Chopra (1947–) has become well known for meditative yoga through his online and DVD yoga programs, probably due to his association with Oprah Winfrey (1954–). But other practitioners who offer DVDs or online courses or appear on television are also popular among people who want to practice at home.

Lavanya Vemsani and Leslie Shafer

See also: Asian Indian American Dance; Karate; Tae Kwon Do; Tai Chi

Further Reading

Chidvilasananda, Gurumayi. *The Yoga of Discipline.* South Fallsburgh, NY: SYDA Foundation, 1996.

Gregoire, Carolyn. "How Yoga Became a $27 Billion Industry—and Reinvented American Spirituality." Huffington Post, December 16, 2013, http://www.huffingtonpost.com/2013/12/16/how-the-yoga-industry-los_n_4441767.html.

Iyengar, B. K. S. *Light on Yoga: Yoga Dipika.* New York: Schocken, 1995.

Shafer, Leslie. "Yoga." In *The Encyclopedia of Wellness: From Açaí Berry to Yo-Yo Dieting,* edited by Sharon K. Zoumbaris, 881–884. Santa Barbara, CA: ABC-CLIO/Greenwood, 2012.

Singleton, Mark. "Body at the Centre: The Postural Yoga Renaissance and Transnational Flows." In *Yoga Traveling: Bodily Practice in Transcultural Perspective,* edited by Beatrix Hauser, 37–56. Heidelberg: Springer, 2013.

YOUTH AND ARTS, ASIAN AMERICAN

Youth is defined as being between the ages of 13 and 24, sometimes slightly younger or older. Asian American youth includes the first generation (those who arrived in the United States after the age of 13), the 1.5 generation (those who arrived between the ages 6 and 12), and the second and later generations (those who are U.S.-born or arrived when they were under the age of 5).

Asian American youths have long been involved in the arts in many forms. Asian American youths as artists conceivably dates back to the arrival of the early immigrant sojourners and settlers in the United States. These initial groups were mostly young male laborers in the 19th century from China, Japan, the Philippines, Korea, and India. Many were teenagers, though more significant numbers were in their 20s. Practically all of them faced minimal to nonexistent opportunities for employment, much less school, in their homelands and ventured to the United States in the hopes of gaining economic prosperity and in the face of restrictive U.S. immigration laws. Women who migrated were significantly fewer, ranging from Japanese women, largely wives of Japanese men, with their children under the Gentlemen's Agreement of 1908 to a number of Chinese young women and girls as young as 6 years old who were sold into prostitution. Though art could not have been formalized in the earliest formations of settlement among these lives, art for certain played a role. Art, whether through the form of visual art, poetry, or music, for instance, provided the means to express material or spiritual loss and gain as well as a coping mechanism that enabled and maintained cultural identity, ties, and continuity. Youths also experienced the opposite through art targeted against them and their communities in the form of aggressions and efforts to dehumanize them by a culturally dominant white population, many of whom were threatened by the labor capacity and lower wages of Asian Americans, through public pictorial and textual representations of the "heathen Chinee" and later the Yellow Peril.

Immigration to the United States in the first half of the 20th century provides rich evidence of the role of art in the lives of youths, including in the form of poetry inscribed on the barrack walls of Angel Island's Immigration Station. Angel Island was the headquarters site of detention, examination, and interrogation for immigrants from the East, the majority of whom were Chinese but included many other Asian and a few East European groups. Children and youths alongside adult men and women immigrated during this era. A number of those who were detained during their youth have provided oral histories of their experiences. Together with the poetry, these oral histories reveal expressions of depression, loss, bad food, fear of deportation, frustration, unfair treatment, and boredom as well as anticipation, eagerness, and hope.

Asian American youth art since the mid-20th century reflects an aesthetic formation that is part of the tradition of both Asian American arts and artists in general while, at the same time, being its own trajectory. Asian American youth arts are also part of both youth culture in the United States in general and Asian American youth culture in particular. This latter distinction is a crucial one, as Asian American youths have largely been portrayed one-dimensionally if at all.

Asian American youth arts emerged with, while fueling the rise of, Asian American racial identity formation beginning in the 1960s. The importance of this unifying pan-ethnic racial identity must not be underestimated. This is the case particularly in the face of historical and ongoing racism, namely Orientalist stereotypes that assign a "forever foreigner" status to a significant and diverse group, thereby denying, ignoring, or minimizing the vast and countless contributions of Asian Americans to U.S. nation building. Asian American youth arts further have addressed and countered images of the model minority that began to appear in popular media during the 1960s, first in the *New York Times Magazine* and later in *U.S. News and World Report*. Asian American youth artists at the same time supersede reactionary and even proactive stances against racism by creating a polycultural genre in its own right that combines elements of what are uniquely Asian, American, and youth culture in combination with other identity or cultural markers.

The next generation of Asian American youth art both continues and strays from political and other forms of arts activism, notably through the cultural medium of hip-hop. Jeff Chang identifies the main pillars of hip-hop style as graffiti, deejaying, and b-boying or b-girling. Emceeing or rapping and spoken word are also central as literary art, while many other artistic media themselves have become "hip-hopified," such as the novel, the short story, photography, film, and graphic and performing arts. Grounded in the lives and expressions of Asian American youths, these projects of hip-hop continue to lead and support the work of social movements, particularly from urban centers such as Oakland, New York City, and Chicago, oftentimes as visionary projects of transformation.

Themes of Asian American youth art extend further beyond the topic of race to cover a wide range of social concerns. Asian American feminists, as politicized women of color, queer of color, and men of color, account for lived experience at the social intersection of race with gender, sexuality, and class. Asian American youth artists are also contributing to and leading the undocu movement, or the movement for putting undocumented peoples in the United States on the pathway to citizenship especially through the Dream Act, which disproportionately affects youths through educational opportunity and the option to join the U.S. military. Asian American youth artists are also addressing

Los Angeles–based hip-hop group Far East Movement performing at the Sleep Train Amphitheater in Wheatland, California, September 3, 2011. Formed in 2003, the group consists of Kev Nish, Prohgress, J-Splif, and DJ Virman. (Randy Miramontez/ Dreamstime.com)

the rights of lesbian, gay, bisexual, transgender, and queer (LGBTQ) people as well as the major social problems that come out of the prison, military, and academic industrial complexes; neoliberalism; and global warming. Online platforms and websites have opened up arts-embedded popular media including *Hyphen* magazine, *KoreAm* magazine, the comic strip Angry Asian Man, and the iconic stereotype-bending figure Angry Asian Girl. Community organizations further the work of Asian American youths in the arts, including youth organization such as AYPAL in Oakland, California, and arts organizations such as the Kearny Street Workshop in San Francisco, California.

In sum, arts produced by Asian American youths, particularly as a social constituency or community organized group in the fabric of U.S. social politics and culture, "can help us to envision the new cultural images we need to grow our souls" and shape the future of Asian America and the United States at large

(Boggs and Kurashige 2011, 36). Asian American youths are in a prime position to develop this capacity to lead and grow future generations in visionary and leadership capacities.

Ruth H. Kim

See also: Arts and Artists (Visual), Asian American; Music and Musicians, Asian American

Further Reading

AYPAL: Building API Community Power, http://aypal.org/.

Boggs, Grace Lee, and Scott Kurashige. *The Next American Revolution: Sustainable Activism in the Twenty-First Century.* Berkeley: University of California Press, 2011.

Chang, Jeff. *Can't Stop, Won't Stop: A History of the Hip-Hop Generation.* New York: St. Martin's, 2005.

Lai, H. Mark, Genny Lim, and Judy Yung. *Island: Poetry and History of Chinese Immigrants on Angel Island, 1910–1940.* Seattle: University of Washington Press, 1991.

Takaki, Ronald T. *Strangers from a Different Shore: A History of Asian Americans.* Revised ed. Boston: Back Bay Books, 1998.

Zhou, Min, and Jennifer Lee. "Introduction: The Making of Culture, Identity, and Ethnicity among Asian American Youth." In *Asian American Youth: Culture, Identity, and Ethnicity,* edited by Min Zhou and Jennifer Lee, 1–30. New York and London: Routledge, 2004.

RECOMMENDED RESOURCES

Adams, Bella. *Asian American Literature*. Edinburgh, UK: Edinburgh University Press, 2008.

Alba, Richard D., Albert J. Raboteau, and Josh DeWind, eds. *Immigration and Religion in America: Comparative and Historical Perspectives*. New York: New York University Press, 2008.

Ambrose, Stephen E. *Nothing Like It in the World: The Men Who Built the Transcontinental Railroad, 1863–1869*. New York: Simon and Schuster, 2000.

American Experience: Transcontinental Railroad. Directed by Mark Swonitzer and Michael Chin. PBS, 2006. DVD.

Ancestors in the Americas. Directed by Loni Ding. Center for Educational Telecommunications, 2001. DVD.

Aoki, Andrew, and Okiyoshi Takeda. *Asian American Politics*. Cambridge, UK: Polity, 2008.

Appadurai, Arjun, Frank J. Korom, and Margaret A. Mills, eds. *Gender, Genre, and Power in South Asian Expressive Traditions*. Philadelphia: University of Pennsylvania Press, 1991.

Asian Women United of California, ed. *Making Waves: An Anthology of Writing by and about Asian Women*. Boston: Beacon, 1989.

Azuma, Eiichiro. *Between Two Empires: Race, History, and Transnationalism in Japanese America*. New York and Oxford: Oxford University Press, 2005.

Bacon, Jean Leslie. *Life Lines: Community, Family and Assimilation among Asian Indian Immigrants*. Oxford: Oxford University Press, 1996.

Bain, David Haward. *Empire Express: Building the First Transcontinental Railroad*. New York: Viking, 1999.

Becoming American: The Chinese Experience. A Bill Moyers Special for Public Affairs Television. DVD, 2003.

Becoming American: Personal Journeys. A Bill Moyers Special for Public Affairs Television. Princeton, NJ: Films for the Humanities & Sciences, 2003. DVD.

Cao, Lan, and Himilce Novas. *Everything You Need to Know about Asian American History.* New York: Plume, 1996.

Carnes, Tony, and Fenggang Yang, eds. *Asian American Religions: The Making and Remaking of Borders and Boundaries.* New York: New York University Press, 2004.

Chan, Jeffery Paul, Frank Chin, Lawson Fusao Inada, and Shawn Wong, eds. *The Big Aiiieeeee! An Anthology of Chinese American and Japanese American Literature.* New York: Meridian, 1991.

Chan, Sucheng. *Asian Americans: An Interpretive History.* New York: Twayne, 1991.

Chan, Sucheng, ed. *Remapping Asian American History.* Walnut Creek, CA: AltaMira, 2003.

Chang, Gordon H., Mark Dean Johnson, Paul J. Karlstrom, and Sharon Spain, eds. *Asian American Art: A History, 1850–1970.* Stanford, CA: Stanford University Press, 2008.

Chang, Iris. *The Chinese in America: A Narrative History.* New York: Viking, 2003.

Chang, Juliana. *Quiet Fire: A Historical Anthology of Asian American Poetry, 1892–1970.* New York: Asian American Writer's Workshop, 1996.

Chang, Roberta, and Wayne Patterson. *A Pictorial History of Koreans in Hawaii, 1903–2003.* Honolulu: University of Hawai'i Press, 2003.

Cheung, King-Kok. *An Interethnic Companion to Asian American Literature.* New York and Cambridge: Cambridge University Press, 1997.

Cheung, King-Kok, and Stan Yogi, eds. *Asian American Literature: An Annotated Bibliography.* New York: MLA, 1988.

Chin, Frank, Jeffery Paul Chan, Lawson Fusao Inada, and Shawn Wong, eds. *Aiiieeeee! An Anthology of Asian-American Writers.* Washington, DC: Howard University Press, 1974.

Chin, Jean Lau, ed. *Relationships among Asian American Women.* Washington, DC: American Psychological Association, 2000.

Chiu, Melissa, Karin Higa, and Susette S. Min, eds. *One Way or Another: Asian American Art Now.* New Haven, CT: Asia Society with Yale University Press, 2006.

Chiu, Monica, ed. *Drawing New Color Lines: Transnational Asian American Graphic Narratives.* Hong Kong: Hong Kong University Press, 2015.

Choy, Catherine Ceniza. *Global Families: A History of Asian International Adoption in America.* New York: New York University Press, 2013.

Chun, Gloria H. *Of Orphans and Warriors: Inventing Chinese-American Culture and Identity.* New Brunswick, NJ: Rutgers University Press, 2000.

Cornell, Daniel, and Mark Johnson, eds. *Asian/American/Modern Art: Shifting Currents, 1900–1970.* Berkeley: University of California Press, 2008.

Danico, Mary Yu, and Franklin Ng. *Asian American Issues*. Westport, CT: Greenwood, 2004.

Daniels, Roger. *Asian America: Chinese and Japanese in the United States since 1850*. Seattle: University of Washington Press, 1990.

Daniels, Roger. *Prisoners without Trial: Japanese Americans in World War II*. New York: Hill and Wang, 2004.

Davé, Shilpa, LeiLani Nishime, and Tasha Oren, eds. *East Main Street: Asian American Popular Culture*. New York: New York University Press, 2005.

Davis, Rocío G. *Begin Here: Reading Asian North American Autobiographies of Childhood*. Honolulu: University of Hawai'i Press, 2007.

Davis, Rocío G., and Sämi Ludwig, eds. *Asian American Literature in the International Context: Readings on Fiction, Poetry and Performance*. Münster, Germany: Lit, 2002.

Desi: South Asians in New York. Shebana Coelho, dir. Center for Asian American Media. DVD, 2000.

Dhingra, Pawan. *Managing Multicultural Lives: Asian American Professionals and the Challenge of Multiple Identities*. Stanford, CA: Stanford University Press, 2007.

Dong, Lan. *Mulan's Legend and Legacy in China and the United States*. Philadelphia: Temple University Press, 2010.

Dong, Lan. *Reading Amy Tan*. Santa Barbara, CA: ABC-CLIO/Greenwood, 2009.

Dong, Lan, ed. *Transnationalism and the Asian American Heroine: Essays on Literature, Film, Myth and Media*. Jefferson, NC: McFarland, 2010.

Dorow, Sara. *Transnational Adoption: A Cultural Economy of Race, Gender, and Kinship*. New York: New York University Press, 2006.

Ebihara, May M., Judy Ledgerwood, and Carol A. Mortland, eds. *Cambodian Culture since 1975: Homeland and Exile*. Ithaca, NY: Cornell University Press, 1994.

Eng, David L., and Alice Y. Hom. *Q & A: Queer in Asian America*. Philadelphia: Temple University Press, 1998.

Espiritu, Yen Le. *Home Bound: Filipino American Lives across Cultures, Communities, and Countries*. Berkeley: University of California Press, 2003.

Feng, Peter X. *Identities in Motion: Asian American Film and Video*. Durham, NC: Duke University Press, 2002.

Foster, Jenny Ryun, Frank Stewart, and Heinz Insu Fenkl, eds. *Century of the Tiger: One Hundred Years of Korean Culture in America, 1903–2003*. Honolulu: University of Hawai'i Press, 2003.

Fowler, Josephine. *Japanese and Chinese Immigrant Activists: Organizing in American and International Communist Movements, 1919–1939*. New Brunswick, NJ: Rutgers University Press, 2007.

Franks, Joel. *Asian Pacific Americans and Baseball: A History*. Jefferson, NC: McFarland, 2008.

Friday, Chris. *Organizing Asian American Labor: The Pacific Coast Canned-Salmon Industry, 1870–1942*. Philadelphia: Temple University Press, 1994.

Fugita-Rony, Dorothy. *American Workers, Colonial Power: Philippine Seattle and the Transpacific West, 1919–1941.* Berkeley: University of California Press, 2003.

Garlough, Christine L. *Desi Divas: Political Activism in South Asian American Cultural Performances.* Jackson: University Press of Mississippi, 2013.

Gee, Emma. *Counterpoint: Perspectives on Asian America.* Los Angeles: Asian American Studies Center, University of California, 1976.

Hall, Gordon, C. Nagayama, and Sumie Okazaki, eds. *Asian American Psychology: The Science of Lives in Context.* Washington, DC: American Psychological Association, 2002.

Hamamoto, Darrell Y., and Sandra Liu, eds. *Countervisions: Asian American Film Criticism.* Philadelphia: Temple University Press, 2000.

Ho, Fred, ed. *Legacy to Liberation: Politics and Culture of Revolutionary Asian Pacific America.* Oakland, CA: AK Press, 2000.

Hongo, Garrett, ed. *The Open Boat: Poems from Asian America.* New York: Anchor, 1993.

Huang, Guiyou. *The Columbia Guide to Asian American Literature since 1945.* New York: Columbia University Press, 2006.

Huang, Guiyou, ed. *Asian American Autobiographers: A Bio-Bibliographical Critical Sourcebook.* Westport, CT: Greenwood, 2001.

Huang, Guiyou, ed. *Asian American Poets: A Bio-Bibliographical Critical Sourcebook.* Westport, CT: Greenwood, 2002.

Hu-DeHart, Evelyn. *Across The Pacific: Asian Americans and Globalization.* Philadelphia: Temple University Press, 1999.

Hune, Shirley, and Gail Nomura, eds. *Asian Pacific Islander American Women: A Historical Anthology.* New York: New York University Press, 2003.

Hyun, Jane. *Breaking the Bamboo Ceiling: Career Strategies for Asians.* New York: HarperCollins, 2005.

In No One's Shadow: Filipinos in America. Naomi De Castro, dir. Center or Asian American Media. DVD, 1988.

Iwamura, Jane Naomi. *Virtual Orientalism: Asian Religions and American Popular Culture.* New York and Oxford: Oxford University Press, 2011.

Jenkins, Esther C., and Mary C. Austin. *Literature for Children about Asians and Asian Americans: Analysis and Annotated Bibliography with Additional Readings for Adults.* Westport, CT: Greenwood, 1987.

Joshi, Khyati Y. *New Roots in America's Sacred Ground: Religion, Race, and Ethnicity in Indian America.* New Brunswick, NJ: Rutgers University Press, 2006.

Kibria, Nazli. *Family Tightrope: The Changing Lives of Vietnamese Americans.* Princeton, NJ: Princeton University Press, 1993.

Kim, Elaine H. *Asian American Literature: An Introduction to the Writings and Their Social Context.* Philadelphia: Temple University Press, 1982.

Kina, Laura, and Wei Ming Dariotis, eds. *War Baby/Love Child: Mixed Race Asian American Art.* Seattle: University of Washington Press, 2013.

King, C. Richard, ed. *Asian American Athletes in Sport and Society*. New York and London: Routledge, 2015.

Ku, Robert Ji-Song, Martin F. Manalansan IV, and Anita Mannur, eds. *Eating Asian America: A Food Studies Reader*. New York: New York University Press, 2013.

Kurahashi, Yuko. *Asian American Culture on Stage: The History of the East West Players*. New York and London: Routledge, 1999.

Lai, Him Mark. *Becoming Chinese American: A History of Communities and Institutions*. Walnut Creek, CA: AltaMira, 2004.

Lai, Him Mark, Genny Lim, and Judy Yung, eds. *Island: Poetry and History of Chinese Immigrants on Angel Island, 1910–1940*. Seattle: University of Washington Press, 1991.

Lawrence, Bruce B. *New Faiths, Old Fears: Muslims and Other Asian Immigrants in American Religious Life*. New York: Columbia University Press, 2002.

Lee, Erika, and Judy Yung. *Angel Island: Immigrant Gateway to America*. New York and Oxford: Oxford University Press, 2010.

Lee, Esther Kim. *A History of Asian American Theatre*. New York and Cambridge: Cambridge University Press, 2006.

Lee, Gary Y., and Nicolas Tapp. *Culture and Customs of the Hmong*. Santa Barbara, CA: ABC-CLIO, 2010.

Lee, Jennifer, and Min Zhou, eds. *Asian American Youth: Culture, Identity, and Ethnicity*. New York and London: Routledge, 2004.

Lee, Jonathan H. X., and Kathleen Nadeau, eds. *Asian American Identities and Practices: Folkloric Expressions in Everyday Life*. Lanham, MD: Lexington Books, 2014.

Lee, Jonathan H. X., Fumitaka Matsuoka, Edmond Yee, and Ronald Nakasone, eds. *Asian American Religious Cultures*. Santa Barbara, CA: ABC-CLIO, 2015.

Lee, Josephine. *Performing Asian America: Race and Ethnicity on the Contemporary Stage*. Philadelphia: Temple University Press, 1997.

Lee, Josephine, Imogene L. Lim, and Yuko Matsukawa, eds. *Re/collecting Early Asian America: Essays in Cultural History*. Philadelphia: Temple University Press, 2002.

Lee, Rachel C., ed. *The Routledge Companion to Asian American and Pacific Islander Literature*. London and New York: Routledge, 2014.

Lee, Rachel C., and Sau-ling Cynthia Wong, eds. *Asian America.Net: Ethnicity, Nationalism, and Cyberspace*. New York and London: Routledge, 2003.

Lee, Robert G. *Orientals: Asian Americans in Popular Culture*. Philadelphia: Temple University Press, 1999.

Leonard, George J., ed. *The Asian Pacific American Heritage: A Companion to Literature and Arts*. New York: Garland, 1999.

Leonard, Karen I. *The South Asian Americans*. Westport, CT: Greenwood, 1997.

Leong, Frederick T. L., ed. *Asian American and Pacific Islander Children and Mental Health*. Santa Barbara, CA: ABC-CLIO/Praeger, 2011.

Leong, Russell. *Asian American Sexualities: Dimensions of the Gay and Lesbian Experience*. New York and London: Routledge, 1996.

Levy, Michael M. *Portrayal of Southeast Asian Refugees in Recent American Children's Books*. Lewiston, NY: E. Mellen, 2000.

Li, David Leiwei, ed. *Asian American Literature*. New York and London: Routledge, 2012.

Li, Guofang, and Lihshing Wang, eds. *Model Minority Myth Revisited: An Interdisciplinary Approach to Demystifying Asian American Educational Experiences*. Charlotte, NC: IAP, 2008.

Lim, Shirley Geok-lin, John Blair Gamber, Stephen Hong Sohn, and Gina Valentino, eds. *Transnational Asian American Literature: Sites and Transits*. Philadelphia: Temple University Press, 2006.

Lim, Shirley Jennifer. *A Feeling of Belonging: Asian American Women's Popular Culture, 1930–1960*. New York: New York University Press, 2005.

Ling, Amy. *Between Worlds: Women Writers of Chinese Ancestry*. New York: Paergamon, 1990.

Ling, Huping ed. *Emerging Voices: Experiences of Underrepresented Asian Americans*. New Brunswick, NJ: Rutgers University Press, 2008.

Liu, Miles Xian, ed. *Asian American Playwrights: A Bio-Bibliographical Critical Sourcebook*. Westport, CT: Greenwood, 2002.

Lowe, Lisa. *Immigrant Acts: On Asian American Cultural Politics*. Durham, NC: Duke University Press, 1996.

Lyman, Stanford Morris. *Chinatown and Little Tokyo: Power, Conflict, and Community among Chinese and Japanese Immigrants to America*. Port Washington, NY: Associated Faculty Press, 1986.

Madsen, Deborah L. *Chinese American Writers*. Farmingham, MI: Gale, 2002.

Mannur, Anita. *Culinary Fictions: Food in South Asian Diasporic Culture*. Philadelphia: Temple University Press, 2010.

McCloud, Aminah Beverly. *Transnational Muslims in American Society*. Gainesville: University Press of Florida, 2006.

Min, Pyong Gap, ed. *Asian Americans: Contemporary Trends and Issues*. Thousand Oaks, CA: Sage, 2005.

Min, Pyong Gap, and Jung Ha Kim, eds. *Religions in Asian America: Building Faith Communities*. Walnut Creek, CA: AltaMira, 2002.

Moon, Krystyn R. *Yellowface: Creating the Chinese in American Popular Music and Performance, 1850s–1920s*. New Brunswick, NJ: Rutgers University Press, 2005.

Nakamura, Lisa. *Digitizing Race: Visual Cultures of the Internet*. Minneapolis: University of Minnesota Press, 2008.

Nakanishi, Don T., and Ellen D. Wu. *Distinguished Asian American Political and Governmental Leaders*. Westport, CT: Greenwood, 2002.

Nakanishi, Don T., and Tina Yamano Nishida, eds. *The Asian American Educational Experience: A Source Book for Teachers and Students*. New York and London: Routledge, 1995.

Nakano, Mei T. *Japanese American Women: Three Generations, 1890–1990.* Berkeley, CA: Mina, 1990.

Nemeto, Kumiko. *Racing Romance: Love, Power, and Desire among Asian American/White Couples.* Rutgers, NJ: Rutgers University Press, 2009.

Ng, Wendy L. *Japanese American Internment during World War II: A History and Reference Guide.* Westport, CT: Greenwood, 2002.

Ngai, Mae M. *Impossible Subjects: Illegal Aliens and the Making of Modern America.* Princeton, NJ: Princeton University Press, 2004.

Nguyen, Tuyen D., ed. *Domestic Violence in Asian American Communities: A Cultural Overview.* Lanham, MD: Lexington Books, 2005.

Nguyen, Viet Thanh. *Race and Resistance: Literature and Politics in Asian America.* New York and Oxford: Oxford University Press, 2002.

Okihiro, Gary Y. *The Columbia Guide to Asian American History.* New York: Columbia University Press, 2001.

Okihiro, Gary Y. *Margins and Mainstreams: Asians in American History and Culture.* Seattle: University of Washington Press, 1994.

Okihiro, Gary Y., Shirley Hune, Arthur A. Hansen, and John M. Liu, eds. *Reflections on Shattered Windows: Promises and Prospects for Asian American Studies.* Pullman: Washington State University Press, 1988.

Ono, Kent A., ed. *Asian American Studies after Critical Mass.* Indianapolis: Wiley-Blackwell, 2004.

Ono, Kent A., and Vincent Pham. *Asian Americans and the Media.* Cambridge, UK: Polity, 2009.

Pak, Jenny Hyun Chung. *Korean American Women: Stories of Acculturation and Changing Selves.* New York and London: Routledge, 2006.

Pang, Valerie Ooka, and Li-Rong Lilly Cheng, eds. *Struggling to Be Heard: The Unmet Needs of Asian Pacific American Children.* Albany: State University of New York Press, 1998.

Park, Clara C., ed. *Asian American Education: Acculturation, Literacy Development, and Learning.* Charlotte, NC: IAP, 2007.

Park, Clara C., and Marilyn Mei-Ying Chi, eds. *Asian-American Education: Prospects and Challenges.* Westport, CT: Bergin and Garvey, 1999.

Patterson, Wayne. *The Korean Frontier in America: Immigration to Hawaii, 1896–1910.* Honolulu: University of Hawai'i Press, 1988.

Pfaelzer, Jean. *Driven Out: The Forgotten War against Chinese Americans.* New York: Random House, 2007.

Posadas, Barbara. *The Filipino Americans.* Westport, CT: Greenwood, 1999.

Ragaza, Angelo. *Lives of Notable Asian Americans: Business, Politics, Science.* New York: Chelsea House, 1995.

Rong, Xue Lan, and Russell Endo, eds. *Asian American Education: Identities, Racial Issues, and Languages.* Charlotte, NC: IAP, 2011.

Rutledge, Paul J. *The Vietnamese Experience in America.* Bloomington: Indiana University Press, 1992.

Sa-I-Gu: From Korean Women's Perspectives. Directed by Dai Sil Kim-Gibson. Center for Asian American Media, 1993. DVD.

Schlund-Vials, Cathy J. *War, Genocide, and Justice: Cambodian American Memory Work.* Minneapolis: University of Minnesota Press, 2012.

Searching for Asian America. Directed by Sapana Sakya, Donald Young, and Kyung Yu. National Asian American Telecommunications Association, 2003. DVD.

Shimizu, Celine. *The Hypersexuality of Race: Performing Asian/American Women on Screen and Scene.* Durham, NC: Duke University Press, 2007.

Shimizu, Celine. *Straitjacket Sexualities: Unbinding Asian American Manhoods in the Movies.* Stanford, CA: Stanford University Press, 2012.

Soh, Sarah C. *The Comfort Women: Sexual Violence and Postcolonial Memory in Korea and Japan.* Chicago: University of Chicago Press, 2008.

Song, Young I., and Ailee Moon. *Korean American Women: From Tradition to Modern Feminism.* Westport, CT: Greenwood/Praeger, 1998.

Srikanth, Rajini. *The World Next Door: South Asian American Literature and the Idea of America.* Philadelphia: Temple University Press, 2004.

Sue, Stanley, and James K. Morishima. *The Mental Health of Asian Americans.* San Francisco: Jossey-Bass, 1982.

Takaki, Ronald T. *Pau Hana: Plantation Life and Labor in Hawaii, 1835–1920.* Honolulu: University of Hawai'i Press, 1983.

Takaki, Ronald T. *Strangers from a Different Shore: A History of Asian Americans.* Boston: Little, Brown, 1989.

Taus, Stacy-Bolstad. *Pakistanis in America.* Minneapolis: Lerner Publications, 2006.

Terada, Yoshitaka, ed. *Transcending Boundaries: Asian Musics in North America.* Osaka, Japan: National Museum of Ethnology, 2001.

Thuy Pelaud, Isabelle. *This Is All I Choose to Tell: History and Hybridity in Vietnamese American Literature.* Philadelphia: Temple University Press, 2011.

Tong, Benson, ed. *Asian American Children: A Historical Guide.* Westport, CT: Greenwood, 2004.

Tran, Barbara, Monique Truong, and Khoi Truong. *Watermark: Vietnamese American Poetry and Prose.* New York: Asian American Writer's Workshop, 1997.

Trinh-Shevrin, Chau, Nadia Shilpi Islam, and Mariano Jose Rey, eds. *Asian American Communities and Health: Context, Research, Policy, and Action.* San Francisco: Jossey-Bass, 2009.

Tsai, Ming. *Blue Ginger: East Meets West Cooking with Ming Tsai.* New York: Clarkson Potter Publishers, 1999.

Tseng, Winston. *Immigrant Community Services in Chinese and Vietnamese Enclaves.* New York: LFB Scholarly Publishing, 2007.

Tu, Thuy Linh Nguyen. *The Beautiful Generation: Asian Americans and the Cultural Economy of Fashion.* Durham, NC: Duke University Press, 2010.

Underwood, Gary. *Happy Lunar New Year! An Asian Festival.* Clayton South, Australia: Blake Education, 2006.

Vang, Chia Youyee. *Hmong America: Reconstructing Community in Diaspora.* Urbana: University of Illinois Press, 2010.

Versluis, Arthur. *American Transcendentalism and Asian Religions.* Oxford and New York: Oxford University Press, 1993.

Võ, Linda Trinh. *Mobilizing an Asian American Community.* Philadelphia: Temple University Press, 2004.

Võ, Linda Trinh, and Rick Bonus, eds. *Contemporary Asian American Communities: Intersections and Divergences.* Philadelphia: Temple University Press, 2002.

Waters, Mary C., Reed Ueda, and Helen B. Marrow, eds. *The New Americans: A Guide to Immigration since 1965.* Cambridge, MA: Harvard University Press, 2007.

Wei, William. *The Asian American Movement.* Philadelphia: Temple University Press, 1993.

Weinberg, Meyer. *Asian-American Education: Historical Background and Current Realities.* Mahwah, NJ: Lawrence Erlbaum, 1997.

Welaratna, Usha. *Beyond the Killing Fields: Voices of Nine Cambodian Survivors in America.* Stanford, CA: Stanford University Press, 1993.

White, Richard. *Railroaded: The Transcontinentals and the Making of Modern America.* New York: Norton, 2012.

Wong, Deborah Anne. *Speak It Louder: Asian Americans Making Music.* New York and London: Routledge, 2004.

Wong, Sau-Ling Cynthia. *Reading Asian American Literature: From Necessity to Extravagance.* Princeton, NJ: Princeton University Press, 1993.

Wong, Sau-Ling Cynthia, and Stephen H. Sumida, eds. *A Resource Guide to Asian American Literature.* New York: MLA, 2001.

Wu, Frank H. *Yellow: Race in America beyond Black and White.* New York: Basic Books, 2002.

Wu, Jean Yu-wen Shen, and Thomas C. Chen, eds. *Asian American Studies Now: A Critical Reader.* New Brunswick, NJ: Rutgers University Press, 2010.

Wu, William F. *The Yellow Peril: Chinese Americans in American Fiction, 1850–1940.* Hamden, CT: Archon Books, 1982.

Xing, Jun. *Asian American through the Lens: History, Representations, and Identities.* Walnut Creek, CA: AltaMira, 1998.

Xu, Wenying. *Eating Identities: Reading Food in Asian American Literature.* Honolulu: University of Hawai'i Press, 2008.

Xu, Wenying. *Historical Dictionary of Asian American Literature and Theater.* Lanham, MD: Scarecrow, 2012.

Yamamoto, Traise. *Masking Selves, Making Subjects: Japanese American Women, Identity, and the Body.* Berkeley: University of California Press, 1999.

Yang, Alice. *Why Asia? Contemporary Asian and Asian American Art.* New York: New York University Press, 1998.

Yin, Xiao-Huang. *Chinese American Literature since the 1850s.* Urbana: University of Illinois Press, 2000.

Yoo, David K. *New Spiritual Homes: Religion and Asian Americans.* Honolulu: University of Hawai'i Press, 1999.

Yoshihara, Mari. *Musicians from a Different Shore: Asians and Asian Americans in Classical Music.* Philadelphia: Temple University Press, 2008.

Yu, Timothy. *Race and the Avant-Garde: Experimental and Asian American Poetry since 1965.* Stanford, CA: Stanford University Press, 2009.

Yung, Judy. *Unbound Feet: A Social History of Chinese Women in San Francisco.* Berkeley: University of California Press, 1995.

Yung, Judy, Gordon H. Chang, and Him Mark Lai, eds. *Chinese American Voices: From the Gold Rush to the Present.* Berkeley: University of California Press, 2006.

Zhao, Xiaojian, and Edward J. W. Park, eds. *Asian Americans: An Encyclopedia of Social, Cultural, Economic, and Political History.* Santa Barbara, CA: ABC-CLIO, 2013.

Zhou, Min, and James V. Gatewood, eds. *Contemporary Asian America: A Multidisciplinary Reader.* New York: New York University Press, 2000.

Zia, Helen. *Asian American Dreams: The Emergence of an American People.* New York: Farrar, Straus, and Giroux, 2000.

ABOUT THE EDITOR
AND CONTRIBUTORS

Editor

Lan Dong is associate professor of English at the University of Illinois, Springfield. She is the author of *Mulan's Legend and Legacy in China and the United States* (2010) and *Reading Amy Tan* (2009) and a number of journal articles, book chapters, and essays on Asian American literature, children's literature, and popular culture. She is the editor of *Transnationalism and the Asian American Heroine* (2010) and *Teaching Comics and Graphic Narratives* (2012). Currently she is working on a project on comics and Asian American experiences.

Contributors

Amanda Solomon Amorao received her PhD in literature from the University of California, San Diego (UCSD). Her research focuses on Philippine writing in English during the period of U.S. control of the islands. She currently serves as the interim associate director of the Culture, Art, and Technology Program at UCSD. She is the executive director of the Kuya Ate Mentorship Program, a grassroots organization providing educational workshops on Filipino history, culture, and identity in local San Diego high schools and middle schools. She is also a member of the Coordinating Committee for the Critical Filipino and Filipina Studies Collective.

Shashikala Muthumal Assella is a doctoral candidate in American and Canadian studies at the University of Nottingham in the United Kingdom. She writes about contemporary South Asian American women's fiction and is interested in postcolonial literature, gender studies, and popular culture. She graduated from Jawaharlal Nehru University in India and Sabaragamuwa University in Sri Lanka and has taught English at the University of Kelaniya and the University of Sabaragamuwa, both in Sri Lanka.

Marta Bladek holds a PhD in English from the Graduate Center, City University of New York. Her research interests include multicultural American novels, postcolonial literature, and theory and literature of trauma.

Joseph Kai-Hang Cheang is a doctoral candidate in Asian American literature at the University of California, Riverside. His research interests include postcolonialism and queer theory. He is currently working on a project examining how the rise of the East has destabilized current trends of racial representation. His master's thesis focuses on the debate on authenticity between Frank Chin and David Henry Hwang, teasing out the writers' divergent viewpoints on identity politics and poetics.

Lilly Catherine Chen received her MA in English from the University of Illinois, Springfield, and her BA in honors English with a minor concentration in Asian literature and languages from the University of Iowa. She has taught English in Taiwan and currently teaches English and writing in Sioux City, Iowa.

Kim Compoc has a BA in women's studies from Agnes Scott College and an MA in English from the University of Hawai'i, Mānoa, where she is currently working on her PhD in English. Her areas of interest are Asian American literature, postcolonial fiction and theory, feminist theory, and American empire.

Anne Cong-Huyen is the digital scholar and coordinator of the Digital Liberal Arts Program at Whittier College in California. She holds a PhD in English from the University of California, Santa Barbara. She was previously an Andrew W. Mellon Postdoctoral Fellow in the Humanities at the University of California, Los Angeles. Her work has appeared in the *Journal of e-Media Studies; Ada: A Journal of Gender, New Media, and Technology;* and *Humanities and the Digital.* She is active in HASTAC and FemTechNet and is a founding member of the collective Transformative Digital Humanities: Doing Race, Ethnicity, Gender, Sexuality, Disability, and Class in DH, which seeks to incorporate critical cultural studies and social justice work into diverse digital humanities activities.

Gerardo Del Guercio is the author of *The Fugitive Slave Law in the Life of Frederick Douglass, an American Slave; Harriet Beecher Stowe's Uncle Tom's Cabin: An American Society Transforms Its Culture;* and the forthcoming book *Perspectives on Edgar Allan Poe: Collected Essays.* He is an English instructor at the YMCA in Montreal, Canada, and is completing his TESOL at York College, City University of New York.

James I. Deutsch is a curator and editor at the Smithsonian Center for Folklife and Cultural Heritage in Washington, D.C. He is also an adjunct professor in the American Studies Department at George Washington University, where he teaches American film history and folklore. Deutsch has taught American studies classes at a number of universities in Armenia, Belarus, Bulgaria, Germany, Kyrgyzstan, Norway, Poland, and Turkey.

Donatella Galella is an assistant professor in the Department of Theatre, Film, and Digital Production at the University of California, Riverside, where she teaches global theater history and Asian American theater. She received her PhD in theater from the Graduate Center, City University of New York. Her research focuses on struggles over race and capital in popular U.S. performance, and her peer-reviewed articles have been published in *Theatre Journal* and *Continuum.* She is the dramaturg in residence of the Leviathan Lab, an Asian American creative studio.

Justin D. García received his PhD in anthropology from Temple University. His research interests include social constructions of race and ethnicity, U.S. immigration, anthropology of sports, and popular culture.

Ben Hamamoto received his BA in cinema from San Francisco State University. He has spent a decade writing about issues that impact the Asian American community for *Youth Outlook, New American Media,* and the *Nichi Bei Times.* He currently works as a research manager at the Institute for the Future, a nonprofit think tank in Palo Alto, California. In addition, he contributes to the *Nichi Bei Weekly* and serves as editor of the National Japanese American Historical Society's official magazine, *Nikkei Heritage.*

Qijun Han, assistant professor in the School of Foreign Studies at Nanjing University of Science and Technology, has a BA in English studies with honors from Nanjing University, China, and an MA and a PhD in American studies from Utrecht University, the Netherlands. Her dissertation, "The Ties That Bind: The Chinese American Family in Transnational Chinese Cinema," examines the cinematic construction of Chinese identities in the United States. She has published several articles on Chinese family culture, cinematic representations of Chinese family conflict in the context of migration, and Chinese cinema in the 1920s.

Lisa K. Hanasono is assistant professor of communication at Bowling Green State University, Bowling Green, Ohio. Her research projects focus primarily on the ways people experience and cope with prejudice, stereotyping, and discrimination. She also studies how individuals and communities work together to prevent and stop discrimination. Hanasono teaches courses on Asian American identities, race and communication, persuasion, interviewing, and communication theory.

Ryan Hata received his MA from San Francisco State University and his BA from Loyola Marymount University. His research is in the fields of communication studies, ethnic studies, and Asian American studies and emphasizes media-related work in terms of equity for minorities, particularly focusing on sports. He is also interested in intercultural communication pertaining to the Olympics.

Candy A. Henry has a PhD in literature and criticism from Indiana University of Pennsylvania. She has over 20 years of experience teaching communication, literature, and composition.

Tammy L. M. Ho is assistant professor of English at Hong Kong Baptist University and a founding coeditor of *Cha: An Asian Literary Journal*.

Caroline Kyungah Hong is assistant professor of English at Queens College, City University of New York. She has published articles on Asian American graphic narratives and popular culture and is currently finishing a book project on Asian American comedy. She is one of three managing editors of the online *Journal of Transnational American Studies*.

Andrew Howe is associate professor of history at La Sierra University in California, where he teaches American history, popular culture, and film studies. His recent publications include book chapters on race and racism in *Star Wars*, the depiction of Latino characters in *Breaking Bad*, and the transformation of the Mohican myth in *Avatar*.

Nancy Kang is assistant professor of multicultural and diaspora literatures at the University of Baltimore. She is the coeditor of *The Culture and Philosophy of Ridley Scott* and coauthor of the forthcoming book *The Once and Future Muse: Poetry and Poetics of Rhina P. Espaillat.* Her other publications include articles in *Canadian Literature,* the *African American Review,* and *MELUS.*

Mary K. Kehoe is a student at Mount Saint Mary College.

Ruth H. Kim is an adjunct professor at the University of San Francisco. She teaches in the Asian Pacific American studies program and the Sociology Department as well as in the human rights education concentration in the School of Education.

Jenny Ungbha Korn has attended Princeton University, Harvard University, and Northwestern University and is now at the University of Illinois, Chicago. She has appeared in video, online, radio, and print stories about race, gender, and online identity, including NPR, CNN, SXSW, Colorlines, and others. Her research examines race and gender online within Facebook, Twitter, YouTube, Tumblr, Chatroulette, blogs, and e-mail.

Vincent Kwan is a graduate student in Asian American studies at San Francisco State University. He received a BA in political science and American ethnic studies from the University of Washington. His current research focuses on the impostor phenomenon and its impact on Asian Americans in education.

Quynh Nhu Le received her PhD from the University of California, Santa Barbara, and is currently assistant professor of English at the University of South Florida, Tampa. Her research emerges at the intersection of comparative ethnic studies, Asian American studies, indigenous critical theory, and hemispheric studies. She is working on a book project that analyzes the cultural politics of Asian and indigenous cross-representations in the post-1968 Americas.

Jonathan H. X. Lee is associate professor of Asian American studies at San Francisco State University who specializes in Southeast Asian and Sino–Southeast Asian American studies. He is the author of *History of Asian Americans: Exploring Diverse Roots* and coeditor of *Encyclopedia of Asian American Folklore and Folklife* and *Asian American Identities and Practices: Folkloric Expressions in Everyday Life.*

Karen Isaksen Leonard, PhD, is a historian and anthropologist at the University of California, Irvine. She has many publications on the social history and anthropology of India and on Punjabi Mexican Americans, South Asian Americans, and Muslim Americans. One of her recent books, *Locating Home: India's Hyderabadis Abroad* (2007), details the construction of identity in the diaspora by emigrants from Hyderabad, India, settling in Pakistan, Britain, Canada, the United States, Australia, and the Persian Gulf states of the Middle East.

Jinhua Li received her MA in English literature from the Beijing Foreign Studies University, China, and her PhD in comparative literature from Purdue University. She is assistant professor of Chinese studies and language at the University of North Carolina, Asheville.

Shoon Lio is assistant professor of sociology and anthropology at the University of Illinois, Springfield. His research interest is the relationship between collective memory and national identity in the United States. Currently he is doing research on gentrification, culture, and the emergence of an Asian hipster cuisine.

Kuilan Liu is associate professor of English and director of Chinese American Literature Research Center at the Beijing Foreign Studies University, China. She received her PhD in Asian American literature from the Beijing Foreign Studies University in 2002 and has taught writing, reading, British and American short stories, modern bildungsroman, and Asian American literature. She has published more than 20 articles in English and Chinese on Asian American literature in mainland China, Hong Kong, the United States, and Canada. Liu is the author of *The Shifting Boundaries: Interviews of Asian American Writers and Critics*, and the editor of *Changing Boundaries and Reshaping Itineraries in Asian American Literary Studies*.

Ann Matsuuchi is an instructional technology librarian and associate professor at LaGuardia Community College, City University of New York. Her research interests include comics, manga, science fiction films and television shows, technology and gender, Wikipedia, and online cultures. Her research also focuses on the work of Samuel R. Delany and Melvin Van Peebles.

Kimberly McKee is an assistant professor in the Department of Liberal Studies at Grand Valley State University in Allendale, Michigan. Using adoption from Korea to the United States as a case study, her book manuscript interrogates the institutional practice of international adoption. The manuscript traces the origins of the transnational adoption industrial complex and challenges the portrayal of international adoption as solely an act of humanitarianism and child rescue. She received her PhD in women's, gender, and sexuality studies from Ohio State University.

Alice L. McLean, PhD, is a lecturer in food studies at the University of the Pacific, San Francisco. A specialist in gastronomic literature and feminist food studies, she is the author of Greenwood's *Cooking in America, 1840–1945* as well as *Aesthetic Pleasure in Twentieth-Century Women's Food Writing: The Innovative Appetites of M. F. K. Fisher, Alice B. Toklas, and Elizabeth David*. In addition to researching and writing books and essays on food culture and culinary literature, McLean served as the honors teaching fellow at Sweet Briar College (2005–2009), where she created and taught a range of food studies courses.

Roger McNamara received his PhD from Loyola University Chicago and is assistant professor of English at Texas Tech University, Lubbock. His research interests include South Asian literature, postcolonial theory, cultural Marxism, and secularism. Currently, he is working on a book manuscript titled *The Contours of Secularism in South Asian Minority Writing*. He has taught courses on Indian literature and film, postcolonial literature, secularism and religion, and African literature.

Sheela Jane Menon is a doctoral candidate in the Department of English at the University of Texas, Austin. Originally from Malaysia, she completed a BA in English with highest honors and a BA in religion at the University of Hawai'i, Mānoa. She earned her MA from the University of Texas, Austin. Her research focuses on Malaysian literature and popular culture, particularly race, nationalism, indigeneity, and multiculturalism in Malaysia.

Patit Paban Mishra is professor of history at Sambalpur University, India, where he specializes in world history, South Asian history, and Southeast Asian history. He received his MA in history from Delhi University, India, and his MPhil and his PhD from Jawaharlal Nehru University, India. He is the author of over 40 research articles and over 900 essays in 75 encyclopedias. He is the author of *The History of Thailand* and a coauthor of *Rapprochement between East Coast of India and Southeast Asia: A Discourse on Cultural Contact*.

Melanie Moore is professor of sociology at the University of Northern Colorado, Greeley. She received her PhD from the University of Washington and recently received a Freeman Fellowship from the Japan Studies Association. Her research and writing focus on community, culture, and identity.

Marco Morini is a research fellow in political science at the University of Padua, Italy. He has been an assistant professor in political science at the International University of Sarajevo, Bosnia and Herzegovina and a post-doctoral research fellow in sociology at Macquarie University, Australia. His main research interests are political behavior and U.S. politics. He has published journal articles on elections, public opinion, and the American presidency.

Sean Morton is an independent scholar since withdrawing in good standing from doctoral research in history and English. He has received a number of degrees from Canadian universities: a HBA in history and an MLIS from Western University; a BA in political science, a BA in ancient history and classical studies, and an MA in English from Trent University; a BA in English and great books from Brock University; an MA in interdisciplinary studies from Laurentian University; and an MA in history from Windsor University.

Kathleen M. Nadeau is professor of anthropology at California State University, San Bernardino. She is the author of *Liberation Theology in the Philippines: Faith in a Revolution* and *The History of the Philippines* and a coauthor of *Women's Roles in Asia*. She is the coeditor of *Encyclopedia of Asian American Folklore and Folklife; Asian American Identities and Practices: Folkloric Expressions in Everyday Life;* and a special issue of *Amerasia: Asian American Folklore: Passages and Practices.* Her work has appeared in *Critical Anthropology, Human Organization,* the *Journal for Scientific Study of Religion, Geografiska Annaler,* the *Philippine Quarterly of Culture and Society, Urban Anthropology,* and other journals and books. Her current research focuses on climate change and resilience in the Philippines.

Cheryl Narumi Naruse is assistant professor of English at the University of Dayton, Ohio, where she teaches postcolonial literature, literary theory, Asian American literature, and writing.

Khoi Nguyen is a writer who lives in San Francisco, California.

Amy Nishimura is associate professor of English at the University of Hawai'i, West Oahu. She teaches gender and sexuality in literature and film, contemporary literature of Hawai'i, composition studies, and Asian American literature. She is working on a book project on the Honouliuli internment site on the island of Oahu.

William Brokaw Noseworthy is a doctoral candidate in the Department of History at the University of Wisconsin, Madison, where he teaches in religious studies and the Department of Languages and Cultures of Asia. His research interests include highland-lowland relations, the history of Indic and Islamic influenced traditions, the history of oceanic spaces, and diaspora history and literature, with a focus on Cambodia and Vietnam. He is the author of a number of articles in English and Vietnamese and a coauthor of a Cham-English-Vietnamese 16,000-word dictionary.

Yuki Obayashi is a doctoral candidate in literature at the University of California, Santa Cruz. Her recent publications include "Interpreting the Vietnam War from a Vietnamese American Perspective" in *The Adaptation of History: Essays on Ways of Telling the Past* and "Paternal Projections of 1.5 Generation Vietnamese American Writers" by the Japanese Association for Migration Studies. She is involved with community services in the Diasporic Vietnamese Artists Network and the Japanese American National Library.

Mary Thi Pham received her MA in Asian American studies from San Francisco State University. Her thesis, "Vietnamese American Memoirs: Writing to Mourn, Reading to Remember," examines three Vietnamese American memoirs and provides a pedagogical framework to integrate Southeast Asian American literature in the classroom.

Eric J. Pido earned his PhD in ethnic studies from the University of California, Berkeley, in 2011. He is assistant professor of Asian American Studies at San Francisco State University. His research and teaching focus on transnational migration and urbanism between the United States and the Philippines. His book *Migrant Returns: Manila, Development, and Transnational Connectivity* is forthcoming in 2016.

Michael J. Polley is associate professor of history at Columbia College, Columbia, Missouri. He has been a frequent contributor of encyclopedia articles on West Asia and the United States since 1989.

Melody Rod-ari is a curator of Asian art at the Norton Simon Museum in California and an adjunct assistant professor of art history at Occidental College, Los Angeles. She completed her doctoral work at the University of California, Los Angeles, where she specialized in the art of Thailand.

Cathy J. Schlund-Vials is associate professor of English and Asian American studies and director of the Asian and Asian American Studies Institute at the University of Connecticut, Storrs. She is the author of *Modeling Citizenship: Naturalization in Jewish and Asian American Writing* and *War, Genocide, and Justice: Cambodian American Memory Work*. She has coedited three collections: *Keywords for Asian American Studies; Asian America: A Primary Source Reader;* and *Disability, Human Rights and the Limits of Humanitarianism.*

Leslie Shafer is a writer who has studied environmental science and has public works and advocacy experience. She is especially interested in environmental health issues.

Talaya Sin received a BA in Asian American studies from the University of California, Davis, and an MA in Asian American studies from San Francisco State University. She was director of programs and development at Cambodian Community Development, Inc., and a research associate at the Prevention Research Center of Pacific Institute of Research and Evaluation. Currently she is a chief project adviser for *Rhythm of the Refugee,* a three-part radio documentary about multigenerational Cambodian refugees in Oakland, California, and coordinates data management and analysis for the Association of Asian Pacific Community Health Organizations's health information technology projects.

Ravindra Pratap Singh is associate professor of English at University of Lucknow, India.

Vipan Pal Singh is assistant professor of English at Government Brijindra College, India. His research focuses on postcolonial studies. His MPhil thesis is titled "Origins of the Postcolonial Theory: A Study of Frantz Fanon's Major Works." He has presented research papers, delivered lectures, and published journal articles. He is a life member of the Forum on Contemporary Theory, Baroda, India, and a member of the Indian Association for Commonwealth Literature and Language Studies. Currently he is completing his doctoral dissertation, "The Problematics of Complicity and Resistance in Selected Works of Edward Said and Homi Bhabha."

Brittany Spurlock received an MA in English from Prairie View A&M University. Since 1997, she has taught English in Katy, a suburb of Houston, where she was named the 2012–2013 District-Wide Teacher of the Year. She writes about biblical devotional studies and has published an autobiographical book,

What Lurks at the Bottom of My Panty Drawer. She is working on a children's book series titled *Laverne's Lone Star Adventures.*

Anantha Sudhakar earned her PhD in English from Rutgers University in 2011. She is assistant professor of Asian American studies at San Francisco State University, where her teaching and research focus on Asian American literature, South Asian American culture, and arts activism.

Marie-Therese C. Sulit was born to immigrant Filipino parents. She earned her PhD in Asian American literature from the University of Minnesota, Twin Cities. As an associate professor at Mount Saint Mary College, Newburgh, New York, she explores the historical and current direction of Filipino American studies and has contributed a number of book chapters on contemporary women writers of the Philippine diaspora.

Hongmei Sun is assistant professor of Chinese at George Mason University, Fairfax, Virginia. She received her PhD in comparative literature from the University of Massachusetts, Amherst.

Joy Takako Taylor holds a PhD in American studies from Washington State University. Her teaching and research interests include Asian Pacific Americans and how they become marginalized through racist and white supremacist discourse. Her master's thesis explores the relationship between Asian Americans and Native Americans and appears in the journal *Life Writing.* Her work on the representations of Asian Pacific Americans in children's literature will appear in an edited collection titled *Growing Up Asian American.*

Junior Tidal received his MS in information science and MS in library science from Indiana University, Bloomington. He is assistant professor and web services and multimedia librarian at New York City College of Technology, City University of New York.

Nicole Topich is a project archivist at Harvard University, Cambridge, Massachusetts. She completed her master's degree in library and information science at the University of Pittsburgh and has assisted a variety of archives and performing arts projects, including the Library of Congress, Philadelphia Dance Projects, and the South Asian American Digital Archive.

Ashley Elisa Truong is a recent graduate of the University of California, Los Angeles, where she completed two bachelor's degrees: one in Asian American

Studies and the other in English. She currently works as a freelance editor and writer in the greater Los Angeles area.

Tom Ue received his PhD in English from University College London in the United Kingdom, where his research examined Shakespeare's influence on the writing of George Gissing. Ue also taught at University College London. He was a visiting scholar in the Department of English at Yale University, the 2011 Cameron Hollyer Memorial Lecturer, and the recipient of an Everett Helm visiting fellowship. He has published a number of essays and is the editor of *World Film Locations: Toronto* and *Dictionary of Literary Biography 377: Twenty-First Century British Novelists*.

Nengher N. Vang has a PhD in history from the University of Minnesota, Twin Cities; an MA in peace studies from the University of Notre Dame; an MA in theology from the Iliff School of Theology; and a BA in sociology from Davidson College. He is currently an assistant professor of history in the Department of History at the University of Wisconsin, Whitewater, where he teaches U.S. transnational history, immigration, comparative race/ethnicity, and the Vietnam War. His research interests are U.S.-Asia relations, American imperialism, social movements, refugee migration, and the transnational politics of diasporic communities in the United States with an emphasis on Hmongs.

Lavanya Vemsani is distinguished professor of history in the Department of Social Sciences at Shawnee State University, Portsmouth, Ohio. She holds a PhD in religious studies from McMaster University, Canada, and a PhD in history from the University of Hyderabad, India. Her research focuses on Indian history and religions. She is the author of *Hindu and Jain Mythology of Balarama* and *Krishna in History, Thought, and Culture: An Encyclopedia of the Lord of Many Names* as well as a number of articles on history and religions of India. She is currently working on two book projects: *India: A New History* and *Ancient Settlement Patterns of South India*. She is the editor of the *International Journal of Dharma and Hindu Studies* and the associate editor of the *Journal of South Asian Religious History*.

Ken Whalen is a lecturer in geography and environmental studies at the Universiti Brunei, Darussalam. He teaches environmental philosophy and geographies of South Asia and Southeast Asia. His research focuses on cultural landscapes, knowledge, and representation.

Joni L. Johnson Williams is a graduate student at Georgia State University.

Cordell D. K. Yee teaches in the integrated program based on fundamental Western works in science, mathematics, music, literature, and philosophy at St. John's College, Annapolis. His research focuses on questions of language. He developed an interest in Chinese calligraphy while working on his essays for *The History of Cartography* and *Approaches and Challenges in a World-Wide History of Cartography.*

INDEX

Page numbers in **boldface** indicate main entries in the volumes.

Confucius, 237; Daoism and, 238–239; decline of, 239; Eno, Robert, on, 238; ethical concepts and practices of, 238; as an ethical-sociopolitical teaching, 238; the Five Bonds, 239; gender roles and, 205; during the Han dynasty, 238; humanism and, 238, 239; influence of, 239; Legalism and, 238; meaning of, 238; New Life Movement, 240; overview of, 237–238, 583; relationships and, 239; "Ruism," 238; as a set of subsidiary guidelines, 240; social harmony, 239; Sun Yat-sen's Three Principles of the People, 239, 240

Cong-Huyen, Anne, 720–721

Consumption and Identity in Asian American Coming-of-Age Novels (Ho), 140

Contemporary Authors Online (2006), 65

The Cook's Canon: Classic Recipes Everyone Should Know (Sokolov), 291

Coquia, Virman, 549

Cornell Bhangra on *America's Got Talent*, 67

Council of Philippine American Organizations (COPAO), 284

court rulings (U.S.): *Chae Chan Ping v. United States*, 213; *Chang Chan et al. v. John D. Nagle*, 697; *Chew Heong v. United States case*, 213; *Ex parte Mitsuye Endo*, 408; *Fong Yue Ting v. United States*, 213; *Hirabayashi v. the United States*, 405, 408; *Korematsu v. United States*, 408; *Lau v. Nichols*, 197; *Loving v. Virginia*, 365; *Lum v. Rice*, 197; *Ozawa v. United States*, 256; *People v. Hall*, 255; *Perez v. Lippold*, 365; *Roldan v. Los Angeles County*, 365; *Tape v. Hurley*, 197, 205; *Thind v. United States*, 256; *United States v. Bhagat Singh Thind*, 58; *Yasui v. United States*, 408

Critical Path Project, 493

Crouching Tiger, Hidden Dragon (2000), 166

Cuoi story, 670

Cuomo, Andrew Mark, 171

The Curse of Quon Gwon: When the Far East Mingles with the West (1916), 163–164

Custred, Glynn, 578

dai jup woey (or *dai dop woey*), 221

Dalai Lamas, 637

Damayan Migrant Workers Association, Inc., 313

dance, Asian American, **241–244**; art and dance studios, 243; Asian American Power and Arts Movements, 243; classical dances, performance of, 243; crossover dance, 243; Filipino patrons' dancing skills, 242; Forbidden City nightclub, 242–243; history and origins, 241; kabuki, 241; Nisei Week celebration, photograph of, 242; regional traditions and contemporary forms, 241–243; taxi dance hall, 242

Dancer Dawkins and the California Kid (Kim), 479

Danh, Binh, 655–656

Daniels, Roger, 400

Dao, Chloe, 618

Daoism, **244–246**; beliefs of, 245; Buddhism and, 244; Cao Cao, 245; Confucianism and, 244; Dao practices, 244; Daoist School of, 246; divisions of, 245; Five Pecks of Rice movement, 245; history and origins, 244; impact of, 246; Laozi, 244, 245; as a lifestyle, 244; Lingbao School of, 245–246; naturalistic and/or mystical religions and, 244; Neo-Confucian school, 244; overview of, 582–583, 644–645; philosophical Daoism, 245; popularity of, 244, 246; Qiu Chuji, 246; Quanzhen School of, 246; religious Daoism, 245; schools of, 245–246; Shangqing School of, 245; significance of, 244; *Tao Te Ching*, 245; as Taoism, 244; Tianshi (Zhengyi) School of, 245; traditions and practices, 244–246; *Writings of Zhuangzi*, 245;

Korean American arts and artists,
444–448; Cha, Theresa Hak Kyung,
445; Chang, Sarah, 446–447; history
and origins, 444; Joo, Michael, 445;
Kim, Byron, 445; Kim, Whanki, 444;
Kim, Yu Yeon, 445; Ligon, Glenn, 445;
Min, Yong Soon, 444–445;
organizations assisting, 445–446; Paik,
Nam June, 444, 447–448; performing
arts and artists, 446–448; visual arts
and artists, 444–445

Korean American children and family,
448–451; acculturation, 450; adoption
of Korean children, 451; child dressed
in traditional clothes, 450 (image);
dietary habits of Korean American
families, 449; divorce, 451; family,
organization of, 449; family living
arrangement, 449; individualism vs.
Confucian collectivism, 450; language
skills, 451; maintaining bonds of
kinship, 449; naming tradition, 449;
popular Korean stories, 449; religions,
450; rite of passage of Korean
American children, 449; role of
women, 450–451

Korean American community
organizations, **452–454**; California
Proposition 187, 452–453;
Immigration and Nationality Act
(1965), 452; Korean American
Association of Greater New York
(KAAGNY), 452; Korean American
Coalition, 452; Korean American
Community Foundation (KACF),
453–454; Korean American Historical
Society (KAHS), 452; Korean
American Sharing Movement
(KASM), 453; National Association of
Korean Americans (NAKA), 453;
National Korean American Service &
Education Consortium (NAKASEC),
453; Nationality Origins Act, 452;
Occasional Papers journal, 452;
professional networking, 454; Treaty of
Amity and Commerce, 452

Korean American films and filmmakers,
454–458; Ahn, Philip, 454, 455, 456
(image); Cho, John Yohan, 456–457;
Cho, Margaret, 454; Chun, Alexandra
Bokyun, 454; Chung, Jamie Jilynn,
457; Dietrich, Joy, 454; Jeong, Ken,
454; Kang, Sung, 455; Lee, Alexander
Sebastien LeeAlexander Sebastien,
455; Lee, Chris Chan, 455; Lee, Ki
Hong, 455; Lee, Lela, 457; Lee,
Patricia Ja, 455; Sohn, Peter, 457;
Wong, Anna May, 456 (image); Yune,
Tommy, 457

Korean American folklore, **458–464**;
Allen, Horace Newton, 462; *Comfort
Woman* (Keller), 461, 462;
contemporary forms, 462–464; creation
story, 462; didactic stories, 461–462;
Edinburgh (Chee), 464–465; etiological
fable, 462; folklore defined, 458; as a
form of retaliation, 459; *Fox Girl*
(Keller), 463; fox girl, or *gumiho*, 459;
Grudge: The Revolt of the Gumiho, 464;
Gumiho (film), 464; "Heavenly Toad"
tale, 462–463; history and origins,
458–459; in illustrated form, 462;
Korean Tales (Newton), 462; Little
Frog story, 463; *Memories of My Ghost
Brother* (Fenkl), 463; *mudang,* or
shaman, 461; *Mudang: Reconciliation
between the Living and the Dead*
(documentary), 461; regional practices
and traditions, 460–462; television
miniseries, 464; *The Thousandth Man*,
464; transmission of, 458–459; Ur
motif, 462; *Yobi, the Five-Tailed Fox*
(film), 464

Korean American food, **465–468**; Asian
pear, 466; BCD Tofu House, 467; beef
and, 466; chicken dishes, 466–467;
contemporary forms, 467–468; fish,
465; fried chicken, 466; *japchae*, 465;
Korea House, 467; Korean restaurants,
467; Lee, Hee-sook, 467; marinated
foods, 466; Mi Cin restaurant, 467;
most popular meat dishes, 466;

(JACCC), 516; Japanese American internment and, 515; Japanese American National Museum (JANM), 516; as a National Historic Landmark District, 515; Onizuka, Ellison S., 517; photograph of, 515; redevelopment of, 515–516; U.S. Japantowns, official, 514–515; Visual Communications (VC), 516–517

Liu, Aimee, 87
Liu, Kuilan, 724
Liu, Lucy (1968–), 164, 168, 575
Liu, Timothy, 194
Locating the Sacred Festival (New York City), 273–274
Locke, Gary, 569
Loh, Vyvyane, 594
Long, Jodi, 227
Long Duk Dong, 223
Loo, Tai Sing, 337
Los Angeles Lantern Festival, 171
Los Angeles Riots (1992), 472, 508
Los Angeles Tribune, 411
Lost Loves (2010), 116
Louie, David Wong, 161, 162, 191
Louie, Edward, 321
Louie, Vivian, 198
Low, Charlie, 147
Lowe, Pardee, 83–84, 188
Lu, Ed, 585
Lu, Pamela, 195
Lu Xun, 239
Luce-Celler Act, 297
Luke, Keye, 224
Lum, Darrell H. Y., 161–162, 336
Lum, Wing Tek, 194
Lum v. Rice case, 196
Lunar New Year, **517–522**; Chinese Lantern Festival, 518; Chun Jie, 520; Chun Jie or Chinese New Year (Spring Festival), 518; contemporary forms and practices in the U.S., 519–521; Korean Americans and, 521; New Year for people of Cambodia, Laos, and Sri

Lank, 518; photograph of a Chinese New Year parade, 519; Seollal, 519, 521; Tet Nguyen Dan festival, 518–519, 520–521; Vietnamese Americans and, 520–521
Lung Kong Tin Yee Association of USA, 331
Luomala, Katharine, 392
Ly, Vi, 657

M. Butterfly (Hwang), 494, 630
Ma, Yo-Yo (1955–), 171, 547, 548, 549 (image)
Madama Butterfly (Puccini, 1903), 263, 543, 628
Magellan, Ferdinand, 314
Magnuson Act (1943), xxxi
Mah, Adeline Yen, 87
Maharishi, Ramana, 342
Mahesh, Maharishi, 75
Mai, Nguyen Thi Tuyet, 681
mail-order brides, 698
Maitri organization, 31
Maivia, Peter, 98
Malaysian American culture, **523–528**; in Chicago, 524; Chinese, Malay, Indian and Others (CMIO), 526; Chinese, Malay, Indian and Others (CMIO) categories, 526; community organizations, 524–525; defining the Malaysian American community, 523; ethnic and religious identities, 526; on Facebook, 524, 525; festivals and celebrations, 525–526; immigrant identity categories, 526–527; Lim, Shirley Geok-lin, 526; Lunar New Year, 525; Malaysia Midwest Games (MGG), 525; Malaysia-America Society, 524, 525; Malaysia-America Society of Washington, D.C., 526; Malaysian Club of Chicago, 525–526; Malaysian Students Association (MASA), 524; Nasi Lemak Project, 526; New Economic Policy, 524; New York Malaysian Association, 526; population statistics concerning